학습 진도표와 함께 목표를 달성해 보세요.

_____의 **Grammar Gateway Basic** 학습 진도표

목표와 다짐을 적어보세요.

나는 _____을 하기 위해

_____년 _____월 _____일까지 이 책을 끝낸다.

학습플랜을 정하세요.

☐ 하루에 UNIT 4개씩 **한 달** 안에 완성
☐ 하루에 UNIT 2개씩 **두 달** 안에 완성
☐ 하루에 UNIT _____개씩 _____ 안에 완성

학습을 마친 UNIT의 번호를 지워 보세요. 복습이 필요한 UNIT은 별도로 표시하고 꼭 복습하세요!

	2	3	4	5	6	7	8	9	10	11	12	13	14	15	16	17	18	19	20
21	22	23	24	25	26	27	28	29	30	31	32	33	34	35	36	37	38	39	40
41	42	43	44	45	46	47	48	49	50	51	52	53	54	55	56	57	58	59	60
61	62	63	64	65	66	67	68	69	70	71	72	73	74	75	76	77	78	79	80
81	82	83	84	85	86	87	88	89	90	91	92	93	94	95	96	97	98	99	100

HACKERS

Grammar Gateway
Basic

해커스 어학연구소

스피킹 · 라이팅 훈련 워크북 & 워크북 MP3
해커스인강 **HackersIngang.com**

PREFACE

Grammar Gateway Basic은
문법을 처음 시작하는 초보 학습자들이 영어의 기초를 탄탄하게 다질 수 있는 기초 영어 문법서입니다.

본 교재는 영어를 모국어로 사용하는 사람들이 어떻게 말하고 쓰는지 분석·관찰하여 가장 중요한 문법 포인트를 총 100개의 UNIT으로 담아냈습니다. 한 UNIT을 2페이지로 구성하여 왼쪽 페이지에서 쉽고 명확하게 설명되어 있는 문법 사항들을 학습한 후, 곧바로 오른쪽 페이지에서 배운 내용을 연습해볼 수 있습니다. 또한, 영문법에 두려움을 가진 학습자를 위해 어려운 문법 용어 대신 쉬운 문법 설명과 다양한 삽화를 통해 재미있게 공부할 수 있도록 하였습니다. 나아가 실생활에서 바로 사용할 수 있는 예문과 다양한 유형의 연습문제를 통해 문법뿐만 아니라 말하기와 쓰기 능력도 기를 수 있습니다.

강의를 들으면서 공부하고 싶은 학습자들은 해커스 동영상강의 포털 해커스인강(HackersIngang.com)에서 동영상강의와 함께 학습이 가능합니다. 더불어, 실시간 토론과 정보 공유의 장인 해커스영어 사이트(Hackers.co.kr)와 점프해커스(JumpHackers.com)에서 교재 학습 중 궁금한 점을 다른 학습자들과 나누고, 다양한 무료 영어 학습 자료를 이용할 수 있습니다.

Grammar Gateway Basic을 통해 막연하고 어렵게만 여겨지는 영문법에 한 걸음 더 가까이 다가설 수 있으실 거라 확신합니다. 여러분의 꿈을 이루는 길에 Grammar Gateway Basic이 함께하기를 기원합니다.

David Cho

CONTENTS

현재와 현재진행

과거와 과거진행

현재완료

미래

CONTENTS

책의 특징

01.
쉽게 이해할 수 있는 문법책,
Grammar Gateway!

· 어려운 문법 용어 대신 설명을 쉬운 말로 풀어 써서
  이해하기 쉽습니다.
· 표와 그래프를 통해 문법 설명을 한눈에 볼 수 있어
  학습자가 보다 쉽게 이해할 수 있습니다.

02.
재미있게 공부할 수 있는 문법책,
Grammar Gateway!

· 생생한 삽화가 그려져 있어 딱딱하기만 했던 영문법을
  재미있게 공부할 수 있도록 도와줄 뿐만 아니라 효과
  적으로 공부할 수 있게 해줍니다.
· 다양한 유형의 연습문제가 수록되어 있어 영문법
  공부에 흥미를 더해줍니다.

03.
끝낼 수 있는 문법책,
Grammar Gateway!

· 한 UNIT이 두 페이지로 구성되어 있어 학습한 내용을
  바로 옆 페이지에서 연습해볼 수 있으며, 부담 없이
  학습을 마칠 수 있습니다.

· 학습 진도표를 활용해 스스로 학습 진도를 점검하며
  꾸준히 공부한다면 책을 완전히 끝낼 수 있습니다.

04.
말하기/쓰기에 활용할 수 있는 문법책,
Grammar Gateway!

· 실생활에서 사용할 수 있는 예문들이 실려 있어 실제
  말하기/쓰기에 바로 적용할 수 있습니다.

· 문장과 대화를 직접 완성해보는 연습을 통해 말하기/
  쓰기 실력을 향상시킬 수 있습니다.

책의 구성

MP3 링크

MP3(HackersIngang.com)로
예문과 문제를 듣고 소리 내어 따라
하며 말하기 연습도 해보세요.

삽화

실제 상황을 보는 듯 생생하고 재미
있는 삽화를 통해 공부할 내용을
효과적으로 파악할 수 있어요.

문법 설명 + 표/그래프

문법 용어를 사용하지 않고 쉽게
풀어 쓴 설명을 읽고, 표/그래프를
통해 내용을 한눈에 확인할 수
있어요.

예문

예문을 통해 문법이 어떻게 활용
되었는지 확인할 수 있어요.

• 예문을 직접 해석해보고, 온라인 무료
  예문 해석 자료(Hackers.co.kr)를
  활용해 내가 해석한 의미가 맞는지
  점검해보세요.

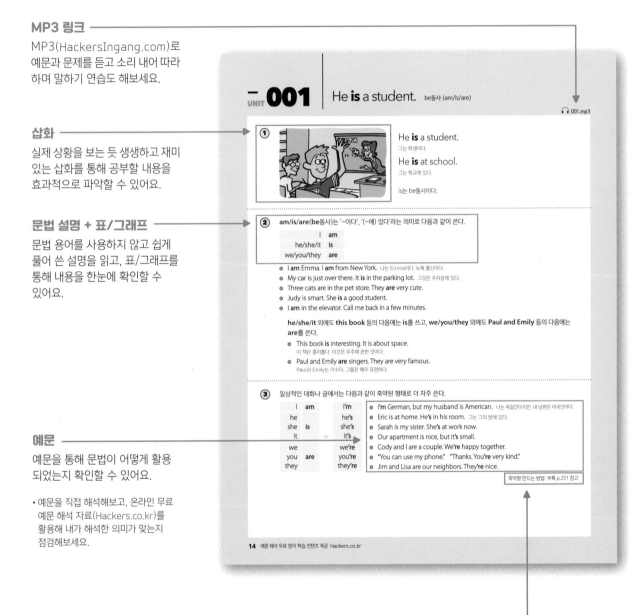

부록 링크

링크를 따라 부록 페이지로
가면 공부에 도움이 되는
내용들을 보충할 수 있어요.

PRACTICE

A. 주어진 주어에 맞게 am/is/are를 써넣고, 축약형을 쓰세요.

1. she _is_ → _she's_
2. we _____ → _____
3. I _____ → _____
4. it _____ → _____
5. they _____ → _____
6. he _____ → _____

B. 그림을 보고 주어진 표현과 am/is/are를 사용하여 문장을 완성하세요.

a photographer	a repairman	in their car	~~on a farm~~	on the stage

1. Mike _is on a farm_ .
2. Jessica _____ .
3. Gary and Troy _____
4. Tony and Anna _____ .
5. Steve _____ .

C. 괄호 안에 주어진 주어와 am/is/are를 사용하여 문장을 완성하세요.

1. (they) Tom and Jill are in Mexico. _They're OR They are_ at the beach.
2. (I) "Hello, _____ Tina." "It's nice to meet you."
3. (it) "This table is from India." " _____ beautiful."
4. (we) Our grandmother is sick, so _____ at the hospital.
5. (you) This steak is delicious. _____ a good cook.
6. (it) My computer is new. _____ very fast.
7. (I) _____ at the mall. I'm with my friends.
8. (she) This is my sister's class photo. _____ in the back.

D. Chris가 자신과 가족을 소개하고 있습니다. 괄호 안에 주어진 단어와 am/is/are를 사용하여 문장을 완성하세요.

AMY JUSTIN JAMES CHRIS LINDA

1. My name _is Chris_ . 2. I _____ . (Chris) (21 years old)
Amy is my sister. 3. Her hobby _____ . (swimming)
4. My brother _____ . His name is Justin. (a high school student)
5. James and Linda _____ . They're from San Francisco. (my parents)

정답 p.266, REVIEW TEST 1 p.216

UNIT 001
Grammar Gateway Basic

문제
재미있고 다양한 문제를 풀어보며 공부한 내용을 바로 연습해볼 수 있어요.

실용지문 문제
대화문, 이메일, 에세이, 광고 등 실생활에서 볼 수 있는 지문을 통해 공부한 내용을 연습할 수 있어요.

REVIEW TEST 링크
링크를 따라가면 여러 UNIT의 내용을 종합적으로 점검할 수 있는 REVIEW TEST를 풀어볼 수 있어요.

문장성분과 품사

기초가 탄탄해야 높은 탑을 쌓을 수 있겠죠? 영어 문장의 기초를 잘 익혀두면 영어를 쉽게 이해할 수 있답니다.
그럼 영어에서 문장을 구성하는 성분들은 무엇인지, 품사는 무엇인지 알아볼까요?

문장성분

주어와 동사

She runs.
주어　동사
그녀는 달린다.

영어 문장에는 주어(She)와 동사(runs)가 꼭 필요합니다.
주어는 어떤 행동이나 상태의 주체가 되는 말로 우리말의 '누가'
또는 '무엇이'에 해당합니다. **동사**는 행동이나 상태를 나타내는
말로 우리말의 '~하다, ~이다'에 해당합니다.

목적어

He drives **the bus**.
주어　동사　　목적어
그는 버스를 운전한다.

주어(He), 동사(drives) 외에 목적어(the bus)를 필요로 하는
문장도 있습니다. **목적어**는 동사가 나타내는 행동의 대상이 되는
말로 우리말의 '~을/를'에 해당합니다.

보어

We are **hungry**.
주어 동사　　보어
우리는 배고프다.

주어(We), 동사(are) 외에 보어(hungry)를 필요로 하는 문장도
있습니다. **보어**는 주어나 목적어의 성질 또는 상태 등을 보충 설명
해주는 말입니다.

수식어

They hike **every weekend**.
주어　동사　　　수식어
그들은 주말마다 등산을 한다.

문장을 구성하는 요소에는 꼭 필요한 성분(They hike) 외에
수식어(every weekend)도 있습니다. **수식어**는 문장에서 없어도
되는 부가적인 요소이지만, 다른 요소를 꾸며주어 문장을 더
풍부하게 하는 말입니다.

품사

명사 우리 주위 모든 것의 이름

girl   desk   music

세상의 모든 것에는 이름이 있습니다. girl, desk, music처럼 우리 주위의 모든 것에 붙여진 이름을 **명사**라고 합니다.

대명사 명사를 대신하는 말

Jack is my brother.
He is a doctor.
대명사

대명사(He)는 앞에 나온 명사(Jack)를 반복하지 않고 대신해서 쓰는 말을 가리킵니다.

동사 동작이나 상태를 나타내는 말

She **plays** the piano.
동사
She **likes** music.
동사

동사(plays, likes)는 '(누가) 무엇을 하는지, 어떠한지'등 사람이나 사물의 동작 또는 상태를 나타내는 말을 가리킵니다.

형용사 명사를 꾸며주는 말

It's a **red** car.
형용사

형용사(red)는 명사(car)를 꾸며서 명사의 상태 또는 특징을 나타내는 말을 가리킵니다.

부사 동사, 형용사, 부사 또는 문장 전체를 꾸며주는 말

It runs **fast**.
부사

부사(fast)는 동사(runs)나 형용사, 부사 또는 문장 전체를 꾸며서 그 의미를 더 자세하게 나타내는 말을 가리킵니다.

접속사 이어주는 말

She has a dog **and** a cat.
접속사

접속사(and)는 두 가지 이상의 대상(a dog, a cat)을 연결하는 말을 가리킵니다.

전치사 명사나 대명사 앞에 쓰는 말

The telephone is **on** the table.
전치사

전치사(on)는 명사(table)나 대명사 앞에 쓰여서 위치, 장소, 시간 등을 나타내는 말을 가리킵니다.

감탄사 감정을 나타낼 때 쓰는 말

Wow!
감탄사

감탄사(Wow)는 기쁘거나, 화가 나거나, 놀랄 때 드는 감정을 표현하는 말을 가리킵니다.

He **is** a student. be동사 (am/is/are)

🎧 001.mp3

①

He **is** a student.
그는 학생이다.

He **is** at school.
그는 학교에 있다.

is는 be동사이다.

② am/is/are(be동사)는 '~이다', '(~에) 있다'라는 의미로 다음과 같이 쓴다.

I	am
he/she/it	is
we/you/they	are

- I **am** Emma. I **am** from New York. 나는 Emma이다. 뉴욕 출신이다.
- My car is just over there. It **is** in the parking lot. 그것은 주차장에 있다.
- Three cats are in the pet store. They **are** very cute.
- Judy is smart. She **is** a good student.
- I **am** in the elevator. Call me back in a few minutes.

he/she/it 외에도 **this book** 등의 다음에는 **is**를 쓰고, **we/you/they** 외에도 **Paul and Emily** 등의 다음에는 **are**를 쓴다.

- This book **is** interesting. It is about space.
  이 책은 흥미롭다. 이것은 우주에 관한 것이다.
- Paul and Emily **are** singers. They are very famous.
  Paul과 Emily는 가수다. 그들은 매우 유명하다.

③ 일상적인 대화나 글에서는 다음과 같이 축약된 형태로 더 자주 쓴다.

I	am		I'm
he			he's
she	is		she's
it		→	it's
we			we're
you	are		you're
they			they're

- I'm German, but my husband is American. 나는 독일인이지만, 내 남편은 미국인이다.
- Eric is at home. He's in his room. 그는 그의 방에 있다.
- Sarah is my sister. She's at work now.
- Our apartment is nice, but it's small.
- Cody and I are a couple. We're happy together.
- "You can use my phone." "Thanks. You're very kind."
- Jim and Lisa are our neighbors. They're nice.

축약형 만드는 방법: 부록 p.251 참고

PRACTICE

A. 주어진 주어에 맞게 am/is/are를 써넣고, 축약형을 쓰세요.

1. she *is* → *she's*
2. we _____ → _____
3. I _____ → _____
4. it _____ → _____
5. they _____ → _____
6. he _____ → _____

B. 그림을 보고 주어진 표현과 am/is/are를 사용하여 문장을 완성하세요.

a photographer	a repairman	in their car	~~on a farm~~	on the stage

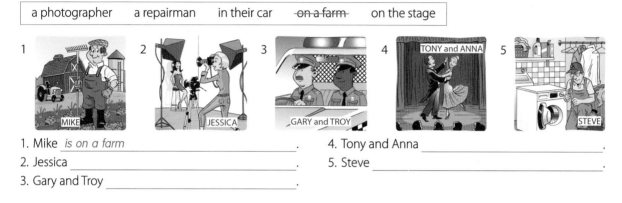

1. Mike *is on a farm* _____.
2. Jessica _____.
3. Gary and Troy _____.
4. Tony and Anna _____.
5. Steve _____.

C. 괄호 안에 주어진 주어와 am/is/are를 사용하여 문장을 완성하세요.

1. (they) Tom and Jill are in Mexico. *They're OR They are* at the beach.
2. (I) "Hello, _____ Tina." "It's nice to meet you."
3. (it) "This table is from India." " _____ beautiful."
4. (we) Our grandmother is sick, so _____ at the hospital.
5. (you) This steak is delicious. _____ a good cook.
6. (it) My computer is new. _____ very fast.
7. (I) _____ at the mall. I'm with my friends.
8. (she) This is my sister's class photo. _____ in the back.

D. Chris가 자신과 가족을 소개하고 있습니다. 괄호 안에 주어진 단어와 am/is/are를 사용하여 문장을 완성하세요.

1. My name *is Chris* _____. 2. I _____. (Chris) (21 years old)
Amy is my sister. 3. Her hobby _____. (swimming)
4. My brother _____. His name is Justin. (a high school student)
5. James and Linda _____. They're from San Francisco. (my parents)

정답 p.266, REVIEW TEST 1 p.216

UNIT 001

Grammar Gateway Basic

UNIT 002 | He **is not** hungry. be동사 부정문

①

I'm full.

긍정 He **is** full. 그는 배부르다.

부정 He **is not** hungry. 그는 배고프지 않다.

---

② **am/is/are + not**: ~이 아니다, (~에) 없다

긍정			부정		
I	am		I	am	
he/she/it	is	→	he/she/it	is	not
we/you/they	are		we/you/they	are	

- I **am not** from Japan. I'm Korean. 나는 일본 출신이 아니다.
- "The dress **is not** in the closet." 옷이 옷장에 없어. "Oh, it's in the washing machine."
- We **are not** busy. Let's watch a movie together.
- I **am not** at school now. Come and see me at the station.
- Carla **is not** in her office. She's out for lunch.
- "These apples **are not** expensive." "Good! Let's get some."

---

③ **I am not, he is not** 등은 다음과 같이 축약된 형태로 더 자주 쓴다.

I	am not		I'm not
he			he's not / he isn't
she	is not		she's not / she isn't
it		→	it's not / it isn't
we			we're not / we aren't
you	are not		you're not / you aren't
they			they're not / they aren't

- I**'m not** tall, but I'm good at basketball. 나는 키가 크지 않다.
- "Where is John?" "He**'s not** here." 그는 여기에 없어.
- We**'re not** brothers. We're cousins.
- Today **isn't** Saturday. It's Sunday.
- Don't worry. You**'re not** late.
- "Those boxes are big." "Yes, but they **aren't** heavy."

  I am not의 축약된 형태는 **I'm not**으로만 쓰는 것에 주의한다.

  - I**'m not** sleepy. I'm just bored. 나는 졸리지 않아.

PRACTICE

A. 괄호 안에 주어진 주어와 am/is/are not을 사용하여 문장을 완성하세요.

1. (I) *I'm not* OR *I am not* an adult. I'm only 15 years old.
2. (this water) __________ cold. It's warm.
3. (you) It's already 8 a.m. and __________ ready for school. Hurry up!
4. (Mark) __________ at the restaurant. He's at the bank.
5. (we) It's lunch time, but __________ hungry.
6. (I) "Are you OK?" "Don't worry. __________ sick anymore."
7. (Sharon) __________ my best friend. We're not close.
8. (my books) __________ in my room. I can't find them.

B. Clara가 잘못된 정보를 말하고 있습니다. am/is/are not을 사용하여 잘못된 정보를 고쳐서 다시 말해보세요.

CLARA

1. Her name is Diane.
2. Richard is 23 years old.
3. Sally and Alex are from Brazil.
4. You are a nurse.
5. Tomorrow is Thursday.

Her name isn't Diane OR *Her name is not Diane*. It's Kate.
__________. He's 25 years old.
__________. They're from Cuba.
__________. I'm a doctor.
__________. It's Friday.

C. am/is/are 또는 am/is/are not을 축약된 형태로 사용하여 문장을 완성하세요.

1. Tara is in France, but she *'s not* OR *isn't* in Paris.
2. Cindy and Luke aren't here. They __________ at the lake.
3. We're not at the airport. We __________ still in the taxi.
4. I __________ sorry I'm late. Let's start the meeting.
5. Moscow isn't a country. It __________ a city.
6. "Do you want some juice?" "No, thanks. I __________ thirsty."
7. My office __________ far from home. It's only three blocks away.
8. I __________ a professional musician, but I can play the guitar well.

D. am/is/are를 사용하여 하와이에 대한 글을 완성하세요. 필요한 경우 부정문으로 쓰세요.

Welcome to Hawaii

1. Hawaii *is* a beautiful island.
The weather is usually warm all year.
2. It __________ cold, even in December.
3. Beautiful beaches __________ in Hawaii too.
4. They __________ close to the airport, but they are popular.
Please enjoy your stay here.

정답 p.266, REVIEW TEST 1 p.216

UNIT 003 | Is she from China? be동사 의문문

🎧 003.mp3

①

Are you from China?

Yes, I am.

긍정 **She is** from China. 그녀는 중국 출신이다.

의문 **Is she** from China? 그녀는 중국 출신인가요?

---

② be동사 의문문에서 **am/is/are**는 주어 앞에 쓴다.

긍정			의문	
I	am		**Am**	I ...?
he/she/it	is	→	**Is**	he/she/it ...?
we/you/they	are		**Are**	we/you/they ...?

- Excuse me. **Am I** near Main Street? 제가 Main가 근처에 있나요?
- "**Is he** your father?" 저분이 네 아버지시니? "No, he's my uncle."
- "**Are we** in the same class?" "Yes. I'm Danny."
- "**Is Diana** in her room?" "No, she's out."
- Your eyes are red. **Are you** tired?
- "**Is it** warm outside?" "Yes. The weather is great."
- "**Are those cookies** good?" "Yes, they're delicious."

---

③ 다음과 같이 의문문에 짧게 답할 수 있다.

	I	am.			I	'm not.
Yes,	he/she/it	is.	**No,**		he/she/it	's not. / isn't.
	we/you/they	are.			we/you/they	're not. / aren't.

- "**Are you** Pamela?" 당신이 Pamela인가요? "**Yes, I am.**" (= Yes, I am Pamela.)
- "**Is the radio** loud?" 라디오가 시끄러운가요? "**No, it's not.**" (= No, it's not loud.)
- "**Is Mom** in the kitchen?" "**Yes, she is.**"
- "**Are the guests** here?" "**No, they aren't.**"

이때, **Yes** 뒤에는 축약형을 사용하지 않는 것에 주의한다.

- "Are you a musician?" "**Yes, I am.**" (Yes, I'm.으로 쓸 수 없음)
- "It's 7 a.m. Is Jason awake?" "**Yes, he is.**" (Yes, he's.로 쓸 수 없음)

PRACTICE

A. am/is/are를 써넣으세요.

1. " _Are_ you in the bathroom?" "Yes, I am."
2. " _____ your cat white?" "No. It's black."
3. "I'm cold." "I am too. _____ the windows closed?"
4. "Excuse me. _____ I at Gate 6?" "No. Gate 6 is not in this terminal."
5. " _____ our car at the repair shop?" "No. It's in the parking garage."
6. "Are you 33 years old?" "Yes. _____ we the same age?"
7. " _____ you an artist?" "Yes. I'm a painter."

B. 괄호 안에 주어진 주어와 am/is/are를 사용하여 의문문을 완성하세요.

1. (Jackie) " _Is Jackie_ _____ in Europe?" "Yes, she is."
2. (it) " _____ cloudy today?" "No. There's not a cloud in the sky."
3. (I) I'm here to see Mr. Smith. _____ in the right building?
4. (you) I can't hear you well. _____ on the subway?
5. (today) " _____ your birthday?" "Yes, it is."
6. (Joel and Mary) " _____ at the theater?" "I think so, but I'm not sure."
7. (she) "My sister is an actress." "Really? _____ famous?"
8. (we) " _____ ready for the meeting?" "Yes. Let's begin."

C. 주어진 의문문을 보고 예시와 같이 짧게 답하세요.

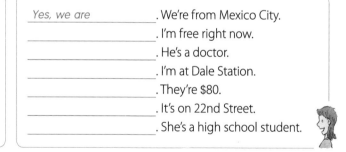

1. Are you and Estevan Mexican?
2. Are you busy?
3. Is Brandon a banker?
4. Are you at the train station?
5. Are these gloves $100?
6. Is your house on 21st Avenue?
7. Is Angela 17 years old?

Yes, we are . We're from Mexico City.
_____ . I'm free right now.
_____ . He's a doctor.
_____ . I'm at Dale Station.
_____ . They're $80.
_____ . It's on 22nd Street.
_____ . She's a high school student.

D. 괄호 안에 주어진 단어들과 am/is/are를 사용하여 Chris와 Chun의 대화를 완성하세요.

CHRIS: Hi. 1. _I'm Chris_ OR _I am Chris_ . (I, Chris)
CHUN: Hi, Chris. 2. _____ . (My name, Chun)
CHRIS: 3. _____ ? (you, from China)
CHUN: 4. Yes, _____ . (I, Chinese)
5. _____ ? (you, in this class)
CHRIS: 6. Yes, I think _____ . (we, in the same class)
It's nice to meet you.

CHRIS

CHUN

UNIT 004 | She **is making** a cake. 현재진행 시제

 004.mp3

①

She **is making** a cake.

그녀는 케이크를 만드는 중이다.

is making은 현재진행 시제이다.

---

② 현재진행 시제는 '(지금) ~하는 중이다'라는 의미로 **am/is/are + -ing**로 쓴다.

I	am (= 'm)	
he she it	is (= 's)	cooking visiting enjoying looking
we you they	are (= 're)	

- ○ Come home soon. I **am cooking** dinner now. 나는 지금 저녁을 요리하는 중이다.
- ○ Ralph isn't here. He **is visiting** his grandparents in Thailand. 그는 태국에서 조부모님을 방문 중이다.
- ○ Thank you for inviting us. We **are enjoying** the party.
- ○ "**I'm looking** for my glasses." "They're on your desk."
- ○ Rebecca **is cleaning** her room right now.
- ○ Jonathan is late for school, but he**'s** still **sleeping**.
- ○ "Look! It**'s snowing**." "Let's go outside."
- ○ Frank and Brenda are in the library. They**'re studying** for an exam.

---

③ **-ing**를 붙일 때 주의해야 할 동사들이 있다.

come → com**ing**	run → ru**nning**	lie → **lying**
take → tak**ing**	sit → si**tting**	tie → **tying**
have → hav**ing**	shop → sho**pping**	die → **dying**

-ing 붙이는 방법: 부록 p.248 참고

- ○ Hurry up! The train is **coming**. 기차가 오고 있어.
- ○ Daniel, you're **running** too fast. Wait for me! 너는 너무 빨리 달리고 있어.
- ○ A couple is **sitting** on the grass, and their dogs are **lying** beside them.
- ○ "Who is in the bathroom?" "Sophie. She's **taking** a shower."

PRACTICE

A. 주어진 동사에 -ing를 붙이세요.

1. ask → *asking*
2. sit → _____
3. write → _____
4. have → _____

5. come → _____
6. shop → _____
7. wait → _____
8. die → _____

B. 그림을 보고 괄호 안에 주어진 표현을 사용하여 현재진행 시제 문장을 완성하세요.

1 　　2 　　3

1. (listen to music) He *'s listening to music* OR *is listening to music* _____ .
   (play with a ball) The dog *is playing with a ball* _____ .
2. (eat popcorn) They _____ .
   (cry) They _____ .
3. (drive) She _____ .
   (ring) The phone _____ .

C. 그림을 보고 주어진 표현을 사용하여 예시와 같이 문장을 완성하세요.

| ~~cross the street~~　　enter the bank　　fly in the sky　　play the violin　　stand at the bus stop |

1. Carl and Rita *are crossing the street* _____ .
2. Jack _____ .
3. Melinda _____ .
4. Two birds _____ .
5. Kim _____ .

D. 괄호 안에 주어진 단어들을 사용하여 현재진행 시제 문장을 완성하세요.

1. (I, pack) *I'm packing* OR *I am packing* _____ for my trip. I'm very excited.
2. (he, have) "Where's Tim?" "_____ lunch at the cafeteria."
3. (the children, help) _____ their dad in the garden. They're planting flowers.
4. (Mitchell, prepare) _____ for a meeting. He's busy.
5. (they, jog) "Where are Alex and Ed?" "_____ in the park."
6. (I, tie) Please stop for a minute. _____ my shoes.
7. (we, sell) _____ tickets for the opera. They are $80 each.
8. (she, get) Maggie is at the hair salon. _____ a haircut.

정답 p.266, REVIEW TEST 1 p.216

UNIT
004

Grammar Gateway Basic

| He **is not driving**. 현재진행 시제 부정문과 의문문

🎧 005.mp3

①

긍정 He **is eating** lunch. 그는 점심을 먹는 중이다.

부정 He **is not driving**. 그는 운전하고 있지 않다.

현재진행 시제 부정문은 **am/is/are + not + -ing**로 쓴다.

I	**am not** (= **'m not**)	
he she it	**is not** (= **'s not / isn't**)	doing using traveling listening
we you they	**are not** (= **'re not / aren't**)	

- I **am not doing** anything. Let's go out. 나는 아무것도 하고 있지 않아.
- I**'m not using** the chair. You can use it. 나는 그 의자를 사용하고 있지 않아.
- Tom is in Seattle with Ann. He **is not traveling** alone.
- "Jane! I'm talking to you." "I think she **isn't listening**."
- It's cloudy, but it**'s not snowing**.
- We **are not working** today. We're on vacation.
- What's wrong? You**'re not looking** well.
- Where are the children? They **aren't playing** in the garden.

②

Is it raining?

Yes, it is.

긍정 It **is raining**. 비가 오는 중이다.

의문 **Is** it **raining**? 지금 비가 오는 중인가요?

현재진행 시제 의문문은 **am/is/are + 주어 + -ing**로 쓴다.

Am	I	
Is	he she it	speaking ...? coming ...? taking ...? working ...?
Are	we you they	

- **Am** I **speaking** too quickly? 제가 너무 빨리 말하고 있나요?
- Where's Bob? **Is** he **coming** home now? 그가 지금 집에 오는 중이니?
- "Sarah's not in her room. **Is** she **taking** a walk?" "Yes, she is."
- "**Is** the printer **working**?" "No, it's broken."
- "**Are** we **winning** the game?" "Yes, we are."
- "It smells good! **Are** you **baking** bread?" "Yes. Are you hungry?"
- "**Are** the subways still **running**?" "No. It's already 1 a.m."

Yes, she is. 또는 **No, I'm not.** 등과 같이 의문문에 짧게 답할 수 있다.

- "**Is** Stacy **studying** now?" Stacy는 지금 공부하는 중인가요? "**Yes, she is.**" (= Yes, she's studying now.)
- "**Are** you **sleeping**?" 너 자고 있니? "**No, I'm not.**" (= No, I'm not sleeping.)

PRACTICE

A. 주어진 동사를 사용하여 현재진행 시제 문장을 완성하세요. 필요한 경우 부정문으로 쓰세요.

enjoy	move	swim	teach	~~watch~~	wear

1. "Can I change the channel?" "Sorry, but I *'m watching* OR *am watching*   this show."
2. The bus _____ because of the traffic.
3. "Is that board game fun?" "Yes. We _____ it a lot."
4. You _____ your seat belt. That's dangerous.
5. Mr. Taylor _____ Russian. It's not German.
6. I _____ because the water is too deep.

B. 괄호 안에 주어진 단어들을 사용하여 현재진행 시제 문장을 완성하세요.

1. (Glen, look) " *Is Glen looking* _____ for me?" "Yes. He's waiting at your office."
2. (my sister, listen) I can't study because _____ to the radio in my room.
3. (you, cry) "_____? What's wrong?" "Don't worry. I'm OK now."
4. (I, sing) "_____ too loudly?" "No. I'm not sleeping anymore, so it's fine."
5. (you and Vicky, bake) "_____ something?" "Yes. We're making a blueberry pie."
6. (the wind, blow) _____ a lot today. Bring your coat.
7. (your brothers, ride) "_____ their bicycles?" "Yes. They're at the park."
8. (Kyle, wear) _____ a new suit. He looks great!

UNIT 005

Grammar Gateway Basic

C. 주어진 의문문을 보고 예시와 같이 짧게 답하세요.

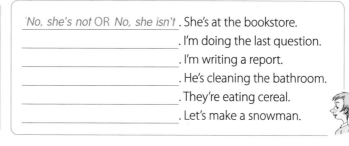

1. Is Helen exercising at the gym?
2. Are you doing your homework?
3. Are you drawing a picture?
4. Is David taking a shower?
5. Are the children having breakfast?
6. Is it snowing outside?

No, she's not OR *No, she isn't* . She's at the bookstore.
_____ . I'm doing the last question.
_____ . I'm writing a report.
_____ . He's cleaning the bathroom.
_____ . They're eating cereal.
_____ . Let's make a snowman.

D. 괄호 안에 주어진 단어들을 사용하여 종업원과 Joe의 대화를 완성하세요. 필요한 경우 부정문으로 쓰세요.

Waitress: 1. *Are you enjoying* _____ your meal? (you, enjoy)
JOE: 2. Yes, _____ pancakes, and they're delicious! (I, have)
Waitress: Good. 3. _____ anything. (you, drink) How about some coffee?
JOE: Yes, please. The restaurant is crowded today.
Waitress: 4. Yes, _____ all pies at half price. (we, sell)
JOE: That's great! Can I have some apple pie, then?

Waitress

JOE

UNIT 006 | They **like** holidays. 일반동사 현재 시제 (1)

🎧 006.mp3

①

They **like** holidays.
그들은 휴일을 좋아한다.

like는 현재 시제이다.

---

② 현재 시제는 다음과 같이 쓴다.

I/we/you/they	visit live exercise
he/she/it	sells sits snows

- I **visit** my aunt in Miami every year. 나는 매년 마이애미에 있는 이모를 방문한다.
- "What is Kevin's job?" "He **sells** cars." 그는 차를 판매해요.
- We **live** in an apartment downtown.
- Sue **sits** next to me in my math class.
- Tom and Ben are at the gym. They **exercise** in the morning.
- It often **snows** here in January.

주어가 **he/she/it** 등일 때 동사 끝에 -s를 붙이는 것에 주의한다.

- Emily **wants** a computer for her birthday. Emily는 생일에 컴퓨터를 원한다.
- My son usually **eats** toast for breakfast. 내 아들은 아침 식사로 주로 토스트를 먹는다.

---

③ -s가 아니라 -es를 붙이는 동사들이 있다.

teach → teaches	go → goes	miss → misses	study → studies
finish → finishes	do → does	pass → passes	fly → flies

-s/-es 붙이는 방법: 부록 p.248 참고

- Professor Kim **teaches** American history. Kim 교수님은 미국사를 가르친다.
- This train **goes** to Washington, DC. 이 열차는 워싱턴 DC까지 간다.
- Alice **misses** her friend Alex. He lives in a different city now.
- Larry **studies** fashion design at college.

단, **have**는 주어가 **he/she/it** 등일 때 **has**로 쓴다.

- I have a dog, and Brian **has** a cat. 나는 개가 있고, Brian은 고양이가 있다.

PRACTICE

A. 둘 중 맞는 것을 고르세요.

1. I (drive / drives) to work every day.
2. The sun is up today. It (shine / shines) in the sky.
3. Kyle and Gary live close to school. They (walk / walks) to school together.
4. We (ride / rides) our bikes on weekends.
5. My cousin likes me a lot. She often (call / calls) me.
6. "My office is in that building." "Oh, you (work / works) for a big company."
7. This jacket is on sale today. It (cost / costs) $30.
8. Scott has short hair. He (get / gets) a haircut every month.

B. 괄호 안에 주어진 동사를 사용하여 문장을 완성하세요. 현재 시제로 쓰세요.

1. (finish) Tate _finishes_ work at 7 p.m. and arrives home at 8 p.m.
2. (carry) My mom _____ a photo of my family in her wallet.
3. (do) Sharon _____ yoga every weekend.
4. (fly) My uncle takes many business trips. He often _____ to Dubai.
5. (have) Jeremy _____ a new hat. It's a gift from his friend.
6. (reach) That plant is very tall. It _____ to the ceiling.
7. (go) Ryan watches a lot of movies. He _____ to the theater every Friday.
8. (pass) "Look at the subway map. This train _____ Cooper station." "Oh, no! We're on the wrong train."

C. 주어진 동사를 사용하여 현재 시제 문장을 완성하세요.

buy	cry	do	have	play	speak	~~take~~

1. William _takes_ a shower every morning.
2. Mark _____ his laundry every Saturday.
3. New York _____ many tall buildings. It's a big city.
4. My parents are from Germany, so I _____ German at home.
5. "Peggy _____ the drums well." "Yes. She's amazing."
6. Babies _____ when they are hungry.
7. Phil and Marco usually _____ bread from a bakery on Larch Street.

D. 괄호 안에 주어진 단어들과 현재 시제를 사용하여 Justin과 Linda의 대화를 완성하세요.

JUSTIN: 1. _I love_ _____ holidays. Especially Christmas! (I, love)
LINDA: Yes, you do. 2. _____ it too, but I don't. (your father, like)
JUSTIN: Why not, Mom?
LINDA: 3. Well, _____ a party every Christmas. (we, have)
          4. _____ everything for the party. (I, prepare)
JUSTIN: I can help. 5. Dad! _____ our help! (Mom, want)
LINDA: Thanks, Justin.

JUSTIN

LINDA

정답 p.267, REVIEW TEST 1 p.216

🎧 007.mp3

①

He **drives** to work every morning.
그는 매일 아침 운전해서 회사에 간다.

② 반복적으로 일어나는 일에 대해 말할 때 현재 시제를 쓴다.

- I often **meet** my friends on Fridays. 나는 금요일에 자주 친구들을 만난다.
- We **go** to the movies every weekend. 우리는 매주 주말에 영화를 보러 간다.
- Jessica **travels** a lot in the summer.
- Mom usually **exercises** at night.
- Naomi **writes** e-mails to her customers sometimes.
- My friend and I **play** golf every day after work.

③ 일반적인 사실에 대해 말할 때도 현재 시제를 쓴다.

- Mexicans **speak** Spanish. 멕시코인들은 스페인어를 쓴다.
- Edward is a lawyer. He **works** for a big company. 그는 큰 회사에서 일한다.
- That store **sells** fresh fruit. Let's go there.
- Peter and Nicole are my neighbors. They **live** next door.
- Some students **wear** uniforms at school.
- Ms. White is a professor. She **teaches** science.

④ 변하지 않는 사실 또는 과학적인 사실을 말할 때도 현재 시제를 쓴다.

- The sun **rises** in the east. 해는 동쪽에서 뜬다.
- Leaves **fall** from trees in autumn. 가을에 나뭇잎이 나무에서 떨어진다.
- Rain **comes** from clouds.
- All birds **have** feathers.
- Owls **hunt** at night.

PRACTICE

A. 다음 스케줄을 보고 Karen의 일상에 대해 말해보세요.

WEEKDAY SCHEDULE

07:00	wake up
08:00	leave home
09:00	start work
NOON	go to lunch
06:00	finish work

1. Karen _wakes up_ at 7 o'clock.
2. She _____ at 8 o'clock.
3. She _____ at 9 o'clock.
4. She _____ at noon.
5. She _____ at 6 o'clock.

B. 괄호 안에 주어진 단어들을 사용하여 문장을 완성하세요.

1. (I, walk) _I walk_ to my office sometimes.
2. (Hannah, wash) _____ her car on weekends.
3. (the post office, open) _____ at 9 a.m. every day.
4. (pandas, eat) _____ for 12 hours a day.
5. (my husband and I, make) _____ dinner together on Fridays.
6. (water, cover) _____ about 75 percent of Earth.

C. 주어진 동사를 사용하여 문장을 완성하세요. 필요한 경우 동사에 -s/-es를 붙이세요.

| bake   close   collect   ~~give~~   jog   like   need |

1. Many people _give_ presents on Christmas.
2. Patrick _____ stamps. It's his hobby.
3. Carl _____ the winter. He hates hot weather.
4. My sister often _____ cookies at home. They taste great.
5. Plants _____ water and sunlight to live.
6. National museums _____ on holidays.
7. Steve is very healthy. He _____ every morning.

D. 다음은 아마존 우림에 대한 정보입니다. 주어진 동사를 사용하여 문장을 완성하세요.

| cut   have   hunt   live   need   ~~rain~~ |

The Amazon rainforest

The Amazon rainforest is in South America.
1. It _rains_ a lot there in the summer.
2. The Amazon rainforest _____ millions of trees.
3. Also, many animals _____ in the rainforest.
They are all important to the global environment.
4. However, some people _____ down the trees.
5. They _____ the animals too.
6. So the rainforest _____ our protection.

정답 p.267, REVIEW TEST 1 p.216

| **He does not like fish.** 현재 시제 부정문

🎧 008.mp3

① I don't like fish.

긍정 She **likes** fish. 그녀는 생선을 좋아한다.

부정 He **does not like** fish. 그는 생선을 좋아하지 않는다.

② 현재 시제 부정문은 **do/does not** + 동사원형으로 쓴다.

I we you they	**do not** (= don't)	work play need swim
he she it	**does not** (= doesn't)	

- "I **do not work** on weekends." 나는 주말에 일하지 않아. "That's good."
- Ray has a guitar, but he **does not play** it much. 그는 그것을 많이 연주하지는 않는다.
- You **don't need** a jacket. It's warm today.
- Dina **doesn't swim**. She's afraid of the water.
- We **don't know** this city well. We're visitors.

일상적인 대화나 글에서는 **do not/does not**보다는 **don't/doesn't**를 더 자주 쓴다.

- My parents **don't travel** a lot. They usually stay at home. 내 부모님은 여행을 많이 다니지 않으신다.
- "The store **doesn't open** early in the morning." 그 가게는 아침에 일찍 열지 않아.
  "Let's go to another store, then."

③ 주어가 he/she/it일 때 **do not**이 아니라 **does not** (= **doesn't**)을 쓰는 것에 주의한다.

- "Is that Anita?" "No, she **doesn't wear** glasses." (she don't wear로 쓸 수 없음)
- Charlie **doesn't eat** meat. He's a vegetarian. (Charlie don't eat으로 쓸 수 없음)
- "I like this hotel. The room **doesn't cost** a lot of money." "It has a nice view too."

이때, **does not** (= **doesn't**) 다음에 동사원형을 쓰는 것에 주의한다.

- Martin **doesn't cook** at home. He usually eats out. (Martin doesn't cooks로 쓸 수 없음)
- This sofa is very big. It **doesn't fit** here. (It doesn't fits로 쓸 수 없음)

PRACTICE

A. 괄호 안에 주어진 표현을 사용하여 부정문을 완성하세요.

1. (have a watch) "What time is it?" "Sorry. I _don't have a watch_ OR _do not have a watch_ ."
2. (understand Chinese) Scott has many Chinese friends, but he _____ .
3. (look well) "You _____ ." "I think I have a cold."
4. (have a lot of homework) "I usually _____ ." "Wow, you're lucky!"
5. (watch TV) Judy _____ . She prefers to read.
6. (make any noise) My apartment is quiet. My neighbors _____ .
7. (clean) Clark _____ his room often. It's usually dirty.

B. 그림을 보고 괄호 안에 주어진 동사를 사용하여 문장을 완성하세요. 필요한 경우 부정문으로 쓰세요.

1
(This is our car.)

2

3
(You're Ted, right?) (Yes, I am.)

4

5
(I hate the rain.)

1. (have) They _have_ _____ a car.
2. (know) He _____ the answer.
3. (remember) She _____ his name.
4. (want) They _____ any more food.
5. (like) She _____ rainy days.

C. 주어진 동사를 사용하여 문장을 완성하세요. 필요한 경우 부정문으로 쓰세요.

| bite | buy | show | snow | ~~talk~~ | work |

1. Bernie _doesn't talk_ OR _does not talk_ much. He's really shy.
2. My brother and I are doctors. We _____ at a hospital.
3. The theater _____ a new play every first week of the month.
4. Don't worry. My dog _____ people.
5. I _____ shoes online. I always try them on at a store.
6. It _____ a lot in Alaska. It's very cold.

D. 괄호 안에 주어진 동사를 사용하여 James와 Linda의 대화를 완성하세요. 필요한 경우 부정문으로 쓰세요.

JAMES

JAMES: What's for dinner, Linda?
LINDA: Fish and salad.
JAMES: Really? 1. I _don't like_ OR _do not like_ fish. (like)
LINDA: I know. 2. You _____ seafood, James. (eat)
But please try some this time.
JAMES: 3. But it _____ good! (smell)
4. And I _____ the taste. (hate)
LINDA: 5. Oh, James. It _____ fine. Try a little. (taste)

LINDA

정답 p.267, REVIEW TEST 1 p.216

UNIT **008**

Grammar Gateway Basic

①

Do you speak English?

Yes, I do.

긍정   You <u>**speak**</u> English. 당신은 영어를 한다.

의문   <u>**Do**</u> you <u>**speak**</u> English? 당신은 영어를 하시나요?

---

②   현재 시제 의문문은 **do/does** + 주어 + 동사원형으로 쓴다.

Do	I we you they	look ...? work ...? like ...? have ...?
Does	he she it	

- **Do I look** OK in this dress? 제가 이 옷을 입으니 괜찮아 보이나요?
- "Andrew is not in his office." "**Does** he **work** from home today?" 그는 오늘 집에서 일하나요?
- **Do you like** Italian food? I know a good restaurant.
- "**Do we have** any milk?" "Look in the fridge."
- "My sister lives in a two-bedroom apartment alone." "**Does** she **need** a roommate?"
- "**Do** your parents **visit** you often?" "Yes. Every week."
- "The new café has several kinds of coffee." "**Does** it **sell** coffee beans too?"

주어가 **he/she/it**일 때 **does**를 쓴다. 이때, **does** + 주어 다음에 동사원형을 쓰는 것에 주의한다.

- "**Does Matthew wear** a uniform at school?" "No. His school doesn't have a uniform." (Does Matthew wears로 쓸 수 없음)
- "Jane is fixing the fence." "**Does she want** any help?" (Does she wants로 쓸 수 없음)

---

③   다음과 같이 의문문에 짧게 답할 수 있다.

Yes,	I/we/you/they	do.	No,	I/we/you/they	don't.
	he/she/it	does.		he/she/it	doesn't.

- "**Do you know** Susie?" Susie를 아나요? "**Yes, I do.**" (= Yes, I know Susie.)
- "**Does** Harry **play** the cello?" Harry는 첼로를 연주하나요? "**No, he doesn't.**" (= No, he doesn't play the cello.)
- "**Do we have** any plans for Friday this week?" "**No, we don't.**"
- "**Does** the new bed **feel** comfortable?" "Yes, it does."

PRACTICE

A. 괄호 안에 주어진 표현을 사용하여 예시와 같이 질문해 보세요.

1. (you, remember me) *Do you remember me* ?   Of course! Hi, Cathy.
2. (Rosa, have a boyfriend) _____ ?   Yes. His name is Mike.
3. (Mr. Gill, need more time) _____ on the report?   Yes. He's very busy.
4. (we, know your phone number) _____ ?   Probably not.
5. (you, own a bicycle) _____ ?   No, but I want one.
6. (the bus, usually arrive) _____ on time?   No, it doesn't.
7. (your kids, like dogs) _____ ?   Yes. They love them.

B. 주어진 단어들과 do 또는 does를 사용하여 의문문을 완성하세요.

| drive | go | know | ~~live~~ | play | talk | work |

1. (Anna) " *Does Anna live* _____ on 3rd Avenue?" "No. Her house is on 4th Street."
2. (we) " _____ that girl?" "Yes. She's in our art class."
3. (your children) " _____ to bed early?" "Yes. They usually sleep before 9 p.m."
4. (Janet) " _____ a blue car?" "No. She has a black van."
5. (Ted) " _____ baseball?" "No. He only watches it on TV."
6. (George) " _____ at a clothing store now?" "Yes, he enjoys his new job."
7. (you) " _____ in French with your French friends?" "No, in English."

C. 주어진 의문문을 보고 예시와 같이 짧게 답하세요.

1. A: Do I need a haircut?
   B: *No, you don't* . Your hair is fine.

2. A: Do you often read magazines?
   B: _____ . It's my favorite hobby.

3. A: Does Steve usually eat out for lunch?
   B: _____ . He always brings his lunch.

4. A: Do you use the Internet a lot?
   B: _____ . I can't work without it.

5. A: Does your daughter go to college?
   B: _____ . She's in high school.

6. A: Do you and Hannah meet often?
   B: _____ . We're very close.

D. Chris는 베트남을 여행 중입니다. 괄호 안에 주어진 단어들과 do 또는 does를 사용하여 Chris와 점원의 대화를 완성하세요. 필요한 경우 부정문으로 쓰세요.

CHRIS: Excuse me. 1. *Do you speak English* ? (you, speak, English)
Clerk: Yes. Can I help you?
CHRIS: 2. _____ . (I, want, some mangoes)
Clerk: 3. Sorry, _____ . (we, have, mangoes)
   How about oranges?
CHRIS: OK. I'll take one. 4. _____ ? (it, taste, good)
Clerk: Sure. Here, you can try it.

CHRIS

Clerk

정답 p.267, REVIEW TEST 1 p.216

UNIT 010 | **I am doing** vs. **I do** 현재진행 시제와 현재 시제 비교

🎧 010.mp3

①

현재진행 시제
He **is playing** a game now.
그는 지금 게임을 하는 중이다.

현재 시제
He **plays** soccer often,
but he's not playing soccer now.
그는 축구를 자주 하지만, 지금은 축구를 하고 있지 않다.

② 현재진행 시제 (I am doing ~)

현재진행 시제는 지금 말하고 있는 시점에 일어나고 있는 일을 나타낸다.

- I'm **jogging** now.
  (지금 조깅을 하고 있음)
- Jeff **isn't wearing** a suit today.
  (오늘 정장을 입고 있지 않음)
- **Is** it **snowing** a lot outside?
- Look! Lena and Nancy **are dancing**.
- Louis **is cooking** Thai food. It smells good.
- My sisters **aren't watching** TV. They're talking.

현재 시제 (I do ~)

현재 시제는 반복적으로 일어나는 일이나 일반적인 사실을 나타낸다.

- I **jog** every morning.
  (매일 아침 조깅을 함)
- Jeff **doesn't** usually **wear** suits.
  (보통 정장을 입지 않음)
- **Does** it **snow** a lot here in December?
- Lena and Nancy **dance** very well.
- Louis **cooks** Thai food often.
- My sisters **don't watch** TV much.

③ 다음과 같은 동사들은 현재진행 시제로 쓰지 않고 주로 현재 시제로 쓴다.

want	love	prefer	know	agree	remember
need	like	hate	believe	understand	forget

- Marie **loves** tea. She drinks it every morning. Marie는 차를 좋아한다.
- Margaret and I are very different. She never **agrees** with me. 그녀는 결코 나와 동의하지 않는다.
- "**Do** you **need** some help?" "Yes. I **don't understand** this question."
- "I sometimes **forget** people's names." "Me too."

④ **have**와 **has**

'(어떤 물건 등을) 가지고 있다'라는 의미로 말할 때는 현재진행 시제로 쓰지 않고 현재 시제로 쓴다.

- Steven **has** a big house. It's beautiful. Steven은 큰 집을 가지고 있다.
  (Steven is having a big house로 쓸 수 없음)

그러나 '~을 먹다'라는 의미로 말할 때는 현재진행 시제와 현재 시제 둘 다 쓸 수 있다.

- I usually **have** dinner with my wife, but now I'**m having** dinner alone.
  나는 보통 아내와 저녁을 먹지만, 지금은 혼자 먹고 있다.

PRACTICE

A. 그림을 보고 괄호 안에 주어진 동사들을 한 번씩 사용하여 문장을 완성하세요.

1
Name: ANTON
Job: car mechanic

2
Name: LIZ
Job: sales clerk

3
Name: GINO
Job: fashion designer

4
Name: GEORGE
Job: painter

1. (fix, eat) Anton _fixes_____ cars. He _'s eating OR is eating___ a sandwich.
2. (ride, work) Liz _____ a horse. She _____ at a shop.
3. (play, design) Gino _____ soccer. He _____ clothes.
4. (paint, sleep) George _____ pictures. He _____ right now.

B. 괄호 안에 주어진 단어들을 사용하여 현재진행 시제 또는 현재 시제 문장을 완성하세요.

1. (he, wash) "Is Dad in the garage?" "Yes. _He's washing OR He is washing_____ the car."
2. (Angela, go) _____ to the dentist every six months.
3. (I, look) "_____ for my cell phone." "Oh, it's on the kitchen table."
4. (the post office, not deliver) _____ mail on Sundays.
5. (we, buy) _____ our groceries at that supermarket every week.
6. (Jason and Fred, not study) _____ now. They're at the gym.
7. (Mr. Smith's phone, ring) _____, but he isn't answering it.

C. 주어진 동사를 사용하여 현재진행 시제 또는 현재 시제 문장을 완성하세요.

attend	hate	~~play~~	remember	spend	swim

1. "Do you have any hobbies?" "I sometimes _play_____ the drums on weekends."
2. Look! There are some ducks in the water. They _____.
3. My brother loves reading. He usually _____ a lot of time at the library.
4. "_____ you _____ Harry's address?" "No, I don't."
5. Nicole is at a church now. She _____ a wedding.
6. Michelle _____ snakes. She's afraid of them.

D. 다음 문장을 읽고 틀린 부분이 있으면 바르게 고치세요. 틀린 부분이 없으면 O로 표시하세요.

1. Howard is knowing my brother. They go to the same school.   _is knowing → knows_
2. Are Matt and Tammy having lunch together now? _____
3. Tom and Sally are at the mall. They shop. _____
4. "I'm not lying. It's not my fault." "I believe you." _____
5. Brian isn't having a car. He takes the bus to work. _____
6. I don't do anything right now. Let's go for a walk. _____

UNIT
010

Grammar Gateway Basic

UNIT 011 | She **was** in the hospital. be동사 과거 시제 (was/were)

①

어제   지금

She **is** at home now.

Yesterday, she **was** in the hospital.
어제 그녀는 병원에 있었다.

---

② was/were는 '~이었다, ~에 있었다'라는 의미로 다음과 같이 쓴다.

I he/she/it	**was**
we/you/they	**were**

- I **was** really happy yesterday. It **was** my birthday. 나는 어제 정말 행복했다.
- "We **were** in Houston last month." 우리는 지난달에 휴스턴에 있었어. "Oh, I like that city."
- "My father **was** a taxi driver many years ago." "What does he do now?"
- You **were** at the theater last night. How was the movie?
- Patricia **was** single last year, but now she's married.
- We **were** at home all day yesterday. We **were** very bored.

   was/were는 축약된 형태로 쓰지 않는 것에 주의한다.

   - "When I **was** young, I **was** interested in airplanes." "Me too." (I's로 쓸 수 없음)
   - Our children were at the zoo yesterday. **They were** so excited. (They're로 쓸 수 없음)

---

③ **am/is**의 과거는 **was**로 쓰고, **are**의 과거는 **were**로 쓴다.

- I **was** a student five years ago. Now I'**m** a teacher.
   나는 5년 전에 학생이었다. 지금은 선생님이다.
- Melisa and Dan **were** in Bangkok last week. Now they'**re** back.
   Melisa와 Dan은 지난주에 방콕에 있었다. 지금은 돌아왔다.
- "It **was** cloudy yesterday, but it'**s** sunny today." "Yes. The sky is very clear."
- Fred and I **are** very close because we **were** roommates for three years.

PRACTICE

A. 각 사람들이 어제 오후 1시에 어디에 있었는지에 대해 말하고 있습니다. 주어진 표현을 사용하여 문장을 완성하세요.

~~at home~~   at school   at a restaurant   at a store

1. I *was at home* _____.

2. I _____.

3. We _____.

4. I _____.

B. 괄호 안에 주어진 주어와 was 또는 were를 사용하여 문장을 완성하세요.

1. (I) *I was* _____ in Italy three weeks ago.
2. (the stars) _____ beautiful last night.
3. (he) "Do you know Mr. Williams?" "Yes. _____ my boss two years ago."
4. (these gloves) "_____ in my car." "Oh, those are mine."
5. (my friends and I) _____ at a concert last weekend.
6. (it) _____ very hot on Sunday, so we were at the pool all day.

C. am/is/are 또는 was/were를 써넣으세요.

1. I can't find my keys. They _____were_____ here a minute ago.
2. I _____ short in middle school. Now I _____ tall.
3. "You _____ in a hurry this morning." "Yes. I _____ late for an appointment."
4. "Jenny _____ sick yesterday." "_____ she OK now?"
5. "Look! These cups _____ $10 each." "Really? They _____ on sale last week."
6. Patrick _____ in London last month. He _____ in Paris now. He _____ very busy these days.

D. am/is/are 또는 was/were를 사용하여 Michael Kim에 대한 글을 완성하세요.

1. Michael Kim _____is_____ a famous pop singer today.
2. He _____ a pilot 10 years ago, but he made a band with his friends.
3. Their albums _____ successful, so the band was very popular.
Last year, Michael left the band. 4. It _____ sad news for his fans.
5. Michael _____ now a solo singer.
6. But he and his friends _____ still close.

정답 p.268, REVIEW TEST 2 p.218

| **He was not cold.** be동사 과거 시제 부정문과 의문문

🎧 012.mp3

①

Close the window! But I'm hot!

어제

긍정 She **was** cold. 그녀는 추웠다.

부정 He **was not** cold. 그는 춥지 않았다.

---

② **was/were** 부정문은 다음과 같이 쓴다.

I he/she/it	was not (= wasn't)
we/you/they	were not (= weren't)

- I **was not** good at math in high school. 나는 고등학교 때 수학을 잘하지 못했다.
- Melanie and I **were not** friends a year ago. Now we're best friends. Melanie와 나는 1년 전에는 친구가 아니었다.
- My vacation was great, but it **wasn't** very long.
- "You **weren't** in the office last week." "I was on a business trip."
- Michelle usually has lunch at the cafeteria, but she **wasn't** there yesterday.

일상적인 대화나 글에서는 **was not/were not**보다는 **wasn't/weren't**를 더 자주 쓴다.

- The museum **wasn't** open last Wednesday. It was a holiday. 박물관은 지난 수요일에 열지 않았다.
- "I like your shoes." "Thanks. They **weren't** expensive, but I think they're nice." 그것들은 비싸지는 않았어.

---

③ **was/were** 의문문은 다음과 같이 쓴다.

Was	I ...?
	he/she/it ...?
Were	we/you/they ...?

- I can't remember the end of the movie. **Was I** asleep? 나 잠들었었니?
- "**Were you** busy yesterday?" 당신은 어제 바빴었나요? "Not really."
- "**Was Tom** at the park this morning?" "No, he was at home."
- "I was late for a meeting with my clients." "**Were they** upset?"
- "I was at Wendy's birthday party." "**Was it** fun?"

다음과 같이 의문문에 짧게 답할 수 있다.

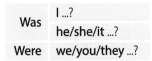

Yes,	I/he/she/it	was.	No,	I/he/she/it	wasn't.
	we/you/they	were.		we/you/they	weren't.

- "**Were you** at the mall last Sunday?" 지난 일요일에 쇼핑몰에 있었니? "**Yes, I was.**" (= Yes, I was at the mall.)
- "**Was the restaurant** OK?" 식당은 괜찮았나요? "**No, it wasn't.**" (= No, it wasn't OK.)
- "**Were your parents** with you at your graduation?" "**Yes, they were.**"

PRACTICE

A. 다음은 어제 Philip에게 있었던 일입니다. was 또는 wasn't를 사용하여 문장을 완성하세요.

1. (tired) Philip _was tired_ .
2. (asleep) He _____ on the bus.
3. (on time) He _____ .
4. (angry) His boss _____ with him.
5. (happy) He _____ .

B. was/were 또는 wasn't/weren't를 써넣으세요.

1. "How was your date last Friday?" "Good. It _was_ nice."
2. Cory and I were at the same school, but we _____ in the same class.
3. The exam _____ easy. My grade isn't very good.
4. The boxes weren't heavy. They _____ empty.
5. The sky _____ clear last night. There wasn't a cloud in the sky.
6. "I can't find the keys. They _____ in the bag." "Here they are!"

C. 괄호 안에 주어진 단어들과 was 또는 were를 사용하여 문장을 완성하세요.

1. (we, on the same flight) " _Were we on the same flight_ ?" "Yes, we were."
2. (Howard, at the meeting) "_____ yesterday?" "No, he wasn't."
3. (you, with Jessica) "_____ on Saturday?" "No. I was with Rob."
4. (Kim and Lucy, there) I was at the picnic last weekend. _____ too.
5. (the baseball game, exciting) "_____." "Yes. It was fun."
6. (your mom, a cook) "_____?" "Yes, she was."
7. (I, in Lisbon) "You were in Portugal last week, right?" "Yes. _____."
8. (you, at the gym) "_____ this morning?" "No. I was at home. Why?"

D. 괄호 안에 주어진 단어들과 was 또는 were를 사용하여 Chris와 Amy의 대화를 완성하세요.

CHRIS: 1. _Were you in class_ this morning? (you, in class)

AMY: 2. No. _____. I'm sick. (I, not, at school)

CHRIS: 3. But you were with me yesterday, and _____. (you, fine)

AMY: I think I have a cold. 4. _____ when we were driving home together. (the window, open)

CHRIS: 5. _____? (you, cold)

AMY: Yes, I was.

CHRIS: Oh, I wasn't. Sorry, that was my fault.

CHRIS

AMY

정답 p.268, REVIEW TEST 2 p.218

UNIT 013 | He **walked** to school yesterday. 일반동사 과거 시제

①

어제

He **walks** to school every day.

He **walked** to school yesterday. 어제 그는 학교에 걸어갔다.

walked는 과거 시제이다.

② '~했다'라는 의미로 과거에 일어난 일에 대해 말할 때 과거 시제를 쓴다. 과거 시제는 주로 동사원형 끝에 **-ed**를 붙인다.

동사원형	clean	finish	watch	laugh	wait
과거 시제	**cleaned**	**finished**	**watched**	**laughed**	**waited**

- "Your house is very clean." "I **cleaned** it last Friday." 나는 지난 금요일에 청소했어.
- The soccer game **finished** at 5 o'clock yesterday. 어제 축구 경기는 5시에 끝났다.
- Eric was bored, so he **watched** TV.
- "Everyone **laughed** at Ken's joke." "Yes. It was very funny."
- "Was the restaurant crowded?" "Yes. We **waited** for an hour."

③ 다음과 같이 **-ed**를 붙일 때 주의해야 할 동사들이 있다.

live → liv**ed**   die → di**ed**   study → stud**ied**   plan → plan**ned**   -(e)d 붙이는 방법: 부록 p.249 참고

- "I **lived** in New Jersey last year." 나는 작년에 뉴저지에 살았어. "Where do you live now?"
- Vincent van Gogh **died** in 1890. 빈센트 반 고흐는 1890년에 사망했다.
- Jenny **studied** medicine for six years. Now, she works at a pharmacy.
- We're so excited. We **planned** our vacation a month ago.

과거 시제로 쓸 때 **-ed**를 붙이지 않고 형태가 달라지는 동사들이 있다.

have → **had**   get → **got**   buy → **bought**   go → **went**   불규칙 동사: 부록 p.246 참고

- Emily **had** bacon and eggs for breakfast this morning. Emily는 오늘 아침에 베이컨과 달걀을 먹었다.
- Mr. Roland **got** a call from his boss. Roland씨는 상사로부터 전화를 받았다.
- "I **bought** a new sofa last week." "Was it expensive?"
- "Noel and Cory are at the café together. Are they friends?" "Yes. They **went** to the same school."

④ 과거 시제는 **yesterday, last week, in 1789**과 같은 표현들과 함께 자주 쓴다.

- The bus **arrived** 20 minutes late **yesterday**. 어제 버스가 20분 늦게 도착했다.
- I **had** a great time at the festival **last week**. 지난주에 나는 축제에서 즐거운 시간을 보냈다.
- George Washington **became** the first president of the United States **in 1789**.

PRACTICE

A. 주어진 동사를 사용하여 과거 시제 문장을 완성하세요.

cry	~~freeze~~	go	invite	play	work

1. The lake _froze_ last winter, so I went skating a lot.
2. I _____ tennis in high school.
3. My neighbors _____ me for dinner last Friday.
4. The baby was sick yesterday. She _____ all night.
5. Joe _____ to the store this morning for some milk.
6. Jessica _____ at a bookstore when she was in college.

B. 괄호 안에 주어진 단어들을 사용하여 현재 시제 또는 과거 시제 문장을 완성하세요.

1. (the company, hire) _The company hired_ new employees three weeks ago.
2. (it, close) "Is the mall still open?" "Yes. _____ at 10 p.m. every day."
3. (Laura and Nick, get) _____ married last year.
4. (Earth, travel) _____ around the Sun.
5. (we, laugh) "Evan has a new costume for Halloween. It looks funny." "I know! _____ a lot."
6. (I, forget) "I'm sorry. _____ your book." "That's OK."
7. (Jeff, fly) _____ to Singapore on business every month.
8. (I, need) It's cold out here! _____ a scarf.

C. 다음 문장을 읽고 틀린 부분이 있으면 바르게 고치세요. 틀린 부분이 없으면 O로 표시하세요.

1. I live in New York a year ago.   _live → lived_
2. We paint our rooms every year.   _____
3. My mom meets my father in 2000.   _____
4. Clara took a trip last summer.   _____
5. It rains a lot yesterday.   _____
6. That actor wins many awards last year.   _____
7. Holly and her brother ate cereal this morning.   _____

D. 괄호 안에 주어진 표현을 사용하여 Justin과 Sandy의 대화를 완성하세요.

JUSTIN

SANDY

JUSTIN: ¹· I _walked to school_ alone this morning. Where were you?
(walk to school)

SANDY: ²· I _____ because I woke up late this morning.
(take the bus)

JUSTIN: Oh. Why?

SANDY: ³· I _____ last night. (go to bed late)
⁴· I _____ . (study for our test)

JUSTIN: What? Do we have a test today?

정답 p.268, REVIEW TEST 2 p.218

UNIT
013

Grammar Gateway Basic

🎧 014.mp3

① 과거 시제 부정문은 **did not** + 동사원형으로 쓴다.

I/he/she/it we/you/they	**did not** (= **didn't**)	enjoy know sleep answer

How was the movie?

I did not enjoy it.

- A: How was the movie?
  B: I **did not enjoy** it. 나는 그것을 즐기지 않았어.
- Bob **didn't know** Janice in high school. They met in college.
  Bob은 고등학교 때 Janice를 알지 못했다.
- We **didn't sleep** much last night because of the storm.
- Mr. Williams called Rose, but she **didn't answer** the phone.

일상적인 대화나 글에서는 **did not**보다는 **didn't**를 더 자주 쓴다.
- "Where is the stapler?" "I don't know. I **didn't take** it." 나는 그것을 가져가지 않았어.
- "Oh, I dropped my phone!" "Don't worry. It **didn't break**." 그것은 고장 나지 않았어.

did not (= **didn't**) 다음에 동사원형을 쓰는 것에 주의한다.
- I **didn't stay** at home last weekend. I went out with my friends. (I didn't stayed로 쓸 수 없음)
- Danny **didn't fix** the printer. I did. (Danny didn't fixed로 쓸 수 없음)

---

② 의문문은 **did** + 주어 + 동사원형으로 쓴다.

Did	I/he/she/it we/you/they	like ...? tell ...? leave ...? rain ...?

MOVIE

Did you **like** the movie?

- A: **Did** you **like** the movie? 너는 그 영화가 좋았니?
  B: It was boring. I fell asleep.
- **Did** Susie **tell** you about her wedding? Susie가 그녀의 결혼식에 대해 얘기했니?
- "**Did** I **leave** my coat here?" "Yes. Here you go."
- The streets are wet. **Did** it **rain**?

did + 주어 다음에도 동사원형을 쓰는 것에 주의한다.
- There was a fire alarm. **Did you hear** it? (Did you heard로 쓸 수 없음)
- "**Did Mr. Green send** you an e-mail?" "No, not yet." (Did Mr. Green sent로 쓸 수 없음)

다음과 같이 의문문에 짧게 답할 수 있다.

Yes,	I/he/she/it we/you/they	**did.**	**No,**	I/he/she/it we/you/they	**didn't.**	

- "**Did** you **take** these pictures?" 네가 이 사진들을 찍었니? "**Yes, I did.**" (= Yes, I took these pictures.)
- "**Did** Mark **get** a haircut?" Mark가 머리를 잘랐니? "**No, he didn't.**" (= No, he didn't get a haircut.)

PRACTICE

A. 다음 목록을 보고 Miranda가 어제 한 일과 하지 않은 일들에 대해 말해보세요.

1. do the laundry   X
2. read the newspaper   X
3. go to the gym   O
4. wash the car   X
5. attend a cooking class   O
6. have lunch with Jackie   O

1. *She didn't do the laundry* OR *She did not do the laundry* .
2. _____ .
3. _____ .
4. _____ .
5. _____ .
6. _____ .

B. 괄호 안에 주어진 단어들을 사용하여 과거 시제 의문문을 완성하세요.

1. (you, lose) *Did you lose* _____ some weight?   Yes. I lost five pounds.
2. (Sarah, pass) _____ her math exam?   Yes. She's so happy.
3. (you, read) _____ this book?   Yes. It was very good.
4. (someone, knock) _____ on the door?   No. I don't think so.
5. (you, get) _____ my invitation? I sent it yesterday.   Yes, I did.
6. (we, miss) _____ the train?   No. We're on time.
7. (Dave, grow up) _____ in France?   No. He's from Italy.
8. (the Smiths, buy) _____ a house?   Yes. It's very nice.

C. 주어진 단어들을 사용하여 과거 시제 문장을 완성하세요. 필요한 경우 부정문으로 쓰세요.

buy	~~cook~~	find	lock	meet	visit

1. (I) *I didn't cook* OR *I did not cook* dinner tonight. I ordered a pizza instead.
2. (you) " _____ these earrings?" "No. I made them."
3. (my friends and I) _____ the Eiffel Tower because we had no time.
4. (Elena) " _____ Tom Cruise on the street!" "She's so lucky!"
5. (we) Oh, _____ the front door. Let's go back home right away!
6. (Jake) " _____ a job." "That's great! I'm happy for him."

D. 괄호 안에 주어진 단어들과 과거 시제를 사용하여 Kate와 Amy의 대화를 완성하세요. 필요한 경우 부정문으로 쓰세요.

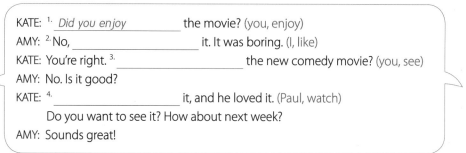

KATE: 1. *Did you enjoy* the movie? (you, enjoy)
AMY: 2. No, _____ it. It was boring. (I, like)
KATE: You're right. 3. _____ the new comedy movie? (you, see)
AMY: No. Is it good?
KATE: 4. _____ it, and he loved it. (Paul, watch)
     Do you want to see it? How about next week?
AMY: Sounds great!

KATE   AMY

정답 p.268, REVIEW TEST 2 p.218

UNIT 015 | He **was playing** the guitar. 과거진행 시제

🎧 015.mp3

①

어제 7시

At 7 o'clock, he was at school.

He **was playing** the guitar.

그는 기타를 연주하는 중이었다.

was playing은 과거진행 시제이다.

---

② 과거진행 시제는 '~하는 중이었다'라는 의미로 was/were + -ing로 쓴다.

I/he/she/it	was	taking studying having cleaning
we/you/they	were	

- I **was taking** a shower when Lisa called. Lisa가 전화했을 때 나는 샤워하는 중이었다.
- Ted **was studying** in London in 2015. Ted는 2015년에 런던에서 공부하고 있었다.
- At 1 o'clock today, we **were having** coffee at a café.
- Benny and Simon **were cleaning** the kitchen this morning.
- "Did you see Joe and Rita?" "They **were talking** with the boss."

---

③ **am/is + -ing**의 과거는 **was + -ing**로 쓰고, **are + -ing**의 과거는 **were + -ing**로 쓴다.

- Vanessa **was sleeping** at 6 a.m. Now, she **is making** breakfast.
  Vanessa는 오전 6시에 자고 있었다. 지금은 아침을 만들고 있다.
- Some kids **were swimming** in the pool a few minutes ago. They **are leaving** now.
  몇몇 아이들이 몇 분 전에 수영장에서 수영하고 있었다. 그들은 지금 떠나고 있다.
- It **was snowing** when I got on the bus. I am home now, and the sun **is shining**.

---

④ 지금 말하고 있는 시점에 일어나고 있는 일에 대해 말할 때 현재진행 시제를 쓴다.

I'm watching a movie now.

과거 ——— 지금 ——— 미래

- **I'm watching** a movie now. I'll call you back.
  나는 지금 영화를 보고 있어.
- "Jen **is looking** for you. She's waiting in your office." Jen이 당신을 찾고 있어요.
  "Oh, I see."
- My classmates and I **are working** on a project right now.

과거의 특정한 시점에 일어나고 있던 일에 대해 말할 때 과거진행 시제를 쓴다.

I **was watching** a movie.

2:00 영화가 시작했음 3:00 4:30 영화가 끝났음

- I **was watching** a movie at 3 o'clock yesterday.
  나는 어제 3시에 영화를 보고 있었어.
- "Jen **was looking** for you an hour ago."
  Jen이 한 시간 전에 당신을 찾고 있었어요.
  "I just met with her."
- My classmates and I **were working** on a project last night.

PRACTICE

A. 다음은 어제 Jay가 파티에 도착했을 때의 모습입니다. 주어진 동사를 사용하여 문장을 완성하세요.

carry	dance	eat	~~sing~~	wave

When Jay arrived at the party…

1. Ann *was singing* _____ a song.
2. Mike and Emma _____ together.
3. Jenny _____ a gift.
4. Jack and Bill _____ cake.
5. Ryan _____ his hand.

B. 주어진 동사를 사용하여 과거진행 시제 문장을 완성하세요.

attend	cross	listen	play	~~wait~~

1. "Why are you late?" "Many people *were waiting* _____ at the taxi stand this morning."
2. Dad _____ to loud music, so he didn't hear the doorbell.
3. Tara and I _____ a swimming class an hour ago.
4. I saw John and Fred at the park. They _____ basketball.
5. "I _____ the street when someone called my name." "Who was it?"

C. 괄호 안에 주어진 단어들을 사용하여 현재진행 또는 과거진행 시제 문장을 완성하세요.

1. (Jim and Monica, drink) *Jim and Monica were drinking* wine together at a bar last night.
2. (they, watch) "Why are there so many people on that hill?" "_____ the sunrise."
3. (Alice, lie) _____ in bed when someone knocked on the door.
4. (I, visit) "Were you in town on Christmas?" "No. _____ my family in Texas."
5. (we, stand) _____ at the bus stop when the accident happened.
6. (he, hold) "Excuse me. I'm looking for Mr. Bell."
   "He's right there. _____ an umbrella in his hand."

D. 괄호 안에 주어진 단어들과 과거진행 시제를 사용하여 Linda와 Justin의 대화를 완성하세요.

LINDA: Justin, you're home late.
JUSTIN: 1. *I was playing* _____ the guitar with my friends. (I, play)
LINDA: I called you a lot, but you didn't answer.
JUSTIN: 2. _____ for a concert. (we, practice)
LINDA: 3. Well, _____ about you. (I, worry)
JUSTIN: Sorry, Mom. 4. _____ loudly, so I didn't hear my phone.
(we, perform)

LINDA

JUSTIN

정답 p.269, REVIEW TEST 2 p.218

UNIT 016 | He **was not practicing.** 과거진행 시제 부정문과 의문문

1 과거진행 시제 부정문은 다음과 같이 쓴다.

I/he/she/it	was not (= wasn't)	practicing waiting
we/you/they	were not (= weren't)	listening jogging

어제 10시

- ◉ He **was not practicing**. He was sleeping. 그는 연습하고 있지 않았다.
- ◉ "Sorry I'm late."
  "Don't worry. We **were not waiting** long." 우리는 오래 기다리고 있지 않았어요.
- ◉ "Can I turn off the radio?" "Sure. I **wasn't listening** to it."
- ◉ Dylan **wasn't jogging** at 8 p.m. He was at home.
- ◉ Sean and Max **weren't eating**. They were still looking at the menu.
- ◉ "Did you see Hilary? Was she with Kyle?" "I saw her, but she **wasn't meeting** him."

....

2 과거진행 시제 의문문은 다음과 같이 쓴다.

Was	I/he/she/it	talking …? working …?
Were	we/you/they	driving …? attending …?

- ◉ **Was** I **talking** too loudly? 내가 너무 크게 말하고 있었니?
- ◉ "**Were** you **working** in Florida in 2017?" 당신은 2017년에 플로리다에서 일하고 있었나요? "No. I was in Seattle."
- ◉ "**Was** Lucy **driving**?" "No. I was driving."
- ◉ **Were** you and Todd **attending** a wedding when I called on Sunday?
- ◉ "**Was** it **raining** when you arrived?" "No. The weather was nice."

다음과 같이 의문문에 짧게 답할 수 있다.

Yes,	I/he/she/it	was.	No,	I/he/she/it	wasn't.
	we/you/they	were.		we/you/they	weren't.

- ◉ "**Was** Diane **washing** her car when you saw her?" 네가 그녀를 봤을 때 Diane이 세차하고 있었니?
  "**Yes, she was.**" (= Yes, she was washing her car.)
- ◉ "**Were** you and your roommate **watching** the soccer game at noon?"
  너와 네 룸메이트는 정오에 축구 경기를 보고 있었니?
  "**No, we weren't.**" (= No, we weren't watching the soccer game.)
- ◉ "**Were** you **fighting** with your friend outside last night?" "**No, I wasn't.**"

PRACTICE

A. 다음은 어제 저녁 7시에 있었던 도난 사건에 대한 경찰과 목격자의 대화입니다. 괄호 안에 있는 단어들을 사용하여 문장을 완성하세요.

Was the thief wearing a cap?

1. (he, wear, a red cap) Yes. *He was wearing a red cap* .

Was a woman sitting on this bench?

2. (a woman, not sit, here) No. _____ .

Were you meeting your friends on the street?

3. (I, meet, them, outside) Yes. _____ .

Was the thief carrying a backpack?

4. (he, not carry, a bag) No. _____ .

B. 괄호 안에 주어진 단어들을 사용하여 과거진행 시제 문장을 완성하세요.

1. (you, read, it) "Where is my book? Did you take it?" "Oh, *were you reading it* _____ ?"
2. (Joe and I, enjoy, the party) _____ , so we didn't sleep much that night.
3. (Evan, write, an e-mail) _____ when I visited him.
4. (we, wait, for the bus) _____ when we saw the accident.
5. (it, snow, there) "_____ when I called you?" "Yes, but it just stopped."
6. (Sally, go, to the bank) "_____ when you saw her?"
   "No. She was going to the hospital."

C. 주어진 단어들을 사용하여 과거진행 시제 문장을 완성하세요. 필요한 경우 부정문으로 쓰세요.

| buy | practice | ~~ride~~ | walk | work |

1. (Nick) *Nick wasn't riding* OR *Nick was not riding* his bicycle. He was on his skateboard.
2. (Victor) "I heard the piano. _____ ?" "Yes, he was."
3. (Eric and I) _____ in the office at noon. We were out for lunch.
4. (I) "I saw you at the mall. Were you shopping?" "Yes. _____ a new tie."
5. (you) You are all wet! _____ home from school when the rain started?

| cook | sit | swim | talk | visit |

6. (we) _____ the food when the guests arrived. It was ready a few minutes later.
7. (I) "Did you ask me something?" "No. _____ to you."
8. (Clara) "_____ this morning?" "No. She was jogging with me."
9. (I) "Why did you move to a different seat?" "_____ in the wrong seat."
10. (you and Pete) _____ your parents last weekend? When I visited your house,
    no one was there.

정답 p.269, REVIEW TEST 2 p.218

UNIT
016

Grammar Gateway Basic

🎧 017.mp3

①

I used to be a football player.

과거　　　지금

He is a golfer now.

He **used to be** a football player.

그는 미식축구 선수였다. (지금은 아니다.)

② **used to + 동사원형**: (과거에는) ~ 했었다 (지금은 아니다)

I/we/you/they he/she/it	used to	be work cry climb

- I'm a music teacher, but I **used to be** a singer. (과거에는 가수였지만 지금은 아님)
- "Do you know Sandra?" "Yes. We **used to work** together." (과거에는 함께 일했지만 지금은 아님)
- When Henry was young, he **used to cry** a lot.
- My sister and I **used to climb** that mountain on weekends. Now she's too busy.

③ **used to**의 부정문은 **didn't use to**로 쓴다.

- I **didn't use to sleep** late. These days, I wake up around 10 o'clock. 나는 늦잠을 자지 않았었다.
- You **didn't use to cook**. When did you start? 당신은 요리하지 않았었잖아요.
- Julia **didn't use to enjoy** rock music, but she listens to it every day now.

의문문은 **did + 주어 + use to ~?**로 쓴다.

- "**Did you use to ride** a bicycle to school?" 너는 학교에 자전거를 타고 갔었니? "Yes. I lived close to school."
- "What **did that company use to make** before phones?" 그 회사가 휴대폰 전에는 무엇을 만들었나요? "Computers."
- "**Did people use to write** letters often?" "Yes. That was the only form of communication."

④ **used to**는 지금은 더 이상 계속되지 않는 과거의 습관이나 상태에 대해 말할 때 쓴다.

- My father **used to smoke** every day, but he doesn't smoke anymore. (과거에는 담배를 피웠지만 지금은 아님)
- I **used to live** alone, but now I have a roommate. (과거에는 혼자 살았지만 지금은 아님)

현재에 대해 말할 때는 **used to**를 쓰지 않는 것에 주의한다.

- Cindy **used to study** French. She **studies** Italian these days. (Cindy uses to study로 쓸 수 없음)
- "Do you play video games?" "I **used to**, but I **don't play** them anymore." (I don't use to play로 쓸 수 없음)

PRACTICE

A. 그림을 보고 used to를 사용하여 예시와 같이 문장을 완성하세요.

1 *I don't play basketball.* / *I play basketball.*

2 *I love dogs.* / *I'm afraid of dogs.*

3 *I like my car.* / *I want a new car.*

4 *We live in New York.* / *We live in San Francisco.*

1. He _used to play_ basketball.
2. He _____ afraid of dogs.
3. He _____ his car.
4. They _____ in San Francisco.

B. 괄호 안에 주어진 동사와 used to를 사용하여 문장을 완성하세요. 필요한 경우 부정문으로 쓰세요.

1. (sleep) My daughter _used to sleep_ with her doll when she was young.
2. (drink) "Does Tim drink coffee?" "Sometimes. He _____ it at all before."
3. (eat) I _____ a lot of spicy food, but it wasn't good for my stomach.
4. (own) "Mike _____ a large van." "Why did he sell it?"
5. (sell) "That shop _____ delicious cookies." "Right. I miss those cookies."
6. (speak) "Maria _____ English well." "I didn't know that. Her English is good."
7. (be) That place _____ a pharmacy. Now it's a bank.

C. 주어진 동사를 사용하여 문장을 완성하세요. used to를 함께 쓰거나 현재 시제로 쓰세요.

| ~~believe~~ exercise go listen remember take |

1. I _used to believe_ in Santa Claus, but I don't anymore.
2. Jennifer _____ every day. She wants to lose some weight.
3. Eddie _____ to hip-hop music. Now he prefers jazz.
4. "Do you know that woman's name?" "Yes. I _____ her name. It's Marsha."
5. The Smiths _____ fishing a lot. They don't have much time these days.
6. "We _____ that bus to the station." "Right. It was always crowded."

D. 주어진 동사와 used to를 사용하여 Chris와 James의 대화를 완성하세요.

| be come have ~~play~~ |

CHRIS

CHRIS: Dad, is this you in the picture?
JAMES: 1. Yes. I _used to play_ football.
CHRIS: Wow. You looked different.
JAMES: I know. 2. I _____ a lot of hair.
  3. And your mom _____ to every game.
CHRIS: Really?
JAMES: Oh, yes. 4. She _____ a cheerleader!

JAMES

정답 p.269, REVIEW TEST 2 p.218

UNIT 017

Grammar Gateway Basic

UNIT 018 | She **has washed** the dishes. 현재완료 시제 (1)

①

> I have washed the dishes.

30분 전   지금

She **has washed** the dishes.
그녀는 설거지를 했다. (지금은 그릇들이 깨끗해졌음)

has washed는 현재완료 시제이다.

---

② 현재완료 시제는 **have/has + 과거분사**로 쓴다.

I/we/you/they	have (= 've)	learned
		worked
he/she/it	has (= 's)	waited

- My children **have learned** English for six years. They're very good at it. 내 아이들은 영어를 6년 동안 배웠다.
- Ann **has worked** for Mr. Lee for a long time, so she knows him well. Ann은 오랫동안 Lee씨를 위해 일했다.
- "When did my client get here?" "He**'s waited** for 10 minutes."

과거분사는 주로 동사원형 끝에 **-(e)d**를 붙인다.

live-lived-**lived**   ask-asked-**asked**   talk-talked-**talked**   -(e)d 붙이는 방법: 부록 p.249 참고

그러나 다음과 같이 형태가 불규칙적으로 변하는 동사도 있다.

have-had-**had**   give-gave-**given**   come-came-**come**   불규칙 동사: 부록 p.246 참고

---

③ 현재완료 시제의 부정문과 의문문은 다음과 같이 쓴다.

부정

I/we/you/they	have not (= haven't)	done
he/she/it	has not (= hasn't)	played

의문

Have	I/we/you/they	finished ...?
Has	he/she/it	stopped ...?

- I **have not done** my homework, so I can't go to bed now. 나는 숙제를 다 하지 못했다.
- Your train to Ottawa is at 8 p.m. today. **Have** you **finished** packing? 짐 싸는 것 다 끝냈니?
- Tiffany used to play the piano, but she **hasn't played** it for 10 years.
- "**Has** the rain **stopped**?" "No, it's still raining."

---

④ 현재완료 시제는 과거부터 현재까지를 포괄하는 시제로, 과거에 있었던 일을 현재와 관련지어 말할 때 쓴다.

- I **have lived** in LA since 2013. (2013년부터 지금까지 LA에 계속 살고 있음)
- "Where's Brian?" "I don't know. He **hasn't answered** my call."
  (지금까지 전화를 받지 않았음)
- "**Have** you **been** to Egypt before?" "Yes. It's a beautiful place."

> I **have lived** in LA.
> 과거   현재 (지금)

PRACTICE

A. 그림을 보고 주어진 동사와 have/has + 과거분사를 사용하여 문장을 완성하세요.

break	eat	~~leave~~	make	paint	take

1. They _'ve left OR have left_ the house.
2. He _____ the vase.
3. She _____ dinner.
4. He _____ the room.
5. They _____ a cake.
6. She _____ her seat.

B. 주어진 동사의 과거형과 과거분사를 쓰세요.

1. give – _gave_ – _given_
2. go – _____ – _____
3. buy – _____ – _____
4. run – _____ – _____
5. play – _____ – _____
6. write – _____ – _____
7. drive – _____ – _____
8. know – _____ – _____
9. send – _____ – _____

C. 괄호 안에 주어진 동사를 사용하여 현재완료 시제 문장을 완성하세요. 필요한 경우 부정문으로 쓰세요.

1. (hear) "Do you know this song?" "Yes. I _'ve heard OR have heard_ it before."
2. (eat) My husband woke up late this morning, so he _____ breakfast.
3. (grow) Your daughter _____ so much! She's an adult now.
4. (speak) Is Edward angry with me? He _____ to me for three days.
5. (ride) "Did you see Dave's new car?" "Yes. We _____ in it already."
6. (see) "I _____ Mary since Monday." "She's in Toronto."

D. 괄호 안에 주어진 단어들을 사용하여 현재완료 시제 의문문을 완성하세요.

1. (you, see my bag) _Have you seen my bag_ ?	Yes. It's under the table.
2. (you, study) _____ for the test?	No, not yet.
3. (Ben, finish the report) _____ ?	No. He's doing it now.
4. (you, read) _____ War and Peace?	No. Is it interesting?
5. (Amanda, call you) _____ ?	No. Maybe she's busy.
6. (the guests, arrive) _____ ?	Yes. They're here.

정답 p.269, REVIEW TEST 3 p.220

UNIT 019 | He **has known** her **for** five years.

현재완료 시제 (2)
현재까지 계속되는 일

🎧 019.mp3

①

Hi, I'm Justin.

2014년 (5년 전)　　　　　지금

Justin met Sandy five years ago.
They're still friends.

He **has known** her **for five years**.
그는 그녀를 5년 동안 알고 지내왔다.

또는 He **has known** her **since 2014**.
그는 그녀를 2014년부터 알고 지내왔다.

---

② 현재완료 시제는 '(과거부터 지금까지) ~해왔다'라는 의미로 말할 때 쓸 수 있다. 이때, **for** 또는 **since**와 자주 함께 쓴다.

have/has + 과거분사 + **for** + 기간 (three months 등): ~ 동안 …해왔다

3개월 동안

I **have studied** French **for three months**.

May　　　　June　　　　July　　　　지금

- I **have studied** French **for three months**. 나는 3개월 동안 프랑스어를 공부해왔다.
- Lily **has lived** in England **for two years**. Lily는 2년 동안 영국에서 살아왔다.
- We **haven't seen** Kathy **for a week**. Did she go somewhere?
- "**Has** this store **been** closed **for a few days**?" "Yes. The owners are on vacation."

have/has + 과거분사 + **since** + 시작된 시점 (May 등): ~부터 …해왔다

5월부터

I **have studied** French **since May**.

May　　　　　　　　　　　　지금

- I **have studied** French **since May**. 나는 5월부터 프랑스어를 공부해왔다.
- Lily **has lived** in England **since 2017**. Lily는 2017년부터 영국에서 살아왔다.
- We **haven't seen** Kathy **since Thursday**. Is she busy these days?
- "**Has** this store **been** closed **since yesterday**?" "Yes. It'll open again tomorrow."

---

③ **How long have/has ~?**: ~한 지 얼마나 되었나요?

- "**How long have you been** here?" 당신은 여기에 온 지 얼마나 되었나요? "For three weeks."
- "Steve collects comic books." "**How long has he collected** them?" 그는 그것들을 모은 지 얼마나 되었니?
- "**How long have you had** your driver's license?" "Since last year."

PRACTICE

A. 그림을 보고 주어진 동사를 사용하여 현재완료 시제 문장을 완성하세요.

| catch | drive | grow | live | stay | ~~study~~ |

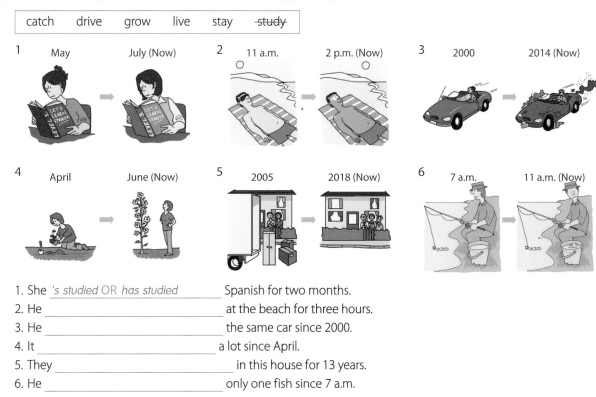

1 May / July (Now)
2 11 a.m. / 2 p.m. (Now)
3 2000 / 2014 (Now)
4 April / June (Now)
5 2005 / 2018 (Now)
6 7 a.m. / 11 a.m. (Now)

1. She _'s studied OR has studied_ Spanish for two months.
2. He _____ at the beach for three hours.
3. He _____ the same car since 2000.
4. It _____ a lot since April.
5. They _____ in this house for 13 years.
6. He _____ only one fish since 7 a.m.

B. 괄호 안에 주어진 표현을 사용하여 현재완료 시제 문장을 완성하세요. for 또는 since를 함께 쓰세요.

1. (lose 10 pounds) "Emily _has lost 10 pounds since_ _____ last month." "Wow. That's amazing!"
2. (be married) Stan and Louise _____ eight years. They have two kids.
3. (not rain) Farmers are worried because it _____ January.
4. (drive his car) Ken _____ nine hours. He's very tired right now.
5. (not talk to Ben) I _____ two weeks. I've been so busy lately.
6. (not eat anything) What's wrong with Luke? He _____ yesterday.
7. (know them) The Jones are our neighbors. We _____ 10 years.

C. How long ~?을 사용하여 예시와 같이 의문문을 완성하세요.

1. A: I work at a coffee shop.
   B: _How long have you worked_ there?

2. A: Kelly can play the flute very well.
   B: _____ it?

3. A: Alex and Sam attend the same school.
   B: _____ the same school?

4. A: My daughter takes ballet lessons.
   B: _____ them?

5. A: Jimmy is sleeping.
   B: _____ asleep?

6. A: I have a roommate.
   B: _____ a roommate?

정답 p.269, REVIEW TEST 3 p.220

UNIT **019**

Grammar Gateway Basic

They **haven't seen** the movie.

현재완료 시제 (3) 지금까지 경험해본 일

🎧 020.mp3

①

We **haven't seen** the movie.

They **haven't seen** the movie.
그들은 그 영화를 본 적이 없다.

② 현재완료 시제는 '(과거부터 지금까지) ~해본 적이 있다'라는 의미로 말할 때 쓸 수 있다.

We **have visited** Europe many times.

과거 ——————————————— 지금

- ● We **have visited** Europe many times. 우리는 유럽에 여러 번 가본 적이 있다.
- ● I **haven't tried** Indian food. Is it good? 나는 인도 음식을 먹어본 적이 없어.
- ● Tony **has met** the president before.
- ● Mandy **hasn't taken** art lessons, but she draws really well.

③ **Have you ever + 과거분사 ~?**: (지금까지) ~해본 적이 있나요?

- ● **Have you ever stayed** up all night? 당신은 밤을 새워본 적이 있나요?
- ● "**Have you ever made** cookies?" 너는 쿠키를 만들어본 적이 있니? "Yes. How about you?"
- ● "**Have you ever heard** of Matt Jonas?" "No. Who is he?"

have/has never + 과거분사: ~해본 적이 전혀 없다

- ● I **have never owned** a pet. 나는 애완동물을 가져본 적이 전혀 없다.
- ● "Sam always studies very hard." "Right. He**'s never failed** an exam." 그는 시험에 떨어진 적이 전혀 없어.
- ● Excuse me. Can we have some forks? We**'ve never used** chopsticks before.

④ **have/has been (to ~)**: (~에) 가본 적이 있다

- ● Mr. Miller **has been to** many countries. Miller씨는 많은 나라에 가본 적이 있다.
- ● "Where does Erika live?" "I don't know. I **haven't been to** her house." 나는 그녀의 집에 가본 적이 없어.
- ● I went to the new restaurant yesterday. **Have** you **been** there?

이때, **have been** 대신에 **have gone**을 쓰지 않도록 주의한다. **have gone**은 '~에 가고 없다'라는 의미이다.

- ● "Have you seen Sue this week?" "She **has gone to** LA for vacation." 그녀는 휴가로 LA에 가고 없어요.
- ● "Is Travis home? Can I talk to him?" "Sorry, but he**'s gone** out." 미안하지만, 그는 나가고 없어.

PRACTICE

A. 주어진 표현과 I've 또는 I've never를 사용하여 예시와 같이 말해보세요.

1. be to Sweden
2. play chess before
3. live in the country
4. ride a roller coaster
5. see a kangaroo
6. have a pet

1. _I've (never) been to Sweden_ .
2. _____ .
3. _____ .
4. _____ .
5. _____ .
6. _____ .

YOU

B. 주어진 표현과 Have you ever ~?를 사용하여 예시와 같이 의문문을 완성하세요.

| be to Paris | eat sushi | go bungee jumping |
| run a marathon | swim in the ocean | watch an opera |

1. A: _Have you ever eaten sushi_ ?
   B: Yes. It's delicious.

2. A: _____ ?
   B: Yes, last year. The music was amazing.

3. A: _____ ?
   B: No. I'm afraid of heights.

4. A: _____ ?
   B: Yes. There are many beaches in my town.

5. A: _____ ?
   B: Yes. It's a beautiful city.

6. A: _____ ?
   B: Yes, but I didn't finish the race.

C. have/has been 또는 have/has gone을 써넣으세요.

1. "Where's Lucy?" "She _'s gone OR has gone_ to bed."
2. Martin _____ to the new park three times. He loved it.
3. "Where is Sarah? She didn't come to work today." "She _____ to Europe for a week."
4. "Is Kyle in his office?" "No. He _____ to the gym."
5. "This street looks familiar, doesn't it?" "You're right. We _____ here before."

D. 괄호 안에 주어진 단어들과 현재완료 시제를 사용하여 Sandy와 Justin의 대화를 완성하세요.

SANDY: ^{1.} I _haven't seen OR have not seen_ this movie. (not see)
^{2.} _____ it? (you, watch)

JUSTIN: No, but it looks like a movie about Russia.
^{3.} _____ to Russia? (you, ever, be)

SANDY: ^{4.} No, I _____ there. (not be)

JUSTIN: I went there last fall.
The culture was interesting, and the food was delicious.
^{5.} _____ Russian food before? (you, eat)

SANDY: ^{6.} No, I _____ it, but I want to. (never, try)

SANDY

JUSTIN

UNIT
020

Grammar Gateway Basic

🎧 021.mp3

①

> How long have you lived in New York?

> We've lived here since 2000.

They **moved** to New York in 2000.
(2000년에 뉴욕으로 이사를 했음)

They **have lived** in New York since 2000.
(2000년부터 지금까지 뉴욕에서 살고 있음)

② Christine **went** to the beach an hour ago.

Christine **has gone** to the beach.

과거   지금

지금과 관련짓지 않고 과거에 끝난 일이나 상황 자체에 대해서만 말할 때는 과거 시제를 쓴다.

- Christine **went** to the beach an hour ago.
  (한 시간 전에 해변에 갔음)
- Mason **changed** his phone number last week.
  (지난주에 전화번호를 바꿨음)
- My boss **didn't attend** yesterday's meeting.
- "Did you **meet** my sister at the mall?"
  "Yes. We had coffee together."

과거에 일어난 일이나 상황이 지금과 관련되어 있음을 말할 때는 현재완료 시제를 쓴다.

- Christine **has gone** to the beach.
  (해변에 가서 지금 여기에 없음)
- Mason **has changed** his phone number.
  (전화번호를 바꿔서 지금은 번호가 다름)
- My boss **hasn't attended** many meetings.
- "**Have** you **met** my sister before?"
  "Of course. I know her very well."

③ 지금까지 어떤 일이 계속되고 있다는 의미로 말할 때는 현재완료 시제를 쓴다. 이때, 과거 시제를 쓰지 않는 것에 주의한다.

- The weather **has been perfect** this week. Let's go for a drive today.
  (지금까지 날씨가 좋은 상태이므로 과거 시제 was perfect로 쓸 수 없음)
- Amanda **has been sick** for a few days. She's still in the hospital.
  (지금까지 아픈 상태이므로 과거 시제 was sick으로 쓸 수 없음)
- "How long **have** you **been here**?" "For an hour. Is Jake here yet?"

④ 이미 지나간 과거의 시점(last night, two days ago 등)에 대해 말할 때는 과거 시제만 쓰는 것에 주의한다.

- "I **watched** a football game **last night**." "How was it?"
  (last night은 이미 지나간 과거 시점이므로 과거 시제 watched를 썼음)
- Aaron is on vacation. He **left** for Hawaii **two days ago**.
  (two days ago는 이미 지나간 과거 시점이므로 과거 시제 left를 썼음)

PRACTICE

A. 주어진 동사를 사용하여 현재완료 시제 또는 과거 시제 문장을 완성하세요.

be	~~call~~	grow	invent	see

1. "Did you meet Pam lately?" "No, but she *called* _____ me."
2. I'm a doctor at this hospital. I _____ here for two years.
3. Alexander Graham Bell _____ the telephone in 1876.
4. I _____ a huge snake at the zoo last weekend.
5. "Your son _____ a lot since last year." "Yes. He's very tall now."

B. 다음 문장을 읽고 틀린 부분이 있으면 바르게 고치세요. 틀린 부분이 없으면 O로 표시하세요.

1. Mary hasn't gone to work yesterday.   *hasn't gone → didn't go*
2. My brother graduated from college last May. _____
3. I didn't use my computer since last Friday. _____
4. Jill knew Ann for 10 years. They are best friends. _____
5. We've stayed in this hotel for a week. Everything has been perfect. _____
6. Tony and his wife have visited India in 2006. _____

C. 괄호 안에 주어진 단어들을 사용하여 현재완료 시제 또는 과거 시제 문장을 완성하세요.

1. A: (you, give) *You gave* _____ me this book last week, and I finished it.
   B: (I, not read) *I haven't read OR I have not read* _____ that book. Did you enjoy it?
2. A: (I, not see) _____ John since last week.
   B: (Brenna, talk) Really? I heard _____ to him today.
3. A: (Ms. Conner, speak) _____ French very well at the meeting.
   B: (she, take) I know. _____ French lessons for a year now.
4. A: (I, join) _____ this company last week. How about you?
   B: (we, work) _____ here for three months.
5. A: (my plane, not arrive) _____ for three hours. Is there a problem?
   B. (it, depart) _____ late from Singapore this morning.

D. 괄호 안에 주어진 단어들을 사용하여 Chun과 Chris의 대화를 완성하세요. 현재완료 시제 또는 과거 시제로 쓰세요.

CHUN: 1. *How long has your family lived* _____ in New York?
(how long, your family, live)

CHRIS: 2. _____ here in 2000. (my parents, move)

CHUN: Where did they live before then?

CHRIS: They lived in San Francisco.

3. _____ in New York? (how long, you, be)

CHUN: 4. _____ here last year. (I, come)

5. _____ here for 10 months. (I, live)

CHUN

CHRIS

정답 p.270, REVIEW TEST 3 p.220

UNIT
021

Grammar Gateway Basic

UNIT 022 | I've just bought this camera. just, already, yet

🎧 022.mp3

① have/has + just + 과거분사: 방금 막 ~했다

- A: I've just bought this camera. 나는 방금 막 이 카메라를 샀어요.
  B: We don't need it, James!
- The plane from Boston has just arrived at the airport.
  보스턴에서 온 비행기가 공항에 방금 막 도착했다.
- "Am I late for the meeting?" "No. We've just started."
- "Excuse me. You've just dropped your wallet."
  "Oh, thank you."

I've just bought this camera.

② have/has + already + 과거분사: (예상보다 앞서) 이미 ~했다

- I've already made plans for Saturday. 나는 이미 토요일의 계획을 세웠어.
- "We need a cake for Dad's birthday."
  "Mom has already baked one." 엄마가 이미 하나 구웠어.
- "Jamie was looking for you." "I've already talked to her."
- "Let's invite Andy to our party." "I've already invited him."

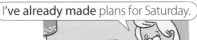

I've already made plans for Saturday.

③ haven't/hasn't + 과거분사 ~ yet (부정문): 아직 ~하지 않았다

- A: Where is Chris?
  B: He hasn't arrived yet. 그는 아직 도착하지 않았어요.
- "Did you do the laundry?"
  "No, I haven't done it yet." 나는 아직 그것을 하지 않았어.
- Don't touch the chair. The paint hasn't dried yet.
- "Is Dr. Lee in her office?" "She hasn't come back from lunch yet."

Have/Has ~ + 과거분사 ~ yet? (의문문): 아직 ~하지 않았나요?

- "Have you eaten dinner yet?" 너는 저녁을 아직 먹지 않았니? "No. I'm so hungry."
- "Has Jake sold his car yet?" Jake가 그의 차를 아직 팔지 않았나요? "Not yet."
- "Has Anna returned from her trip yet?" "No. She'll be back next week."

Where is Chris?

He hasn't arrived yet.

④ just, already, yet은 현재완료 시제와 함께 쓸 수도 있고, 과거 시제와 함께 쓸 수도 있다. 이때, 의미 차이가 없다.

- I've just finished cleaning. 또는 I just finished cleaning.
  나는 방금 막 청소를 마쳤다.
- Monica has already spent all of her money. 또는 Monica already spent all of her money.
  Monica는 이미 그녀의 돈을 다 썼다.
- "Did we miss the bus?" "No, it hasn't come yet." 또는 "No, it didn't come yet."
- Have Marie and Darcy moved to their new apartment yet?
  또는 Did Marie and Darcy move to their new apartment yet?

PRACTICE

A. 그림을 보고 주어진 동사와 just를 사용하여 현재완료 시제 문장을 완성하세요.

dive	~~leave~~	meet	open

1. She *'s just left* OR *has just left* _____ the house.
2. He _____ into the pool.
3. The mall _____ .
4. They _____ each other.

B. 괄호 안에 주어진 단어들과 already를 사용하여 현재완료 시제 문장을 완성하세요.

1. I don't see Clara's car in the parking lot.
2. Let's go out for some coffee.
3. Does our boss need this report?
4. Let's send Mom a birthday card.

(she, leave) *She's already left* OR *She has already left* _____ .
(we, have) _____ coffee.
(he, read) No. _____ it.
(I, send) _____ her one.

C. 괄호 안에 주어진 단어들과 yet을 사용하여 예시와 같이 현재완료 시제 문장을 완성하세요. 필요한 경우 부정문으로 쓰세요.

1. (I, take, it) "Did you take the Spanish class?" "No. *I haven't taken it yet* OR *I have not taken it yet* ."
2. (you, visit, him) "My uncle is in the hospital." " _____ ?"
3. (he, start, it) "Is Mr. Collins working on the new project?" "No. _____ ."
4. (I, see, him) "Kevin came back from his vacation." "Really? _____ !"
5. (Lily, call you, back) " _____ ?" "Maybe she forgot."

D. 괄호 안에 주어진 단어들과 현재완료 시제를 사용하여 James와 Linda의 대화를 완성하세요. 필요한 경우 부정문으로 쓰세요.

JAMES: ¹· Linda, *I've just bought a new camera* ! (I, just, buy, a new camera)
LINDA: What? But you bought one a month ago!
JAMES: Yes, but this one is really nice.
　　　　²· And _____ . (I, already, pay, the money)
LINDA: What will you do with the other one?
　　　　³· _____ ! (you, use, it, yet)
JAMES: ⁴· Well, _____ to Chris. (I, just, give, that one)
　　　　So then, can I have the new camera?

JAMES

LINDA

정답 p.270, REVIEW TEST 3 p.220

| She **will** run tomorrow. 미래 시제 (1) will

🎧 023.mp3

①

She **runs** every day.
She **ran** yesterday.

She **will run** tomorrow.
그녀는 내일 달릴 것이다.

will run은 미래 시제이다.

---

② 미래 시제는 '~할 것이다'라는 의미로 **will** + 동사원형으로 쓴다.

I/we/you/they	**will**	be
he/she/it	(= **'ll**)	need
		like

- I **will be** in the office this afternoon. 저는 오늘 오후에 사무실에 있을 거예요.
- It's cold outside. You**'ll need** a coat. 너는 코트가 필요할 거야.
- "I've got some flowers for Jane." "That's sweet. She**'ll like** them a lot."

---

③ **will**은 미래의 사실이나 미래에 일어날 것이라고 생각하는 일에 대해 말할 때 쓴다.

- Sharon **will be** 18 years old next year. Sharon은 내년에 18살이 될 것이다.
- "I'm worried about the test on Wednesday." "Don't worry. You**'ll do** fine." 너는 잘할 거야.

will은 미래에 어떤 일을 할 것이라고 말하고 있는 시점인 지금 결정하는 경우에도 쓴다.

- "Larry, the music is too loud!" "OK. I**'ll turn** down the volume." (음량을 줄이기로 지금 결정함)
- I think we're lost. I**'ll ask** for directions. (길을 물어보기로 지금 결정함)

---

④ **will**의 부정문과 의문문은 다음과 같이 쓴다.

부정

I/we/you/they	**will not**	make
he/she/it	(= **won't**)	tell
		leave

의문

Will	I/we/you/they	go ...?
	he/she/it	finish ...?
		snow ...?

- "The baby is sleeping." "OK. I **will not make** any noise." 시끄럽게 하지 않을게요.
- "**Will** you **go** to the library this week?" 이번 주에 도서관에 갈 거니? "Yes. I want to borrow some books."
- "We're planning a surprise party for Patty." "All right. I **won't tell** her about it."
- "**Will** Rob **finish** the report by noon?" "I hope so."
- "I'll be a few minutes late." "Take your time. We **won't leave** without you."
- "**Will** it **snow** tomorrow?" "Maybe."

PRACTICE

A. 괄호 안에 주어진 단어들과 will을 사용하여 문장을 완성하세요.

1. (the class, begin) _The class will begin_ soon. Let's sit over here.
2. (you, find) "Where is Mr. Gill's office?" "Go to the 7th floor. _____ it next to the elevator."
3. (they, win) The Tigers won last year's championship. _____ this year's championship too.
4. (she, return) Polly has gone to her swimming class. _____ home in an hour.
5. (we, need) Laura's family will join us for dinner. _____ a table for five people.
6. (it, help) "This machine is not working." "Check the manual. _____."

B. 주어진 표현과 I'll을 사용하여 문장을 완성하세요.

| drive | lend you | ~~see you~~ | take it |

1. Bill, _I'll see you_ _____ later.
   Goodbye.
2. You look tired. _____.
3. _____ some money.
   I lost my wallet.
4. Yes, I love it! _____.
   Do you like the jacket?

C. 주어진 동사와 will 또는 won't를 사용하여 문장을 완성하세요.

| call | explain | forget | ~~love~~ | sleep | stop | take |

1. "I'm planning a trip to Jeju Island." "It's beautiful there. You _'ll love OR will love_ it."
2. "Is the museum far from here?" "No. We can walk. It _____ long."
3. "Your appointment is next Tuesday at 2:30." "I'll write it down. I _____."
4. "I don't understand this question." "Ask Bob. He _____ it to you."
5. The bus _____ at 24th Avenue next Friday. The road will be closed for a parade.
6. Don't drink too much coffee. You _____ well.
7. "Judy hasn't arrived yet." "OK. I _____ her."

D. 괄호 안에 주어진 단어들과 will을 적절히 배열하여 문장을 완성하세요.

1. (to work / tomorrow / you / drive) "_Will you drive to work tomorrow_?" "Probably."
2. (we / the train / miss) Hurry up. We don't have enough time. _____!
3. (you / me / at the airport / meet) "_____?" "No. At your hotel."
4. (be / here / she / in a minute) "Where's Ann?" "She's on the phone. _____."
5. (the chicken salad / I / have) "Are you ready to order?" "Yes. _____, please."
6. (travel / this fall / your family) "_____?" "Yes. We'll visit Vietnam for a week."
7. (Jonathan / pass / the exam) "_____?" "Well, he studied hard for it."
8. (it / I / change) "That tie doesn't match your suit." "Really? _____, then."

정답 p.270, REVIEW TEST 4 p.222

🎧 024.mp3

①

> I'm going to make dinner.

He**'s going to make** dinner.
그는 저녁 식사를 준비할 것이다.

is going to make는 미래 시제이다.

---

② '~할 것이다'라는 의미로 미래의 일에 대해 말할 때 **be going to + 동사원형**을 쓸 수도 있다.

I	am		**be**
he/she/it	is	going to	**meet**
we/you/they	are		**visit**
			stay

- It**'s going to be** very hot today. 오늘은 매우 더울 것이다.
- I talked to Joe about the picnic. We**'re going to meet** tomorrow at 9:30. 우리는 내일 9시 30분에 만날 것이다.
- Lisa **is going to visit** her parents. She**'s going to stay** with them for a week.

---

③ 이미 하기로 결정한 미래의 일에 대해 말할 때 **be going to + 동사원형**을 쓴다.

- Susan **is going to move** to Chicago. She has a new job there. (시카고로 이사하기로 이미 결정했음)
- "Roy **is going to get** married!" "I know. He already told me." (결혼하기로 이미 결정했음)

be going to는 지금 상황을 근거로 미래에 어떤 일이 확실히 일어날 것이라고 말할 때도 쓴다.

- The sun is going down. It**'s going to be** dark soon. (해가 지고 있는 것을 보아 곧 어두워질 것임)
- The bus is leaving! We**'re going to miss** it. (버스가 떠나고 있는 것을 보아 버스를 놓칠 것임)

---

④ **be going to**의 부정문과 의문문은 다음과 같이 쓴다.

부정

I	am			**exercise**
he/she/it	is	not	going to	**take**
we/you/they	are			**win**

의문

Am	I			**study** ...?
Is	he/she/it		going to	**clean** ...?
Are	we/you/they			**visit** ...?

- I**'m not going to exercise** tonight. I'm too tired. 나는 오늘 밤에 운동하지 않을 거야.
- "Jess will attend B.C. College."
  "That college is famous for journalism. **Is** she **going to study** that?" 그녀는 그것을 공부할 것이니?
- Ryan just bought a car. He**'s not going to take** the subway anymore.
- "**Are** you **going to clean** your room?" "Yes, but I'm going to take a shower first."
- We're losing now. We **aren't going to win** this game.
- "Jim and Sophie will come to our town." "**Are** they **going to visit** us?"

PRACTICE

A. 주어진 동사와 be going to를 사용하여 문장을 완성하세요. 필요한 경우 부정문으로 쓰세요.

be	graduate	leave	~~read~~	relax	rent	take

1. I bought a new book. I *'m going to read* OR *am going to read* _____ it during my vacation.
2. OK, class. We _____ a break. Come back in 10 minutes.
3. "My plane _____ soon." "OK. Have a good trip!"
4. My friend wants to take another class at college. She _____ this year.
5. We _____ in the office next Monday. It's a holiday.
6. "You look tired." "Yes. I _____ for a few minutes."
7. I _____ that apartment. It's very old and dirty.

B. 그림을 보고 주어진 표현과 be going to를 사용하여 문장을 완성하세요.

have a sale	~~play golf~~	take an exam	watch a movie

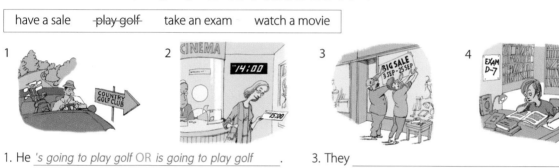

1. He *'s going to play golf* OR *is going to play golf* _____ .
2. She _____ .
3. They _____ .
4. She _____ .

C. 괄호 안에 주어진 단어들과 be going to를 사용하여 문장을 완성하세요.

1. (I, attend) *I'm going to attend* OR *I am going to attend* a seminar tomorrow. It's about African art.
2. (Tina, meet) "_____ us at the train station?" "Yes. At 10 o'clock."
3. (I, see) _____ the musical tonight. I'm so excited!
4. (you, buy) "_____ that car?" "I'm not sure."
5. (Brian, join) "_____ us for lunch." "Good! I haven't seen him for years."
6. (they, get) Andy proposed to Hannah. _____ married soon.
7. (it, hurt) "You have a cold. I'll give you a shot." "_____ ?"

D. 괄호 안에 주어진 단어들과 be going to를 사용하여 Linda와 James의 대화를 완성하세요.

LINDA

LINDA: I'm so hungry.
JAMES: Don't worry. 1. *I'm going to make* _____ dinner soon. (I, make)
LINDA: Oh good. What are you going to cook?
JAMES: 2. _____ chicken and rice. It's easy. (I, cook)
3. _____ ready in 30 minutes. (it, be)
LINDA: Great! 4. _____ some help? (you, need)
JAMES: 5. Thanks, but _____ your help. (I, not need)

JAMES

정답 p.271, REVIEW TEST 4 p.222

UNIT
024

Grammar Gateway Basic

She**'s leaving** tomorrow. 미래 시제 (3) 미래를 나타내는 현재진행과 현재 시제

🎧 025.mp3

①

I'm leaving tomorrow.

She**'s leaving** tomorrow.
그녀는 내일 떠날 예정이다.

The plane **leaves** at 10 o'clock.
비행기는 10시에 떠날 예정이다.

is leaving은 현재진행 시제 형태이고, leaves는 현재 시제 형태이지만 둘 다 미래의 일을 나타내고 있다.

---

② 구체적으로 계획을 세워 둔 미래의 일(약속, 예약 등)에 대해 말할 때 **am/is/are + -ing**를 쓴다.

- I**'m seeing** Bob on Friday. We**'re going** to the opera. 우리는 금요일에 Bob을 만날 예정이다. 오페라를 보러 갈 예정이다.
- Michelle and I **are having** dinner tonight. Will you join us? Michelle과 나는 오늘 밤에 저녁 식사를 할 예정이야.
- Sally **isn't moving** to Florida. She changed her mind.
- "**Is** Jack **returning** to the office today?" "Yes. At around 5 p.m."

이때, **am/is/are + -ing**는 현재가 아닌 미래의 일을 나타내는 것에 주의한다.

- I**'m starting** a new job tomorrow. 나는 내일 새 일을 시작할 예정이다. (새 일을 시작하고 있다는 뜻이 아님)
- George **is not coming** home tonight. George는 오늘 밤 집에 올 예정이 아니다. (집에 오고 있지 않다는 뜻이 아님)

이때, **am/is/are + -ing** 대신 **am/is/are going to + 동사원형**을 쓸 수도 있다.

- I**'m opening** my new business next month.
  또는 I**'m going to open** my new business next month. 저는 다음 달에 새로운 사업을 시작할 예정이에요.
- **Are** you **running** in the marathon on Sunday?
  또는 **Are** you **going to run** in the marathon on Sunday? 너는 일요일에 마라톤에서 뛸 예정이니?

---

③ 대중교통, 수업 등 이미 짜여 있는 시간표, 일정표상의 일에 대해 말할 때는 미래의 일이라도 현재 시제를 쓸 수 있다.

- The train **arrives** in Paris at 7 p.m. (기차 시간에 대해 말하고 있으므로 현재 시제 arrives를 썼음)
- "Why are you going to bed now? It's only 9 o'clock."
  "My class **starts** early in the morning." (수업 시간에 대해 말하고 있으므로 현재 시제 starts를 썼음)
- The TV show **doesn't end** at 5:30. It **ends** at 6.
- "**Does** your soccer team **play** here on May 13?" "Yes, and on June 13."

개인의 계획이나 일정에 대해 말할 때는 현재 시제가 아닌 **am/is/are + -ing**를 쓰는 것에 주의한다.

- Terry and Rachel are getting married soon. They **are buying** a house next week.
  (They buy로 쓸 수 없음)
- Carla **is not studying** in Sweden next year. She**'s going** to Finland instead.
  (Carla studies, She goes로 쓸 수 없음)

PRACTICE

A. 다음 수첩을 보고 am/is/are + -ing를 사용하여 Stephanie의 다음 주 일정에 대해 말해보세요.

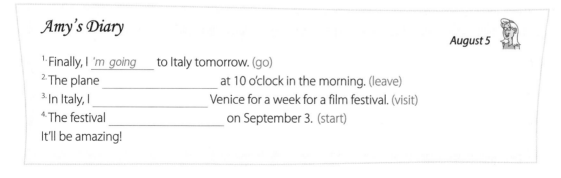

Monday
Play golf

Tuesday

Wednesday
See a movie with Kim

Thursday
Take a swimming lesson

Friday
Visit my grandparents

Saturday
Attend Karen's wedding

Sunday
Leave for Brazil

1. She *'s playing golf* OR *is playing golf* _____ on Monday.
2. She _____ with Kim on Wednesday.
3. She _____ on Thursday.
4. She _____ on Friday.
5. She _____ on Saturday.
6. She _____ on Sunday.

B. 다음 시간표를 보고 괄호 안에 주어진 동사를 사용하여 예시와 같이 현재 시제 문장을 완성하세요.

1 Movie Schedule		2 Flight Departures		3 Train Arrivals		4 Class Schedule	
5:30	*Funny People*	12:30	London	1:00	New York	9:00	Computer
6:30	*Space War*	2:15	Berlin	2:00	Boston	10:30	English

1. (start) *Funny People* _*starts at 5:30*_ .
2. (leave) I'm going to Berlin. My flight _____ .
3. (arrive) Jerome is coming from Boston. His train _____ .
4. (begin) My computer class _____ .

C. 괄호 안에 주어진 단어들과 am/is/are + -ing 또는 현재 시제를 사용하여 문장을 완성하세요.

1. (I, fly) "When are you going to China?" " _*I'm flying* OR *I am flying*_ there tomorrow night."
2. (you, stay) "_____ at a hotel during your vacation?" "Yes. I've already made a reservation."
3. (the plane, depart) _____ in 30 minutes. Let's hurry.
4. (Brenda, move) _____ to a new house next month. She's very excited.
5. (it, begin) "When does the school holiday start?" " _____ next Wednesday."
6. (the meeting, finish) _____ at 10 p.m. I'll call you then.
7. (I, meet) Ms. Edmonds doesn't have much time this morning, so _____ her at noon.

D. 다음은 Amy의 일기입니다. 괄호 안에 주어진 동사와 am/is/are + -ing 또는 현재 시제를 사용하여 문장을 완성하세요.

Amy's Diary

August 5

1. Finally, I *'m going* to Italy tomorrow. (go)
2. The plane _____ at 10 o'clock in the morning. (leave)
3. In Italy, I _____ Venice for a week for a film festival. (visit)
4. The festival _____ on September 3. (start)
It'll be amazing!

정답 p.271, REVIEW TEST 4 p.222

UNIT 025

Grammar Gateway Basic

UNIT **026** | He **can** speak Italian. *can, could*

🎧 026.mp3

①

He **can speak** Italian.
그는 이탈리아어를 할 수 있다.

He **can't speak** Japanese.
그는 일본어를 할 수 없다.

② **can + 동사원형: ~할 수 있다**

어떤 일을 할 수 있는 능력 또는 어떤 일이 일어날 가능성이 있다고 할 때 **can**을 쓴다.

I/we/you/they he/she/it	can	ride eat dance sing

- I **can ride** a bike. 나는 자전거를 탈 수 있다.
- We **can eat** at the hotel. It has a restaurant. 우리는 호텔에서 식사할 수 있어.
- Peter **can dance** well. He **can sing** well too.
- Wendy **can meet** me tomorrow. She doesn't have any classes.

③ **can**의 부정문과 의문문은 다음과 같이 쓴다.

부정

I/we/you/they he/she/it	cannot (= can't)	cook talk

의문

Can	I/we/you/they he/she/it	play ...? take ...?

- I **cannot cook** very well, so my husband makes our meals. 나는 요리를 잘하지 못한다.
- "**Can** you **play** the guitar?" 너는 기타를 연주할 줄 아니? "Yes. I've played for many years."
- "Peggy isn't answering her phone." "She **can't talk** to you now. She's in a meeting."
- "**Can** we **take** pictures inside the museum?" "No. Sorry."

④ 과거에 대해 말할 때는 **could**를 쓴다.

긍정

I/we/you/they he/she/it	could	swim see

부정

I/we/you/they he/she/it	could not (= couldn't)	walk find

- Ten years ago, Liz **could swim** 50 meters in 30 seconds. 10년 전에 Liz는 30초에 50미터를 수영할 수 있었다.
- Sorry I'm late. I **could not walk** fast because the streets were icy. 길이 얼어서 저는 빠르게 걸을 수 없었어요.
- The sky was clear yesterday evening, so we **could see** the stars.
- John and Stacy looked everywhere, but they **couldn't find** their photo album.

PRACTICE

A. 주어진 동사와 can 또는 can't를 사용하여 문장을 완성하세요.

fix	~~go~~	join	stay	talk	understand	wear

1. "Sara _can't go OR cannot go_ to the beach with us today." "Really? That's too bad."
2. You should take the computer to Tom. He _____ computers.
3. "Let's discuss this now. Where should we go?" "The meeting room is empty, so we _____ there."
4. "Tony! Let's go to the mall." "I _____ you. I have a lot of homework."
5. "You _____ shoes inside the house." "Sorry. I didn't know that."
6. "My friends are coming to our town for vacation. Can I bring them home?" "Sure. They _____ here."
7. Steve speaks very fast. I _____ him.

B. 괄호 안에 주어진 단어들과 can을 사용하여 대화를 완성하세요.

1. (you, climb) _Can you climb_ that tree?
2. (your parrot, talk) _____?
3. (Karen, help) _____ you with your report?
4. (you, attend) _____ the company picnic?
5. (your husband, drive) _____ a truck?
6. (you, tell) _____ me the meaning of this word?

No. I can't.
Yes. It can say hello and goodbye.
No. She's busy.
Of course I can.
No, but he can drive a motorcycle.
Sure. What is the word?

C. 괄호 안에 주어진 동사와 can/can't 또는 could/couldn't를 사용하여 문장을 완성하세요.

1. (take) "Where is City Hall?" "On Main Street. You _can take_ the subway over there."
2. (see) Can we move to different seats? I _____ the movie well from here.
3. (walk) My brother is only 10 months old, but he _____!
4. (buy) When I was a child, I _____ a soda for 25 cents. Everything was so cheap.
5. (remember) "When is Lisa's birthday? I _____." "It's May 8."
6. (ride) Kelly _____ a bicycle last week, but now she can.
7. (have) "This room is too small for a party." "Then we _____ the party in another room."
8. (answer) "Ask Ron about this. He's smart." "I did, but he _____ it."

D. 괄호 안에 주어진 단어들과 can 또는 could를 사용하여 Justin과 Sandy의 대화를 완성하세요.

JUSTIN: I talked to an Italian man on the street today.
SANDY: Oh. 1. _Can you speak_ Italian? (you, speak)
JUSTIN: A little. 2. But _____ English too. (he, understand)
SANDY: That's good. 3. _____ Italian when I was young. (I, speak)
4. Now, _____ anything. (I, not remember)
JUSTIN: My friend is teaching me Italian every Friday night.
SANDY: Really? 5. _____ you? (I, join)
JUSTIN: Sure. 6. _____ if you want to. (you, come)

JUSTIN

SANDY

정답 p.271, REVIEW TEST 5 p.224

He **might** play soccer. _{might, may}

①

He **might play** soccer.
그는 축구를 할지도 모른다.

He **might not play** soccer.
그는 축구를 하지 않을지도 모른다.

---

② **might + 동사원형: ~할지도 모른다**

어떤 일이 일어날 가능성이 있다고 할 때 **might**를 쓴다.

I/we/you/they he/she/it	might	come see be have

- I **might come** to work after lunch because I have a dentist appointment. 저는 점심 이후에 회사에 올지도 몰라요.
- Let's go to Hollywood! We **might see** a famous person. 우리는 유명한 사람을 볼지도 몰라.
- "Where's Eric?" "I'm not sure. He **might be** in his bedroom."
- "Do you have our room key?" "No. Ask Monica. She **might have** it."

---

③ **might**의 부정문은 다음과 같이 쓴다.

I/we/you/they he/she/it	might not	finish go enjoy remember

- I have a lot of work to do. I **might not finish** it all today. 나는 오늘 다 끝내지 않을지도 모른다.
- We **might not go** skiing this weekend. There's not much snow. 우리는 이번 주말에 스키를 타러 가지 않을지도 모른다.
- Thomas **might not enjoy** this movie. He doesn't like comedies.
- Tina **might not remember** her uncle. She has met him only once.

---

④ **might**와 동일한 의미로 **may**도 쓸 수 있다.

- Jeff **might work** late tonight. 또는 Jeff **may work** late tonight.
  Jeff는 오늘 밤늦게까지 일할지도 모른다.
- Anne **might take** an art class next year. 또는 Anne **may take** an art class next year.
  Anne은 내년에 미술 수업을 들을지도 모른다.

  일상 대화에서는 **may**보다 **might**를 더 자주 쓴다.
  - "I'll pick you up at 7 p.m." "6:30 **might be** better. We don't want to be late." 6시 30분이 더 좋을지도 몰라요.

PRACTICE

A. 주어진 대화를 보고 might를 사용하여 상황에 맞게 문장을 완성하세요.

1. BILL （ Are you meeting Jenny tomorrow? ）　　（ I'm not sure. I'll ask her. ） TOM

2. JANE （ Are you traveling by train? ）　　（ I'm thinking about it. ） ROBERT

3. MACY （ Are you going to Martin's wedding? ）　　（ Maybe. ） SUSAN

4. PETER （ Are you moving next month? ）　　（ I don't know yet, but it's possible. ） RACHEL

1. Tom _might meet Jenny tomorrow_ .
2. Robert _____ .
3. Susan _____ .
4. Rachel _____ .

B. 괄호 안에 주어진 동사와 might 또는 might not을 사용하여 문장을 완성하세요.

1. (win) Our soccer team is playing well. We _might win_ the game.
2. (help) Fred isn't very busy today. He _____ us with our homework.
3. (come) "Emma is sick. She _____ with us." "That's too bad."
4. (try) "Have you been to that restaurant?" "No, but I _____ it next week."
5. (fit) This dress looks too small. It _____ me.
6. (like) Carla and Jake _____ seafood. Let's cook some steaks.
7. (invite) "Do you have plans for this Friday?" "Well, we _____ some friends to our house."
8. (buy) I _____ that suitcase. It's very expensive.
9. (be) "Where is Steve?" "He's not in the office. He _____ at the gym."
10. (rain) There are dark clouds in the sky. It _____ .

C. 주어진 동사와 might를 사용하여 Paul과 Chris의 대화를 완성하세요. 필요한 경우 부정문으로 쓰세요.

be	go	have	~~play~~

PAUL: 1. I _might play_ soccer tomorrow. Can you come?
CHRIS: 2. I want to go, but I _____ time.
PAUL: Why not?
CHRIS: 3. I _____ to see my grandparents.
PAUL: How about Sunday?
CHRIS: 4. The weather _____ good. I heard it's going to rain.
PAUL: Well, OK. Maybe we can play together next week.

정답 p.271, REVIEW TEST 5 p.224

UNIT **027**

Grammar Gateway Basic

UNIT 028 | **Can I** use your phone?   Can/Could I ~?, Can/Could you ~?, May I ~?

🎧 028.mp3

①

Can I use your phone?

Can I use your phone?

네 휴대폰을 써도 될까?

Can you come to the party?

Can you come to the party?

파티에 와주시겠어요?

---

② **Can I ~?**: ~해도 될까요?

- It's very late. **Can I** stay here tonight? 제가 오늘 밤 여기에서 머물러도 될까요?
- "**Can I** bring my friend to the picnic?" 내가 소풍에 내 친구를 데려가도 될까? "Of course."
- "I don't have a pen. **Can I** borrow yours?" "Here you go."
- "**Can I** pay by credit card?" "Sure."

Can I ~?와 같은 의미이지만 더 공손하게 말할 때 **Could I ~?** 또는 **May I ~?**를 쓸 수 있다.

- "**Could I** ask you something?" 제가 무언가 물어봐도 될까요? "Sure. What is it?"
- "**May I** check my e-mail on your computer?" 당신의 컴퓨터로 제 이메일을 확인해도 될까요? "All right."
- "I need that box from the top shelf, but I can't reach it." "**Could I** help you with that?"
- **May I** leave now? I have another meeting after this.

---

③ **Can you ~?**: ~해주시겠어요?

- "**Can you** lend me 10 dollars?" 10달러를 빌려주시겠어요? "Sorry. I didn't bring my wallet."
- "It's hot in this room. **Can you** open the window for me?" 창문을 열어 주시겠어요? "OK. Just a moment."
- "**Can you** recommend a good restaurant in this town?" "The Thai Grill is good."
- "**Can you** take my picture, please?" "Sure. Say cheese!"

Can you ~?와 같은 의미이지만 더 공손하게 말할 때 **Could you ~?**를 쓸 수 있다.

- I'm sorry. **Could you** say that again? 다시 말씀해주시겠어요?
- "**Could you** give this document to Jason?" 이 서류를 Jason에게 주시겠어요? "No problem."

    Can/Could you ~? 대신 **May you ~?**는 쓸 수 없는 것에 주의한다.

    - **Can you** show me the way, please? 또는 **Could you** show me the way, please? 저에게 길을 알려주시겠어요?
      (May you show me the way, please?로 쓸 수 없음)
    - **Can you** wash the dishes for me? 또는 **Could you** wash the dishes for me? 저 대신 설거지 좀 해주시겠어요?
      (May you wash the dishes for me?로 쓸 수 없음)

PRACTICE

A. 그림을 보고 주어진 표현과 Can I ~?를 사용하여 의문문을 완성하세요.

close the window	~~come in~~	get some water	take this seat

1. _Can I come in_ ?
2. _____ ?
3. _____ ?
4. _____ ?

B. 괄호 안에 주어진 동사와 May I ~? 또는 Can you ~?를 사용하여 의문문을 완성하세요.

1. (have) " _May I have_ _____ a cup of coffee?" "OK. Do you want milk in it?"
2. (help) "These bags are heavy." " _____ you with them?"
3. (call) _____ me back in five minutes? I'm meeting with a client now.
4. (look) "I can't turn the heater on." " _____ at it for you?"
5. (borrow) _____ some money? I just need a few dollars.
6. (check) I sent you an e-mail this morning. _____ it?
7. (buy) Are you still at the supermarket? _____ me some eggs?

UNIT 028

C. 괄호 안에 주어진 표현과 Could you ~?를 사용하여 의문문을 완성하세요.

1. (take me home) _Could you take me home_ ?
2. (come to my office) _____ ?
3. (sign this form) _____ , please?
4. (read me another story) _____ ?
5. (move your car) _____ ?
6. (tell me your name) _____ ?

Of course.
What time?
OK.
No. It's time for bed.
Sure.
It's Jennifer.

D. 괄호 안에 주어진 단어들과 Can I ~? 또는 Can you ~?를 사용하여 Kate와 Amy의 대화를 완성하세요.

KATE: 1. Amy, _can I use your phone_ ? (use, your phone)
AMY: Sure. Where's your phone?
KATE: I left it at home. 2. Oh, _____ your password? (tell, me)
AMY: It's 2947.
KATE: Hmm. It doesn't work. 3. _____ again? (say, the number)
AMY: 4. _____ ? I'll do it for you. (see, it)
KATE: Oh, thank you!

KATE

AMY

UNIT 029 | He **must** wear a seat belt. must

🎧 029.mp3

①

You **must wear** your seat belt.

He **must wear** a seat belt.

그는 반드시 안전벨트를 착용해야 한다.

---

② **must + 동사원형: (반드시) ~해야 한다**

어떤 일을 반드시 해야 한다고 할 때 **must**를 쓴다.

I/we/you/they he/she/it	must	arrive buy show

- You **must arrive** on time for work. 당신은 회사에 제시간에 도착해야 해요.
- The concert isn't free. We **must buy** tickets. 우리는 표를 사야 한다.
- Travelers **must show** their passport before they get on the plane.

  단, 과거에 대해 말할 때는 **must**를 쓸 수 없다. 이때는 **had to**를 쓴다.
  - Nancy **had to pay** for my lunch yesterday because I had no money. Nancy가 어제 내 점심을 사야 했다.
  - Mr. Smith had a lot of work last night, so he **had to stay** late. 그는 늦게까지 있어야 했다.

---

③ **must not + 동사원형: ~해서는 안 된다**

어떤 일을 해서는 안 된다고 할 때 **must not**을 쓴다.

I/we/you/they he/she/it	must not	run cross bring

- Children **must not run** near the pool. 아이들은 수영장 근처에서 뛰어선 안 된다.
- You **must not cross** the street when the light is red. 빨간불일 때 길을 건너선 안 된다.
- Visitors **must not bring** any food into the museum.

---

④ '분명히 ~할 것이다'라는 의미로 어떤 일에 대해 강하게 확신할 때도 **must**를 쓴다.

- "Elisa has lived in France for 10 years." "She **must speak** French very well." 그녀는 분명히 프랑스어를 잘할 거야.
- Jill and Peter **must like** each other a lot. They are always together. Jill과 Peter는 분명히 서로를 많이 좋아할 것이다.
- "We're leaving for Malaysia tomorrow." "You **must be** really excited!"

'분명히 ~하지 않을 것이다'라는 의미로 말할 때는 **must not**을 쓴다.

- Ken is still sleeping. He **must not have** class today. 그는 분명히 오늘 수업이 없을 것이다.
- Shana's room is always dirty. She **must not clean** it often. 그녀는 분명히 자주 청소하지 않을 것이다.
- This store **must not sell** hats. I don't see any here.

PRACTICE

A. 주어진 동사와 must 또는 must not을 사용하여 각 표지의 의미에 대해 말해보세요.

~~park~~	smoke	stop	take	turn off

1. You *must not park* here.
2. You _____ now.
3. You _____ here.
4. You _____ pictures.
5. You _____ your cell phone.

B. must 또는 had to를 써넣으세요.

1. "Can I borrow your car tonight, Dad?" "OK, but you *must* be careful."
2. Mr. Smith wasn't in his office, so I _____ leave him a message.
3. Brenda _____ quit the softball team. She was too busy at school.
4. We _____ finish the report by 3 o'clock tomorrow.
5. The restaurant was full last night, so we _____ go to another place.
6. You _____ return this equipment before next Tuesday.

C. 주어진 동사와 must를 사용하여 대화를 완성하세요. 필요한 경우 부정문으로 쓰세요.

~~be~~	feel	have	hurt	know	miss	read

1. The diamond on that ring is so big!
2. Sara caught a bad cold.
3. I haven't seen my mom for a year.
4. Nick just met Andrea for the first time.
5. I cut my finger.
6. The children are still playing outside.
7. Mark has so many books at home.

It *must be* really expensive.
She _____ very well.
You _____ her.
He _____ her well.
It looks bad. It _____.
They _____ homework today.
He _____ a lot.

D. 괄호 안에 주어진 동사와 must를 사용하여 James와 Justin의 대화를 완성하세요. 필요한 경우 부정문으로 쓰세요.

JAMES: 1. Justin, you *must wear* your seat belt. (wear)
JUSTIN: I know, Dad. Don't worry.
JAMES: Safety is very important, Justin.
2. You _____ that. (forget)
JUSTIN: I won't. 3. Also, I _____ all the mirrors before I drive. (check)
JAMES: Right. 4. And you _____ too fast. (go)

JAMES

JUSTIN

정답 p.272, REVIEW TEST 5 p.224

UNIT
029

Grammar Gateway Basic

UNIT 030 | He **has to** leave now. have to

🎧 030.mp3

①

I'm late. I **have to leave** now.

He **has to leave** now.

그는 지금 떠나야 한다.

---

② **have/has to + 동사원형: (반드시) ~해야 한다**

어떤 일을 반드시 해야 한다고 할 때 **have/has to**를 쓴다.

I/we/you/they	**have to**	hurry
		wear
he/she/it	**has to**	return

- We **have to hurry**. The movie starts soon. 우리는 서둘러야 한다.
- Terry **has to wear** a suit tomorrow. He has a job interview. Terry는 내일 정장을 입어야 한다.
- That's not my book. I **have to return** it to the library.

  have/has to와 같은 의미로 **must**를 쓸 수도 있다. 단, 일상 대화에서는 **have/has to**를 주로 쓴다.
  - You **must be** quiet in the hall. 또는 You **have to be** quiet in the hall. 복도에서는 조용히 해야 한다.

---

③ **don't/doesn't have to + 동사원형: ~할 필요가 없다**

어떤 일을 할 필요가 없다고 할 때 **don't/doesn't have to**를 쓴다.

I/we/you/they	**don't**		worry
		have to	see
he/she/it	**doesn't**		go

- You **don't have to worry**. Everything will be OK. 너는 걱정할 필요 없어.
- Scott canceled his appointment. He **doesn't have to see** the doctor today. 그는 오늘 진찰을 받지 않아도 된다.
- We **don't have to go** to school this Friday. It's a national holiday.

그러나 **don't/doesn't have to**와 **must not**은 다음과 같은 의미 차이가 있으므로 주의한다.
- Daisy lives near her office, so she **doesn't have to drive** to work. (사무실 근처에 살기 때문에 운전해서 갈 필요가 없음)
  Andy had a lot of wine, so he **must not drive** tonight. (와인을 많이 마셨기 때문에 운전해서는 안 됨)

---

④ **have/has to**의 과거는 **had to**로 쓴다.
- It was cold last night, so I **had to put** on my jacket. 나는 재킷을 입어야 했다.

don't/doesn't have to의 과거는 **didn't have to**로 쓴다.
- We **didn't have to cook** yesterday because we ordered pizza. 우리는 어제 요리할 필요가 없었다.

PRACTICE

A. 그림을 보고 주어진 동사와 have to를 사용하여 문장을 완성하세요.

~~carry~~ see use wait

1. You *have to carry* an umbrella.

2. I _____ a dentist.

3. We _____ here.

4. We _____ the stairs.

B. 주어진 동사와 have/has to 또는 don't/doesn't have to를 사용하여 문장을 완성하세요.

ask attend call pay ~~study~~ take teach

1. Tim has a test tomorrow. He *has to study* _____ tonight.
2. I've never played chess before. You _____ me.
3. Diane feels better today, so she _____ the medicine anymore.
4. Mr. Roy _____ me back. I'll visit his office.
5. "Can I leave work early today?" "You _____ Mr. Nelson first. He's right there."
6. The jeans are on sale, so I _____ a lot.
7. "Is Melanie joining us for lunch on Saturday?" "No. She _____ a wedding."

C. 괄호 안에 주어진 동사와 have/has to 또는 must를 사용하여 문장을 완성하세요. 필요한 경우 부정문으로 쓰세요.

1. (come) The show starts at 7 p.m. You *must not come* _____ late.
2. (write) Tim _____ the essay today. He can do it tomorrow.
3. (run) We _____. The bus isn't at the station yet.
4. (be) "Could I have a cup of tea?" "Sure, but it's very hot. You _____ careful."
5. (park) "You _____ in front of the entrance." "Sorry. I'll move my car."
6. (pack) We're going on camping this afternoon. We _____ now!
7. (bring) You _____ anything to the party. We already have enough food.
8. (leave) Bianca _____ now. She's going to miss the last train.

D. 괄호 안에 주어진 단어들과 had to 또는 didn't have to를 사용하여 예시와 같이 문장을 완성하세요.

1. (she, stay, in the hospital) Gina hurt her leg, so *she had to stay in the hospital* last week.
2. (we, stop, at the gas station) _____ because we didn't have much gas.
3. (I, tell, John) _____ about my job. He already knew about it.
4. (Allan, buy, a ticket) The concert was free, so _____.
5. (I, change, my clothes) "Why are you late?" "Sorry. _____."

정답 p.272, REVIEW TEST 5 p.224

UNIT
030

Grammar Gateway Basic

🎧 031.mp3

①

You should go home.

He **should go** home.
그는 집에 가는 것이 좋겠다.

---

② should + 동사원형: ~하는 것이 좋겠다

어떤 일을 하는 것이 좋겠다고 제안할 때 **should**를 쓴다.

I/we/you/they he/she/it	should	be have see

- The soup is very hot. You **should be** careful. 조심하는 것이 좋겠어.
- We **should have** a party. It'll be fun. 우리 파티를 하는 것이 좋겠다.
- "Samantha has a toothache." "Again? She **should see** a dentist."

---

③ **should**의 부정문은 다음과 같이 쓴다.

I/we/you/they he/she/it	should not (= shouldn't)	drive drink smoke

- You look so tired. You **should not drive**. 너는 운전하지 않는 게 좋겠다.
- I'm going to bed soon. I **shouldn't drink** coffee. 나는 커피를 마시지 않는 게 좋겠어.
- Frank **shouldn't smoke**. It's not good for his health.

---

④ Should I ~?: ~하는 것이 좋을까요?

- I think my hair is too long. **Should I get** a haircut? 제가 머리를 자르는 것이 좋을까요?
- "**Should I bring** an umbrella?" 제가 우산을 가져가는 것이 좋을까요? "Yes. It might rain this afternoon."
- "**Should I wear** a tie to the wedding?" "No. You don't have to."
- "What **should I cook** for dinner tonight?" "How about chicken?"

---

⑤ should는 I think 또는 I don't think와 함께 자주 쓴다.

I think ~ should ...	- Sue is angry at me. I **think** I **should talk** to her. 내 생각에 그녀와 얘기해보는 것이 좋겠어. - I **think** we **should go**. Our train arrives soon.
I don't think ~ should ...	- I **don't think** we **should buy** a new car. 내 생각에 우리가 새 차를 사지 않는 것이 좋겠어. - It's dark outside. I **don't think** you **should leave**.

PRACTICE

A. 그림을 보고 주어진 동사와 should를 사용하여 문장을 완성하세요.

buy	~~call~~	speak	wash

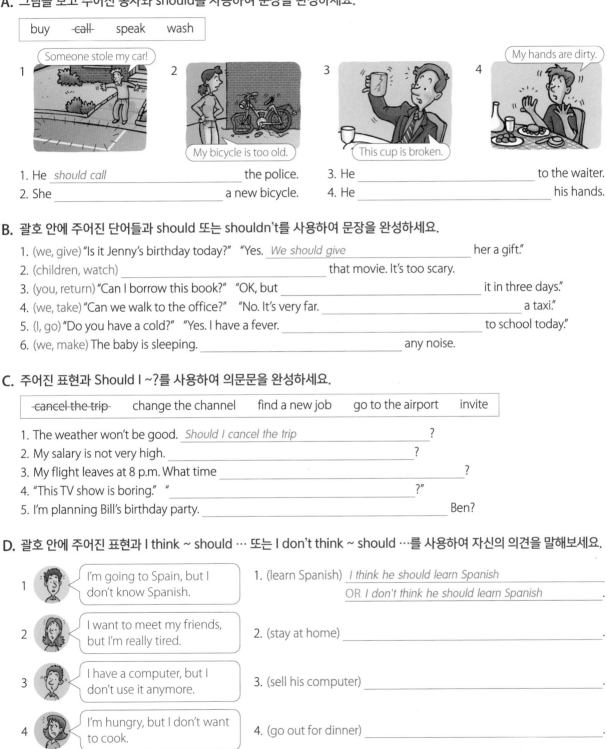

1 Someone stole my car!

2 My bicycle is too old.

3 This cup is broken.

4 My hands are dirty.

1. He _should call_ the police.
2. She _____ a new bicycle.
3. He _____ to the waiter.
4. He _____ his hands.

B. 괄호 안에 주어진 단어들과 should 또는 shouldn't를 사용하여 문장을 완성하세요.

1. (we, give) "Is it Jenny's birthday today?" "Yes. _We should give_ _____ her a gift."
2. (children, watch) _____ that movie. It's too scary.
3. (you, return) "Can I borrow this book?" "OK, but _____ it in three days."
4. (we, take) "Can we walk to the office?" "No. It's very far. _____ a taxi."
5. (I, go) "Do you have a cold?" "Yes. I have a fever. _____ to school today."
6. (we, make) The baby is sleeping. _____ any noise.

C. 주어진 표현과 Should I ~?를 사용하여 의문문을 완성하세요.

~~cancel the trip~~	change the channel	find a new job	go to the airport	invite

1. The weather won't be good. _Should I cancel the trip_ _____ ?
2. My salary is not very high. _____ ?
3. My flight leaves at 8 p.m. What time _____ ?
4. "This TV show is boring." "_____?"
5. I'm planning Bill's birthday party. _____ Ben?

D. 괄호 안에 주어진 표현과 I think ~ should … 또는 I don't think ~ should …를 사용하여 자신의 의견을 말해보세요.

1 I'm going to Spain, but I don't know Spanish.

1. (learn Spanish) _I think he should learn Spanish_
   OR _I don't think he should learn Spanish_ .

2 I want to meet my friends, but I'm really tired.

2. (stay at home) _____ .

3 I have a computer, but I don't use it anymore.

3. (sell his computer) _____ .

4 I'm hungry, but I don't want to cook.

4. (go out for dinner) _____ .

정답 p.272, REVIEW TEST 5 p.224

🎧 032.mp3

Would you help us, please?

Would you help us, please?
저희를 도와주시겠어요?

---

② 상대방에게 어떤 일을 해달라고 요청할 때 **Would you + 동사원형**을 쓴다.

Would you ~?: ~해주시겠어요?

- I feel cold. **Would you close** the window, please? 창문을 닫아주시겠어요?
- **Would you get** me a glass of water, please? 물 한 잔 주시겠어요?
- "**Would you drive** me to work, please?" "Sure."

Would you ~?와 같은 의미로 **Can/Could you ~?**를 쓸 수도 있다.

- **Can you give** me some advice? 또는 **Could you give** me some advice? 제게 조언을 해주실 수 있나요?
- **Can you pass** me the pen? 또는 **Could you pass** me the pen? 그 펜을 제게 건네주실 수 있나요?

---

③ 상대방에게 무언가를 권하거나, 어떤 일을 하자고 제안할 때 **Would you like ~?**를 쓴다.

Would you like ~?: ~을 드릴까요?

- "Did you enjoy your meal? **Would you like some dessert** now?" 이제 디저트를 드릴까요? "That will be great."
- "**Would you like a newspaper**?" 신문을 드릴까요? "No, thanks."

Would you like to + 동사원형 ~?: ~ 하실래요?

- "**Would you like to join** us for lunch?" 우리와 점심 같이 하실래요? "Sure."
- "**Would you like to go** fishing on Saturday?" 토요일에 낚시하러 가실래요? "Sorry, I can't. I have to work."

---

④ 상대방에게 무언가를 달라고 하거나, 어떤 일을 하고 싶다고 말할 때 **I would like ~ (= I'd like ~)**를 쓴다.

I would like ~: ~을 주세요

- "Can I help you?" "Yes. **I would like two tickets**, please." 표 두 장 주세요.
- "**I'd like a room**, please." 방 하나 주세요. "For one person?"

I would like to + 동사원형: ~하고 싶어요

- **I would like to introduce** you to Mr. Murphy. Murphy씨에게 당신을 소개하고 싶어요.
- **I'd like to thank** you for your interest in our company. 저희 회사에 대한 관심에 대해 감사드리고 싶습니다.

PRACTICE

A. 주어진 동사와 Would you ~?를 사용하여 의문문을 완성하세요.

answer	bring	~~call~~	drive	show	turn off

1. *Would you call* _____ me when you get this message?
2. David, I can't sleep. _____ the TV, please?
3. I feel sick. _____ me some medicine?
4. Karen, _____ the phone? I can't get it right now.
5. _____ me home? I didn't bring my car today.
6. _____ me the way to the hospital? It should be near here.

B. 주어진 표현과 Would you like ~?를 사용하여 상황에 맞게 의문문을 완성하세요.

an orange	~~some cookies~~	some ice cream	some wine

1. *Would you like some cookies* ?

2. _____ _____ ?

3. _____ _____ ?

4. _____ _____ ?

UNIT 032

Grammar Gateway Basic

C. 괄호 안에 주어진 표현과 Would you like ~? 또는 Would you like to ~?를 사용하여 대화를 완성하세요.

1. (a drink) *Would you like a drink* _____ ?
2. (go shopping) _____ ?
3. (some bread) _____ ?
4. (a map) _____ ?
5. (see the menu) _____ ?
6. (play golf) _____ this Sunday?

Thanks, but I'm good.
OK. Where?
No, thanks. I'm full.
Yes, please.
Thank you.
That sounds fun.

D. 괄호 안에 주어진 표현과 I'd like ~ 또는 I'd like to ~를 사용하여 대화를 완성하세요.

1. A: (a coffee) *I'd like a coffee OR I would like a coffee* , please.
   B: Hot or cold?

2. A: (study biology) _____ _____ in college.
   B: Me too!

3. A: Hello. Where are you traveling to?
   B: (a ticket) _____ _____ to Boston.

4. A: (invite you) _____ _____ to my Christmas party.
   B: That's very kind of you.

5. A: (that blue sweater) _____ _____ , please.
   B: Here you are, ma'am.

6. A: Do you have any plans for vacation?
   B: (visit Europe) _____ _____ .

정답 p.272, REVIEW TEST 5 p.224

UNIT 033 | The window **was broken.** 수동태

🎧 033.mp3

①

능동태 Someone **broke** the window.

수동태 The window **was broken.** 창문이 깨졌다.

---

② 사람이나 사물이 '~되다'라고 말할 때 수동태를 쓴다. 수동태는 **am/is/are** + 과거분사로 쓴다.

긍정·부정

am/is/are	(not)	spoken allowed grown parked

의문

Am	I	
Is	he/she/it	given ...? hurt ...?
Are	we/you/they	

- Spanish **is spoken** in Mexico. 멕시코에서는 스페인어가 사용된다.
- Children **are not allowed** in this pool. 어린이들은 이 수영장에 들어오는 것이 허락되지 않는다.
- "**Is** wine **given** to every guest here?" "Yes. The hotel provides it for free."
- Bananas **are grown** in tropical countries.
- "Where's your car? It **isn't parked** outside." "I didn't bring it today."
- Did my dog bite you? **Are** you **hurt**?

---

③ 수동태의 과거는 **was/were** + 과거분사로 쓴다.

긍정·부정

was/were	(not)	made discovered destroyed

- "This doll **was made** in Russia." 이 인형은 러시아에서 만들어졌어. "Wow! It's so pretty."
- Vitamin C is in food, but it **wasn't discovered** until 1928. 비타민C는 1928년까지 발견되지 않았다.
- Several buildings **were destroyed** during the storm.

---

④ will, can, must 등과 함께 쓸 때는 **will/can/must** 등 + **be** + 과거분사로 쓴다.

긍정·부정

will can must 등	(not)	be	served repaired answered

- Dinner **will be served** in a minute. 잠시 후에 저녁 식사가 제공될 것입니다.
- Unfortunately, your phone **cannot be repaired**. 안타깝지만, 당신의 휴대폰은 수리될 수 없어요.
- All the questions on this form **must be answered**.

PRACTICE

A. 괄호 안에 주어진 동사를 사용하여 수동태 문장을 완성하세요. 현재 시제로 쓰세요.

1. (lock) The office door _is locked_ at 10 o'clock.
2. (write) I can't read this book. It _____ in Italian.
3. (not require) The museum is free, so tickets _____.
4. (make) Those shoes look great on you! _____ they _____ of leather?
5. (deliver) "Do you read the newspaper?" "Yes. It _____ to my home every morning."
6. (not use) Look at the old car. That kind of car _____ much these days.
7. (bake) "That bakery has fresh pies." "_____ those pies _____ every day?"

B. 괄호 안에 주어진 단어들을 사용하여 수동태 문장을 완성하세요. 현재 시제 또는 과거 시제로 쓰세요.

1. A: (our team, move) _Our team was moved_
   _____ to the 3rd floor last week.
   B: Did any other teams change floors?

2. A: How old is that building?
   B: (it, build) _____ in 1910.

3. A: (my dog, wash) _____
   _____ every weekend.
   B: Really? You take good care of your dog.

4. A: Did you go to the concert last night?
   B: (it, cancel) No. _____.

5. A: Is Tom a famous artist?
   B: (his paintings, display) Yes. _____
   _____ at many galleries.

6. A: (these photos, take) _____
   _____ last year.
   B: Your hair has grown a lot since then.

C. 주어진 동사들을 사용하여 수동태 문장을 완성하세요.

announce	~~make~~	pay	show	wear

1. (must not) The same mistake _must not be made_ again.
2. (can) Casual clothes _____ to the office on Fridays.
3. (cannot) This movie _____ to children. There is too much violence in it.
4. (will not) The winners of the contest _____ until tomorrow.
5. (must) The credit card bill _____ every month.

D. 다음은 도로 공사 안내문입니다. 둘 중 맞는 것을 고르세요.

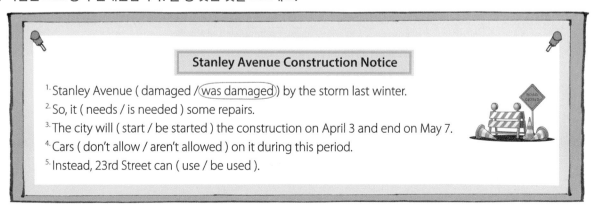

Stanley Avenue Construction Notice

1. Stanley Avenue (damaged /(was damaged)) by the storm last winter.
2. So, it (needs / is needed) some repairs.
3. The city will (start / be started) the construction on April 3 and end on May 7.
4. Cars (don't allow / aren't allowed) on it during this period.
5. Instead, 23rd Street can (use / be used).

정답 p.273, REVIEW TEST 6 p.226

UNIT
033

Grammar Gateway Basic

She **caught** a fish. A fish **was caught**.

능동태와 수동태 비교

🎧 034.mp3

①

She **caught** a fish.
그녀는 물고기를 잡았다.

A fish **was caught**.
물고기가 잡혔다.

② 능동태는 사람이나 사물이 '~하다'라는 의미이다.

- Nate **washes** the floors every evening.
  Nate는 저녁마다 바닥을 청소한다.
- Helen **didn't pay** the phone bill.
  Helen은 전화 요금을 지불하지 않았다.
- **Did** someone **invite** Jane?
- I **will fix** the bicycle.
- You **can find** the stapler on my desk.

수동태는 사람이나 사물이 '~되다'라는 의미이다.

- The floors **are washed** every evening.
  바닥이 저녁마다 청소된다.
- The phone bill **wasn't paid**.
  전화 요금이 지불되지 않았다.
- **Was** Jane **invited**?
- The bicycle **will be fixed**.
- The stapler **can be found** on my desk.

③ 수동태 문장에서 누구 또는 무엇에 의해서 일어난 일인지 말하고 싶을 때는 주로 **by**를 쓴다.

능동태 | Many people | **speak** English.

수동태 English **is spoken** | **by** many people |. 영어는 많은 사람들에 의해 말해진다.

능동태 / 수동태

(am/is/are)
- Ms. Wright **teaches** my son.
  Wright씨는 내 아들을 가르친다.
  → My son **is taught by** Ms. Wright.
  내 아들은 Wright씨에 의해 가르쳐진다.
- The farmers **grow** these pears.
  → These pears **are grown by** the farmers.

(was/were)
- Shakespeare **wrote** *Hamlet*.
  셰익스피어는 햄릿을 썼다.
  → *Hamlet* **was written by** Shakespeare.
  햄릿은 셰익스피어에 의해 쓰였다.
- The airline **canceled** all flights.
  → All flights **were canceled by** the airline.

(will, can, must 등)
- The company **will hold** a seminar.
  회사가 세미나를 열 것이다.
  → A seminar **will be held by** the company.
  세미나가 회사에 의해 열릴 것이다.
- Visitors **must not touch** the painting.
  → The painting **must not be touched by** visitors.

PRACTICE

A. 그림을 보고 주어진 동사를 사용하여 능동태 또는 수동태 문장을 완성하세요. 과거 시제로 쓰세요.

find	grow	hit	~~make~~	send

1. The vase *was made* _____ in 1563.
2. The flowers _____ by John.
3. A ball _____ the girl.
4. The rice _____ in China.
5. They _____ a box under the bed.

B. 주어진 동사를 사용하여 수동태 문장을 완성하세요. 현재 시제 또는 과거 시제로 쓰세요.

keep	repair	~~sell~~	tell	use	wear

1. Our house *was sold* _____ yesterday. We're moving to a new house next week.
2. "The meeting starts at 4:30." "Are you sure? I _____ 5:00."
3. "Excuse me, where is the ham?" "It _____ in the big fridge, next to the beef."
4. My car _____ this morning. I can drive to work now.
5. Computers _____ in almost every house today.
6. Those shoes are expensive because they _____ by Elvis Presley when he was alive.

C. 다음 문장을 읽고 틀린 부분이 있으면 바르게 고치세요. 틀린 부분이 없으면 O로 표시하세요.

1. The house cleans on Saturdays.   *cleans → is cleaned*
2. The pizza will deliver to your home.   _____
3. I hope you were enjoyed your meal.   _____
4. Beef must cook at a high temperature.   _____
5. My sunglasses stole yesterday at the mall.   _____
6. These magazines are published every month.   _____
7. Does food allow in the library?   _____
8. Jimmy was broken his leg twice last year.   _____

D. 주어진 문장을 보고 by를 사용하여 수동태 문장을 완성하세요.

1. My husband wrote the letter.   *The letter was written by my husband* .
2. The Millers invited me.   _____ .
3. Mr. Lee designed those buildings.   _____ .
4. The author will sign the book.   _____ .
5. Many tourists visit this place.   _____ .
6. John Baird invented the television.   _____ .
7. An accident can cause a traffic jam.   _____ .

정답 p.273, REVIEW TEST 6 p.226

UNIT
034

Grammar Gateway Basic

Is the water hot? 의문문 (1)

①

> Is the water hot?

긍정 The water **is** hot. 물이 뜨겁다.

의문 **Is** the water hot? 물이 뜨거운가요?

---

② **be동사/현재완료 시제/조동사** 의문문은 다음과 같이 쓴다.

be동사

Am/Is/Are		
Was/Were	주어	...?

● **Are you** from Canada? 당신은 캐나다 출신인가요?
● "**Was the weather** good in Miami?" 마이애미의 날씨는 좋았나요? "Yes. It was sunny."

현재완료 시제

Have		tried ...?
Has	주어	arrived ...?

● **Have you tried** Indian food before? 너는 인도 음식을 먹어본 적 있니?
● Carl hasn't come yet. **Has Dave arrived**? Dave는 도착했나요?

조동사

Will		become ...?
Can 등	주어	open ...?

● **Will Bob become** a famous actor? Bob은 유명한 배우가 될까?
● I can't open this jar. **Can you open** it? 당신이 이걸 열어줄 수 있나요?

---

③ 일반동사 의문문은 주어 앞에 **do/does/did**를 쓴다.

Do		know ...?
Does	주어	live ...?
Did		meet ...?

● **Do you know** this song? 너는 이 노래를 아니?
● "Jenna lives in England." "**Does she live** in London?" 그녀는 런던에 사나요?
● "We met Mr. Jacobs last night." "**Did you meet** his wife too?"

일반동사 의문문에는 **be동사**를 쓰지 않는 것에 주의한다.

● "**Do** you **have** a pen?" "No, but I have a pencil." (Are you have ~?로 쓸 수 없음)
● "**Does** this computer **work**?" "I think so." (Is this computer work?로 쓸 수 없음)
● "**Did** Jerry **come** to your wedding?" "Yes, he did."

---

④ **who, what** 등은 동사 앞에 쓴다.

● "**Who is** your best friend?" 너의 가장 친한 친구가 누구니? "Michelle."
● "**What did** you **eat** for breakfast?" 너는 아침 식사로 무엇을 먹었니? "Pancakes."
● I was worried about you. **Where have** you **been** all day?
● "**When will** you **be** home tonight?" "Around midnight."
● "**How can** you **forget** my birthday?" "I'm so sorry."

PRACTICE

A. 괄호 안에 주어진 단어들을 적절히 배열하여 문장을 완성하세요.

1. (go / you / will) You don't look very well. _Will you go_____ to the doctor today?
2. (are / the cookies) "_____ in the oven." "Oh, I forgot about that."
3. (Ted / done / has) "Can I take Ted to the park with me?" "_____ his homework?"
4. (live / Mitchell / does) "_____ with his parents?" "No. With his brother."
5. (Julie / was / sleeping) "_____ when you called?" "Yes. I woke her up."
6. (should / take / we) We've studied for three hours. _____ a break.
7. (you / found / have) "_____ your keys yet?" "No. I'm still looking for them."
8. (ask / I / you / can) "I'm sorry, but _____ a question?" "Sure. What is it?"

B. be동사/do/have를 적절한 형태로 써넣으세요.

1. _Is_____ Kristin a nurse?	No. She's a doctor.
2. _____ you talked to Jane lately?	Yes. I spoke to her yesterday.
3. _____ Tina work in China?	Yes. She's in Beijing.
4. _____ Debbie spend a lot of money last weekend?	Not too much.
5. _____ you going to the seminar next month?	I haven't decided yet.
6. _____ Mr. Riley sold his car yet?	I'm not sure. I'll ask him.
7. _____ you wearing a new tie yesterday?	Yes. Did you like it?
8. _____ you have any plans for Saturday?	I'm visiting my parents.

C. 다음 문장을 읽고 틀린 부분이 있으면 바르게 고치세요. 틀린 부분이 없으면 O로 표시하세요.

1. Are you remember that woman's name?   _Are → Do_
2. Should I sign on this paper?   _____
3. Where was Joel grow up?   _____
4. Does Kelly travel a lot for work?   _____
5. Who the girl is in the picture?   _____
6. Has Jenny called you yet?   _____
7. What you bought at the grocery store yesterday?   _____

D. 괄호 안에 주어진 단어들을 적절히 배열하여 대화를 완성하세요.

1. A: I found my wallet!
   B: (was / your car / in / it)
   _Was it in your car_____ ?

2. A: (are / moving to / Australia / you / when)
   _____ ?
   B: Next year.

3. A: I'm seeing Thomas tonight.
   B: (him / will / meet / where / you)
   _____ ?

4. A: (you / my office / come to / can)
   _____ by 10 a.m.?
   B: Sure. I'll be there.

정답 p.273, REVIEW TEST 7 p.228

UNIT **035**

Grammar Gateway Basic

UNIT 036 | Who is he? 의문문 (2) who, what, which

🎧 036.mp3

① who는 '누구'라는 의미로 사람에 대해 물을 때 쓴다.

Who is he?

He is my favorite singer.

- A: **Who** is he? 그는 누구니?
  B: He's my favorite singer.
- "**Who** are you meeting tonight?" 너는 오늘 밤에 누구를 만날 거니? "Billy."
- "**Who** will you ask for help with this project?" "Gwen and Brian."
- "**Who** did you see at the mall?" "My roommate Sam."

② what은 '무엇'이라는 의미로 사물 또는 정보에 대해 물을 때 쓴다.

What is it?

It's a gift for my friend.

- A: **What** is it? 그게 뭐니?
  B: It's a gift for my friend.
- "**What** can I do for you?" 제가 무엇을 해드릴까요? "Can I have a drink?"
- "**What** do you usually wear to work?" "A suit."
- This box is heavy. **What's** in it?

what + 명사는 '무슨 ~, 몇 ~'이라는 의미로 사물 또는 정보에 대해 물을 때 쓸 수 있다.
- "**What magazine** are you reading?" 너는 무슨 잡지를 읽고 있니? "*Home Design*."
- "**What time** does the class start?" 수업이 몇 시에 시작하니? "It starts at 5 o'clock."

③ which는 '어떤 것'이라는 의미로 사물에 대해 물을 때 쓴다.

Which do you want?

Tea, please.

- A: **Which** do you want? 당신은 어떤 것을 원하나요?
  B: Tea, please.
- **Which** is closer, Chicago or Dallas? 시카고와 댈러스 중 어느 곳이 더 가깝나요?
- "**Which** does Joe want, cake, pie, or a muffin?" "He wants cake."
- We're going to the mall. **Which** should we take, the train or the bus?

which + 명사는 '어떤 ~'이라는 의미로 사람과 사물 모두에 대해 물을 때 쓸 수 있다.
- "**Which boy** is Jack?" 어떤 소년이 Jack인가요? "He's wearing jeans."
- "**Which dress** do you like best?" 당신은 어떤 옷을 가장 좋아하나요? "The black one."

④ which와 what

제한적으로 주어진 몇 가지 사항 중에서 선택하는 경우에는 주로 **which**를 쓴다.
- "We have chicken and fish. **Which** would you like?" "I'll have the fish."
  (chicken과 fish로 선택할 사항이 제한적으로 주어졌으므로 Which를 씀)
- "**Which** sport do you like, baseball, basketball, or soccer?" "Baseball is my favorite."
  (야구, 농구, 축구로 선택할 사항이 제한적으로 주어졌으므로 Which를 씀)

그러나 선택할 사항이 제한적으로 주어지지 않은 경우에는 주로 **what**을 쓴다.
- "**What** do you want for dinner tonight?" "Anything is OK."
  (선택할 음식의 종류를 제한적으로 주지 않았으므로 What을 씀)
- "**What** year were you born?" "1994."
  (태어난 연도를 제한적으로 묻지 않았으므로 What을 씀)

PRACTICE

A. 그림을 보고 괄호 안에 주어진 단어들과 who 또는 what을 사용하여 의문문을 완성하세요. 과거 시제로 쓰세요.

1  2 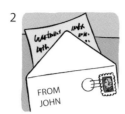 3  4

1. (she, pay) " *Who did she pay* ?" "Jill."
2. (John, send) " _____ ?" "A letter."
3. (they, visit) " _____ ?" "Larry."
4. (he, eat) " _____ ?" "Some pizza."

B. 괄호 안에 주어진 단어들을 적절히 배열하여 의문문을 완성하세요.

1. (what / your major / was) " *What was your major* _____ in college?" "I studied art and history."
2. (sports / what / you / play / do) " _____ ?" "Basketball."
3. (you / inviting / are / who) "I'm having a party next week." " _____ ?"
4. (that store / sell / what / does / fruit) " _____ ?" "Apples and pears."
5. (should / who / I / contact) " _____ for reservations?" "John Murphy."
6. (the problem / what / is) " _____ ?" "Nothing. Everything is fine."

C. 그림을 보고 주어진 명사와 which를 사용하여 의문문을 완성하세요.

book	car	~~restaurant~~	shirt

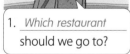
1. *Which restaurant*
should we go to?

2. _____
should I buy?

3. _____
do you recommend?

4. _____
do you like?

D. who/what/which 중 가장 적절한 것을 써넣으세요.

1. *Who* did you meet at Ken's wedding?
2. I'm not sure how to get outside. _____ door is the exit?
3. " _____ does Mr. Taylor teach?" "History."
4. " _____ is that woman?" "My neighbor."
5. _____ island did you visit in Indonesia, Java or Bali?
6. " _____ did you do last night?" "I stayed at home."
7. "Korea and Greece are having a soccer match tomorrow." " _____ team do you think will win?"
8. " _____ time does the next bus come?" "It comes at 9 o'clock."

정답 p.273, REVIEW TEST 7 p.228

Where is the bathroom? 의문문 (3) where, when, why

🎧 037.mp3

①

> Where is the bathroom?
>
> Over there.

Where is the bathroom?

화장실이 어디인가요?

where은 '어디'라는 의미로 장소를 물을 때 쓴다.

- "**Where** is Ralph working these days?" 요즘 Ralph는 어디에서 일하고 있니? "At a hospital."
- That necklace is so pretty. **Where** did you get it? 그것을 어디에서 샀니?
- "**Where** can I find an ATM?" "Across the street."
- "**Where** are we meeting Mr. Kim?" "In the lobby."

Where ~ from?: 어디에서 왔나요?

- "**Where** are you **from**?" 당신은 어디에서 오셨나요? "I'm from Brazil."
- "**Where** did this package come **from**?" 이 소포는 어디에서 온 건가요? "It's from my company."

②

> When is your flight?

When is your flight?

네 비행편이 언제니?

when은 '언제'라는 의미로 시간 또는 날짜를 물을 때 쓴다.

- "**When** is Cindy's birthday?" Cindy의 생일이 언제니? "March 21."
- "**When** does the new museum open?" 새 박물관이 언제 여나요? "Next month."
- "I'm sorry, but I'm busy now. I'll call you later." "**When** can you call me back?"
- "**When** do you watch TV?" "I watch TV after dinner."

③

> Why are you crying?
>
> I'm reading a sad story.

Why are you crying?

왜 울고 있어?

why는 '왜'라는 의미로 이유를 물을 때 쓴다.

- "**Why** are you studying Italian?" 왜 이탈리아어를 공부 중인가요? "I use it at work."
- "**Why** did you take a taxi?" 왜 택시를 탔니? "Because I was in a hurry."
- "**Why** has Terry been in her room all day?" "She isn't feeling well."
- "Jeff is in Africa right now." "Really? **Why** did he go there?"

PRACTICE

A. where/when/why를 써넣으세요.

1. *When*   does the next train for Chicago leave?
2. _____ is Tom upset?
3. _____ did Simon get married?
4. _____ can I return these shoes?
5. _____ are your hands dirty?
6. _____ should I go on vacation?

At 12 o'clock.
He lost his cell phone.
Last month.
The customer service counter.
I was fixing the car.
How about Mexico?

B. 괄호 안에 주어진 단어들을 적절히 배열하여 의문문을 완성하세요.

1. (quit / did / why / you) *Why did you quit*   your job? I thought you liked it.
2. (be / will / your parents / when) "_____ home?" "I'm not sure."
3. (do / live / where / you) I live in Seattle. _____ ?
4. (why / wear / should / I) "_____ sunglasses?" "The sun is very strong today."
5. (bringing / you / why / are) _____ a coat? Are you going somewhere?
6. (where / from / is / she) "That's the new student in my class." "Really? _____ ?"
7. (Sharon / leaving / when / is) _____ for London? Is it next week?

UNIT 037

C. where/when/why를 사용하여 예시와 같이 의문문을 완성하세요.

1. *Where do you park your car*   ?
2. _____ ?
3. _____ ?
4. _____ ?
5. _____ ?

I park my car on Ivory Street.
Ivan left the office an hour ago.
The bus comes in 10 minutes.
The mall is closed because it's a holiday.
You can find the elevator in the lobby.

D. 다음은 Chris와 Chris의 삼촌 Simon의 통화 내용입니다. 둘 중 맞는 것을 골라 Chris와 Simon의 대화를 완성하세요.

CHRIS: Hello. Uncle Simon! Thank you for inviting me to Greece.
SIMON: Chris, I miss you so much.
     1. ((When) / Where) are you coming?
CHRIS: Next Monday. 2. (Where / Why) should we meet?
SIMON: Let's meet at the airport.
     3. (When / Where) does your flight arrive?
CHRIS: At 3:30. 4. (When / Where) are we going after we meet?
     Can we go to Santorini first?
SIMON: 5. Sure, but (where / why) do you want to go there?
CHRIS: I saw some pictures online. It looks very beautiful there.

CHRIS

SIMON

정답 p.273, REVIEW TEST 7 p.228

How can I help you? 의문문 (4) how

①

How can I help you?

How can I help you?
어떻게 도와드릴까요?

how는 '어떻게'라는 의미로 방법을 물을 때 쓴다.

- "**How** can I get to the library?" 도서관까지 어떻게 갈 수 있나요? "Take Bus 202."
- **How** do you say "tree" in German? 독일어로 '나무'를 어떻게 말하나요?
- "**How** did Jim break his leg?" "He fell while he was skiing."
- "**How** do I open this door?" "Here, use this key card."

② **how + be동사**: ~은 어떤가요?

- **How is** the weather today? 오늘 날씨는 어떤가요?
- "**How was** your trip to Hong Kong?" 홍콩 여행은 어땠나요? "It was so much fun!"
- "**How are** you these days?" "I'm very busy."

③ **how + 형용사/부사**: 얼마나 ~

How   형용사/부사

How	long	have you known Lucy?" (얼마나 오래)	"For six years."
How	far	is the train station?" (얼마나 멀리)	"Just a few kilometers."
How	fast	can a cheetah run?"	"I'm not sure."
How	often	do you exercise?"	"Twice a week."

④ '얼마나 많이'라는 의미로 **how many/much**를 쓸 수 있다.

- "Could I have some cookies, please?" "**How many** do you want?" 얼마나 많이 원하니?
- "Put some salt in the soup." "**How much** should I put?" 얼마나 많이 넣는 것이 좋을까요?

   how much는 가격을 물을 때도 쓸 수 있다.

- "This is a nice watch. **How much** is it?" 이것은 얼마인가요? "That one is $800."

how many/much 뒤에 명사를 쓸 수도 있다.

- "**How many guests** are coming for dinner?" 저녁 식사에 얼마나 많은 손님이 올 건가요? "Maybe 10."
- "**How much time** do you need?" 얼마나 많은 시간이 필요한가요? "It will take about 30 minutes."

PRACTICE

A. 괄호 안에 주어진 단어들과 how를 적절히 배열하여 의문문을 완성하세요.

1. (I / can / contact) *How can I contact*_____ you?
2. (you / come / did) _____ to Germany?
3. (can / turn off / I) _____ the heater?
4. (do / get to / your kids) _____ school?
5. (prepare / we / should) _____ for the party?

Here's my phone number.
I took a train from Italy.
Just push that button.
They usually walk.
Let's cook some food first.

B. 주어진 문장을 보고 how + be동사를 사용하여 의문문을 완성하세요.

1. *How are you*_____ today? Are you still sick?
2. _____? Was it good?
3. _____?
4. _____?
5. _____ in Hawaii?

I'm OK. I feel better.
Yes. The concert was excellent.
The food tastes bad. I don't like it.
My parents are fine.
My holiday was great.

C. 주어진 형용사 또는 부사와 how를 사용하여 의문문을 완성하세요.

far	~~fast~~	long	many	much	much	often	old	tall

1. " *How fast*_____ was Dan driving?" "I don't know, but it was over the speed limit."
2. "Your little brother is very cute. _____ is he?" "He's six years old."
3. "These apples were on sale." "_____ were they?"
4. "_____ do you check your e-mail?" "Once a day."
5. "_____ is the park from your house?" "Three miles."
6. "Sorry, but you have to wait. The restaurant is full." "_____ do we have to wait?"
7. "_____ cash do you have? Can I borrow some?" "I only have credit cards."
8. "_____ is Carl?" "I think he's 180 cm."
9. "_____ children do you have?" "I have two daughters."

D. 괄호 안에 주어진 단어들을 적절히 배열하여 점원과 Amy의 대화를 완성하세요.

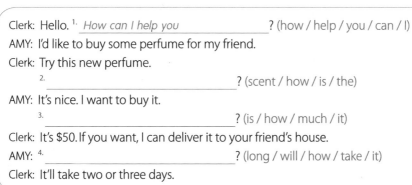

Clerk: Hello. 1. *How can I help you*_____? (how / help / you / can / I)
AMY: I'd like to buy some perfume for my friend.
Clerk: Try this new perfume.
2. _____? (scent / how / is / the)
AMY: It's nice. I want to buy it.
3. _____? (is / how / much / it)
Clerk: It's $50. If you want, I can deliver it to your friend's house.
AMY: 4. _____? (long / will / how / take / it)
Clerk: It'll take two or three days.

정답 p.274, REVIEW TEST 7 p.228

🎧 039.mp3

①

The stars are very pretty, **aren't they**?

The stars are very pretty, **aren't they**?
별들이 매우 예뻐, 그렇지 않니?

aren't they와 같이 문장 끝에 붙여 말하는 짧은 의문문을
부가의문문이라고 한다.

부가의문문은 상대방에게 동의를 구하거나 자신의 말이 맞는지 물을 때 쓴다.

● It's going to rain tomorrow, **isn't it**? 내일 비가 올 거야, 그렇지 않니?
● You aren't reading this book, **are you**? 넌 이 책을 읽고 있지 않아, 그렇지?

② 긍정문 끝에는 부정 부가의문문을 쓴다. 이때, 부가의문문의 주어는 항상 대명사로 쓴다.

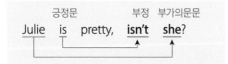

긍정문　　　　부정　부가의문문
Julie　is　pretty,　**isn't　she**?

● It was a long trip, **wasn't it**? 긴 여행이었어요, 그렇지 않나요?
● Ellen enjoys surfing, **doesn't she**? Ellen은 서핑하는 것을 즐기죠, 그렇지 않나요?
● You can drive, **can't you**?
● "Mark and Tina will come to see us tonight, **won't they**?" "I'm not sure."

부정문 끝에는 긍정 부가의문문을 쓴다. 이때에도 부가의문문의 주어는 대명사로 쓴다.

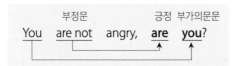

부정문　　　　긍정　부가의문문
You　are not　angry,　**are　you**?

● The roller coaster wasn't scary at all, **was it**? 그 롤러코스터는 전혀 무섭지 않았어, 그렇지?
● Sam doesn't like me, **does he**? Sam은 나를 좋아하지 않아, 그렇지?
● You haven't seen Bob lately, **have you**?
● "Sophie can't speak French, **can she**?" "I don't know."

③ 부가의문문에 '~하다/이다'라는 긍정의 의미는 **Yes**로 답하고, '~하지 않다/아니다'라는 부정의 의미는 **No**로 답한다.

● "You know this song, **don't you**?" "**Yes**, I do." 네, 저는 이 노래를 알아요. (= Yes, I know this song.)
● "The food was very good, **wasn't it**?" "**No**, it was awful." 아니요, 그것은 끔찍했어요. (= No, the food wasn't very good.)
● "You haven't heard this story, **have you**?" "**Yes**, I've heard it many times!"
● "Jack doesn't smoke, **does he**?" "**No**, he doesn't."

PRACTICE

A. 주어진 긍정문에 맞게 부가의문문을 써넣으세요.

1. These sunglasses are yours, _aren't they_ ?
2. You locked the door, _____ ?
3. Your parents live in New York, _____ ?
4. Mary has been to Morocco, _____ ?
5. You can fix the computer, _____ ?
6. Tomorrow is Tuesday, _____ ?

B. 주어진 부정문에 맞게 부가의문문을 써넣으세요.

1. Bill doesn't like sports, _does he_ ?
2. You haven't met Ronald, _____ ?
3. I'm not wrong, _____ ?
4. Joseph can't play the guitar, _____ ?
5. You aren't coming to the meeting, _____ ?
6. We don't work this weekend, _____ ?

C. 주어진 문장을 보고 적절한 부가의문문을 써넣으세요.

1. You went shopping today, _didn't you_ ?
2. The soccer game was great, _____ ?
3. You can't speak Japanese, _____ ?
4. It's not cold outside, _____ ?
5. You have ridden a horse before, _____ ?
6. Your sister doesn't like spaghetti, _____ ?
7. Tom and Megan are having a baby next year, _____ ?

Yes, I did.
Yes, it was exciting.
No, I can't.
No. It's very warm today.
Yes, I have.
No, she doesn't.
Yes, they are.

D. 상황에 맞게 Yes 또는 No를 써넣으세요.

1. You are from Russia, aren't you?
2. Sally can't swim, can she?
3. This umbrella is mine, isn't it?
4. You haven't had lunch yet, have you?
5. You don't drink soda, do you?
6. Jane's children are cute, aren't they?

Yes , I'm Russian.
_____ . She is afraid of water.
_____ , it's yours.
_____ . I'm very hungry.
_____ , I never drink it.
_____ . They're nice too.

E. Justin이 망원경으로 별을 보고 있습니다. 적절한 부가의문문을 사용하여 Chris와 Justin의 대화를 완성하세요.

CHRIS: ¹·The stars are very pretty, _aren't they_ ?
JUSTIN: I can't see anything.
CHRIS: Really? What's wrong?
　　　　²·The lens is OK, _____ ?
JUSTIN: I think so. ³·You checked it before we left home, _____ ?
CHRIS: Yes, I did. ⁴·You've opened the lens cap, _____ ?
JUSTIN: Whoops. I forgot!

CHRIS

JUSTIN

Do you know **where the station is**? 간접의문문

🎧 040.mp3

①

Do you know **where the station is**?

Where is the station?
↓
Do you know **where the station is**?

역이 어디에 있는지 아시나요?

where the station is와 같이 문장 안에 포함된 의문문을
간접의문문이라고 한다.

---

② 의문사가 있는 의문문을 간접의문문으로 쓸 때 **의문사 + 주어 + 동사**로 쓴다.

be동사, 조동사 등을 포함하는 의문사 의문문을 간접의문문으로 말할 경우

의문사 + **be 동사, will/can 등** + 주어		간접의문문 의문사 + 주어 + **be동사, will/can 등**
○ Who is Holly?		**who** Holly **is**. (누가 Holly인지)
○ How has Peter been?	I don't know	**how** Peter **has been**. (Peter가 어떻게 지내는지)
○ Where can we find a gas station?		**where** we can find a gas station.

일반동사를 포함하는 의문사 의문문을 간접의문문으로 말할 경우

의문사 + **do/does/did** + 주어 + 동사		간접의문문 의문사 + 주어 + 동사
○ What do you like?		**what** you like? (당신이 무엇을 좋아하는지)
○ When does the store close?	Could you tell me	**when** the store closes? (그 상점이 언제 닫는지)
○ Why did Carol leave early?		**why** Carol left early?

간접의문문에는 **do/does/did**를 쓰지 않는 것에 주의한다.

○ Can you tell me **what you study in college**? (Can you tell me what do you study in college로 쓸 수 없음)
○ I'm not sure **where Jason lives**. (I'm not sure where does Jason live로 쓸 수 없음)

---

③ 의문사가 없는 의문문을 간접의문문으로 쓸 때는 **if/whether + 주어 + 동사**로 쓴다. 이때, **if**와 **whether**는
'~인지 아닌지'라는 의미이다.

if/whether + 주어 + 동사

○ Does Sam speak Greek?		**if** Sam **speaks** Greek. **whether** Sam **speaks** Greek. (Sam이 그리스어를 하는지 아닌지)
	I wonder	
○ Is Jane coming to the meeting?		**if** Jane **is coming** to the meeting. **whether** Jane is coming to the meeting. (Jane이 회의에 올 것인지 아닌지)

PRACTICE

A. 괄호 안에 주어진 단어들을 적절히 배열하여 문장을 완성하세요.

1. (where / is / the bus stop) Could you tell me _where the bus stop is_ ?
2. (Emily / why / was / late) Do you know _____ ?
3. (I / parked / my car / where) I don't remember _____ .
4. (in the report / I / should / what / write) I don't know _____ .
5. (John / will / be back / when) I'm not sure _____ .
6. (called / why / the manager / me) Do you know _____ ?
7. (you / answer / how / can / this question) Please tell me _____ .

B. 옆집에 Tony와 Sue 부부가 이사 왔습니다. Do you know를 사용하여 Tina가 궁금해하는 것들을 질문하세요.

1. When did they move here?
2. Where did they live before?
3. What does Tony do?
4. How many children do they have?
5. What are their hobbies?

TINA

Do you know when they moved here ?
_____ ?
_____ ?
_____ ?
_____ ?

C. 주어진 의문문을 보고 간접의문문을 사용하여 문장을 완성하세요. if 또는 whether를 함께 사용하세요.

1. Did Greg finish his report?   I don't know _if (OR whether) Greg finished his report_ .
2. Did many people come to the party?   I'm not sure _____ .
3. Is Annie going to visit us tomorrow?   Could you tell me _____ ?
4. Have you seen my brother?   I wonder _____ .
5. Can Joey play the violin?   I'm not sure _____ .
6. Has Hannah gone home?   Do you know _____ ?

D. Amy는 어떤 관광객을 만났습니다. 괄호 안에 주어진 단어들을 적절히 배열하여 관광객과 Amy의 대화를 완성하세요.

Tourist

AMY

Tourist: 1. Excuse me. Could you tell me _how I can get to the airport_ ?
      (get / can / how / I / to the airport)
AMY: Sure. It's easy. You can take the subway.
Tourist: 2. Do you know _____ ? (the station / where / is)
AMY: It's right down the street.
Tourist: 3. Can you tell me _____ ?
      (how / can / a ticket / I / buy)
AMY: I'll help you with that.
Tourist: 4. I wonder _____ by 5 p.m.
      (if / will / at the airport / arrive / I)
AMY: Don't worry. It only takes 30 minutes.

정답 p.274, REVIEW TEST 7 p.228

UNIT
040

Grammar Gateway Basic

Exercising is good for health. -ing와 to + 동사원형

🎧 041.mp3

①

Exercising is good for health.
운동하는 것은 건강에 좋다.

---

② '~하는 것'이라는 의미로 **-ing**를 주어로 쓸 수 있다.

- **Painting** is fun. I really enjoy it. 그림 그리는 것은 재미있다.
- **Traveling** can cost a lot of money. 여행하는 것은 돈이 많이 들 수 있다.
- "I'm still sleepy. I have to wake up." "**Drinking coffee** might help."

-ing를 목적어로도 쓸 수 있다.

- I enjoy **playing cards**. 나는 카드놀이를 하는 것을 즐긴다.
- We just finished **cleaning the house**. 우리는 방금 집을 청소하는 것을 끝냈다.
- "Do you mind **opening the window**? It's hot in here." "No. Go ahead."

---

③ 다음과 같이 **-ing** 뒤에 여러 단어를 함께 쓸 수 있다.

- **Learning a foreign language** takes a long time. (외국어를 배우는 것)
- **Washing your hands before meals** is important. (식사 전에 손을 씻는 것)

- Jack avoids **taking the subway in the morning**. (아침에 지하철을 타는 것)
- I suggest **wearing that blue dress to the party**. (파티에 그 파란 드레스를 입는 것)

---

④ '~하는 것, ~하기'라는 의미로 **to + 동사원형**도 목적어로 쓸 수 있다.

- I didn't expect **to see you**. What brings you here? 당신을 볼 것을 기대하지 않았어요.
- Benny wants **to buy a car**. Benny는 차를 사기를 원한다.
- Lisa isn't good at math, so her brother offered **to help her**.

to + 동사원형도 주어로 쓸 수 있지만 자주 쓰지는 않는다. **to + 동사원형**보다는 **-ing**를 주로 쓴다.

- **Smoking** is not allowed in this restaurant. 이 식당에서 담배를 피우는 것은 허용되지 않는다. (= To smoke)
- It's raining. **Bringing an umbrella** was a good idea. 우산을 가져오는 것은 좋은 생각이었어. (= To bring an umbrella)

---

⑤ 다음과 같이 **to + 동사원형** 뒤에도 여러 단어를 함께 쓸 수 있다.

- Is Megan planning **to study in Europe next year?** (내년에 유럽에서 공부하는 것)
- We hope **to work with you again**. (당신과 다시 함께 일하기)

PRACTICE

A. 주어진 동사를 -ing로 사용하여 문장을 완성하세요.

~~collect~~   lose   make   plant   swim   watch   wear

1. I have a lot of comic books at home. *Collecting* them is my favorite hobby.
2. _____ weight is hard. I exercise every day, but it doesn't help.
3. I want to avoid _____ a reservation for a room on Saturday. It's too expensive.
4. You should put on your sunglasses. _____ them protects your eyes.
5. "What do you usually do on weekends?" "I enjoy _____ old movies."
6. _____ in this lake is not safe. It's very deep.
7. _____ trees helps the environment.

B. 괄호 안에 주어진 표현들을 적절히 배열하여 문장을 완성하세요. 동사를 -ing로 쓰세요.

1. (to work / drive) Traffic is bad in the morning. *Driving to work* _____ takes a long time.
2. (read / that book) I finished _____ last night. It was very good.
3. (about her / talk) I think Bill likes Diane. He keeps _____.
4. (eat / too much food) _____ can cause a stomachache.
5. (with these old shoes / run) _____ hurts my feet. I should get new ones.

C. 주어진 표현에 대해 자신의 생각과 가까운 것에 표시하고 -ing를 사용하여 예시와 같이 말해보세요.

make friends	☐ easy	☐ difficult	1. *Making friends is easy* OR *Making friends is difficult* .
ride a roller coaster	☐ exciting	☐ scary	2. _____ .
take a taxi	☐ cheap	☐ expensive	3. _____ .
travel alone	☐ safe	☐ dangerous	4. _____ .
play chess	☐ fun	☐ boring	5. _____ .

D. 각 사람의 말을 보고 괄호 안에 주어진 동사와 to + 동사원형을 사용하여 예시와 같이 문장을 완성하세요. 현재 시제로 쓰세요.

 JOE ⟨ Can we go camping this weekend? ⟩
1. (want) Joe *wants to go camping this weekend* .

 MILA ⟨ I should visit my grandparents tomorrow. ⟩
4. (plan) Mila _____ _____ .

HENRY ⟨ I will be home by 6. ⟩
2. (promise) Henry _____ _____ .

 DANIEL ⟨ My dream is to win a Nobel Prize. ⟩
5. (hope) Daniel _____ _____ .

BELLA ⟨ I have to finish the report by Monday. ⟩
3. (need) Bella _____ _____ .

 LUCY ⟨ The interview went well. Maybe I'll get the job. ⟩
6. (expect) Lucy _____ _____ .

정답 p.274, REVIEW TEST 8 p.230

①

He is making pizza.

He **enjoys cooking**.

그는 요리하는 것을 즐긴다.

He **wants to open** a restaurant.

그는 음식점을 열기를 원한다.

enjoys 뒤에 cooking을 썼고, wants 뒤에는 to open을 썼다.

---

② 다음과 같은 동사 뒤에는 '~하는 것, ~하기'라는 의미로 말할 때 **-ing**를 쓴다.

enjoy	finish	keep	mind	**-ing**
avoid	give up	practice	suggest	(writing, raining, waiting 등)

- "I **finished writing** my essay." 나는 에세이 쓰는 것을 끝냈어. "Great. Can I read it?"
- It **kept raining** for three days. 3일 동안 계속 비가 내렸다.
- "Do you **mind waiting** a moment?" "No problem."
- Sophie is **avoiding going** to the dentist because she is scared.
- "Ken will **give up teaching** and go to law school." "Really? Does he want to be a lawyer?"
- Jane and I take a Chinese class together. We **practice speaking** Chinese every day.
- We don't **suggest staying** at that hotel. The service isn't good.

  이때, **-ing** 대신 **to + 동사원형**을 쓰지 않도록 주의한다.
  - Jake **finished painting** the fence. (finished to paint로 쓸 수 없음)

---

③ 다음과 같은 동사 뒤에는 '~하는 것, ~하기'라는 의미로 말할 때 **to + 동사원형**을 쓴다.

want	need	hope	expect	**to + 동사원형**
decide	plan	promise	offer	(to worry, to get, to see 등)
choose	ask	learn	refuse	

- "Alan, are you OK?" "You don't **need to worry** about me. I'm fine." 나에 대해 걱정할 필요 없어.
- I **hope to get** a reply from you soon. 저는 당신으로부터 곧 답변을 얻길 바랍니다.
- We can **expect to see** a lot of snowfall this winter.
- "Have you **decided to take** the job?" "Yes. I will start next week."
- "What are you doing this weekend?" "I'm **planning to attend** a wedding on Saturday."
- Ben **promised to be** here at 4, but he hasn't arrived yet.
- "Jackie and Allison **offered to bring** some cake to the party." "That's great!"

  이때, **to + 동사원형** 대신 **-ing**를 쓰지 않도록 주의한다.
  - I **promised to go** out for dinner with you tonight, but I can't. (promised going으로 쓸 수 없음)

PRACTICE

A. 둘 중 맞는 것을 고르세요.

1. "The meeting is at 3:30, right?" "It was, but Ms. Bill asked (changing / (to change)) the time."
2. I've been busy with too much work, so I suggested (hiring / to hire) more people.
3. "You promised (doing / to do) all your homework tonight." "OK, I'll do it."
4. I was going to offer (helping / to help) with your report, but you already finished it.
5. My roommate is practicing (singing / to sing) in her room.
6. I told John some ghost stories, but he refused (believing / to believe) in them.

B. 그림을 보고 주어진 표현을 사용하여 문장을 완성하세요. -ing 또는 to + 동사원형으로 쓰세요.

buy this house	clean the bathroom	~~get some gas~~	look at me	open the door	play the flute

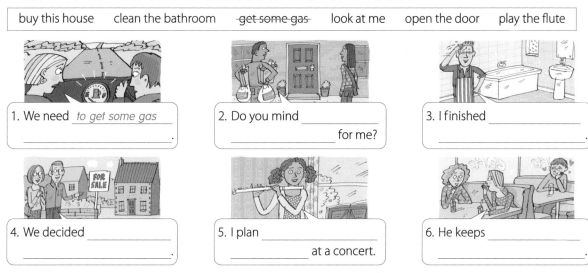

1. We need *to get some gas* _____ .

2. Do you mind _____ _____ for me?

3. I finished _____ _____ .

4. We decided _____ _____ .

5. I plan _____ _____ at a concert.

6. He keeps _____ _____ .

C. 주어진 동사들을 사용하여 예시와 같이 문장을 완성하세요.

become	drive	~~ride~~	smoke	spend

1. (learn) "When did you *learn to ride* _____ a motorcycle?" "Last year."
2. (choose) "Why did you _____ a writer?" "I love writing short stories."
3. (avoid) Julie _____ a car at night.
4. (expect) I didn't _____ so much money at the mall today.
5. (give up) "My father _____ a year ago." "You must be proud of him."

D. 괄호 안에 주어진 동사들을 사용하여 Linda와 James의 대화를 완성하세요. 필요한 경우 동사의 형태를 바꾸세요.

LINDA

LINDA: What are you thinking about, James?
JAMES: 1. I *want to open* _____ a restaurant. (want, open)
LINDA: 2. But you _____ to your office. (enjoy, go)
JAMES: 3. I do, but I _____ my own business. (hope, have)
LINDA: It will be hard, you know.
JAMES: I know. 4. But I don't _____ hard. (mind, work)

JAMES

정답 p.275, REVIEW TEST 8 p.230

UNIT 043 | They **like visiting/to visit** museums. -ing와 to + 동사원형 모두 뒤에 올 수 있는 동사

🎧 043.mp3

①

They **like visiting** museums.

또는 They **like to visit** museums.

그들은 박물관을 방문하는 것을 좋아한다.

---

② 다음과 같은 동사 뒤에는 -ing와 to + 동사원형을 둘 다 쓸 수 있다.

like	love	prefer	hate	-ing (skating, living 등)
start	begin	continue		to + 동사원형 (to skate, to live 등)

- Polly **loves skating**. 또는 Polly **loves to skate**. Polly는 스케이트 타는 것을 좋아한다.
- Do you **prefer living** in the city or in the country?
  또는 Do you **prefer to live** in the city or in the country? 당신은 도시에 사는 것을 선호하나요 또는 시골에 사는 것을 선호하나요?
- I **hate doing** the dishes. 또는 I **hate to do** the dishes.
- When did you **start studying** French? 또는 When did you **start to study** French?
- Leaves **begin falling** in October. 또는 Leaves **begin to fall** in October.
- Harry will **continue working** at the bank. 또는 Harry will **continue to work** at the bank.

---

③ 다음과 같은 동사 뒤에도 -ing와 to + 동사원형을 둘 다 쓸 수 있다. 단, -ing를 쓸 때와 to + 동사원형을 쓸 때 의미가 다르다.

stop	**-ing** ~하는 것을 멈추다
	to + 동사원형 ~하기 위해 (하던 일을) 멈추다

- Please **stop making** noise. I can't sleep. 소음 내는 것을 멈춰주세요.
- There are some nice dresses at that store. Let's **stop to look**. 우리 보기 위해 멈춰보자.
- Paula **stopped listening** to the radio and turned on the TV.
- "Can we **stop to eat** something?" "Sure. What do you want?"

try	**-ing** (시험 삼아) ~해보다
	to + 동사원형 ~하려고 노력하다

- "Planning a wedding is so tiring." "You should **try hiring** a wedding planner." 웨딩 플래너를 고용해보는 게 좋겠다.
- After graduating, Tina will **try to get** a job at a marketing company. Tina는 마케팅 회사에 취직하려고 노력할 것이다.
- "My computer isn't working." "You should **try turning** off its power and on again."
- I **tried to talk** to Jessica, but she was still upset.

PRACTICE

A. 괄호 안에 주어진 동사를 -ing 또는 to + 동사원형으로 사용하여 문장을 완성하세요.

1. (find) We expected _to find_____ Mr. Miller in his office, but he wasn't there.
2. (go) We avoid _____ to the mall on Sundays. It's very crowded.
3. (feel) "When did you begin _____ sick?" "This morning."
4. (join) Greg and I refused _____ the golf club because it cost too much.
5. (write) Thomas continued _____ the novel until it was finished.
6. (drive) I don't like _____ in the snow. It's very dangerous sometimes.
7. (learn) My grandmother keeps _____ new things. She's learning about smartphones these days.

B. 주어진 동사와 stop을 사용하여 문장을 완성하세요.

ask	buy	laugh	take	~~walk~~	worry

1. Can we _stop walking_____ now? My feet hurt.
2. The movie was so funny. I couldn't _____ .
3. "I think we're lost." "We should _____ for directions."
4. "I'm so nervous about my speech." "_____ about it so much."
5. Can we _____ some milk at the store? We don't have any at home.
6. Let's _____ a picture here. The view from this mountain is beautiful.

C. 주어진 동사를 사용하여 문장을 완성하세요.

call	finish	go	~~invite~~	take

1. Why wasn't Joel at the party?
2. Are you done writing the report?
3. Have you been to the new theater?
4. I've never done yoga.
5. Did you speak to Bob?

I tried _to invite_____ him, but he was busy.
Almost. I'll try _____ it by 2.
No. Let's try _____ there tomorrow.
You should try _____ a lesson.
No. I'm trying _____ him now.

D. 다음 문장을 읽고 틀린 부분이 있으면 바르게 고치세요. 틀린 부분이 없으면 O로 표시하세요.

Picasso – A great artist

1. Picasso started studying art when he was four. _____O_____
2. He practiced to draw at school until he was 16. _____
3. Picasso always loved experiencing new things. _____
4. So, he decided moving to Paris. _____
5. He was very poor, but he didn't give up to paint. _____
6. He continued making artwork until he died in 1973. _____

정답 p.275, REVIEW TEST 8 p.230

UNIT
043

Grammar Gateway Basic

She **wants him to clean** the room. 동사 + 사람 + to + 동사원형

🎧 044.mp3

①

> I want you to clean the room.

She **wants him to clean** the room.
그녀는 그가 방을 치우기를 원한다.

---

② **want + 사람 + to + 동사원형: ~가 …하기를 원하다**

- I'm really tired, so I **want you to drive**. 저는 당신이 차를 운전해주기를 원해요.
- Jenny didn't **want Albert to buy** the TV. It was too expensive. Jenny는 Albert가 그 TV를 사는 것을 원하지 않았다.
- I'm going to the store. Do you **want me to get** anything for you?

  want 뒤에 **to + 동사원형**만 쓸 수도 있다. 다음과 같은 차이에 주의한다.

  - I **want to help** him. 나는 그를 돕기를 원해요.
    I **want you to help** him. 나는 당신이 그를 돕기를 원해요.

---

③ 다음과 같은 동사 뒤에도 사람 + to + 동사원형을 쓸 수 있다.

advise   allow   ask   expect   teach   tell

	동사	사람	to + 동사원형	
The doctor	advised	Judy	to drink more water.	의사는 Judy에게 물을 더 마시라고 조언했다.
We didn't	expect	Fred	to win the race.	우리는 Fred가 경주를 이길 것이라고 기대하지 않았다.
Can you	teach	me	to dance?	

---

④ **make/have/let + 사람 + 동사원형: ~가 …하게 하다**

	make/have/let	사람	동사원형	
Bob and Helen	made	me	wait	for an hour. Bob과 Helen은 내가 한 시간 동안 기다리게 했다.
Erin	had	Tom	move	some furniture. Erin은 Tom이 가구들을 옮기게 했다.
	Let	me	introduce	myself.

이때, 동사원형 대신 **to + 동사원형**을 쓰지 않도록 주의한다.

- Exercising **makes me feel** healthy. (makes me to feel로 쓸 수 없음)

---

⑤ **help + 사람 + 동사원형: ~가 …하는 것을 돕다**

	help	사람	동사원형	
Can you	help	me	find	the post office? 제가 우체국을 찾는 것을 도와주시겠어요?
I	helped	Sean	do	his homework. 나는 Sean이 숙제를 하는 것을 도와주었다.

이때, 동사원형 대신 **to + 동사원형**을 쓸 수도 있다.

- I'll **help you hang** that picture. 또는 I'll **help you to hang** that picture. 네가 그 그림을 거는 것을 도와줄게.

PRACTICE

A. 괄호 안에 주어진 단어들과 want를 사용하여 대화를 완성하세요.

1. A: (you, come) I _want you to come_ to my wedding.
   B: Of course! I'll be there.

2. A: Let's stay at home tonight.
   B: (us, have) Actually, Leo and Marcy _____ _____ dinner with them.

3. A: (me, move) Do you _____ those boxes upstairs?
   B: Thanks, but I can do it.

4. A: John isn't here yet.
   B: (you, call) I don't have my phone now, so I _____ him.

B. 각 사람의 말을 보고 괄호 안에 주어진 동사를 사용하여 예시와 같이 문장을 완성하세요. 과거 시제로 쓰세요.

JOE < Bill, can you close the window?
1. (ask) Joe _asked Bill to close the window_ .

JAY < Ben, you can use the camera.
2. (allow) Jay _____ .

LYNN < Brian, could you answer the phone?
3. (tell) Lynn _____ .

DIANA < David will call back soon.
4. (expect) Diana _____ .

TIM < Nick, please speak louder.
5. (want) Tim _____ .

ANNA < Nancy, you should go to bed.
6. (advise) Anna _____ .

C. 주어진 동사를 사용하여 예시와 같이 문장을 완성하세요.

| ~~bake~~ | buy | drive | pay | run | stay |

1. Lana makes delicious cookies, so I had _her bake_ some for me.
2. My wife wants me to lose weight. She makes _____ every morning now.
3. "Where is Larry?" "I had _____ some eggs and butter."
4. I want to use Dad's car, but he won't let _____ it.
5. "Did you and Lucy find a hotel?" "No, but my friend let _____ at her house."
6. Jim and Cody broke a vase in the store, so the clerk made _____ for it.

D. 주어진 동사와 help를 사용하여 예시와 같이 도와주겠다고 제안하세요.

| answer | carry | find | ~~prepare~~ | wash |

1. I have to make dinner.
2. I lost my passport.
3. These bags are heavy.
4. I don't understand this question.
5. My dog is so dirty.

I can _help you prepare_ OR _help you to prepare_ it.
I will _____ it.
I can _____ them.
I can _____ it.
I will _____ your dog.

They're running **to catch** the bus.

목적을 나타내는 to + 동사원형과
명사 + to + 동사원형

🎧 045.mp3

①

> Oh, no! We're going to miss it!

They're running **to catch** the bus.
그들은 버스를 타기 위해 뛰어가고 있다.

'~하기 위해'라는 의미로 말할 때 **to** + 동사원형을 쓸 수 있다.

○ I must study hard **to pass** the exam. 나는 시험에 합격하기 위해 열심히 공부해야 한다.

○ "How can I help you?" "I'm here **to meet** Mr. Johnson." 저는 Johnson씨를 만나기 위해 왔어요.

○ We usually go to a bar **to drink** some wine on Friday nights.

○ "Where's Fred?" "He went out **to play** baseball."

이때, **to** + 동사원형 대신 **in order to** + 동사원형도 쓸 수 있다. 단, 일상 대화에서는 **to** + 동사원형을 더 자주 쓴다.

○ A lot of effort is necessary **(in order) to succeed**. 성공하기 위해 많은 노력이 필요하다.

○ Tickets are required **(in order) to enter** the theater. 극장에 들어가기 위해 표가 요구된다.

- -

②

> It's **time to go**!

It's **time to go**.
가야 할 시간이에요.

'~할 …'이라는 의미로 말할 때 다음과 같이 명사 뒤에 **to** + 동사원형을 쓸 수 있다.

time	**to go**	갈 시간
key	**to open**	열 열쇠
line	**to buy**	살 줄
place	**to stay**	머물 장소
money	**to spend**	쓸 돈

○ "Do you have a **key to open** this cabinet?" "It's not locked." 이 캐비닛을 열 열쇠를 가지고 있나요?

○ The **line to buy** tickets for last night's game was very long. We had to wait for an hour.
어젯밤 경기의 티켓을 살 줄은 매우 길었다.

○ Are there any hotels nearby? I need a **place to stay**.

○ I can't go shopping. I have no **money to spend**.

PRACTICE

A. 그림을 보고 주어진 표현을 사용하여 예시와 같이 문장을 완성하세요.

~~get a haircut~~	return a book	see the pandas	send a package	visit his friend

1. She went to the *hair salon to get a haircut* .
2. He went to the _____ .
3. He went to the _____ .
4. She went to the _____ .
5. They went to the _____ .

B. 주어진 표현과 to를 사용하여 문장을 완성하세요.

buy some ice cream	get some fresh air	help him
make an appointment	stay healthy	~~take a nap~~

1. Derek got up at 5 o'clock this morning. He wanted to go home early *to take a nap* .
2. I opened the window _____ .
3. A boy fell down the stairs, so Ben stopped _____ .
4. I'm going to the supermarket _____ .
5. You should exercise regularly _____ .
6. I'm not feeling well, so I'm calling the doctor's office _____ .

C. 괄호 안에 주어진 단어들을 적절히 배열하여 문장을 완성하세요. to를 함께 쓰세요.

1. (sit / place) There's no *place to sit* here. We should go to another café.
2. (time / visit) I don't have _____ my grandparents these days.
3. (ask / questions) Can we meet this afternoon? I have some _____ you.
4. (games / play) I'm bored. Do you have any _____ ?
5. (book / read) It'll be a long trip. You should take a _____ .
6. (share / snacks) "Let's have a picnic tomorrow." "Should I bring some _____ ?"

D. 괄호 안에 주어진 단어들과 to를 적절히 배열하여 James와 Linda의 대화를 완성하세요.

JAMES

LINDA

JAMES: 1. Linda, it's *time to go* ! (go / time)
LINDA: I need five more minutes.
2. I just have a few _____ . (things / do)
JAMES: Please hurry! 3. I have _____ . (finish / work)
4. I've also got _____ . (meetings / attend)
LINDA: OK. 5. Then, there's no _____ . (talk / time)
JAMES: All right. I'll wait in the car.

정답 p.275, REVIEW TEST 8 p.230

UNIT **045**

Grammar Gateway Basic

🎧 046.mp3

①

a **bag**

three **bags**

a **bag** → three **bags**

단수   복수

사람 또는 사물이 하나인 경우를 **단수**, 둘 이상인 경우를 **복수**라고 한다.

단수	a **bag**	one **girl**	this **car**	my **son**
복수	three **bags**	some **girls**	these **cars**	your **sons**

② 명사의 복수를 쓸 때 명사 끝에 주로 **-s**를 붙인다.

this desk → these desk**s**   a cat → some cat**s**   one apple → two apple**s**   my friend → my friend**s**

- These **desks** are made of wood. 이 책상들은 나무로 만들어졌다.
- "My **friends** bought a birthday gift for me." 내 친구들이 나에게 생일 선물을 사 줬어. "What did you get?"

다음과 같이 **-s**를 붙일 때 주의해야 할 명사가 있다.

-sh/-ch/-s/-x/-z/-o + es	dish → dish**es**	church → church**es**	potato → potato**es**	예외) kilo → kilo**s**
-y → -ies	baby → bab**ies**	lady → lad**ies**	party → part**ies**	예외) day → day**s**
-f/-fe → -ves	calf → cal**ves**	knife → kni**ves**	self → sel**ves**	wife → wi**ves**

- Steve usually washes the **dishes** after dinner. Steve는 보통 저녁 식사 후에 설거지를 한다.
- Look at those **babies**. They're so cute! 저 아기들 좀 보세요.
- "Can you put these **knives** in the drawer?" "Sure."
- Americans usually attend many **parties** during the holiday season.
- "The weather is very nice these **days**." "Yes. It's perfect for a picnic."

명사의 복수형: 부록 p.249 참고

③ 다음과 같이 복수의 형태가 불규칙한 명사가 있다.

a **person** → some **people**   my **foot** → my **feet**

a **woman** → many **women**   a **child** → a lot of **children**

- Some **people** can write with both hands. 몇몇 사람들은 양손으로 글을 쓸 수 있다.
- I can't walk anymore. My **feet** hurt. 내 발이 아프다.
- There are many **women** in our office.
- A lot of **children** don't eat vegetables.

PRACTICE

A. 주어진 명사를 복수로 쓰세요.

1. doctor → *doctors*
2. foot → _____
3. day → _____
4. lady → _____

5. child → _____
6. bench → _____
7. party → _____
8. wife → _____

9. knife → _____
10. kilo → _____
11. loaf → _____
12. friend → _____

B. 그림을 보고 적절한 명사를 써넣으세요. 단수 또는 복수로 쓰세요.

1  2  3  4

1. There are some *cats* _____ in the basket.
2. He is carrying _____.

3. The _____ are crying.
4. She is buying some _____.

C. 다음 문장을 읽고 틀린 부분이 있으면 바르게 고치세요. 틀린 부분이 없으면 O로 표시하세요.

1. "How many day do you work each week?" "Only three."   _____ *day → days*
2. I need to buy two loaf of bread.   _____
3. How many child do you have?   _____
4. I wear a uniform at work.   _____
5. My daughter likes peach, so she eats them every day.   _____
6. Two boy are playing in the pool. Who are they?   _____
7. Many womans go shopping on the day after Christmas.   _____
8. "I want to sit down." "Oh, there is a bench."   _____
9. Jody took a photography class. She enjoys taking photoes.   _____
10. I've lived in many big cities since I was young.   _____

D. Paul과 Chris는 캠핑을 가려고 합니다. 괄호 안에 주어진 명사를 사용하여 Paul과 Chris의 대화를 완성하세요.

PAUL   (PAUL 그림)

CHRIS   (CHRIS 그림)

PAUL: What can I bring for the camping trip?
CHRIS: ¹·Can you bring five *potatoes* _____ ? (potato)
PAUL: Sure. ²·Do you have a camping _____ ? (knife)
CHRIS: ³·I have three camping _____ . (knife)
        I'll bring them.
PAUL: Good. ⁴·How many _____ are coming? (person)
CHRIS: Six. ⁵·And don't forget to wear a warm _____ . (jacket)
        It's cold in the mountains.
PAUL: OK.

UNIT 047 | a girl, water 셀 수 있는 명사와 셀 수 없는 명사 (1)

🎧 047.mp3

① 명사에는 셀 수 있는 명사와 셀 수 없는 명사가 있다.

셀 수 있는 명사

a girl

three hats

girl	hat	dog	apple
brother	pen	bird	flower

셀 수 없는 명사

water

music

water	music	snow	sugar
air	time	money	news

셀 수 없는 명사: 부록 p.252 참고

② 셀 수 있는 명사는 단수 또는 복수로 쓸 수 있다.

- Do you have a **pencil**? 너 연필 한 자루 있니?
- I have a **brother** and two **sisters**. 나는 한 명의 남자 형제와 두 명의 여자 형제가 있다.
- Have you seen my **gloves**? I can't find them.

셀 수 있는 명사를 단수로 쓸 때는 주로 **a** 또는 **an**을 함께 쓴다.

- Does Leo have **a dog**? Leo는 개 한 마리가 있니?
- I ate **an egg** for breakfast. 나는 아침으로 달걀 하나를 먹었다.

    자음으로 시작하는 단수명사 앞에는 **a**, 모음으로 시작하는 단수명사 앞에는 **an**을 함께 쓴다.

- **A boy** is standing by the window. 한 소년이 창문가에 서 있다.
- I think I lost **an earring**. 내가 귀걸이 한 짝을 잃어버린 것 같아.

    이때, 단어의 첫 번째 철자가 아니라 발음에 따라서 **a** 또는 **an**을 함께 쓰는 것에 주의한다.

- Joseph teaches physics at **a university**. (university의 첫 음이 [ju]로 발음되므로 a를 썼음)
- Mr. Roberts is out, but he'll return in **an hour**. (hour의 첫 음이 [a]로 발음되므로 an을 썼음)

③ 셀 수 없는 명사는 앞에 숫자를 붙이거나, 뒤에 **-s**를 붙일 수 없다.

- I bought **water** and **milk** at the store. (one water and one milk로 쓸 수 없음)
- "Do you enjoy listening to **music**?" "Yes. I really like pop songs." (musics로 쓸 수 없음)
- I asked Tony for **information** about the seminar.

셀 수 없는 명사 앞에는 **a** 또는 **an**도 역시 쓸 수 없다.

- There is **snow** on the road. Drive carefully. (a snow로 쓸 수 없음)
- Can you give me some **advice**? (an advice로 쓸 수 없음)

PRACTICE

A. 괄호 안에 주어진 명사를 사용하여 문장을 완성하세요. 필요한 경우 a 또는 an을 사용하세요.

1. (rice) I'd like _rice_ with my steak, please.
2. (air) This city has clean _____.
3. (rain) There will be _____ this evening.
4. (umbrella) I'd like to get _____.

5. (taxi) Let's take _____ to the airport.
6. (salt) Could you bring me some _____?
7. (man) I saw _____ with purple hair.
8. (orange) Can I have _____?

B. 그림을 보고 주어진 명사를 사용하여 문장을 완성하세요. 필요한 경우 a 또는 an을 함께 사용하거나 복수로 쓰세요.

| apple | bicycle | ~~milk~~ | snow | sugar |

1. The man is drinking _milk_ .
2. There are _____ on the tree.
3. There is a lot of _____ on the street.

4. She is riding _____.
5. There is _____ in the jar.

| baby | dog | flower | music | water |

6. She is holding _____.
7. He is walking with _____.
8. He is listening to _____.

9. There is _____ in the glass.
10. She has _____ in her garden.

C. 다음 문장을 읽고 틀린 부분이 있으면 바르게 고치세요. 틀린 부분이 없으면 O로 표시하세요.

1. I wanted to take a shower, but there was no hot waters. _waters → water_
2. Robert exercises for half an hour in the morning. _____
3. I need some egg and butter for the cake. _____
4. I'd like to get an information about the train schedule. _____
5. Ann is teacher. She teaches history. _____
6. I forgot my wallet. Could you lend me some money? _____
7. I don't have much times now. I'll call you later. _____

정답 p.276, REVIEW TEST 9 p.232

UNIT 048 | some **fish**, **a glass of** water 셀 수 있는 명사와 셀 수 없는 명사 (2)

🎧 048.mp3

① 다음과 같은 명사들은 단수와 복수를 같은 형태로 쓴다.

단수	a **fish**	a **sheep**	a **deer**
복수	some **fish**	eight **sheep**	many **deer**

- Look! Some **fish** are swimming in the water. 몇몇 물고기들이 물속에서 헤엄치고 있어.
- Mr. Anderson has eight **sheep** and a horse on his farm. Anderson씨는 농장에 양 여덟 마리와 말 한 마리가 있다.
- We saw many **deer** during our camping trip.

② 다음과 같이 두 개의 부분이 모여 하나의 사물을 이루는 경우에는 항상 복수로 쓴다.

pajamas   scissors   jeans   shorts
glasses   pants   headphones

- I like my **pajamas**. They're very comfortable. 나는 내 잠옷을 좋아한다.
- Can I borrow your **scissors** for a minute? 당신의 가위를 잠깐 빌릴 수 있을까요?
- "Do you wear **jeans** often?" "No, I don't."

glasses

pajamas

위의 명사들을 셀 때는 **a pair of/two pairs of** 등을 함께 쓴다.

- I got **a pair of shorts** for my birthday. (반바지 한 벌)
- I have **two pairs of glasses**. I use one pair at home and the other pair at work. (안경 두 쌍)

③ 다음과 같은 셀 수 없는 명사들은 단위를 나타내는 표현을 사용하여 수나 양을 말할 수 있다.

a glass of water   **two cans of soda**   **three bottles of juice**

a glass of water 물 한 잔	**a can of** soda 탄산음료 한 캔	**a bottle of** juice 주스 한 병
a cup of coffee 커피 한 잔	**a loaf of** bread 빵 한 덩어리	**a piece of** cake/paper 케이크 한 조각/종이 한 장
a carton of milk 우유 한 통	**a box of** cereal 시리얼 한 박스	**a slice of** pizza 피자 한 조각

- Can I have **a glass of water**? 물 한 잔 마실 수 있을까요?
- I need **two loaves of bread** and **a box of cereal**. 저는 빵 두 덩어리와 시리얼 한 박스가 필요해요.
- "What did you have for lunch?" "I ate **two slices of pizza**."

이때, **two bottles of juices** 등으로 쓸 수 없는 것에 주의한다.

- "Are there any drinks?" "There are **two bottles of juice** in the fridge." (two bottles of juices로 쓸 수 없음)
- How many **cartons of milk** are sold in a week? (cartons of milks로 쓸 수 없음)

단, 음료를 주문하는 상황에서는 다음과 같이 **a/two** 등을 함께 쓸 수도 있다.

- Would you like **a soda**? 또는 Would you like **a can of soda**? 탄산음료 한 캔 드시겠어요?
- **Two coffees**, please. 또는 **Two cups of coffee**, please. 커피 두 잔 주세요.

PRACTICE

A. 괄호 안에 주어진 명사를 사용하여 문장을 완성하세요. a 또는 an을 함께 쓰거나 복수로 쓰세요.

1. (glove) I bought new _gloves_ , but they are too small for me.
2. (pant) "I'd like to buy these _____ ." "Sure. What size do you need?"
3. (fish) "I went fishing last weekend." "Did you catch many _____ ?"
4. (key) "I found _____ on the floor." "Oh, it's mine."
5. (glass) Cindy has worn _____ for many years.
6. (sheep) Some _____ are sleeping on the grass. They look peaceful.
7. (apple) _____ is good for breakfast if you're busy in the morning.

B. 그림을 보고 a glass of, two bottles of 등의 표현을 사용하여 문장을 완성하세요.

> *I am buying ...*
> 1. (wine) _two bottles of wine_ .
> 2. (milk) _____ .
> 3. (cake) _____ .
> 4. (soda) _____ .
> 5. (bread) _____ .

C. 다음 문장을 읽고 틀린 부분이 있으면 바르게 고치세요. 틀린 부분이 없으면 O로 표시하세요.

1. I'll have an orange juice, please.   O
2. Julia bought two box of cereals for her kids. _____
3. The market on Hill Street sells many fish and vegetables. _____
4. "My feet are cold." "Well, you're not wearing sock." _____
5. When I went hiking last weekend, I saw three deers. _____
6. "Would you like a coffee?" "Yes. With some sugar, please." _____
7. We will bring a bottle of wine to dinner tomorrow. _____
8. There is a lot of snows on the street. _____
9. "I need two pieces of papers." "OK. Here you go." _____

D. Linda는 식당에서 주문을 하고 있습니다. 괄호 안에 주어진 명사들과 of를 사용하여 Linda와 종업원의 대화를 완성하세요.

LINDA:

LINDA: ¹·Could I have three _pieces of cake_ ? (piece, cake)
²·And four _____ , please. (slice, pizza)
Waiter: Certainly. Would you like anything to drink?
LINDA: ³·Yes, a _____ and
two _____ . (cup, coffee) (can, soda)
⁴·Oh, and a _____ . (bottle, water)
Waiter: Really? You're ordering a lot!
LINDA: Yes. My husband and two sons are coming.

Waiter

정답 p.276, REVIEW TEST 9 p.232

UNIT
048

Grammar Gateway Basic

🎧 049.mp3

①

We need **a lamp**.

They need **a lamp**.
그들은 램프가 하나 필요하다.

막연한 램프 하나를 의미하므로 a를 썼다.

특별히 정해지지 않은 막연한 사람 또는 사물 하나를 말할 때는 **a** 또는 **an**을 쓴다.
- **A woman** is walking down the street. (막연한 여자 한 명을 의미하므로 a를 썼음)
- Brenda is looking for **an office** to rent. (막연한 사무실 하나를 의미하므로 an을 썼음)
- "Do you have **a car**?" "Yes. I bought one a month ago."

②

It's too bright!

The lamp is too bright.
그 램프는 너무 밝다.

어떤 램프를 의미하는지 명확하므로 the를 썼다.

어떤 사람 또는 사물을 가리키는지 명확할 때나, 특정한 사람 또는 사물을 말할 때는 **the**를 쓴다.
- I saw you on the street. Who was **the woman** with you? (같이 있던 특정한 여자를 의미하므로 the를 썼음)
- It's almost 6 o'clock. I'm leaving **the office**. (어떤 사무실을 의미하는지 명확하므로 the를 썼음)
- "Is **the car** in front of the store yours?" "Yes, it is."

일반적인 사람 또는 사물에 대해 말할 때는 **the**를 쓰지 않는다. 특정한 사람 또는 사물에 대해 말할 때 **the**를 쓰는 것에 주의한다.
- I like **cats**. (일반적인 고양이들을 의미하므로 the를 쓰지 않음)
  The cats in this shop are so cute. (이 가게의 고양이들이라는 특정한 고양이들을 의미하므로 the를 썼음)
- Winter is my favorite season. I don't like hot **weather**.
  "What was **the weather** like in California?" "It was very warm."

③ 어떤 대상에 대해 처음 말할 때는 **a** 또는 **an**을 쓰고, 그 대상을 다시 말할 때는 **the**를 쓴다.
- I got **an e-mail** from Jenny this morning. **The e-mail** was about today's meeting.
  (e-mail을 앞에서 언급했으므로 The e-mail로 썼음)
- I ate **a sandwich** and **a salad** for lunch. **The sandwich** was very good, but I didn't like **the salad**.
  (sandwich와 salad를 앞에서 언급했으므로 The sandwich와 the salad로 썼음)

PRACTICE

A. 그림을 보고 주어진 명사와 a/an 또는 the를 함께 사용하여 문장을 완성하세요.

apple	bill	~~bus~~	car	office	ticket

1. Let's take _the bus_____ .

2. Can I have _____ ?

3. I'd like _____ , please.

4. Is Ms. Lee in _____ ?

5. Did you pay _____ ?

6. Hi. We want to buy _____ .

B. 주어진 단어와 a/an 또는 the를 함께 사용하여 문장을 완성하세요.

accident	cake	exam	~~food~~	funny joke	heater	phone	window

1. A: How was _the food_____ at that Thai restaurant?
   B: It was very good.

2. A: Why is the traffic so slow?
   B: I think there was _____ .

3. A: Which dessert do you want?
   B: I want _____ on the blue plate.

4. A: Why are you smiling?
   B: I just heard _____ .

5. A: Look out _____ . It's snowing!
   B: Let's go outside and make a snowman!

6. A: Can you answer _____ ? I'm busy.
   B: Of course.

7. A: Is there _____ in here? It's cold.
   B: Yes. I'll turn it on for you.

8. A: Do we have _____ tomorrow?
   B: Yes, we do. Did you study for it?

C. 괄호 안에 주어진 명사와 a/an 또는 the를 함께 사용하여 문장을 완성하세요.

1. (gloves) Nancy sent me some nice gloves. _The gloves_____ are very warm.
2. (question) "I have _____ for you." "OK. Go ahead."
3. (water) _____ in this river is very clear.
4. (umbrella) It's raining outside. Do you have _____ ?
5. (key) I need to open the cabinet. Where is _____ ?
6. (book) "I'm reading an interesting book." "What's _____ about?"
7. (problem) I have _____ with my computer. I should take it to the repair shop.
8. (mountain) There is _____ near my hometown. I often go hiking there.
9. (suit) I got a suit and a book for my birthday. My wife gave me _____ .
10. (orange) I'd like to buy _____ . Do you have any?

정답 p.276, REVIEW TEST 9 p.232

본 교재 동영상강의 HackersIngang.com **111**

Grammar Gateway Basic

I want to travel **the world.** the를 쓰는 경우와 쓰지 않는 경우

🎧 050.mp3

① 다음과 같은 경우 명사 앞에 주로 **the**를 쓴다.

the				
	세상에 하나밖에 없는 것	the world	the sun	the moon
	자연환경	the sky	the sea	the ocean
	국가/도시 등에 하나밖에 없는 것	the army	the police	the government
	방송, 매체	the radio	the Internet	

- I want to travel **the world.** 나는 세계를 여행하고 싶어.
- Look at the color of **the sky.** It's beautiful. 하늘 색깔 좀 봐.
- John was in **the army** 20 years ago.
- I always listen to **the radio** in the morning.

the sun   the radio

악기를 연주한다고 할 때 악기 이름 앞에 **the**를 쓴다.

- "Can you play **the guitar**?" 너는 기타를 연주할 수 있니? "Not very well."
- Helen practices **the piano** every day, so she's good at it.
  Helen은 매일 피아노를 연습한다.

the police   the piano

---

② 다음과 같은 경우는 명사 앞에 **the**를 쓰지 않는다.

~~the~~			
운동	basketball	football	tennis
학과목	biology	history	marketing
식사	breakfast	lunch	dinner

- Ted and Mike play **basketball** every Sunday. Ted와 Mike는 일요일마다 농구를 한다.
- My daughter is studying **biology** at college. 내 딸은 대학에서 생물학을 공부한다.
- "Have you eaten **breakfast** yet?" "Yes, I have."

---

③ 다음과 같은 장소에 간다고 할 때는 **the**를 쓴다.

go to the movies   go to the station   go to the bank
go to the theater   go to the airport   go to the post office

- "Do you want to **go to the movies** tomorrow?" 너는 내일 영화관에 가고 싶니? "Sure."
- Dad **went to the bank** yesterday. 아빠는 어제 은행에 갔다.
- "Which subway line **goes to the airport**?" "The blue line."
- "Are you **going to the post office**?" "Not now. I'm going there this afternoon."

단, 집/직장에 가거나 있다고 할 때는 **the**를 쓰지 않는다.

go home   go to work
at home   at work

- Joanne **went home** early because she had a cold. Joanne은 집에 일찍 갔다.
- "How do you know Jonathan?" "We met **at work**." 우리는 직장에서 만났어요.

주의해야 할 the 용법: 부록 p.252 참고

PRACTICE

A. 그림을 보고 주어진 명사를 사용하여 문장을 완성하세요. 필요한 경우 the를 함께 쓰세요.

golf	math	moon	~~piano~~	radio

1. She is playing _the piano_ .
2. She is listening to _____ .
3. He is playing _____ .

4. They are looking at _____ .
5. He's studying _____ at school.

B. 괄호 안에 주어진 명사를 사용하여 문장을 완성하세요. 필요한 경우 the를 함께 쓰세요.

1. (lunch) I had _lunch_ with Eric today. We went to a Mexican restaurant.
2. (ocean) Michael likes to go surfing in _____ .
3. (history) "Are you taking _____ classes this year?" "No, I'm not."
4. (Internet) "What time does the flight arrive?" "Let me check on _____ ."
5. (government) _____ is going to build a new road in my hometown.
6. (baseball) I like watching _____ . It's very exciting.
7. (breakfast) I usually eat pancakes for _____ .
8. (world) "How many countries are there in _____ ?" "Maybe around 200?"

C. 주어진 명사와 go (to)를 사용하여 문장을 완성하세요. 필요한 경우 the를 함께 쓰세요.

airport	bank	home	movies	~~post office~~	work

1. Would you send these packages when you _go to the post office_ ?
2. I must _____ now. My parents are coming, and I need to clean the house.
3. Let's _____ early. I don't want to miss our flight.
4. "Would you like to _____ tonight?" "Sure. I haven't seen any films recently."
5. "What time do you _____ in the morning?" "I have to be in the office by 8:30."
6. "I have to _____ to get some money." "It closes at 4, so you should hurry."

D. 다음 문장을 읽고 틀린 부분이 있으면 바르게 고치세요. 틀린 부분이 없으면 O로 표시하세요.

1. I need to go to station. Can you give me a ride?   _go to station → go to the station_
2. I called police because someone stole my car.   _____
3. "Where were you last night?" "I was at work."   _____
4. You shouldn't look at sun directly. You can damage your eyes.   _____
5. We usually don't stay at the home during the summer. We like to travel.   _____
6. "Did you go to the theater yesterday?" "Yes. I saw a funny play."   _____
7. Do you study the politics in college?   _____

정답 p.276, REVIEW TEST 9 p.232

UNIT 050

Grammar Gateway Basic

She is my friend. 사람과 사물을 가리키는 대명사

🎧 051.mp3

①

This is Kate. **She** is my friend.
I met **her** in high school.

This is <u>Kate</u>.

She is my friend. 그녀는 내 친구야.
I met **her** in high school. 나는 고등학교 때 그녀를 만났어.

She와 her는 Kate를 가리키는 대명사이고, 이미 한 번 언급한 Kate를
반복해서 말하지 않기 위해 썼다.

② 대명사 I/we/you 등은 문장에서 주어 역할을 한다.

사람		사물	
(나는) **I**		(그것은) **It** was beautiful.	
(우리는) **We**		(그것들은) **They** were beautiful.	
(너는, 너희들은) **You**	saw Danny.		
(그는) **He**			
(그녀는) **She**			
(그들은) **They**			

- I'm thirsty. Can **I** have some water? 나는 목이 말라요. 물 좀 마실 수 있을까요?
- "Is Stephanie home?" "**She** is in her room." 그녀는 그녀의 방에 있어요.
- "Have **you** met your new neighbors?" "Yes. **They**'re very nice."
- **We** washed our car on the weekend. **It** looks nice and clean now.

③ 대명사 me/us/you 등은 문장에서 목적어 역할을 한다.

	사람			사물	
	me.	(나를, 나에게)		**it.**	(그것을, 그것에게)
	us.	(우리를, 우리에게)	I bought	**them.**	(그것들을, 그것들에게)
Danny saw	**you.**	(너를/너희를, 너에게/너희에게)			
	him.	(그를, 그에게)			
	her.	(그녀를, 그녀에게)			
	them.	(그들을, 그들에게)			

- My dad drives **me** to school every day. 매일 아빠가 나를 학교에 차로 데려다주신다.
- "Have you seen Ryan lately?" "I met **him** last week." 나는 지난주에 그를 만났어.
- I sent **you** some flowers. Did you get **them**?
- This hat is for Rob. I bought **it** in Sweden.

전치사 뒤에는 항상 목적어 역할을 하는 대명사를 쓴다.
- I'm going to the park. You should come **with me**. (전치사 with 뒤에 me를 썼음)
- Is Bianca in her office? I'd like to talk **to her** for a minute. (전치사 to 뒤에 her를 썼음)

PRACTICE

A. 둘 중 맞는 것을 고르세요.

1. "Is Laura back yet?" "I'm not sure. I haven't seen (her / she)."
2. "Did your package arrive today?" "Yes. I received (them / it) this morning."
3. "Is Steve feeling okay?" "No. (He / Him) has a headache."
4. "I want to move this sofa to my room. Can you help (I / me)?" "Of course."
5. "Do you remember Matthew and Julie?" "(They / Them) were in our class, right?"
6. My brother and I are going to the beach. You should join (we / us).

B. 그림을 보고 I/we/me/us 등을 한 번씩 사용하여 문장을 완성하세요.

1. _I_ am Sam.
People call _me_ Sammy.

2. I know _____ very well.
_____ lives next door.

3. _____ is my uncle. I don't
see _____ very often.

4. I like _____.
Do _____ like me?

5. _____ are friends.
People like _____.

6. _____ are my grandparents.
I love _____ very much.

C. 적절한 대명사를 써넣으세요.

1. Do you enjoy movies?
2. What are they building over there?
3. You should call Mr. Green now.
4. Are we going to the party?
5. Would you like some tomatoes?
6. Did you and Tim go to the museum yesterday?

Yes, but I don't watch _them_ often.
_____ is a new hotel.
I'm busy. I'll contact _____ later.
Yes. Bruce invited _____.
No, thanks. _____ don't look fresh.
Yes. _____ saw many beautiful paintings.

D. 다음 문장을 읽고 틀린 부분이 있으면 바르게 고치세요. 틀린 부분이 없으면 O로 표시하세요.

1. "Nicole hasn't arrived yet." "Then we should wait for she." _she → her_
2. "Look at this photo from high school." "Us look so young!" _____
3. "Do you need help with the report?" "No. I'm almost done." _____
4. "Where did you get that sweater?" "My grandmother gave it to I." _____
5. "What's this?" "It is a gift for you." _____
6. "Are those earrings diamonds?" "No. Them are made of glass." _____

정답 p.276, REVIEW TEST 9 p.232

①

It is Monday.
월요일이다.

It is snowing.
눈이 오고 있다.

② 다음과 같은 경우에 **it**을 주어로 쓸 수 있다.

시간을 말할 때
- ○ "What time is **it** now?" "**It's** 5 o'clock." 5시예요.
- ○ **It's** noon. Let's go to lunch. 정오다.
- ○ **It's** time to go. We should leave now.

날짜를 말할 때
- ○ "What's the date today?" "**It's** October 10th." 10월 10일이에요.
- ○ **It's** the first day of September. Time has gone so fast. 9월의 첫째 날이다.
- ○ We're going to a concert. **It's** on March 2nd.

요일을 말할 때
- ○ "What day is **it** today?" "**It's** Friday." 금요일이에요.
- ○ **It's** Saturday. What should we do? 토요일이야.
- ○ **It** can't be Monday already! I'm so sad.

날씨를 말할 때
- ○ Let's go on a picnic. **It's** very sunny today. 오늘 아주 화창해.
- ○ **It's** raining outside. Did you bring an umbrella? 밖에 비가 오고 있어.
- ○ **It's** going to be hot all week.

거리를 말할 때
- ○ Don't worry. **It's** only one kilometer to the gas station. 주유소까지 겨우 1킬로미터 떨어져 있다.
- ○ "Is your house close?" "Yes. **It's** a short walk from here." 여기서 잠깐만 걸으면 돼.
- ○ "How far is **it** from London to Paris?" "**It's** about 300 miles."

계절을 말할 때
- ○ **It's** snowing! Is **it** winter already? 벌써 겨울이야?
- ○ **It's** almost spring. It is my favorite season of the year. 거의 봄이다.

③ 시간, 날짜 등을 말할 때 **it**은 '그것'이라는 의미가 아니다. 사물을 가리키는 **it**과 의미 차이에 주의한다.
- ○ **It's** 1:50 right now. The meeting will start soon. 지금은 1시 50분이다. ('그것은 1시 50분이다'라는 의미가 아님)
  "What's in the box?" "A belt. **It's** a gift for my dad." 그것은 아빠를 위한 선물이야.
- ○ **It** was very windy at the beach last weekend.
  I enjoyed this book. **It** was very interesting.

PRACTICE

A. 주어진 표현과 it을 사용하여 예시와 같이 문장을 완성하세요.

12:30	close	summer	~~Thursday~~	warm

1. Is today Wednesday?
2. What time is it?
3. How is the weather today?
4. Is it far from here to the hospital?
5. What season is it now in Australia?

No, *it's Thursday* OR *it is Thursday* _____ .
_____ .
_____ .
No, _____ .
_____ there.

15 miles	8 o'clock	~~cloudy~~	December 25th	Tuesday

6. *It's cloudy* OR *It is cloudy* _____ outside.
7. _____ today.
8. _____ to the museum.
9. _____ tomorrow!
10. _____ already.

Yes. It's going to rain this afternoon.
Is it? I thought it was Monday.
That's far. We should take a taxi.
I know! I love Christmas.
Really? I should get ready for work.

UNIT 052

B. 적절한 대명사를 써넣으세요.

1. "How's your brother?"   " *He* 's doing well, thanks."
2. I can't open the door. _____ 's locked.
3. These boots were on sale, so _____ weren't very expensive.
4. "I called you this morning, but _____ didn't answer." "I didn't have my phone with me."
5. _____ 's almost midnight. You should go to bed.
6. "Sam and I have great news. _____ are getting married!" "Congratulations!"
7. "What is today's date?" " _____ 's February 1st."
8. " _____ 's already winter." "I hope it doesn't snow a lot."

C. 다음은 Amy가 여행 중에 Kate에게 보낸 엽서입니다. 괄호 안에 주어진 표현과 it을 사용하여 문장을 완성하세요.

Dear Kate,

1. *It's July 11th* OR *It is July 11th* _____ today, and I'm in Capri, Italy. (July 11th)
2. _____ there? (midnight)
3. _____ here, and I just finished my lunch. (2 p.m.)
What's the weather like there?
4. _____ here, so _____ . (summer) (very warm)
Capri is so beautiful. You should come with me next time!

AIR MAIL

Love, Amy

정답 p.277, REVIEW TEST 9 p.232

Grammar Gateway Basic

UNIT 053 | That's **my** camera. 소유를 나타내는 표현

🎧 053.mp3

① '(누구)의'라는 의미로 소유를 나타낼 때, 명사 앞에 **my/our/your** 등을 쓴다.

-은/는	I	we	you	he	she	they	it
-의	**my**	**our**	**your**	**his**	**her**	**their**	**its**

- A: What's this?
  B: That's **my camera**! 그것은 내 카메라야!
- Brian and I are getting married. **Our wedding** is on April 21.
  우리의 결혼식은 4월 21일이에요.
- "What's **your name**?" "I'm Bella Smith."
- I can't find Mr. Tyler. He's not in **his office**.

이때, **its**와 **it's** (= **it is**)를 혼동하지 않도록 주의한다.

- I don't wear this jacket these days. **Its** zipper is broken, and **it's** too small.
  그것의 지퍼는 고장이 났고, 그것은 너무 작다.
- There's a flower in my yard. I don't know **its** name, but **it's** beautiful.
  그것의 이름은 모르지만, 그것은 아름답다.

② **mine/ours/yours** 등: (누구)의 것

-은/는	I	we	you	he	she	they
-의	my	our	your	his	her	their
-의 것	**mine**	**ours**	**yours**	**his**	**hers**	**theirs**

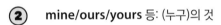

- This car is **mine**. I got it yesterday. 이 차는 내 것이야.
- Excuse me? I think these seats are **ours**. 이 좌석들은 저희의 것인 것 같은데요.
- That's my cup. **Yours** is on the table.
- "Is this Tom's backpack?" "Yes, it's **his**."

mine/ours/yours 등의 뒤에는 명사를 쓰지 않는 것에 주의한다.

- I lent Diane my laptop because **hers** was not working. (hers laptop으로 쓸 수 없음)
- My neighbors have a son. My son often plays with **theirs**. (theirs son으로 쓸 수 없음)

③ **my/our/your** 등 또는 **mine/ours/yours** 등은 **a/an** 또는 **the**를 함께 쓰지 않는다.

- I have a meeting with **my boss** tomorrow. (a my boss로 쓸 수 없음)
- "Which phone is **yours**?" "The small one." (the yours로 쓸 수 없음)

④ **Whose** + 명사 ~?: 누구의 ~인가요?

- "**Whose scissors** are these?" 누구의 가위인가요? "Sophie was just here. Maybe they're hers."
- "**Whose magazine** is this?" 누구의 잡지인가요? "It's mine. Do you want to read it?"
- "There are some gloves on the sofa." "**Whose gloves** are they?"
- "**Whose party** are you attending tonight?" "Paul's. It's his birthday."

PRACTICE

A. 그림을 보고 괄호 안에 주어진 명사와 my/our/your 등을 사용하여 상황에 맞게 문장을 완성하세요.

1. (house) This is
   our house .

2. (bag) This is
   _____ .

3. (key) It's
   _____ .

4. (dog) This is
   _____ .

5. (ball) It's
   _____ .

B. mine/ours/yours 등을 써넣으세요.

1. Is this your ticket?
2. Can I borrow this book?
3. Is this Rachel's purse?
4. Cody, are these my socks?
5. Is this Mr. and Mrs. Brown's car?

Yes, it's _mine_ .
Ask Bill. It's _____ .
No, it's not _____ .
Yes, they are _____ .
No, it's not _____ .

C. my/our/your 등 또는 mine/ours/yours 등을 사용하여 문장을 완성하세요.

1. "I lost my pen." "You can use _mine_ ."
2. The book has an interesting title, but _____ story wasn't very good.
3. "Where's _____ office?" "I work in a building downtown."
4. We didn't sleep well last night. _____ neighbors were too noisy.
5. "Did Ms. Spears bring a suitcase?" "Yes. The black one is _____."
6. "Does this house belong to your aunt and uncle?" "Yes, and that car is _____ too."

D. 괄호 안에 주어진 단어를 사용하여 예시와 같이 대화를 완성하세요. 질문을 할 때는 whose를 함께 쓰세요.

1. A: (tent) *Whose tent* _____ can I borrow?
   B: (we) You can use _ours_ .

2. A: (glasses) _____ are these?
   B: (he) Ask Jim. Maybe they're _____ .

3. A: (wallet) _____ is this?
   B: (you) Oh, I thought it was _____ .

4. A: (scarf) _____ is on the chair?
   B: (she) Kim was wearing it. It must be _____ .

E. my/our/your 등 또는 mine/ours/yours 등을 사용하여 Justin과 Chris의 대화를 완성하세요.

JUSTIN: Chris! 1. Is this _your_ camera? I found it in Ginger's house.
CHRIS: 2. Yes, that's _____! Ginger, you bad dog!
JUSTIN: And look, there is a watch. 3. Is it _____ too?
CHRIS: No. 4. Dad lost _____ watch a few days ago.
　　　 5. It's probably _____.
JUSTIN: And Ginger also took a ball from someone!
CHRIS: Um, Justin. That's Ginger's ball.

JUSTIN

CHRIS

정답 p.277, REVIEW TEST 9 p.232

🎧 054.mp3

①

It's my book.

LOST and FOUND

It's **Amy's** book.

그것은 Amy의 책이다.

---

② '(누구)의'라는 의미로 사람의 소유를 나타낼 때 -**'s**를 쓴다.

Mr. Wright's	job
Karen's	room
children's	toys
brother's	name

- "What's **Mr. Wright's job**?" Wright씨의 직업이 무엇인가요? "He's a lawyer."
- **Karen's room** is upstairs. She's probably in her room. Karen의 방은 위층에 있어.
- "Where are the **children's toys**?" "I put them in the closet."
- My **brother's name** is Jeff. He's at university.

그러나 -**s**로 끝나는 복수명사의 끝에는 **'**만 쓴다.

parents'	anniversary
the Grays'	house
artists'	paintings
neighbors'	garden

- Today is my **parents' anniversary**. 오늘은 부모님의 결혼기념일이다.
- "Is this **the Grays' house**?" 여기가 Gray씨 댁인가요? "No. Theirs is next door."
- There are many **artists' paintings** in this museum.
- Our **neighbors' garden** is beautiful. It has many flowers.

---

③ 무엇을 가리키는지 명확히 알 수 있는 경우에는 '(누구)의 것'이라는 의미로 명사 없이 -**'s**만 쓸 수도 있다.

- "I like your hat." "Thanks. It's **my sister's**." (my sister's = my sister's hat)
- "Whose bicycle is that?" "It's **our kids'**." (our kids' = our kids' bicycle)
- "Is that your suit?" "No. It's **Jim's**. I borrowed it for my job interview."
- This isn't my laptop. It's **Tammy's**.

---

④ 사람이 아니라 사물에 대해 말할 때는 -**'s** 대신 **of**를 주로 쓴다.

- "Can you play chess?" "No. I don't know **the rules of the game**." 나는 그 게임의 규칙을 몰라.
- **The time of the flight** has changed. It will leave at 7:40. 그 항공편의 시간이 변경되었다.
- The company is on **the 10th floor of the building**.
- "I found a good restaurant downtown." "What's **the name of the restaurant**?"

그러나, 사람에 대해 말할 때는 **of**가 아니라 -**'s**를 주로 쓴다.

- Do you know **Jessie's phone number**? Jessie의 전화번호를 아니?
- Excuse me. Are you **Mr. Green's wife**? Green씨의 아내신가요?
- "Have you seen my blue skirt?" "Yes. It's in **Sally's closet**."
- "Is he **Jason's brother**?" "Yes. His name is Toby."

PRACTICE

A. 주어진 단어들과 -' 또는 -'s를 사용하여 문장을 완성하세요.

boat	husband	~~name~~	presents	problems	voice

1. (your dentist) "What's _your dentist's name_ ?" "John Williams."
2. (Laura) "What does _____ do?" "He is an engineer."
3. (our kids) My wife and I wrapped _____ on Christmas Eve.
4. (your brother) "Is that _____ ?" "Yes. He sometimes uses it to go fishing."
5. (Richard) _____ is amazing. He's a great singer.
6. (her friends) Wendy always listens to _____ . She's a good friend.

B. 그림을 보고 상황에 맞게 문장을 완성하세요.

I lost my wallet. 1 Emma
Where is my coat? 2 Scott
We lost our cat. 3 The Andersons
Where are my gloves? 4 Lucy
I lost my phone. 5 Kevin

1. "This wallet was on the floor." "It's _Emma's_ ."
2. "Is this your coat?" "No. It might be _____ ."
3. "Whose cat is that?" " _____ ."
4. "I found these gloves." "They're _____ ."
5. "Whose phone is this?" "I think it's _____ ."

C. 괄호 안에 주어진 단어들을 적절히 배열하여 문장을 완성하세요. of를 함께 사용하세요.

1. (this street / the name) "Do you know _the name of this street_ ?" "Yes. It's 3rd Avenue."
2. (this chair / the price) "What's _____ ?" "It's $200."
3. (the title / the book) "I'm looking for a book." "What's _____ ?"
4. (the number / your hotel room) Could you tell me _____ ?
5. (the mountain / the top) We walked to _____ . It was beautiful.
6. (the year / the start) Patricia moved to England at _____ .

D. 다음 문장을 읽고 틀린 부분이 있으면 바르게 고치세요. 틀린 부분이 없으면 O로 표시하세요.

1. I found the watch of Sam under the desk.   _the watch of Sam → Sam's watch_
2. The ending of the program was very surprising.   _____
3. "Whose car is that?" "It's my parents's."   _____
4. Please write your name at the page's top.   _____
5. My husband and I couldn't go to Rose' wedding.   _____
6. Andrew's favorite sport is soccer.   _____
7. "Where is Jack?" "He is in Mr. Cowan office."   _____
8. Do you know the meaning of this word?   _____
9. The best friend of Mia is Natalie.   _____
10. We're going to stay at the Smiths' house this summer. _____

정답 p.277, REVIEW TEST 9 p.232

UNIT **054**

Grammar Gateway Basic

| **She is looking at herself.** -self

🎧 055.mp3

①

She is looking at **herself**. 그녀는 그녀 자신을 보고 있다.
　주어　　　　　　　　목적어

'그녀 자신을'이라고 말하기 위해 herself를 썼다.
이때, herself와 she는 같은 사람이다.

② '~ 자신'이라는 의미로 말할 때 -self를 쓴다.

-은/는	I	you (단수)	he	she	we	you (복수)	they
-을/를	me	you	him	her	us	you	them
-self	**myself**	**yourself**	**himself**	**herself**	**ourselves**	**yourselves**	**themselves**

○ I'm going to start learning piano this year. I promised **myself**. 나는 나 자신에게 약속했다.
○ You can do it. You have to trust **yourself**. 너는 너 자신을 믿어야 해.
○ Gary isn't careful. He often cuts **himself** while shaving.
○ Tom and Jenny are taking a photo of **themselves**.

③ 주어와 목적어가 같은 사람일 때 -self를 쓴다.

I'm so handsome!

○ **Justin** is talking to **himself**.
　(Justin과 himself는 같은 사람임)
○ "Where did you learn English?" "I taught **myself**."
　(I와 myself는 같은 사람임)
○ **Alison** made **herself** a salad.

주어와 목적어가 서로 다른 사람일 때는 -self를 쓰지 않고 me/him 등을 쓰는 것에 주의한다.

You look great!

○ **Justin** is talking to **him**.
　(Justin과 him은 다른 사람이므로 himself로 쓸 수 없음)
○ **My brother** taught **me** English.
　(My brother와 me는 다른 사람이므로 myself로 쓸 수 없음)
○ Tina was hungry, so **Alison** made **her** a salad.

④ **by -self**: 혼자, 스스로
○ I've lived **by myself** since 2008. 나는 2008년부터 혼자 살고 있다.
○ "Can you carry the table **by yourself**?" 탁자를 너 스스로 운반할 수 있니? "Sure. It's not heavy."

⑤ **Make yourself at home**: 편히 쉬세요
○ Welcome to my place. Please **make yourself at home**. 편히 쉬세요.

Help yourself: 마음껏 드세요
○ "Can I have some more bread?" "Of course. **Help yourself**." 마음껏 드세요.

PRACTICE

A. -self를 써넣으세요.

1. Susan became the captain of her football team. She must be proud of _herself_ .
2. "I'll see you next week." "OK. Take care of _____."
3. The meeting didn't go well, but it's not our fault. We shouldn't blame _____.
4. "These paintings are nice. Did you take an art class?" "No. I taught _____."
5. "Why is Carlos in the hospital?" "He injured _____ during the baseball game."

B. 그림을 보고 상황에 맞게 him/her 또는 himself/herself를 써넣으세요.

1    2    3

4 MAGGIE   5   6 I'm Dave.

1. She is talking to _herself_ .
2. She cut _____ with a knife.
3. The police officer stopped _____ .

4. Maggie is giving _____ a present.
5. He hurt _____ .
6. He is introducing _____ .

C. 주어진 문장을 보고 by -self를 사용하여 문장을 완성하세요.

1. Did you go to the beach alone?
2. Did your mom make dinner for you?
3. Did Jake go to the park with his friends?
4. Kevin, were you shopping alone?
5. Was Claire playing games with her friend?
6. Are you and your wife traveling with your kids?

Yes. _I went to the beach by myself_ .
No. _____ .
No. _____ .
Yes. _____ .
No. _____ .
No. _____ .

D. me/you 등 또는 myself/yourself 등을 사용하여 Amy와 Kate의 대화를 완성하세요.

AMY: Kate, come in. ¹·Make _yourself_ at home.
KATE: ²·Thanks for inviting _____ to your Halloween party.
AMY: There are some cookies on the table. ³·Help _____ .
KATE: ⁴·Did you make these cookies by _____?
AMY: No. ⁵·My mom made _____ .
KATE: What about the room decorations? They're very nice.
AMY: Thanks. ⁶·I did them by _____ .

AMY

KATE

정답 p.277, REVIEW TEST 9 p.232

UNIT
055

Grammar Gateway Basic

🎧 056.mp3

①

How much is **this**? 이것은 얼마예요?
How much are **these**? 이것들은 얼마예요?

How much is **that**? 저것은 얼마예요?
How much are **those**? 저것들은 얼마예요?

② '(여기) 이 사람, 이것'이라는 의미로 가까이에 있는 대상을 가리켜서 말할 때 **this**를 쓴다.

- "**This** is my cousin, Alex." 이 사람은 내 사촌 Alex야.
  "It's nice to meet you."
- **This** tastes really good. Did you make it?
  이것은 정말 맛이 좋다.
- "Can I try **this** on?"
  "Sure. The fitting room is over here."

둘 이상의 대상을 가리켜서 말할 때는 **these**를 쓴다.

- **These** are my friends. Their names are Dave and Janine. 이 사람들은 내 친구들이야.
- "Which shoes should I buy?"
  "**These** are nice." 이것들이 좋네요.
- "Whose pens are **these**?"
  "They're mine."

'(저기) 저 사람, 저것'이라는 의미로 멀리 있는 대상을 가리켜서 말할 때는 **that**을 쓴다.

- "Is **that** your cousin?" 저 사람이 네 사촌이니?
  "I'm not sure. I can't see him very well."
- **That** smells very delicious. What did you cook?
  저것은 정말 맛있는 냄새가 난다.
- "Can I try **that** on?"
  "Sure. I'll get it for you if you wait here."

둘 이상의 대상을 가리켜서 말할 때는 **those**를 쓴다.

- "Are **those** your friends over there?"
  저기에 저 사람들이 네 친구들이니? "Yes, they are."
- I'd like **those** on the shelf, please.
  선반 위에 저것들을 주세요.
- "Whose pens are **those** on the table?"
  "They're Fred's."

③ **this/these, that/those** 뒤에 명사를 함께 쓸 수도 있다.

this + 단수명사 또는 셀 수 없는 명사

- **This box** is very light. What's in it?
  이 상자는 아주 가볍다.
- Thank you again for visiting our museum.
  The exit is **this way**. 출구는 이쪽입니다.

these + 복수명사

- Here you are. Try **these sandwiches**.
  이 샌드위치들을 먹어 봐.
- I'm sorry, but you can't sit here. **These seats** are reserved. 이 좌석들은 예약되어 있어요.

that + 단수명사 또는 셀 수 없는 명사

- Is **that box** heavy? Do you need some help?
  저 상자는 무겁나요?
- You took the wrong road.
  The museum is **that way**. 박물관은 저쪽이에요.

those + 복수명사

- Jerry made **those sandwiches** for our picnic.
  Jerry가 우리 소풍을 위해 저 샌드위치들을 만들었다.
- "Where should we sit?"
  "**Those seats** are ours." 저 좌석들이 우리 것이야.

PRACTICE

A. 그림을 보고 괄호 안에 주어진 명사와 this 또는 that을 사용하여 문장을 완성하세요.

1. (word) What does _this word_ mean?

2. (book) Is _____ _____ yours?

3. (painting) Look at _____ _____ !

4. (ring) I'll take _____ _____ !

B. 둘 중 맞는 것을 고르세요.

1. "These scissors aren't sharp." "Here, try (these / those)."
2. "What is (this / that) on the wall over there?" "It looks like a spider!"
3. (These / Those) are my brother's friends. Let's go and say hello.
4. "Are you wearing a new suit?" "Yes, (this / that) is new."
5. "What is (this / that) on the water?" "I'm not sure. It's too far away."
6. "(This / That) restaurant is amazing." "I know. I come here often."
7. Can you see (these / those) buildings across the street?
8. "What are you holding in your hand?" "(These / Those) are the invitations for my birthday party."

UNIT 056

C. 그림을 보고 괄호 안에 주어진 명사와 this/these 또는 that/those를 사용하여 예시와 같이 가격을 물으세요.

1	2	3
4	5	6

1. (lamp) _How much is this lamp_ ?
2. (socks) _____ ?
3. (cake) _____ ?
4. (spoons) _____ ?
5. (perfume) _____ ?
6. (sunglasses) _____ ?

D. Kate와 Amy가 쇼핑을 하고 있습니다. this/these 또는 that/those를 사용하여 Kate와 Amy의 대화를 완성하세요.

KATE: ¹·Amy, do you like _this_ shirt?

AMY: Not really. ²·I like _____ shirt over there.

KATE: ³·But it looks very nice with _____ shoes here.

AMY: Really? ⁴·I think _____ shoes on that shelf are better.

KATE: ⁵·_____ are for men!

KATE

AMY

🎧 057.mp3

①

I'd like to buy **a melon**.

How about this **one**?

How about this **one**?

이것은 어떤가요?

I'd also like some **oranges**.

How about these fresh **ones**?

How about these fresh **ones**?

이 신선한 것들은 어떤가요?

앞서 말한 명사를 다시 말할 때 명사 대신 **one** 또는 **ones**를 쓸 수 있다.

- "May I borrow **a pencil**?" "Sure. You can take **one**." (one = a pencil)
- "I like these **socks**." "Well, I prefer the **ones** with stripes." (ones = socks)

② 한 사람 또는 한 개의 사물을 말할 때는 **one**을 쓴다.

- "Which **boy** is your son?" "The **one** in the white shirt." (one = a boy)
- I'm looking for **a hotel**. Could you suggest **one**? (one = a hotel)
- "You should take **a taxi**." "Where can I catch **one**?"

둘 이상의 사람 또는 사물을 말할 때는 **ones**를 쓴다.

- We want to be **cheerleaders**. The **ones** at our school are very popular. (ones = cheerleaders)
- Can you bring me my **glasses**? They are the **ones** on the desk. (ones = glasses)
- "Which **jeans** are on sale?" "The **ones** outside the store."

③ **one**과 **ones** 앞에 형용사를 함께 쓸 수 있다.

a(n)/the 등 + 형용사 + one

- "That is a famous building."
  "It looks like **an old one**." 그것은 오래된 것처럼 보여요.
- All of these ties are nice, but I think I'll buy **the blue one**. 저는 파란 것을 살까 해요.
- "This store has a lot of dolls."
  "Yes. I really like **this little one**."

some/the 등 + 형용사 + ones

- Let's buy some snacks. There are **some good ones** at this store. 이 가게에 몇몇 좋은 것들이 있다.
- The small envelopes are $2, and **the large ones** are $3. 큰 것들은 3달러이다.
- Let's get some roses. **These yellow ones** are pretty.

④ **Which one(s) ~?**: 어느 것(들) ~?

- "**Which one** is your bicycle?" 어느 것이 네 자전거니? "It's the red one on the left."
- "Ally can speak four languages." "Really? **Which ones**?" 어느 것들?
- There are so many dogs. **Which one** is yours?
- **Which ones** do you like better, the red gloves or the purple ones?

PRACTICE

A. one 또는 ones를 써넣으세요.

1. Do you have a pet?
2. Which painting is your favorite?
3. What do you think of these pants?
4. I need to find a good dentist.
5. Does anyone have an eraser?
6. These sodas are warm.

No, I don't have _one_____.
I like the _____ with bright colors.
I think the black _____ are better.
I know a good _____. He's very kind.
I have _____. Here you go.
The _____ in the fridge are cold.

B. 주어진 형용사와 one 또는 ones를 사용하여 문장을 완성하세요. a/an 또는 some을 함께 쓰세요.

bigger	~~black~~	cheap	chocolate	exciting	important	new

1. "Do you have any brown boots?" "No, we don't. But we have _some black ones_____."
2. "Our toaster is very old." "You're right. We need _____."
3. These earphones are expensive. Do you have _____?
4. There is a meeting tomorrow. It's _____, so I have to go.
5. "Did you bake blueberry cookies?" "Yes. Try _____ too. I just made them."
6. "I can't put all these clothes in the suitcase." "I have _____. You can borrow it."
7. Did you watch the baseball game last night? It was _____.

C. 그림을 보고 Which one ~? 또는 Which ones ~?를 사용하여 상황에 맞게 의문문을 완성하세요.

1. _Which one_____
   is Andy?
2. _____
   are Mary's?
3. _____
   is Ted's house?
4. _____
   goes to London?
5. _____
   do you like?

D. 괄호 안에 주어진 단어와 one 또는 ones를 사용하여 Linda와 점원의 대화를 완성하세요.

LINDA

LINDA: Hello. I'd like to buy a melon.
Clerk: 1. How about _this one_____? It's from Turkey. (this)
LINDA: No, thank you. 2. I want the _____ over there. (big)
        I'd also like some apples.
        3. Do you have any _____? (green)
Clerk: 4. No. We only have _____. (red)
LINDA: OK. I'll take them.

Clerk

UNIT 058 | There are **some** children on the bus. some과 any

🎧 058.mp3

① '몇몇의, 약간의'라는 의미로 사람 또는 사물의 불특정한 수나 양에 대해 말할 때 명사 앞에 **some** 또는 **any**를 쓴다.

some은 주로 긍정문에 쓴다.

- There are **some children** on the bus. 버스에 몇몇 아이들이 있다.
- We spent **some time** in the mountains last weekend.
  우리는 지난 주말에 산에서 약간의 시간을 보냈다.
- "What did you buy for Sandra?" "I got **some flowers**."

any는 주로 부정문과 의문문에 쓴다.

- There aren't **any children** on the bus. 버스에 아이들이 한 명도 없다.
- I'm tired today because I didn't get **any sleep** last night.
  나는 어젯밤에 잠을 하나도 못 잤다.
- "Do you have **any plans** for Saturday?"
  "Yes. I'm visiting my parents."

  단, 권유나 요청을 할 경우에는 의문문에 **some**을 주로 쓴다.
  - "Can I offer you **some advice**?" 당신에게 약간의 조언을 해도 될까요? "Of course."

② 명사 없이 **some** 또는 **any**만 쓸 수도 있다.

- "We have some ice cream." "Oh, I want **some**." (some = some ice cream)
- "Did you see any dolphins at the zoo?" "No. There weren't **any**." (any = any dolphins)

③ '누군가, 무언가, 어딘가'라는 의미로 정확히 알 수 없는 사람, 사물, 장소에 대해 말할 때 다음과 같은 표현을 쓴다.

사람	someone/somebody	anyone/anybody
사물	something	anything
장소	somewhere	anywhere

- "**Someone** left this briefcase in the lobby." 누군가 로비에 이 서류 가방을 두고 갔어요. "Oh. That's mine."
- I'm going to the supermarket. Do you need **anything**? 너 무언가 필요하니?
- "Where is Jen's office?" "It's **somewhere** on Washington Avenue."

someone, something 등은 주로 긍정문에 쓰고, **anyone, anything** 등은 주로 부정문과 의문문에 쓴다.

- "**Something** smells great!" 무언가 좋은 냄새가 나! "It's my perfume. Do you like it?"
- "Is **anyone** sitting here?" 여기에 누군가 앉나요? "No. Have a seat."
- We haven't traveled **anywhere** lately.

  단, 권유나 요청을 할 경우에는 의문문에 **someone, something** 등을 주로 쓴다.
  - "Can you bring **something** to drink here?" 마실 무언가를 여기에 가져올 수 있니? "Sure."

PRACTICE

A. 주어진 명사와 some 또는 any를 사용하여 문장을 완성하세요.

| friends | money | ~~pancakes~~ | paper | rest | snow | sports | trains |

1. "What are you cooking?" "I'm making _some pancakes_ for breakfast."
2. It was warm last winter, so there wasn't _____.
3. We need to buy _____ for the printer.
4. "Does Sandra play _____?" "I think she plays hockey."
5. "There aren't _____ to London tonight, right?" "Actually, we have one at 8."
6. Jacob used to live in Australia, so he has _____ there.
7. You should get _____. You look very tired.
8. I lost my wallet, so I don't have _____ now.

B. some 또는 any를 써넣으세요.

1. It's so quiet in this room.
2. Let's buy some shampoo.
3. There are no chairs in this room.
4. The weather is very clear today.
5. Have you seen any movies lately?
6. Can I have a steak?

Should we turn on _some_ music?
I have no money right now. Do you have _____?
Oh, I'll bring _____.
Yes. There aren't _____ clouds in the sky!
No, I haven't watched _____.
Sure. Would you like _____ wine with it?

UNIT
058

Grammar Gateway Basic

C. 그림을 보고 someone/somebody/something/somewhere를 써넣으세요.

Where is my umbrella?

I'm hungry.

Who is it?

Where are they going?

1. _Someone_ OR _Somebody_ took his umbrella.
2. He wants _____ to eat.
3. _____ is knocking on the door.
4. They're going _____.

D. someone/something 등 또는 anybody/anywhere 등을 써넣으세요.

1. "Did _anyone_ OR _anybody_ call me?" "Yes. Your sister left a message for you."
2. "Where does Sienna live?" "She lives _____ in Brooklyn."
3. William is angry because _____ parked a car in front of his house again.
4. "Are you busy?" "No. I'm not doing _____ right now."
5. "Would you like _____ to read?" "A newspaper, please."
6. "I haven't seen Ben _____ today." "He went to his brother's wedding."
7. _____ is wrong with the washing machine. It's not working.
8. "Has _____ heard from John?" "He called me this morning."

🎧 059.mp3

①

Sorry, all the rooms are full.

There are **no rooms**.

방이 없다.

---

② '~이 없다'라는 의미로 말할 때 **no + 명사**를 쓴다.
- Ms. White has three sons but **no daughters**. White씨는 세 명의 아들이 있지만 딸이 없다.
- That sofa is too big for our apartment. There's **no space** for it. 그것을 위한 공간이 없다.
- "I want to meet you this afternoon." "Sorry, I have **no time**."

---

③ **no + 명사** 대신에 **not ~ any + 명사**를 쓸 수도 있다.
- I have **no questions**. 또는 I don't have **any questions**. 저는 질문이 없어요.
- There are **no girls** in my class. 또는 There aren't **any girls** in my class. 내 수업에는 여자애들이 없다.

---

④ **no + 명사** 대신에 **none**을 쓸 수도 있다.
- "How much pizza is left?" "**None**. Jeff ate it all." (None = No pizza)
- "Do you have any pets?" "No. I have **none**." (none = no pets)

  no는 명사와 함께 쓰지만 **none**은 명사와 함께 쓰지 않는 것에 주의한다.
  - I checked for messages, but there were **none**. (none messages로 쓸 수 없음)
  - "Did you buy an umbrella?" "No. The store had **none**." (none umbrellas로 쓸 수 없음)

---

⑤ '아무 ~도 …않다'라는 의미로 말할 때 다음과 같은 표현을 쓴다.

사람	no one/nobody
사물	nothing
장소	nowhere

- "Who is that boy?" "He must be new to this town. **No one** knows him." 아무도 그를 몰라.
- We have **nothing** to eat. We should go to the grocery store. 우리는 먹을 것이 아무것도 없다.
- "Where did you go last weekend?" "**Nowhere**. I stayed at home."

---

⑥ **no + 명사, no one, nothing** 등은 **not**과 함께 쓰지 않는다.
- There are **no classes** on Sunday. (there are not no classes로 쓸 수 없음)
- Claire told a joke, but **nobody** laughed. (nobody didn't laugh로 쓸 수 없음)

PRACTICE

A. 주어진 명사와 no를 사용하여 문장을 완성하세요.

| bread | children | choice | money | rain | ~~seats~~ | tickets | windows |

1. There were _no seats_ on the bus, so I had to stand.
2. "I want to make some sandwiches." "We have _____ at home. Should we go to the bakery?"
3. There's _____ in my wallet. I spent it all.
4. There are _____ for the 11 a.m. show. They're sold out.
5. "Why are you moving to Dubai?" "My company is moving there. I have _____."
6. _____ are allowed in the playground after 8 p.m.
7. It was cloudy last night, but there was _____.
8. Our garage has _____, so it's always dark.

B. no/any/none을 써넣으세요.

1. "How many people are coming today?" "_None_. The meeting was canceled."
2. I couldn't take _____ pictures in the museum. _____ cameras were allowed.
3. Mike bought two suits at the mall, but I bought _____.
4. There weren't _____ buildings here 10 years ago. Those are all new.
5. The library was very quiet. There was _____ noise.
6. There aren't _____ cups on the table. Could you get some?
7. "How many cousins do you have?" "_____."

C. no one/nobody/nothing/nowhere를 써넣으세요.

1. "_No one_ OR _Nobody_ was hurt in the accident." "That's good news."
2. "There's _____ to park the car here." "Let's try the next street."
3. "What's that sound?" "It's _____. Just the wind."
4. "This gallery is boring." "Yes. There's _____ to see here. Let's go."
5. I have to get a bookshelf. There's _____ to put these new books.
6. If _____ wants the last piece of pizza, I'll eat it.

D. no/any/none을 사용하여 Paul과 호텔 직원의 대화를 완성하세요.

PAUL

PAUL: Hello. Is there a room here?
Clerk: Yes, there is one. How many people are staying?
PAUL: 1. There are _no_ other people. It's just me.
How much is the room?
Clerk: 2. It's $30 for a night, but it has _____ wi-fi.
PAUL: 3. Well, the other hotels didn't have _____ rooms. I'll take that one.
Clerk: OK. Do you have any bags? I'll help you with them.
PAUL: 4. I have _____. Thanks for the offer.

Clerk

정답 p.278, REVIEW TEST 10 p.234

UNIT 059

Grammar Gateway Basic

🎧 060.mp3

①

There are **many cars** on the road.
도로에 많은 차가 있다.

There isn't **much sugar** in the spoon.
숟가락에 많은 설탕이 있지 않다.

many + 복수명사: 많은 ~

- I invited **many friends** to my house.
  나는 많은 친구들을 집으로 초대했다.
- There are **many birds** in the garden.
  많은 새들이 정원에 있다.

many는 긍정문, 부정문, 의문문 모두에 쓴다.

- Ted can speak **many different languages**.
  Ted는 다른 언어를 많이 할 줄 안다.
- **Many stores** don't open on Sundays.
  일요일에는 많은 상점들이 문을 열지 않는다.
- How **many brothers** do you have?

much + 셀 수 없는 명사: 많은 ~

- We haven't had **much rain** lately.
  최근에 많은 비가 오지 않았다.
- Do you use **much oil** in your cooking?
  요리에 기름을 많이 사용하나요?

much는 주로 부정문과 의문문에 쓴다.

- I don't have **much work** to do today.
  나는 오늘 할 일이 많지 않다.
- Did you get **much sleep** last night?
  어젯밤에 많이 잤나요?
- How **much time** does it take to get to the airport?

② **a lot of/lots of**: 많은 ~

a lot of/lots of는 복수명사와 셀 수 없는 명사 앞에 모두 쓸 수 있다.

- **A lot of people** go shopping at the mall before the holidays. 많은 사람들이 연휴 전에 쇼핑몰로 쇼핑을 하러 간다.
- My mom gives me **lots of advice** about life. 엄마는 나에게 인생에 관한 많은 조언을 주신다.

a lot of/lots of는 긍정문, 부정문, 의문문 모두에 쓴다.

- I'm so full! I ate **a lot of food** for dinner. 나는 저녁에 많은 음식을 먹었어.
- Luke likes music, but he doesn't attend **a lot of concerts**. 그는 많은 콘서트에 참석하지는 않는다.
- "Did you visit **lots of places** in New Zealand?" "Yes, I did."

③ 명사 없이 **many** 또는 **much**만 쓸 수도 있다.

- Maria likes flowers. She grows **many** in her yard. (many = many flowers)
- "Do we have any cheese for the burgers?" "Yes, but there isn't **much**." (much = much cheese)

명사 없이 **a lot of/lots of**를 쓸 수 없다. 이때는 **a lot**을 쓴다.

- "How much money did you spend today?" "**A lot**." (A lot = A lot of money)
- "I want to buy these shoes. They're very pretty!" "But you already have **a lot**." (a lot = a lot of shoes)

PRACTICE

A. 그림을 보고 괄호 안에 주어진 명사와 There are many 또는 There isn't much를 사용하여 문장을 완성하세요.

1 2 3 4 5

1. (book) _There are many books_   on the bookshelf.
2. (space) _____ in the fridge.
3. (money) _____ in the wallet.

4. (kids) _____ on the playground.
5. (bread) _____ in the basket.

B. 괄호 안에 주어진 명사와 many 또는 much를 사용하여 문장을 완성하세요. 필요한 경우 명사를 복수로 쓰세요.

1. (orange) _Many oranges_   are grown in Florida.
2. (interest) "Do you like playing basketball?" "No. I don't have _____ in sports."
3. (furniture) We don't have _____ in our house. Let's buy some this weekend.
4. (cup) "How _____ do we need?" "Well, there are 12 guests."
5. (dog) There are _____ in my neighborhood. They bark too much.
6. (information) "Did you find _____ for your trip?" "No, not yet."
7. (time) Hurry up! We don't have _____ .

C. 주어진 명사와 a lot of를 사용하여 문장을 완성하세요.

~~books~~	coffee	fun	noise	vegetables

1. "Do you have to read _a lot of books_   for your history class?" "Yes. The class is very hard."
2. You should stop drinking _____ . It might be bad for your health.
3. "Do you eat _____ ?" "Yes. I especially like carrots."
4. "Did you have _____ yesterday?" "Yes, I did."
5. My roommates were making _____ last night. I couldn't sleep.

D. much/a lot/a lot of 중 더 적절한 것을 써넣으세요.

1. "Let's go out!" "I can't. I have _a lot of_   things to do."
2. It's raining a lot, but there isn't _____ wind.
3. "Can you bring me a pen from the desk?" "Which one do you want? There are _____ ."
4. "Are there many mistakes in my report?" "Yes. You made _____ ."
5. This lamp doesn't use _____ electricity.
6. The meeting is very important. We should prepare _____ .
7. "Are there _____ parks in your city?" "No. There's only one."
8. "How many people bought that book?" "_____ . I think it'll be a best-seller."
9. I spend _____ time with my family on weekends.
10. Please don't put _____ salt in the soup. It'll taste bad.

정답 p.278, REVIEW TEST 10 p.234

UNIT
060

Grammar Gateway Basic

①

There are **a few cookies**.
약간의 쿠키가 있다.

There is **a little milk**.
약간의 우유가 있다.

'몇몇의, 약간의'라는 의미로 **a few** 또는 **a little**을 쓸 수 있다.

a few + 복수명사

- Sue bought **a few magazines** at the store.
  Sue는 가게에서 몇 권의 잡지를 샀다.
- Can I talk to you for **a few minutes**?
  몇 분간 이야기할 수 있나요?
- It's late, but **a few restaurants** might be open.

a little + 셀 수 없는 명사

- Nick had **a little wine** at dinner.
  Nick은 저녁 식사 때 약간의 와인을 마셨다.
- Can I have **a little salt** in my soup?
  제 수프에 약간의 소금을 넣을 수 있을까요?
- There's **a little ice** on the streets. Walk carefully.

②

There are **few cookies**.
쿠키가 거의 없다.

There is **little milk**.
우유가 거의 없다.

'거의 없는'이라는 의미로 **few** 또는 **little**을 쓸 수 있다.

few + 복수명사

- We see **few stars** in the sky these days.
  요즘에는 하늘에서 별을 거의 볼 수 없다.
- The store just opened, so it has **few customers**.
  그곳에 손님이 거의 없다.
- There were **few cars** on the road this morning.

little + 셀 수 없는 명사

- Eric spends **little money** on clothes.
  Eric은 옷에 돈을 거의 쓰지 않는다.
- I have **little knowledge** about physics.
  나는 물리학에 대한 지식이 거의 없다.
- We had **little snow** this year.

③ **a few/a little**과 **few/little**의 의미 차이에 주의한다.

- The party was fun. **A few** people came.
  (몇 명의 사람들이 왔다.)
  The party was boring. **Few** people came.
  (사람들이 거의 오지 않았다.)

- I don't have to leave now. I have **a little** time.
  (약간의 시간이 있다.)
  I have to leave now. I have **little** time.
  (시간이 거의 없다.)

④ 명사 없이 **(a) few** 또는 **(a) little**만 쓸 수도 있다.

- My brother reads many books, but I read **few**. (few = few books)
- "Is there any paper in the printer?"   "There's **a little**." (a little = a little paper)

PRACTICE

A. 그림을 보고 주어진 명사와 a few 또는 a little을 사용하여 문장을 완성하세요. 필요한 경우 명사를 복수로 쓰세요.

~~hair~~	rose	ticket	water

1

2

3

4

1. He has *a little hair*   .
2. There is   in the cup.

3. There are   in the vase.
4. She has   .

B. 주어진 명사와 few 또는 little을 사용하여 문장을 완성하세요. 필요한 경우 명사를 복수로 쓰세요.

car	information	letter	space	~~student~~	sugar

1. The test was very difficult. *Few students*   passed it.
2. The police are still looking for the thieves. They have   about them.
3.   were on the road after midnight. It was almost empty.
4. There is   in this pie, so it's not very sweet.
5. I can't put this sofa in the garage. There is   .
6. People write   these days. They usually use e-mail.

C. a few/few 또는 a little/little을 써넣으세요.

1. Tim is out of the office. He'll be back in *a few*   hours.
2. My sister has   interest in cooking. She always eats out.
3. "Could you give me   help? I don't understand this question." "Sure."
4. "Would you like some grapes?" "Yes, I'll have   ."
5. I found   errors in your report. You did a good job.
6. I had   time to prepare for my speech, so it wasn't good.
7. "Would you like some pepper on your pasta?" "   , please."
8. Our baseball team didn't play well this year. They won   games.

D. a few/few 또는 a little/little을 사용하여 Justin과 Amy의 대화를 완성하세요.

JUSTIN

JUSTIN: We should eat something before we leave for the movie.
AMY: ¹·But we just ate *a little*   chocolate. You also had some cake.
JUSTIN: ²·Yes, but I had   pieces. I'm still hungry.
AMY: ³·We have   tomatoes in the fridge.
    We can make some soup.
JUSTIN: That will take too long. ⁴·There's   time.
AMY: OK. ⁵·Let's just get   snacks at the theater then.

AMY

정답 p.278, REVIEW TEST 10 p.234

UNIT
061

Grammar Gateway Basic

UNIT 062 | **All** dogs have tails. all과 every

①

All dogs have tails.

또는 **Every dog** has a tail.

모든 개들은 꼬리가 있다.

---

② '모든 ~'이라는 의미로 말할 때 **all** 또는 **every**를 쓸 수 있다.

all + 복수명사/셀 수 없는 명사

- Nancy often goes to the zoo. She loves **all animals**. 그녀는 모든 동물을 사랑한다.
- **All bread** at this bakery is baked every morning. 이 빵집의 모든 빵은 매일 아침마다 구워진다.
- There are restrooms on **all floors** of the building.

every + 단수명사

- **Every book** in this library is in English. 이 도서관에 있는 모든 책은 영어로 되어 있다.
- I open **every window** when I get up. 나는 일어나면 모든 창문을 연다.
- **Every painting** in this gallery is for sale.

---

③ **all + 복수명사**를 주어로 쓸 때는 복수동사를 쓰고, **all + 셀 수 없는 명사**를 주어로 쓸 때는 단수동사를 쓴다.

- **All banks close** on Sundays. (All banks closes로 쓸 수 없음)
- "**Is all wine** made from grapes?" "No. There are many different kinds." (Are all wine으로 쓸 수 없음)

every + 단수명사를 주어로 쓸 때는 단수동사를 쓴다.

- In my school, **every class has** 30 students. (every class have로 쓸 수 없음)
- I couldn't get into the office because **every door was** locked. (every door were로 쓸 수 없음)

---

④ **all + day, week, month** 등: ~ 종일, ~ 내내

- I'm hungry. I haven't eaten anything **all day**. 나는 하루 종일 아무것도 먹지 않았다.
- Tanya went to London in June and stayed there **all month**. Tanya는 6월에 런던에 가서 한 달 내내 그곳에서 지냈다.

every + day, week, month 등: ~마다, 매~

- I take a shower **every day**. 나는 날마다 샤워를 한다.
- "Do you visit your parents often?" "Yes. I visit them **every week**." 나는 매주 그들을 방문해.

---

⑤ '모든 ~'이라는 의미로 사람, 사물, 장소에 대해 말할 때 다음과 같은 표현을 쓴다.

사람	everyone/everybody	• The concert was amazing. **Everyone** enjoyed it. 모든 사람이 그것을 즐겼다.
사물	everything	• "How was your vacation?" "**Everything** was perfect." 모든 것이 완벽했어.
장소	everywhere	• You need to clean your room. Your clothes are **everywhere**.

PRACTICE

A. all 또는 every를 써넣으세요.

1. _Every_ desk in our classroom is new.
2. I like _____ kinds of ice cream.
3. _____ shop on the street was crowded.
4. _____ flights were canceled yesterday.
5. There are books on _____ shelf in the library.
6. _____ plants need water and sunlight.

B. 그림을 보고 주어진 단어들을 사용하여 문장을 완성하세요. 필요한 경우 명사를 복수로 쓰세요.

~~cat~~ flower man seat student

1. (every) _Every cat_ _____ is white.
2. (all) _____ wear uniforms.
3. (every) _____ is red.
4. (every) _____ is taken.
5. (all) _____ wear glasses.

C. 괄호 안에 주어진 단어들과 all 또는 every를 적절한 형태로 사용하여 문장을 완성하세요. 현재 시제로 쓰세요.

1. (advice, be) We need ideas for the project. _All advice is_ _____ welcome.
2. (languages, have) _____ rules of grammar.
3. (story, have) _____ a beginning and an ending.
4. (children, need) _____ parents' care.
5. (rain, come) _____ from clouds.
6. (table, be) " _____ taken. We have to wait." "OK."

D. 괄호 안에 주어진 명사와 all 또는 every를 사용하여 문장을 완성하세요.

1. Did you sleep much last night?	(night) No. I watched TV _all night_ .
2. What do you do on the weekend?	(weekend) I go to the mountains _____ .
3. Do you read a lot of books?	(month) Yes. I read 10 books _____ .
4. You promised to call me, but you didn't.	(week) Sorry. I've been busy _____ .
5. Did you have fun at the beach yesterday?	(day) Yes. We swam _____ .
6. How often do you jog?	(morning) I jog _____ .

E. everyone/everybody/everything/everywhere를 써넣으세요.

1. Thank you for the meal. _Everything_ was so good!
2. Mr. and Mrs. Adams traveled _____ in Asia after they retired.
3. I've tried _____, but the computer is still not working.
4. "Has _____ arrived?" "No. Ken isn't here yet."
5. There are clothes _____. You need to pick them up.

정답 p.279, REVIEW TEST 10 p.234

UNIT
062

Grammar Gateway Basic

UNIT 063 | He wants **both.** both, either, neither

🎧 063.mp3

①

> I want **both.**

He wants **both.**
(베이글과 머핀 둘 다)

both (+ 복수명사): 둘 다, 두 ~ 모두

- Alan likes baseball and basketball. He enjoys playing **both.** 그는 둘 다 하는 것을 좋아한다.
- I've been to Rome twice. **Both times** were wonderful. 두 번 모두 좋았다.
- "Does Karen speak English or Spanish?" "She can speak **both.**"
- Look **both ways** before you cross the street.

②

> **Either** is fine.

Either is fine.
(베이글과 머핀 둘 중 아무것이나 하나)

either (+ 단수명사): 둘 중 아무것이나 하나, 두 ~ 중 아무것이나 하나

- "Do you want chicken or fish?" "**Either** is OK." 둘 중 아무거나 괜찮아요.
- We can stay at **either hotel.** Both seem nice. 우리는 두 호텔 중 아무 곳에서나 묵어도 괜찮아요.
- "Do you want to go to the beach or the lake?" "I'm fine with **either.**"
- "Should we meet at your house or mine?" "**Either place** is good."

③

> I like **neither.**

He likes **neither.**
(베이글이나 머핀 둘 다 아님)

neither (+ 단수명사): 둘 다 아닌, 두 ~ 모두 아닌

- I'm not buying these dresses. **Neither** looks good on me. 둘 다 나에게 어울리지 않는다.
- "Which house has a garage?" "**Neither house** has one." 두 집 모두 없어.
- I have two printers at home, but **neither** is working.
- "Which should we take, the bus or the subway?" "Let's take **neither.** We should take a taxi."

PRACTICE

A. 그림을 보고 괄호 안에 주어진 명사와 both 또는 neither를 사용하여 문장을 완성하세요. 필요한 경우 명사를 복수로 쓰세요.

1 　　　　2 　　　　3

4 　　　　5 　　　　6

1. (man) *Neither man* _____ is wearing glasses.
2. (woman) _____ have long hair.
3. (seat) _____ is taken.
4. (car) _____ are in the garage.
5. (store) _____ is open.
6. (baby) _____ are one year old.

B. both/either/neither를 써넣으세요.

1. "Do you like horror movies or action movies?" " *Neither* _____. I like comedies."
2. "Which bag is yours?" "_____ are mine. I brought two."
3. "Should I leave the box here or on your desk?" "It doesn't matter. Just leave it _____ place."
4. "How were your math and science exams?" "Terrible. _____ was easy."
5. Our company always uses _____ sides of a paper to save money.
6. "Could we meet on Friday or Saturday?" "You can pick a date. I can see you _____ day."

C. 괄호 안에 주어진 명사와 both/either/neither를 사용하여 문장을 완성하세요. 필요한 경우 명사를 복수로 쓰세요.

1. Where should we park our car?
2. Who wrote these books?
3. Which has two bedrooms?
4. Which month is better for you to visit, May or June?
5. Do you want some juice? I have apple and lemon.

(side) *Either side* _____ of the street is fine.
(novel) _____ were written by Sam.
(house) _____ have two bedrooms.
(month) _____ is OK.
(kind) No. _____ sounds good.

D. both/either/neither를 사용하여 Wilson 가족의 대화를 완성하세요.

LINDA: Do you want a muffin or a bagel, Justin?
JUSTIN: 1. *Neither* _____. I already ate some toast.
LINDA: OK. What about you, Amy?
AMY: 2. _____ is fine. I don't mind.
JAMES: 3. Linda, I want _____. And some butter, please!
LINDA: No, James. 4. You can have _____ a bagel or a muffin.
　　　 5. You can't have _____. Please choose one.

JUSTIN

AMY　JAMES

LINDA

정답 p.279, REVIEW TEST 10 p.234

UNIT 064 | all of the pie, most of the pie all/most/some/none of ~

🎧 064.mp3

①

all of the pie
파이 전부

most of the pie
파이 대부분

some of the pie
파이 약간

none of the pie
파이가 없음

---

② 특정한 사람 또는 사물을 가리킬 때 **all/most/some/none** 뒤에 **of ~**를 쓸 수 있다.

all most some none	of	the/my/these 등 + 명사 it/us/you/them

- **All of my friends** like playing football. 내 친구들 전부는 축구를 하는 것을 좋아한다.
- "Have you talked to your new classmates?" "Yes. **Most of them** are friendly." 그들 대부분은 상냥해.
- **Some of the clothes** in the store are on sale.
- We took a taxi to the airport because **none of us** could drive.

---

③ **all/most of ~** 등은 특정한 대상에 대해 말할 때 쓴다.

- I've met **all of the people** in our company.
  (우리 회사에 있는 사람들 전부)
- **Most of these cars** are expensive.
  (이 차들 대부분)
- **Some of the songs** on this album are good.
- I've read **none of the books** on the shelf yet.

all/most 등 + 명사는 일반적인 대상에 대해 말할 때 쓴다.

- **All people** have secrets.
  (일반적인 사람들 전부)
- **Most cars** use gas.
  (일반적인 차들 대부분)
- I like to listen to **some songs** when I'm jogging.
- **No books** are published without titles.

---

④ **both/either/neither** 뒤에도 **of ~**를 쓸 수 있다.

both either neither	of	the/my/these 등 + 복수명사 us/you/them

- **Both of my parents** are teachers. (부모님 두 분 모두)
- "Should I wear a red tie or a blue one?"
  "**Either of those colors** matches your suit." (두 가지 색깔 중 아무거나)
- "Have Brad and Andy arrived?"
  "No. **Neither of them** is here yet."

PRACTICE

A. 그림을 보고 all/most/some/none of를 사용하여 예시와 같이 문장을 완성하세요. them을 함께 쓰세요.

1-4

5-8

1. *All of them*   are in the kitchen.
2. _____ are standing.
3. _____ are sitting at the table.
4. _____ are wearing yellow shirts.

5. _____ have red ribbons.
6. _____ have green ribbons.
7. _____ are open.
8. _____ are under the Christmas tree.

B. 괄호 안에 주어진 단어들을 적절히 배열하여 문장을 완성하세요.

1. (our neighbors / of / have children / some) *Some of our neighbors have children* .
2. (those fish / all / of / did you / catch) _____ ?
3. (none / of / liked it / us) The movie was boring. _____ .
4. (some / I / my cousins / often visit / of) _____ in New York.
5. (the shops / of / most / are expensive) I don't really like this street. _____ .
6. (of / were here / these buildings / none) _____ 10 years ago.
7. (put / most / I / mine / of) My sister never saves her money, but _____ in a bank.

C. 괄호 안에 주어진 단어들을 사용하여 문장을 완성하세요. 필요한 경우 of를 함께 쓰세요.

1. (none, you) Why did everyone come late? Did *none of you* know the schedule?
2. (some, animals) _____ sleep during the day.
3. (most, the work) "Do you need help with the dishes?" "No. _____ is done."
4. (all, animals) We should protect _____ . They're important for the environment.
5. (most, trees) _____ lose their leaves in the winter.
6. (some, these muffins) "Would you like _____ ?" "Sure. I'll take one."
7. (all, them) I've tried on these sweaters, and I want to buy _____ .
8. (none, my friends) The hotel had a nice pool, but _____ could swim.

D. 괄호 안에 주어진 표현과 both/either/neither of를 사용하여 문장을 완성하세요.

1. (them) "Which table do you want to sit at?" " *Either of them* is OK."
2. (our cars) _____ are in the repair shop. Can you give us a ride?
3. (his parents) "Jason is really tall." " _____ is tall, so it's very unusual."
4. (the restaurants) I'm fine with _____ . You can choose.
5. (us) My friend and I like singing, but _____ likes dancing.
6. (you) Jenna will need _____ . Those chairs are heavy, so three people should carry them.

정답 p.279, REVIEW TEST 10 p.234

🎧 065.mp3

①

He's wearing a black jacket.
그는 검은 재킷을 입고 있다.

He's tall.
그는 키가 크다.

black과 tall은 형용사이다.

---

② 형용사를 써서 사람이나 사물의 상태 또는 특징을 말할 수 있다.

형용사 + 명사

- "Have you met Dr. Morris?" "Yes. He's a **nice man.**" 그는 좋은 사람이야.
- We bought a house with a **pretty garden.** 우리는 예쁜 정원이 있는 집을 샀다.
- Frank is writing a **short story** about his family.
- My sister has **blond hair**, and I have **brown hair.**
- "What is your **favorite sport**?" "Hockey."
- "Let's eat out tonight." "OK. How about **Mexican food**?"

be동사 + 형용사

- "**I'm thirsty.** Can I have a glass of water?" 저는 목이 말라요. "Of course."
- Don't touch that pan. It**'s hot.** 그것은 뜨겁다.
- Charlie's old apartment **wasn't big**, but it **was expensive.**
- "**Is** that new restaurant **good**?" "No. I'll never go there again."
- Let's go home. It'll **be dark** soon.
- "Can I help you carry your bags?" "No, thanks. They **aren't heavy.**"

---

③ **look/smell/sound 등 + 형용사**

look + 형용사: ~해 보이다	- You **look sad**. What happened? 너 슬퍼 보여. - "Tony **looks different** today." "Really? Well, I didn't notice."
smell + 형용사: ~한 냄새가 나다	- What is this? It **smells strange.** 이상한 냄새가 나요. - This perfume **smells nice.** I'd like to buy it.
sound + 형용사: ~하게 들리다	- Claire told a joke, but it didn't **sound funny** at all. 그것은 전혀 재미있게 들리지 않았다. - Do you know this song? It **sounds great.**
taste + 형용사: ~한 맛이 나다	- This cake **tastes sweet.** Try some. 이 케이크는 달콤한 맛이 나. - The soup **tastes great.** Can I have some more?
feel + 형용사: ~하게 느끼다	- My daughter graduated from college. I **feel proud.** 나는 자랑스럽게 느낀다. - William lives alone, so he **feels lonely** sometimes.

PRACTICE

A. 그림을 보고 주어진 형용사와 명사를 하나씩 사용하여 문장을 완성하세요.

| blue | ~~cloudy~~ | long | old | + | car | ~~day~~ | eyes | hair |

1. It is a *cloudy day* _____ .
2. She has _____ .

3. They are driving an _____ .
4. He has _____ .

B. 주어진 단어들을 사용하여 문장을 완성하세요.

| cold | empty | medical | ~~new~~ | pink |

1. (suit) "Are you wearing a *new suit* _____?" "Yes. I bought it yesterday."
2. (weather) I don't like _____ , so I hate winter.
3. (roses) I ordered some _____ for my wife, but I got red ones!
4. (seats) On the subway, we had to stand because there were no _____ .
5. (school) "Is your brother a student?" "Yes. He goes to _____ ."

UNIT
065

Grammar Gateway Basic

C. 그림을 보고 괄호 안에 주어진 형용사와 look/smell/sound/taste/feel을 사용하여 문장을 완성하세요.

1. (nice) You *look nice* _____ .
2. (delicious) It _____ .
3. (scared) I _____ .
4. (good) It _____ .
5. (great) It _____ .
6. (happy) They _____ .

D. 주어진 단어들을 사용하여 Amy와 Kate의 대화를 완성하세요.

| black | kind | tall | ~~old~~ |

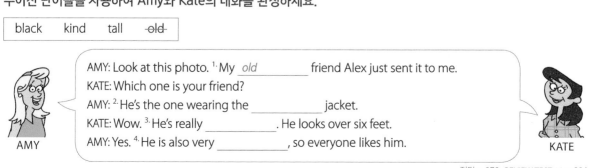

AMY: Look at this photo. [1.] My *old* _____ friend Alex just sent it to me.
KATE: Which one is your friend?
AMY: [2.] He's the one wearing the _____ jacket.
KATE: Wow. [3.] He's really _____ . He looks over six feet.
AMY: Yes. [4.] He is also very _____ , so everyone likes him.

AMY

KATE

정답 p.279, REVIEW TEST 11 p.236

UNIT 066 | They are walking **carefully**. 부사

🎧 066.mp3

①

They are walking **carefully**.
그들은 조심스럽게 걷고 있다.

carefully는 부사이다.

---

② 행동이나 일이 '어떻게' 일어나는지를 말할 때 부사를 쓸 수 있다. 부사는 일반적으로 형용사 끝에 **-ly**를 붙인다.

형용사	clear	quick	quiet	regular	slow
부사	clear**ly**	quick**ly**	quiet**ly**	regular**ly**	slow**ly**

- I bought new glasses, so now I can see **clearly**. 나는 이제 선명하게 볼 수 있다.
- Jack, come **quickly**! It's snowing outside! 빨리 와!
- Please shut the door **quietly**. Everybody is sleeping.
- "Do you visit the dentist **regularly**?" "Yes. I go once a year."
- Traffic was moving **slowly** because of an accident.

---

③ **-ly**를 붙일 때 주의해야 할 부사가 있다.

-y → -ily	easy → eas**ily**	busy → bus**ily**
-le → -ly	gent**le** → gent**ly**	comfortab**le** → comfortab**ly**
-ic → -ically	dramat**ic** → dramat**ically**	automat**ic** → automat**ically**
불규칙	**good → well**	

형용사에 -ly 붙이는 방법: 부록 p.249 참고

- Most children can learn foreign languages **easily**. 대부분의 아이들은 외국어를 쉽게 배울 수 있다.
- Jenna **gently** held her baby in her arms. Jenna는 그녀의 아기를 부드럽게 그녀의 팔에 안았다.
- This city has changed **dramatically** since last year. There are many new buildings.
- Our computer is very old, but it still runs **well**.
- Firefighters are **busily** spraying water on the fire.
- "What are you going to do this weekend?" "I'll stay and watch TV **comfortably** at home."
- I wake up **automatically** at 6 o'clock. It's an old habit.

---

④ 다음과 같이 **-ly**로 끝나지만 부사가 아니라 형용사인 단어도 있다.

friendly (친절한)   **lovely** (사랑스러운)   **silly** (어리석은)   **ugly** (못생긴)   **lonely** (외로운)

- My new neighbors are **friendly**. I really like them. 나의 새 이웃들은 친절하다.
- "Where did you get that **lovely** dress?" 어디에서 그 사랑스러운 드레스를 샀나요? "At the mall."
- "Sorry. I made a **silly** mistake." "That's OK."
- "Should we get that lamp?" "No. I think it's **ugly**."
- "My grandfather lives alone." "You should visit him often. He might feel **lonely**."

PRACTICE

A. 그림을 보고 주어진 형용사를 부사로 사용하여 문장을 완성하세요.

bright	comfortable	nervous	quick	~~sudden~~

1   2   3   The interview is in 5 minutes.   4   5

1. *Suddenly*_____, the door closed.
2. He is running _____ across the road.
3. They are waiting _____.
4. He is sitting _____.
5. The sun is shining _____.

B. 적절한 부사를 사용하여 예시와 같이 문장을 완성하세요.

1. Your paintings are wonderful. You paint pictures *wonderfully*_____.
2. There will be heavy rain tomorrow. It will rain _____.
3. Peter is a simple person. He likes to live _____.
4. Our wedding was perfect. Everything was planned _____.
5. My neighbor's dog is so noisy. The dog barks _____.
6. The Tigers and the Eagles are both good teams. They always play _____.
7. The computer program is automatic. It will be updated _____.

C. 주어진 동사와 부사를 하나씩 사용하여 예시와 같이 문장을 완성하세요.

drive	solve	speak	~~visit~~	walk	+	angrily	~~happily~~	loudly	quickly	safely

1. I like my grandmother, so I always *visit*_____ her house *happily*_____.
2. Would you _____? I can't hear you.
3. "Why did Collin _____ out of the room _____?" "We just had a fight."
4. "It's too dark. You might not see other cars very well." "Yes. I'll _____."
5. You studied a lot. I think you can _____ these questions _____.

D. 다음 문장을 읽고 틀린 부분이 있으면 바르게 고치세요. 틀린 부분이 없으면 O로 표시하세요.

1. Olivia is a friend girl. Everyone likes her.   *friend → friendly*
2. This is a lovely scarf. It looks well on you.
3. "I saw a ghost!" "Don't be silly. It was a shadow."
4. People should talk quiet in public places.
5. "Can you hear the beautifully violin sound?" "Yes. Who's playing it?"
6. I don't like living abroad. It feels lonely.
7. Oh, I forgot to call you. I'm terrible sorry about that.
8. The temperature has dropped dramatically this morning.

정답 p.280, REVIEW TEST 11 p.236

UNIT
066

Grammar Gateway Basic

He's **nervous**. He's waiting **nervously**.

형용사와 부사 비교

🎧 067.mp3

①

He's **nervous**.
그는 초조하다.

He's waiting **nervously**.
그는 초조하게 기다리고 있다.

형용사는 사람이나 사물이 어떠한지를 나타낼 때 쓴다.

- Jake is a **nice** guy. Everyone likes him.
  Jake는 좋은 사람이다.
- Our new bed is **comfortable**.
  우리의 새 침대는 편안하다.
- This book has a **happy** ending.
- The music is **loud**.
- Mike got a **bad** grade on his test.
- Why does Sam look **angry**?
- Jane is a **quick** runner.

부사는 행동이나 일이 어떻게 일어나는지를 나타낼 때 쓴다.

- Jake always dresses **nicely**.
  Jake는 항상 옷을 멋지게 입는다.
- We slept **comfortably** last night.
  우리는 어젯밤에 편안하게 잤다.
- The story ends **happily**.
- Tom is playing the guitar **loudly**.
- Mike did **badly** on his test.
- Sam just walked out **angrily**. What's wrong?
- Look! Why is Jane running so **quickly**?

② 다음과 같이 형용사와 부사 두 가지 모두로 쓸 수 있는 단어가 있다.

	형용사	부사
late	It's **late**. It's almost midnight. 늦었어.	I got home **late** last night. Everyone was asleep. 나는 어젯밤에 집에 늦게 왔다.
long	Sarah has **long** hair. Sarah는 긴 머리를 가졌다.	Let's walk to the park. It doesn't take **long**. 오래 걸리지 않는다.
hard	My father is a **hard** worker. 내 아버지는 열심히 일하시는 분이다.	The soccer team is practicing **hard**. 축구팀이 열심히 연습하고 있다.
fast	Nicole's car is **fast**. Nicole의 차는 빠르다.	Nicole talks **fast**. Nicole은 말을 빨리한다.
early	I had an **early** breakfast. 나는 이른 아침 식사를 했다.	Mr. Jenkins arrived **early** for his interview. Jenkins씨는 면접에 일찍 도착했다.

PRACTICE

A. 둘 중 맞는 것을 고르세요.

1. "Which shoes do you like?" "These ones. They feel (comfortable / comfortably)."
2. I don't like history. It is not (interesting / interestingly) to me.
3. Ben and Anna were talking (serious / seriously) when I saw them just a minute ago.
4. Lisa is a very (smart / smartly) student. She knows everything.
5. "Today is Valerie's birthday." "Oh no! I (complete / completely) forgot."
6. It was raining (heavy / heavily) when I woke up this morning.
7. I heard a (strange / strangely) sound last night. Did you hear anything?
8. You should exercise (regular / regularly) to stay healthy.

B. 주어진 형용사를 사용하여 문장을 완성하세요. 필요한 경우 형용사를 부사로 바꾸어 쓰세요.

beautiful	~~exciting~~	fast	hard	late	safe

1. "How was the soccer game?" "It was so _exciting_ ! Our team won."
2. We need to get to the theater _____. The show starts in 10 minutes.
3. "The concert was great. The singer sang _____." "I agree. I loved her voice."
4. We finally finished the project! Thank you for your _____ work.
5. I'm sorry I'm _____. There was so much traffic.
6. Did the train arrive _____? I was worried because of the bad weather.

C. 다음 문장을 읽고 틀린 부분이 있으면 바르게 고치세요. 틀린 부분이 없으면 O로 표시하세요.

1. Please walk slowly. We don't need to hurry. _____O_____
2. Golf isn't an easily sport. You must practice often. _____
3. I visit that café frequent. It's my favorite place. _____
4. I have to get up early tomorrow. I'm going to the airport. _____
5. "What happened?" "I don't know. The car stopped sudden." _____
6. This painting is lovely! We should buy it. _____
7. Your car looks nice. Is it newly? _____
8. The children are playing noisy on the playground. _____

D. 주어진 형용사를 사용하여 Linda와 Justin의 대화를 완성하세요. 필요한 경우 형용사를 부사로 바꾸어 쓰세요.

late	long	nervous	quick	~~terrible~~

LINDA: What's wrong, Justin? You look sick.
JUSTIN: 1. I have a _terrible_ toothache. It hurts a lot.
LINDA: 2. You should see the dentist _____.
JUSTIN: 3. But I feel _____ when I go to the dentist.
LINDA: 4. Please don't wait too _____.
        5. Go before it's too _____!

LINDA

JUSTIN

정답 p.280, REVIEW TEST 11 p.236

UNIT
067

Grammar Gateway Basic

UNIT **068** | He **always** eats cereal for breakfast. always, often, never ...

🎧 068.mp3

①

| MON | TUE | WED | THU | FRI | SAT | SUN |

He **always** eats cereal for breakfast.

그는 항상 아침으로 시리얼을 먹는다.

---

② 어떤 일을 얼마나 자주 하는지를 말할 때 다음과 같은 부사를 쓴다.

always	**usually**	**often**	**sometimes**	**rarely**	**never**
(항상)	(보통)	(자주)	(가끔)	(좀처럼 ~하지 않는)	(전혀 ~하지 않는)

- I **always** take a shower in the morning. 나는 항상 아침에 샤워를 한다.
- John **usually** wakes up around 7 a.m. John은 보통 오전 7시쯤 일어난다.
- You **often** give me advice. It helps a lot.
- We **sometimes** invite some neighbors to our house on weekends.
- It **rarely** snows here in October.
- Diana **never** drinks coffee at night.

---

③ always, often, never 등은 다음과 같이 쓴다.

일반동사 앞

- Ben **always** checks his e-mail when he arrives at the office. Ben은 사무실에 도착하면 항상 이메일을 확인한다.
- We **rarely** cook dinner these days. We **usually** eat out. 우리는 요즘에 좀처럼 저녁을 요리하지 않는다. 보통 외식한다.
- I **often** travel abroad with a friend, but I **sometimes** go alone.

be동사 뒤

- This hotel is **usually** full during the summer. 이 호텔은 보통 여름 동안에 꽉 찬다.
- I am **rarely** late for work, but my coworkers are **often** late. 나는 좀처럼 직장에 늦지 않지만, 내 동료들은 자주 늦는다.

will/can 등의 뒤

- I will **never** take a taxi to the airport again. It cost over $50! 나는 다시는 절대 공항까지 택시를 타지 않을 거야.
- You can **always** call me when you need help. 네가 도움이 필요할 때 항상 나한테 전화해도 돼.
- We should **often** visit our parents when we have time.

have/has와 과거분사 사이

- We have **never** been to Africa. 우리는 아프리카에 가본 적이 전혀 없다.
- Lynn has **always** lived in this town. Lynn은 항상 이 도시에서 살아왔다.

PRACTICE

A. 둘 중 맞는 것을 고르세요.

1. The bus (rarely / (usually)) comes late, so I don't take it to school.
2. "You used to go fishing (often / rarely). Do you still go regularly?" "No. I'm very busy these days."
3. "Do you drive a lot?" "Only (always / sometimes). I prefer to walk most places."
4. Tommy (never / usually) eats breakfast at home. He eats at a café every morning.
5. We (rarely / sometimes) go to bed late. We are always asleep before 10 p.m.
6. The shopping mall (always / never) has clothing sales, but there weren't any lately.
7. I see you and your dog on 2nd Street a lot. Do you (never / usually) walk there?

B. 다음의 활동들을 얼마나 자주 하는지 always/often/never 등을 사용하여 예시와 같이 자신에 대해 답해보세요.

How often do you …?

1. wear jeans
2. exercise
3. watch movies
4. read books
5. clean your room
6. listen to music

I always wear jeans OR *I never wear jeans*   .
_____ .
_____ .
_____ .
_____ .
_____ .

YOU

C. 괄호 안에 주어진 단어들을 적절히 배열하여 문장을 완성하세요.

1. (a lot of traffic / is / usually / there) *There is usually a lot of traffic*   in the morning.
2. (always / smiling / is / she) Julia seems happy all the time. _____ .
3. (often / plays / Nick) _____ chess with his sister.
4. (never / we / will / move) _____ to the city. We enjoy living in the country.
5. (should / never / you / leave) _____ a baby alone.
6. (Danny / meets / sometimes) _____ his cousins from Belgium.
7. (always / can / you / talk) _____ to me when you have any problems.
8. (finish / rarely / we) _____ work before 8 o'clock.
9. (I / free / am / usually) _____ on Sundays.

D. 주어진 의문문을 보고 괄호 안에 주어진 부사를 사용하여 현재완료 시제 문장을 완성하세요.

1. Have you visited that restaurant?
2. Has your son ever been late for class?
3. Have you wanted to go to Spain?
4. Has Lily ridden in a boat before?
5. Have you ever felt lonely?

(often) I *'ve often visited* OR *have often visited*   there.
(rarely) No. He _____ late for class.
(always) Yes. We _____ to go.
(never) No. She _____ in a boat before.
(sometimes) Yes. I _____ lonely.

정답 p.280, REVIEW TEST 11 p.236

UNIT 069 | The bag is **too** small. too

🎧 069.mp3

①

It's too small!

The bag is **too small**.
가방이 너무 작다.

---

② **too + 형용사/부사**

'(필요 이상으로) 너무 ~한/~하게'라는 의미로 말할 때 **too**를 쓴다.

- Our washing machine is **too old**. We need a new one. 우리 세탁기는 너무 낡았다.
- "I lost my wallet again!" "You lose things **too easily**." 넌 물건을 너무 쉽게 잃어버려.
- Can I turn on the heater? The room is **too cold**.

---

③ **too + 형용사** 뒤에 **for ~** 또는 **to ~**를 함께 쓸 수도 있다.

too + 형용사 + for + 사람: (사람)에게 너무 ~한

- Can you help me? This box is **too heavy for me**. 이 상자는 저에게 너무 무거워요.
- This movie is **too scary for kids**. 이 영화는 아이들에게 너무 무섭다.
- "Is the tea **too hot for you**?" "No, it's OK."

too + 형용사 + to + 동사원형: …하기에는 너무 ~한

- You're only 15 years old. You're **too young to drive**. 너는 운전을 하기에는 너무 어려.
- The supermarket is already closed. It's **too late to buy** groceries. 식료품을 사기에는 너무 늦다.
- I was **too excited to sleep** before the trip, so I stayed awake all night.

---

④ '너무 많은 ~'이라는 의미로 말할 때 **too many/too much ~**를 쓸 수 있다.

too many + 복수명사

- **Too many people** are waiting in line. Let's come back later. 너무 많은 사람들이 줄을 서서 기다리고 있다.
- I made **too many mistakes** on my exam. 나는 시험에서 너무 많은 실수를 했다.

too much + 셀 수 없는 명사

- Don't spend **too much time** on the Internet. 인터넷상에서 너무 많은 시간을 쓰지 마.
- The children are making **too much noise**. I can't read my book here. 아이들이 너무 많은 소음을 내고 있다.

명사 없이 **too many**나 **too much**만 쓸 수도 있다.

- "I'm taking eight classes a day." "Eight? You're taking **too many**." (too many = too many classes)
- I don't have money for my bills. I spent **too much** last month. (too much = too much money)

PRACTICE

A. 그림을 보고 주어진 형용사와 too를 사용하여 문장을 완성하세요.

dark	fast	high	long	~~small~~

1. This bag is
   too small .

2. It's _____
   _____.

3. It's _____
   _____.
   I can't see you.

4. They're _____
   _____.

5. It's _____
   _____.

B. 주어진 형용사와 too ~ for …를 사용하여 예시와 같이 문장을 완성하세요.

~~big~~	early	expensive	hard	spicy

1. Do you want half of my burger? It's _*too big for me*_ _____.
2. We cannot afford to buy that sofa. It's _____.
3. This soup is _____. Can I have a glass of water?
4. Andrew didn't do well on the test. The questions were _____.
5. "Let's meet at 7 p.m." "Henry and Cathy finish work at 8 o'clock. 7 p.m. will be _____."

C. 주어진 표현들을 하나씩 사용하여 문장을 완성하세요.

too busy	~~too full~~	too heavy	+	~~to eat~~	to go	to lift
too large	too sick			to take	to see	

1. "Would you like some ice cream?" "No, thanks. I'm _*too full to eat*_ dessert."
2. I've got a bad cold. I'm _____ to class today.
3. "Should I move the piano in my room?" "It weighs more than 50 kg. It's _____ by yourself."
4. "This museum is huge." "Yes. It's _____ everything in one day."
5. I'm so tired, but I'm _____ a break.

D. 괄호 안에 주어진 명사와 too many 또는 too much를 사용하여 문장을 완성하세요. 필요한 경우 명사를 복수로 쓰세요.

1. (salt) Jenny is not a good cook. She always puts _*too much salt*_ in her food.
2. (rain) "How was your trip?" "I didn't enjoy it because there was _____."
3. (word) This article is very long. It has _____.
4. (car) There are _____ on the road. Let's just walk to the station.
5. (food) I have a stomachache. I had _____.
6. (tourist) _____ visit the Louvre Museum. It's always crowded.

정답 p.280, REVIEW TEST 11 p.236

UNIT
069

Grammar Gateway Basic

UNIT 070 | They aren't big **enough.** enough

🎧 070.mp3

① 형용사/부사 + **enough**

'충분히 ~한/~하게'라는 의미로 말할 때 **enough**를 쓴다.

These pants aren't **big enough.**

- His pants don't fit. They aren't **big enough.**
  그것은 충분히 크지 않다.
- Did I write this report **quickly enough**? It only took me two days.
  제가 이 보고서를 충분히 빠르게 썼나요?
- Mike can get into law school. He's **smart enough.**
- Tina was late for work. She didn't wake up **early enough.**

형용사 + enough + for + 사람: (사람)에게 충분히 ~한

- This book is **easy enough for children.** 이 책은 아이들에게 충분히 쉽다.
- "Is the TV **loud enough for you?**" TV 소리가 당신에게 충분히 큰가요? "Yes, it's fine."

형용사 + enough + to + 동사원형: …하기에 충분히 ~한

- The weather is **cold enough to go** ice skating today. 날씨가 스케이트를 타러 가기에 충분히 춥다.
- I like Mary, but I'm not **brave enough to tell** her. 나는 그녀에게 말하기에 충분히 용감하지 않다.

---

② **enough** + 복수/셀 수 없는 명사

'충분한 ~'이라는 의미로 말할 때 **enough ~**를 쓸 수 있다.

- There aren't **enough seats** on the bus. 버스에 충분한 자리가 없다.
- I got **enough sleep** last night. 나는 어젯밤에 충분한 수면을 취했다.
- "Can we stay at your house tonight?"
  "Of course. There are **enough bedrooms.**"
- "Do we have **enough bread** for lunch?"
  "I'm not sure. Maybe we need some more."

enough + 명사 + for + 사람: (사람)에게 충분한 ~

- I'll drive. There's **enough space for everyone** in my car. 제 차에 모두에게 충분한 공간이 있어요.
- Jane didn't buy **enough tickets for all of us.** She only bought four. Jane은 우리 모두에게 충분한 표를 사지 않았다.

enough + 명사 + to + 동사원형: …하기에 충분한 ~

- Did you save **enough money to pay** the rent? 당신은 집세를 내기에 충분한 돈을 모았나요?
- I don't have **enough time to finish** my homework. 내가 숙제를 끝내기에 충분한 시간이 없다.

---

③ 명사 없이 **enough**만 쓸 수도 있다.

- "Do we need to stop for gas?" "No. We have **enough.**" (enough = enough gas)
- "I'd like some cream for my coffee." "Here you go. Is that **enough?**" (enough = enough cream)

PRACTICE

A. 그림을 보고 주어진 형용사와 enough를 사용하여 문장을 완성하세요.

large	long	loud	~~strong~~	tall

1. She is _strong enough_____.
2. Her voice isn't _____.
3. The space is _____.

4. The boy is _____.
5. His arm isn't _____.

B. 주어진 단어와 enough를 사용하여 문장을 완성하세요.

close	hungry	information	~~jobs~~

1. The new company will provide _enough jobs_____ for 500 people.
2. I'm just going to have a salad. I'm not _____ for a steak.
3. Let's walk to the mall. It's _____ from here.
4. I couldn't find _____ on the Internet for my essay.

doctors	hard	paper	wide

5. Is there _____? I have to print out over 100 pages.
6. Ray tried to score a goal, but he didn't kick the ball _____.
7. We always have to wait at that hospital. There aren't _____.
8. "Do you think this table will fit in the elevator?" "Yes. The door is _____."

C. 괄호 안에 주어진 단어들과 enough를 사용하여 문장을 완성하세요. for 또는 to를 함께 쓰세요.

1. (good, sell) Tim's paintings are _good enough to sell_____. He's an excellent artist.
2. (big, two people) The hotel room had a very small bed. It wasn't _____.
3. (old, drink) My daughter isn't _____ beer. She's only 15.
4. (comfortable, me) I'm not going to buy these shoes. They're not _____.
5. (lucky, meet) During my trip to LA, I was _____ my favorite actor.

D. 괄호 안에 주어진 단어들과 enough를 적절히 배열하여 문장을 완성하세요.

1. (cook / potatoes / to) I'm going to the grocery store. I don't have _enough potatoes to cook_____.
2. (for / books / the students) Our school library doesn't have _____.
3. (get to the station / to / time) "We're late!" "Don't worry. There's _____."
4. (stay healthy / to / exercise) Eric should jog more often. He doesn't do _____.
5. (for / toys / all of our cousins) It's Christmas, so I brought _____.

정답 p.280, REVIEW TEST 11 p.236

UNIT 070

Grammar Gateway Basic

| # The mountain is **so** high. so

🎧 071.mp3

①

The mountain is **so high!**

The mountain is **so high**.
산이 매우 높아요.

---

② **so + 형용사/부사**

'매우'라는 의미로 형용사 또는 부사의 뜻을 강조할 때 **so**를 쓴다.

- This cake is **so good**. Can I have some more? 이 케이크는 매우 맛있어요.
- Can you slow down? You're walking **so fast**. 너는 매우 빠르게 걷고 있어.
- Are you getting married? I'm **so happy** for you!
- I am tired because I got up **so early** this morning.

---

③ '매우 많은 ~'이라는 의미로 말할 때 **so many/much ~**를 쓸 수 있다.

so many + 복수명사

- Katie received **so many gifts** on her birthday. Katie는 생일에 매우 많은 선물을 받았다.
- I made **so many friends** during the trip. 나는 여행 중에 매우 많은 친구들을 사귀었다.
- "Why do you need **so many boxes**?" "I'm moving to a new apartment."
- "I'm sorry. I made **so many mistakes**." "Don't worry. It's OK."

so much + 셀 수 없는 명사

- My kids bring me **so much joy**. 내 아이들은 나에게 매우 많은 즐거움을 가져다준다.
- You should stop drinking **so much coffee**. Then, you'll sleep better.
  너는 매우 많은 커피를 마시는 것을 그만두는 것이 좋겠어.
- "How was the concert?" "It was great. We had **so much fun**."
- I spend **so much time** on the Internet. Maybe I should do something else.

---

④ 명사 없이 **so many**나 **so much**만 쓸 수도 있다.

- I don't know how many guests were at the party. There were **so many**. (so many = so many guests)
- Did you eat all the ice cream? You've eaten **so much**! (so much = so much ice cream)
- "Which book do you want to borrow?" "You have **so many**. It's hard to choose."
- Mr. Pitt taught history, art and math. I've learned **so much** from him.

PRACTICE

A. 그림을 보고 주어진 형용사와 so를 사용하여 문장을 완성하세요.

~~full~~	heavy	long	small	tall

1. I'm _so full_ _____.

2. It's _____ _____.

3. These bags are _____.

4. The line is _____.

5. His hands are _____.

B. 괄호 안에 주어진 명사와 so many 또는 so much를 사용하여 문장을 완성하세요.

1. (snow) "I've never seen _so much snow_ _____ in my life!" "Me neither. It's very beautiful."
2. (passengers) "There were _____ on the bus." "Was it during rush hour?"
3. (food) "Jason cooked _____." "Right. We couldn't eat it all."
4. (questions) "I have _____ for you." "OK. You can ask me now."

C. 주어진 명사와 so many 또는 so much를 사용하여 문장을 완성하세요.

clothes	countries	gas	languages	sisters	~~space~~	sugar	water

1. "How's your new room?" "I love it. It has _so much space_ _____."
2. I have _____. I need another closet.
3. "I can speak English, French and Japanese." "Wow! You speak _____."
4. I'm not going to buy that car. It uses _____.
5. You're wasting _____. Please turn off the shower.
6. You shouldn't eat _____. It's not good for your health.
7. Rick has been to _____. He visited every part of Europe.
8. Carla has _____. She comes from a large family.

D. 괄호 안에 주어진 단어와 so를 사용하여 Linda와 James의 대화를 완성하세요. 필요한 경우 many 또는 much를 함께 쓰세요.

LINDA

LINDA: Look, James! 1. The trees and mountains are _so beautiful_ ! (beautiful)
JAMES: 2. Yes, and it's _____ here. (quiet)
3. There are _____ in the city. (people)
LINDA: I know. Well, let's start climbing the mountain.
JAMES: 4. But the mountain is _____! (high)
5. It'll take _____. (time)
LINDA: Oh, come on, James. Let's just go!

JAMES

정답 p.281, REVIEW TEST 11 p.236

UNIT
071

Grammar Gateway Basic

🎧 072.mp3

①

fast (빠른)　　　　　faster (더 빠른)

A car is fast.

An airplane is **faster.**

비행기가 더 빠르다.

faster는 비교급이다.

---

② '더 ~한/~하게'라는 의미로 말할 때 비교급을 쓴다. 비교급은 일반적으로 형용사/부사 끝에 **-er**을 붙인다.

형용사/부사	hard	high	cold	quiet
비교급	hard**er**	high**er**	cold**er**	quiet**er**

- "Japanese is hard to learn." "I think Chinese is **harder**." 나는 중국어가 더 어려운 것 같아.
- This roller coaster goes high, but that one goes **higher**. 이 롤러코스터는 높이 올라가지만, 저것이 더 높이 올라간다.
- Take your jacket. It might get **colder** tonight.
- This café is noisy. Do you know a **quieter** place?

---

③ 비교급 + **than** ~: ~보다 더 …한/…하게

'~보다'라는 의미로 비교의 대상을 말할 때 비교급 뒤에 **than** ~을 쓴다.

- Silver is **cheaper than** gold. 은이 금보다 더 싸다.
- Ms. Jenner is **kinder than** Mr. Carter. Jenner씨는 Carter씨보다 더 친절하다.
- Sound travels **slower than** light.
- I want a **lighter** racket **than** this one. Can you show me another one?

---

④ **than** 다음에는 다음과 같은 두 가지 형태를 쓸 수 있다.

than	me/him/you 등
	I am/he is/you do 등

- Larry is one year **older than me**. 또는 Larry is one year **older than I am**.
  Larry는 나보다 한 살 더 많다.
- Frank is tall, but his brother is **taller than him**. 또는 Frank is tall, but his brother is **taller than he is**.
  Frank의 형은 그보다 키가 더 크다.
- I always come to work **earlier than you**. 또는 I always come to work **earlier than you do**.

단, **than** 다음에는 **I am/he is** 등 보다 **me/him** 등을 더 자주 쓴다.

- Sharon is **stronger than me**. Sharon은 나보다 힘이 더 세다.
- "How old is Mr. Brown's wife?" "She is five years **younger than him**." 그녀는 그보다 다섯 살 더 어려요.

PRACTICE

A. 주어진 단어의 비교급을 사용하여 문장을 완성하세요.

cold	old	small	~~soft~~	soon	sweet

1. This lotion is great. My skin feels _*softer*_ now.
2. These sandals are too big. Do you have a _____ size?
3. "I think this sauce needs to be _____." "OK. I'll add some more sugar."
4. This winter is _____ than the last one.
5. "I'll finish the report by Friday." "I need it _____. How about Thursday?"
6. "Do you have any sisters?" "Yes. I have two _____ sisters. They're 25 and 28."

B. 그림을 보고 주어진 단어의 비교급과 than을 사용하여 문장을 완성하세요.

long	short	warm	~~young~~

1. Peter is _*younger than Nicole*_ .
2. Mike is _____ .
3. Miami is _____ .
4. The Nile is _____ .

C. 주어진 문장을 보고 괄호 안에 주어진 단어를 사용하여 예시와 같이 다시 말해보세요.

1. One pound is lighter than one kilogram.
   → (heavier) One kilogram _*is heavier than one pound*_ .
2. Theo has higher grades than Nathan.
   → (lower) Nathan _____ .
3. Beth has lighter hair than Jessie.
   → (darker) Jessie _____ .
4. Steel is stronger than aluminum.
   → (weaker) Aluminum _____ .
5. The countryside is quieter than the city.
   → (noisier) The city _____ .

D. 비교급과 than을 사용하여 예시와 같이 두 가지 형태로 문장을 완성하세요.

1. Sean is rich, but Matt is _*richer than him* OR *richer than he is*_ .
2. I'm smart, but my brother is _____ .
3. My wife and I are tall, but our children are _____ .
4. Mary is fast, but John is _____ .
5. I can dive deep, but my dad can dive _____ .
6. High school students study hard, but college students usually study _____ .

정답 p.281, REVIEW TEST 11 p.236

UNIT
072

Grammar Gateway Basic

①  The sofa is **bigger** than the chair.
소파가 의자보다 더 크다.

The chair is **more expensive** than the sofa.
의자가 소파보다 더 비싸다.

---

② -er을 붙일 때 주의해야 할 단어들이 있다.

형용사/부사	nice	wide	big	thin	early	pretty
비교급	nic**er**	wid**er**	big**ger**	thin**ner**	earl**ier**	prett**ier**

- I can't decide which car to buy. This one is **nicer**, but that one is **bigger**. 이것이 더 좋지만, 저것이 더 크다.
- "Does the movie start at 8:30?" "No. It's **earlier** than that. It starts at 7:45." 그것보다 더 일러.
- I like this TV, but I still want a **wider** one.
- "Have you seen Jeff lately? He has gotten **thinner**." "Yes. He has been sick for two weeks."
- "Lucy changed her hairstyle." "I just saw her. She looks **prettier**."

비교급 만드는 방법: 부록 p.250 참고

---

③ 다음과 같이 긴 단어는 앞에 **more**를 쓴다.

형용사/부사	beautiful	carefully	comfortable	expensive
비교급	**more** beautiful	**more** carefully	**more** comfortable	**more** expensive

- I think roses are **more beautiful** than lilies. 나는 장미가 백합보다 더 아름다운 것 같아.
- "I fell off my bike again." "You should ride **more carefully**." 너는 더 조심히 타는 게 좋을 것 같아.
- Let's sit there. Those chairs look **more comfortable**.
- Diamonds are usually **more expensive** than pearls.

  -er로 끝나는 비교급 앞에는 **more**를 쓰지 않는 것에 주의한다.
  - Can you walk **faster**? I'm in a hurry. (more faster로 쓸 수 없음)
  - Water is **healthier** than soda. (more healthier로 쓸 수 없음)

---

④ 다음과 같이 형태가 불규칙적으로 변하는 단어들이 있다.

형용사/부사	good	bad	far
비교급	**better**	**worse**	**farther**

- We should listen to others to make **better** decisions.
  우리는 더 나은 결정을 하기 위해 다른 사람들의 말을 듣는 것이 좋겠다.
- I put some salt in this soup, and now it tastes **worse**!
  내가 이 수프에 약간의 소금을 넣었는데, 이제 맛이 더 안 좋아졌어!
- Which is **farther** from here, LA or San Francisco?

PRACTICE

A. 주어진 단어의 비교급을 쓰세요.

1. long → *longer*
2. thin → _____
3. easy → _____
4. interesting → _____
5. bad → _____

6. low → _____
7. early → _____
8. big → _____
9. serious → _____
10. far → _____

11. wide → _____
12. close → _____
13. good → _____
14. strong → _____
15. important → _____

B. 그림을 보고 비교급을 사용하여 예시와 같이 문장을 완성하세요.

expensive	far	fast	heavy	~~high~~

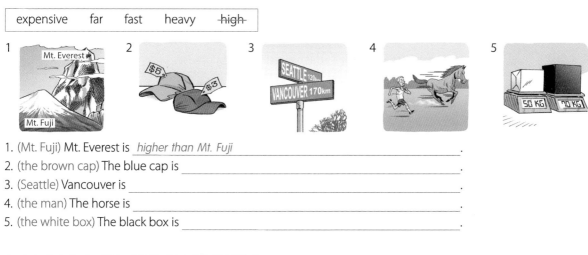

1. (Mt. Fuji) **Mt. Everest is** *higher than Mt. Fuji* .
2. (the brown cap) **The blue cap is** _____ .
3. (Seattle) **Vancouver is** _____ .
4. (the man) **The horse is** _____ .
5. (the white box) **The black box is** _____ .

C. 주어진 단어의 비교급을 사용하여 문장을 완성하세요.

carefully	cheap	~~close~~	happy	hot	large	useful

1. I moved into a new apartment. It's *closer* to my office.
2. "I don't see my red boots here." "Try looking _____."
3. This summer is _____ than last year. We use the air conditioner all day long.
4. "I'm writing an essay, but the textbook isn't helping." "Use the Internet. You'll find _____ information."
5. These pants are too small for me. Do you have a _____ size?
6. "Are you taking a plane?" "No, it's too expensive. The train is _____."
7. "Do you like your new job?" "Yes. I'm _____ than before."

D. 다음 문장을 읽고 틀린 부분이 있으면 바르게 고치세요. 틀린 부분이 없으면 O로 표시하세요.

1. The meeting room is too small. We need a more big place.   *more big → bigger*
2. Health is more important than wealth. _____
3. This puzzle is too difficult. Let's do the more easy one. _____
4. Can you speak louder? I can't hear you. _____
5. Riding a motorcycle is dangerous than driving a car. _____
6. I hope tomorrow's weather will be good than today. _____

정답 p.281, REVIEW TEST 11 p.236

UNIT **073**

Grammar Gateway Basic

Chris is **the tallest** person. 최상급

🎧 074.mp3

①
JUSTIN AMY CHRIS

Amy is taller than Justin. Chris is taller than Amy.

Chris is **the tallest** person.

Chris가 가장 키가 큰 사람이다.

the tallest는 최상급이다.

---

② '가장 ~한'이라는 의미로 말할 때 최상급을 쓴다. 최상급은 주로 형용사/부사 끝에 **-est**를 붙이고, **the**와 함께 쓴다.

형용사/부사	deep	long	new	bright
최상급	the deep**est**	the long**est**	the new**est**	the bright**est**

- Lake Baikal is **the deepest** lake in Russia. 바이칼호는 러시아에서 가장 깊은 호수이다.
- Emily has worked here **the longest**. She started 20 years ago. Emily는 여기에서 가장 오래 일했다.
- That gym just opened. It's **the newest** gym in the city.
- Sirius is **the brightest** star in the night sky.

---

③ 최상급을 만들 때 주의해야 할 단어들이 있다.

형용사/부사	close	large	big	hot	early	easy
최상급	the clos**est**	the larg**est**	the bi**ggest**	the hot**test**	the earl**iest**	the eas**iest**

다음과 같이 긴 단어(2음절 이상)는 앞에 **most**를 쓴다.

형용사/부사	popular	crowded	widely
최상급	the **most** popular	the **most** crowded	the **most** widely

다음과 같이 형태가 불규칙적으로 변하는 단어들이 있다.

형용사/부사	good	bad	far
최상급	the **best**	the **worst**	the **farthest**

최상급 만드는 방법: 부록 p.250 참고

- "Where is **the closest** bank from here?" 여기에서 가장 가까운 은행이 어디에 있나요? "Just around the corner."
- That hotel has **the biggest** swimming pool in town. 저 호텔은 시내에서 가장 큰 수영장을 가지고 있다.
- "Have you waited long?" "No, but Tina has. She arrived the **earliest**."
- This is **the most popular** song these days. Everyone listens to it.
- I had **the best** birthday! It was so fun.

  -est로 끝나는 최상급 앞에는 **most**를 쓰지 않는 것에 주의한다.
  - The library is **the largest** building on campus. (the most largest로 쓸 수 없음)

---

④ 다음과 같이 명사 없이 최상급만 쓸 수도 있다.
- I'm **the youngest** in my family. 나는 우리 가족 중에서 가장 어리다.
- "Do you have a cheaper camera?" "No. That's **the cheapest** in the store." 그것이 가게에서 가장 싼 거예요.

PRACTICE

A. 주어진 단어의 비교급과 최상급을 쓰세요.

1. low   - *lower*   - *the lowest*
2. beautiful - _____ - _____
3. good   - _____ - _____
4. clean   - _____ - _____

5. hot   - _____ - _____
6. happy   - _____ - _____
7. large   - _____ - _____
8. bad   - _____ - _____

B. 주어진 단어들을 사용하여 문장을 완성하세요. 최상급으로 쓰세요.

busy	creative	delicious	fresh	~~hard~~	strong

1. (decision) Choosing a college was *the hardest decision* _____ of my life.
2. (person) Cindy has many good ideas. She is _____ on my team.
3. (animals) Elephants can lift heavy things. They're one of _____ .
4. (man) Mr. Miller is _____ in our office. He always works late.
5. (dish) "Is the curry here good?" "Yes. It is _____ at this restaurant."
6. (vegetables) "That market sells _____ in town." "I should buy some carrots there, then."

C. 그림을 보고 주어진 단어의 비교급과 최상급을 사용하여 예시와 같이 문장을 완성하세요.

expensive	~~fast~~	high	young

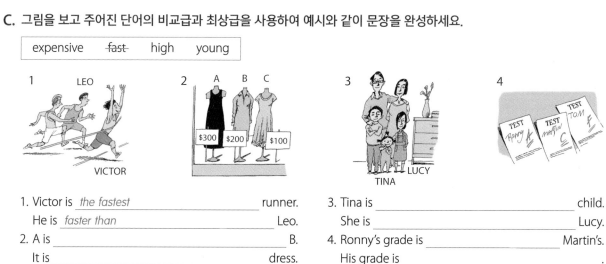

1. Victor is *the fastest* _____ runner.
   He is *faster than* _____ Leo.
2. A is _____ B.
   It is _____ dress.

3. Tina is _____ child.
   She is _____ Lucy.
4. Ronny's grade is _____ Martin's.
   His grade is _____ .

D. 다음 운동선수들에 대한 정보를 보고 괄호 안에 주어진 단어의 최상급을 사용하여 예시와 같이 문장을 완성하세요.

	JIMMY	STEVEN	KEVIN
Height	194 cm	190 cm	206 cm
Weight	81 kg	86 kg	92 kg
Age	23	25	19
Ranking	1st	3rd	2nd

1. (tall) Kevin *is the tallest* _____ .
2. (old) Steven _____ .
3. (good) Jimmy _____ player.
4. (heavy) Kevin _____ .
5. (short) Steven _____ .

정답 p.281, REVIEW TEST 11 p.236

UNIT 075 | Chris is **as** heavy **as** Paul. as ~ as

075.mp3

①

Chris is **as heavy as** Paul.

Chris는 Paul만큼 무겁다. (즉, 둘의 몸무게가 같음)

② **as + 형용사/부사 + as**

'~만큼 …한/…하게'라는 의미로 말할 때 **as ~ as**를 쓸 수 있다.

- I know Julie's sister. She's **as beautiful as** Julie. 그녀는 Julie만큼 아름답다.
- Mason speaks French **as well as** a native speaker. Mason은 원어민만큼 프랑스어를 잘한다.
- The film was **as interesting as** the book.
- Anita is 16 years old. She is **as old as** me.

③ **not as + 형용사/부사 + as ~**: ~만큼 …하지 않은/…하지 않게

- These cookies are **not as good as** Laura's. 이 쿠키들은 Laura의 것만큼 맛있지 않다.
- I don't watch the news **as often as** my dad. 나는 아빠만큼 뉴스를 자주 보지 않는다.
- "It's very hot this summer." "Yes, but it's **not as hot as** last year."
- William doesn't jog **as regularly as** before. He's busy these days.

not as ~ as와 같은 의미로 **비교급 + than**도 쓸 수 있다.

- This lamp is **not as bright as** that one. 이 램프는 저것만큼 밝지 않다.
  또는 That lamp is **brighter than** this one. 저 램프는 이것보다 더 밝다.
- Terry doesn't eat **as quickly as** his brother.
  또는 Terry's brother eats **more quickly than** Terry.

④ **as ~ as possible**: 가능한 한 ~하게

as soon as possible	가능한 한 빨리
as long as possible	가능한 한 오래
as early as possible	가능한 한 일찍

- Please come home **as soon as possible**. 가능한 한 빨리 집에 와.
- We'll wait for you **as long as possible**. 우리는 너를 가능한 한 오래 기다릴 거야.
- "Let's leave **as early as possible** to avoid traffic." "Good idea."

PRACTICE

A. 그림을 보고 주어진 단어와 as ~ as를 사용하여 문장을 완성하세요.

cheap	fast	heavy	~~long~~	new	tall

1	JENNY	I've lived in Seoul for two years. I've lived in Seoul for two years.	TED	4	ROBERT	I'm 175 cm tall. I'm 175 cm tall.	FRED
2	JIM	I can run 100 meters in 17 seconds. I can run 100 meters in 17 seconds.	ANNA	5	JASON	My luggage weighs 30 kg. My luggage weighs 30 kg.	JOY
3	HELEN	My shoes cost only $20. My shoes cost only $20.	SARAH	6	NICK	I bought a new car yesterday. I bought a new car yesterday.	PAULA

1. Ted has lived in Seoul *as long as*   Jenny.
2. Anna can run _____ Jim.
3. Helen's shoes are _____ Sarah's.

4. Robert is _____ Fred.
5. Jason's luggage is _____ Joy's.
6. Paula's car is _____ Nick's.

B. 주어진 문장을 보고 not as ~ as를 사용하여 예시와 같이 문장을 완성하세요.

1. Katie was born in 1990. Tom was born in 1992.
2. I can eat three donuts. Jim can eat five donuts.
3. The park is 5 km away. The mall is 10 km away.
4. Sally goes to work at 9. Ian goes to work at 8.
5. This tower is 5 m tall. That tower is 7 m tall.
6. It's 3 degrees in Beijing. It's 9 degrees in Tokyo.

(old) Tom *isn't as old as Katie* OR *is not as old as Katie*
(much) I _____.
(far) The park _____.
(early) Sally _____.
(high) This tower _____.
(cold) Tokyo _____.

C. B의 문장을 비교급과 than을 사용하여 예시와 같이 다시 말해보세요.

1. Katie *is older than Tom*   .
2. Jim _____.
3. The mall _____.
4. Ian _____.
5. That tower _____.
6. Beijing _____.

D. 주어진 단어와 as ~ as possible을 사용하여 문장을 완성하세요.

carefully	loud	often	quickly	~~soon~~

1. I can't talk now, but I'll call you back *as soon as possible*   .
2. There are glasses in those boxes, so carry them _____.
3. This is our favorite restaurant. We come here _____.
4. I still can't hear the music. Turn up the volume _____.
5. The meeting won't take long. We'll finish _____.

UNIT 075

Grammar Gateway Basic

I'll meet you **at** the bus stop. 장소 전치사 at, in, on (1)

🎧 076.mp3

①

at the bus stop
버스 정류장에서

in the living room
거실 안에서

on the floor
바닥 위에서

'(어디)에/에서'라는 뜻으로 장소를 말할 때 **at, in, on**을 쓸 수 있다.

- I'll meet you **at the bus stop.** (버스 정류장에서)
- They're watching TV **in the living room.** (거실 안에서)
- My sister is doing yoga **on the floor.**

② 어떤 지점에 있다고 말할 때 **at**을 쓴다.

> **at** the mall   **at** the door/window   **at** the desk   **at** the corner   **at** the traffic light

- I bought this coat **at the mall.** It was on sale. (쇼핑몰에서)
- "Who's **at the door?**" "It might be Ted." (문 앞에)
- You can leave your room key **at the desk** in the hotel lobby.
- Go straight and turn right **at the corner.** Then you'll see the bookstore.
- All cars must stop **at the traffic light** when the light is red.

③ 어떤 공간 안에 있다고 말할 때는 **in**을 쓴다.

> **in** the room   **in** the box   **in** the forest   **in** Paris   **in** the car

- Tim is talking on the phone **in the room.** (방 안에서)
- Please put these books **in the box.** (상자 안에)
- I was hiking **in the forest**, and I saw a bear.
- Michelle will spend this summer **in Paris.**
- "I think I left my gloves **in the car.**" "Should we go back?"

④ 어떤 표면에 또는 표면 위에 있다고 말할 때는 **on**을 쓴다.

> **on** the wall   **on** the table   **on** the ceiling   **on** the sofa   **on** the bench

- The clock **on the wall** isn't working. It needs new batteries. (벽에)
- "Have you seen my bag?" "Yes. It's **on the table.**" (탁자 위에)
- Look! There's a bee **on the ceiling**!
- "Where's Tony?" "He's lying **on the sofa.**"
- Don't sit **on the bench.** I just painted it.

PRACTICE

A. 그림을 보고 at/in/on을 사용하여 문장을 완성하세요.

1. There are three people *in* the room.
2. A picture is hanging _____ the wall.
3. A dog is sleeping _____ the floor.
4. There are apples _____ the basket.
5. A man is sitting _____ the desk.

6. A woman is standing _____ the window.
7. There are flowers _____ the vase.
8. There are toys _____ the box.
9. A cat is sitting _____ the sofa.
10. A little boy is standing _____ the door.

B. at/in/on을 써넣으세요.

1. I studied English *in* Canada four years ago.
2. "Why is Dad _____ the garage?" "He's fixing the car."
3. "Where did you see Nick?" "_____ the bus stop."
4. There was a lot of trash _____ the ground after the hurricane.
5. The people _____ the bench are eating sandwiches.
6. "Where are we getting off?" "_____ the next station."
7. "What's that _____ the shelf?" "It's raspberry jam. I made it yesterday."
8. "Is there any juice _____ the fridge?" "No. There's only water."

C. 괄호 안에 주어진 표현과 at/in/on을 사용하여 Justin과 James의 대화를 완성하세요.

JUSTIN: Dad, I'm bored. Where's Chris?
JAMES: 1. He's *in his room* . (his room)
2. He's studying _____. (his desk)
JUSTIN: Oh. Then where's Amy?
JAMES: 3. She's doing yoga _____. (the living room)
JUSTIN: Well, what about Mom?
JAMES: 4. She's _____. (the mall)
If you're bored, you could read something.
5. There are some magazines _____. (the table)

JUSTIN

JAMES

정답 p.282, REVIEW TEST 12 p.238

UNIT

076

Grammar Gateway Basic

① **at**을 사용한 다음과 같은 표현이 있다.

직장·학교 등 일상적으로 다니는 장소	**at** work **at** the doctor's (office)	**at** home **at** somebody's (house)	**at** school	**at** church
역·공항	**at** the station	**at** the airport		
행사·공연·경기	**at** a party	**at** a concert	**at** a baseball game	

- I don't have to wear a suit **at work**. (회사에서)
- "Can you wait for me **at the station**?" "OK. I'll be there." (역에서)
- I was **at a party** last night. I had a great time.
- Sally wasn't feeling well, so she stayed **at home**.
- Last night, we had dinner **at Laura's**.

② **in**을 사용한 다음과 같은 표현이 있다.

하늘·태양 등 자연환경	**in** the world	**in** the sky	**in** the ocean
책·사진 등 인쇄물	**in** a book	**in** a picture	**in** a newspaper
(어떤 장소에서) ~하는 중인	**in** bed (침대에 누워 있는 중인/잠자는 중인) **in** the hospital (병원에 입원 중인)	**in** prison/jail (감옥에 수감 중인)	

- Mount Everest is the highest mountain **in the world**. (세계에서)
- "Have you ever heard of Isaac Newton?" "Yes. I read about him **in a book**." (책에서)
- "What were you doing this morning? I called you five times!" "Sorry. I was **in bed**."
- Look! Can you see those stars **in the sky**?
- Jim is **in the hospital**. He's having surgery tomorrow.

③ **on**을 사용한 다음과 같은 표현이 있다.

거리	**on** 2nd Avenue	**on** Main Street	
층	**on** the first floor	**on** the 3rd floor	
교통수단	**on** the train 예외) **in** the car	**on** the bus **in** the taxi	**on** the plane

- "Is your office **on 2nd Avenue**?" "Yes. It's not far from here." (2번가에)
- "Excuse me. I'm looking for the restroom." "It's **on the first floor**." (1층에)
- I bought a newspaper to read **on the train**.
- I saw a famous actor **on the plane** yesterday.
- "Where is your luggage?" "I put it **in the car**."

PRACTICE

A. 그림을 보고 주어진 장소와 at/in/on을 사용하여 문장을 완성하세요.

2nd Avenue	a birthday party	~~school~~	the bus	the sky

1. The students are _at school_____.
2. The bookstore is _____.
3. They are _____.

4. There are birds _____.
5. They are _____.

B. at/in/on을 써넣으세요.

1. "I can't see you _in_____ the picture." "I'm there, at the back."
2. "Are you going out tonight?" "I might just watch TV _____ home."
3. Mr. Brown's house is _____ Oak Street.
4. Could you meet me _____ the airport? I'll arrive at 12 p.m.
5. "Is the cafeteria _____ the 2nd floor?" "No. The 3rd floor."
6. "Where's your brother?" "He's waiting _____ the car."

C. 주어진 표현과 at/in/on을 사용하여 문장을 완성하세요.

a book	Ann's house	prison	the concert
the first floor	the train	~~the world~~	

1. Whales are the largest animals _in the world_____.
2. "What kind of music will the bands play _____?" "Jazz, I think."
3. Sorry I'm late. I fell asleep _____ and missed my stop.
4. I was _____ last night. Her room is so big.
5. "Where did you find that information?" "_____ from the library."
6. The thief was _____ for two years because he stole expensive jewelry.
7. "Excuse me. Where's customer service?" "It's _____ of this building."

D. 괄호 안에 주어진 장소와 at/in/on을 사용하여 Sandy와 Amy의 대화를 완성하세요.

SANDY: Where's Justin today?
1. I didn't see him _at school_____. (school)
AMY: 2. He's sick and needs to stay _____. (bed)
3. He was _____ this morning. (the doctor's office)
SANDY: 4. The one _____? (Main Street)
AMY: 5. Yes, but he is feeling better, and he's _____ now. (home)

AMY

SANDY

정답 p.282, REVIEW TEST 12 p.238

🎧 078.mp3

①

in front of: ~ 앞에
- The bus stop is **in front of my house**. (내 집 앞에)
- Daniel is waiting for you **in front of the station**. (역 앞에서)
- Jessica can speak well **in front of people**.

behind: ~ 뒤에
- "Where is my scarf?" "It's **behind the chair**." (의자 뒤에)
- I sit **behind Tate** in history class. (Tate 뒤에)
- "Can I park my car **behind the building**?" "Sorry, but you can't."

②

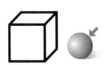

by, next to: ~ 옆에
- We had a picnic **by the lake** last weekend. (호수 옆에서)
- "Who's the girl **next to Jake**?" "Angela. She's from Canada." (Jake 옆에)
- "I'll meet you **by the elevator**." "OK. Sounds good."
- Philip is my neighbor. His house is **next to mine**.

③

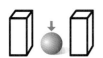

between: (명확히 구분된 둘 이상의 사람·사물) 사이에
- That's my brother. He's standing **between Emily and Lynn**. (Emily와 Lynn 사이에)
- The bank is **between the mall and the pharmacy**. (쇼핑몰과 약국 사이에)
- I can't decide **between the cake, the donut, and the cookie** for dessert.

among: (명확히 구분되어 있지 않은 셋 이상의 그룹·집단) 중에
- Joan is the tallest girl **among the students** in her class. (학생들 중에)
- The children are hiding **among the trees**. (나무들 중에)
- Who is the best player **among the team members**?

④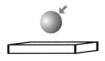

over: ~ 위에
- A lamp is hanging **over the table**. (탁자 위에)
- It started raining, so Dave held an umbrella **over her head**. (머리 위에)
- Can you see the rainbow **over that river**?

under: ~ 아래에
- I found a coin **under the sofa**. (소파 아래에서)
- "My slippers are missing." "Did you look **under the bed**?" (침대 아래에)
- When we went to Paris, we took a picture **under the Eiffel Tower**.

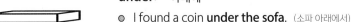

PRACTICE

A. 그림을 보고 in front of/behind/by/next to를 써넣으세요.

1. Sarah is *in front of* _____ Ben.
2. Tom is standing _____ Mary.
3. There is someone _____ the curtain.
4. The kids are walking _____ the woman.
5. Nicolas is sitting _____ Nancy.

B. 그림을 보고 between/among/over/under를 써넣으세요.

1. The bench is *between* _____ two large trees.
2. There are clouds _____ the mountains.
3. There is a cat _____ several dogs.
4. A man is sleeping _____ the tree.
5. Mike is sitting _____ the two men.

C. 둘 중 맞는 것을 고르세요.

1. "Who is Mr. Nelson?" "The man standing ((between) / among) Mr. Smith and Mr. Miller."
2. I can't see the professor. The man (behind / in front of) me is too tall.
3. "Can I sit (next to / over) you?" "Sorry. This seat is taken."
4. There is a police car (in front of / behind) us. Why is it following us?
5. In China, the Great Wall is the most popular place to visit (over / among) tourists.
6. There is a park (by / between) my house. I go there often.
7. There's a new exit sign (over / among) the door. We put it there yesterday.
8. I woke up on Christmas morning and found many presents (under / over) the Christmas tree.

D. James와 Linda는 외출 후에 집으로 돌아가려고 합니다. 둘 중 맞는 것을 골라 James와 Linda의 대화를 완성하세요.

JAMES

JAMES: Where are you going?
  1. Our car is ((in front of) / over) the supermarket.
LINDA: 2. No, we parked it (between / behind) the store.
JAMES: Wait! I found it. 3. It's (next to / among) that bank.
LINDA: Where? I don't see it.
JAMES: 4. There's a white car (under / between) the truck and the van.
LINDA: That's not ours. Oh, I just remembered! We took the subway!

LINDA

정답 p.282, REVIEW TEST 12 p.238

UNIT **078**

Grammar Gateway Basic

Where is this letter **from**? 방향 전치사

🎧 079.mp3

① from: ~으로부터　　to: ~으로

 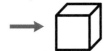

up: ~ 위로　　down: ~ 아래로

- Where is this letter **from**? (어디로부터)
- I'm traveling **to Europe** next week. (유럽으로)
- Susie's family came **from Vietnam**.
- We went **to the museum** last weekend.

- Jim went **up the ladder** to fix the roof. (사다리 위로)
- A rock is rolling **down the hill**. (언덕 아래로)
- Look! A spider is climbing **up the wall**.
- Firefighters are coming **down the stairs**.

② into: ~ 안으로　　out of: ~ 밖으로

over: ~을 넘어서　　under: ~ 아래로

- Ann poured soda **into the glasses**. (유리잔 안으로)
- Ken took his keys **out of his pocket**. (주머니 밖으로)
- Please come **into my office**.
- Can you take the bread **out of the oven**?

- We're flying **over the Grand Canyon**! (그랜드 캐니언을 넘어서)
- I'm walking **under the bridge**. (다리 아래로)
- A cat jumped **over the chair**.
- The dolphins just passed **under the boat**.

③ through: ~을 통과해서　　across: ~을 가로질러

 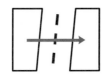

along: ~을 따라서　　around: ~을 돌아서

- The Nile flows **through Egypt**. (이집트를 통과해서)
- Don't walk **across the road**. (도로를 가로질러)
- We carried the piano **through the door**.
- The actors danced **across the stage**.

- I jogged **along the beach** for an hour. (해변을 따라서)
- The boats sail **around the island**. (섬을 돌아서)
- Flowers are growing **along the lake**.
- Jane rode her bicycle **around the track**.

④ on: ~ 위에　　off: ~에서 (떨어져)

past: ~을 지나서　　toward: ~ 쪽으로

- Can you put the bags **on the sofa**? (소파 위에)
- Sam fell **off the bed** and woke up. (침대에서 떨어져)
- I'll leave this report **on your desk**.
- We need to get **off the train** soon.

- I drive **past the mall** every day. (쇼핑몰을 지나서)
- The bird flew **toward the tree**. (나무 쪽으로)
- We went **past the bus stop** by mistake.
- The children ran **toward their parents**.

PRACTICE

A. 그림을 보고 괄호 안에 주어진 동사와 적절한 전치사를 사용하여 문장을 완성하세요. 현재진행 시제로 쓰세요.

along	~~into~~	out of	over	up

1. (dive) She *'s diving into* OR *is diving into* the pool.
2. (go) The car _____ the bridge.
3. (get) They _____ school.

4. (drive) The car _____ the river.
5. (walk) She _____ the stairs.

across	around	off	past	through

6. (pass) The train _____ the tunnel.
7. (go) The car _____ the bank.
8. (fall) He _____ the table.

9. (walk) She _____ the street.
10. (drive) The car _____ the fountain.

B. 주어진 전치사를 써넣으세요.

~~around~~	down	into	over	to	under

1. "Where is the zoo?" "Go *around* that corner, and you'll find it on the left."
2. "The elevator is broken. We have to ride _____ the escalator." "Oh, no! We're on the top floor."
3. I found Andy. He was hiding _____ his desk!
4. The baseball player hit the ball _____ the fence! It's a home run!
5. "Did you spend your vacation in Hawaii?" "No, I went _____ Bali."
6. Ted read the letters and threw them _____ the trash can.

from	off	on	out of	through	toward

7. My neighbors moved here _____ Chicago last year. They lived there for a few years.
8. John is running _____ the finish line. I think he'll win the race!
9. "Ouch! You stepped _____ my foot." "Oh, I'm sorry."
10. Rachel didn't like the picture, so she took it _____ the wall.
11. A storm passed _____ the city last night. Many houses were damaged.
12. You should get _____ bed! You're late for school!

정답 p.282, REVIEW TEST 12 p.238

UNIT **079**

Grammar Gateway Basic

①

at 5:30 **on Monday** **in July**

5시 30분에 월요일에 7월에

'(시간)에'라는 뜻으로 시간을 말할 때 **at, on, in**을 쓸 수 있다.

- "What time does the plane arrive?" "It arrives **at 5:30.**" (5시 30분에)
- Do you want to go hiking **on Monday**? (월요일에)
- Angela is moving to Sydney **in July**.

② **at**

| 시각 | **at** 10:30 | **at** noon | **at** 3 o'clock |
| 식사 | **at** breakfast | **at** lunch | **at** dinner |

- Every night, I go to sleep **at 10:30.** (10시 30분에)
- We can talk about our business trip **at lunch.** (점심 식사 때)
- The library opens **at noon** on Sunday.
- "I had a good time **at dinner** last night." "I'm glad to hear that."

③ **on**

요일	**on** Wednesday/Saturday	**on** Friday night/Sunday morning
평일·주말	**on** weekdays/a weekday	**on** weekends/the weekend
날짜·기념일	**on** May 21 **on** my birthday	**on** our anniversary

- I have an interview **on Wednesday.** (수요일에)
- We work late **on weekdays**, so we sleep in **on weekends**. (주중에, 주말에)
- "My wedding is **on May 21.** Can you come?" "Of course I can!"
- I usually get a call from my parents **on my birthday**.

④ **in**

월·계절	**in** January/June/December	**in** (the) spring/summer/fall/winter
세기·연도	**in** the 19th century	**in** 2018
오전·오후·저녁	**in** the morning/afternoon/evening	예외) **at** night

- It often snows here **in January.** (1월에)
- Cars were invented **in the 19th century.** (19세기에)
- I always go to the park for a walk early **in the morning**.
- The tennis court has lights, so we can play **at night**.

PRACTICE

A. 그림을 보고 적절한 명사와 at/on/in을 사용하여 문장을 완성하세요.

1  2  3  4  5

1. Patrick's birthday is *on Friday* .
2. Carol got the message _____ .
3. The building was built _____ .
4. He often exercises _____
5. Gina is having lunch with Greg _____ .

B. at/on/in을 써넣으세요.

1. I'll tell you about my plans *at* dinner tonight.
2. My parents are going to move into a new house _____ Saturday.
3. "I'm going to bed. I'll see you _____ breakfast." "OK. Good night."
4. "When are you leaving for London?" "_____ January 15."
5. New York is very beautiful _____ the fall.
6. "Kelly was born _____ 1975." "Wow, she looks so young."
7. We're going to a concert today. It starts _____ noon.
8. I can't watch TV _____ weekdays. I'm too busy.

C. 괄호 안에 주어진 표현과 at/on/in을 사용하여 문장을 완성하세요.

1. (Sunday) "I'm going to play baseball *on Sunday* ." "That will be fun."
2. (February) The new mall will open _____ .
3. (lunch) "Do you check your e-mails _____ ?" "No, not usually."
4. (10 a.m.) The meeting is _____ tomorrow morning.
5. (our anniversary) My husband gave me a necklace _____ .
6. (the 20th century) Christmas trees started becoming popular _____ .
7. (the evening) Amanda takes her dog for a walk _____ .
8. (Saturday night) We're going to a bar _____ . Can you join us?

D. 괄호 안에 주어진 표현과 at/on/in을 사용하여 Justin과 Sandy의 대화를 완성하세요.

JUSTIN: 1. I'm having a party *on my birthday* . (my birthday)
SANDY: When is your birthday? 2. Is it _____ ? (the weekend)
JUSTIN: No. It's this Friday.
3. The party starts _____ . (11 o'clock)
SANDY: 4. Sorry. I can't go _____ . (the morning)
5. Can you meet me _____ or _____ ?
(the afternoon) (night) I'll buy you dinner.

JUSTIN   SANDY

정답 p.283, REVIEW TEST 12 p.238

① **during**과 **for**

during + the day, the basketball game 등: ~ 동안에

- Bats sleep **during the day**. (낮 동안에)
- Terry got hurt **during the basketball game**. (농구 경기 동안에)
- I went to Italy **during the holidays**.
- "Did you visit many places **during your trip** to Ireland?" "Yes, we did."

for + a second, three years 등: ~ 동안 (내내)

- "Can I talk to you **for a second**?" "Sure." (잠시 동안)
- Holly has studied French **for three years**. (3년 동안)
- I have known Kevin **for a long time**.
- We cleaned the house **for two hours**, but it's still dirty.

> **during**과 **for** 모두 '~ 동안'이라는 뜻이지만, 언제 일어나는지를 말할 때는 **during**을 쓰는 것에 비해, 얼마나 오래 계속되는지를 말할 때는 **for**를 쓰는 것에 주의한다.

- I usually exercise **during lunch**. I feel refreshed.
  (언제 운동을 했는지를 말하기 위해 during을 썼음)

  I usually exercise **for an hour**. I do yoga first, then I jog.
  (얼마나 오래 운동을 계속 했는지를 말하기 위해 for를 썼음)

- We are going to travel in Asia **during the summer**. I hope it's not too hot when we go.
  We are going to travel in Asia **for two months**. We'll spend our whole vacation there.

② **in**과 **within**

in + 10 minutes, two hours 등 (기간): ~ 후에

- "Are you ready?" "Not yet. I'll be ready **in 10 minutes**." (10분 후에)
- The store will close **in two hours**. (두 시간 후에)
- Harry and Julie will get married **in one month**.
- It's my mom's birthday **in a few days**. I have to buy a gift for her.

within + 15 minutes, four days 등 (기간): ~ 이내에

- I can get there **within 15 minutes**, so I'll see you soon. (15분 이내에)
- Please pay this bill **within four days**. (4일 이내에)
- You should return the book **within three weeks**. There is a fee if you're late.
- Tickets for the show were sold out **within a couple of hours**.

PRACTICE

A. 다음은 Howard 여행사의 여행 일정 중 일부입니다. 일정을 보고 during 또는 for를 써넣으세요.

DAY 2 SCHEDULE	
09:00 ~ 11:00	Swimming at the beach
11:00 ~ 12:00	**[Free time]** - You can take pictures.
12:00 ~ 13:00	**[Lunch time]** - You can take a break.
13:00 ~ 15:00	Visiting the museum
15:00 ~ 18:00	Going to Central Park
18:00 ~ 20:00	**[Dinner time]** - You can go shopping.

1. Tourists will go swimming _for_ two hours.
2. They can take pictures _____ their free time.
3. They can take a break _____ lunch time.
4. They will visit the museum _____ two hours.
5. They will go to Central Park _____ three hours.
6. They can go shopping _____ dinner time.

B. 괄호 안에 주어진 표현과 during 또는 for를 사용하여 대화를 완성하세요.

1. How long has Jimmy been asleep?	(about 10 hours) _For about 10 hours_ .
2. When did you get a haircut?	(the weekend) _____ .
3. How long have you collected stamps?	(eight years) _____ .
4. When did Amber leave the office?	(our meeting) _____ .
5. When were these pictures taken?	(the winter) _____ .
6. How long should I cook this sauce?	(five minutes) _____ .
7. How long have you worked here?	(about four months) _____ .

C. 둘 중 맞는 것을 고르세요.

1. The race lasted 50 minutes. All the runners finished (during / (within)) an hour.
2. "It's noon right now. Let's meet at 12:30." "OK. I'll see you (in / during) 30 minutes."
3. People cannot smoke (during / for) the flight.
4. I have played the flute (in / for) three years, but I can't play very well.
5. Frank was very nervous (within / during) his first job interview.
6. The winner of the contest will be announced (for / within) two weeks.
7. The lecture will begin (in / for) exactly 45 minutes. Please don't be late.

D. 다음 문장을 읽고 틀린 부분이 있으면 바르게 고치세요. 틀린 부분이 없으면 O로 표시하세요.

1. The guests will come in an hour, so dinner should be ready by then. O
2. I didn't sleep well yesterday. I woke up several times for the night. _____
3. It's Friday already! Our vacation starts next Friday, so it's within a week. _____
4. Sam wants to stay at my house during one night. _____
5. I've lived in this city for a month. I moved here four weeks ago. _____
6. We have a 60-minute lunch break, so we must eat in an hour. _____
7. I couldn't open my eyes during the horror movie. It was so scary! _____

정답 p.283, REVIEW TEST 12 p.238

① **from ~ to** …: ~부터 …까지

- The café is open **from 2 to 9 p.m.** (오후 2시부터 9시까지)
- I work five days a week, **from Monday to Friday.** (월요일부터 금요일까지)
- "How long will you stay in Africa?" "**From January to March.**"
- Mr. Chan was the president **from 2013 to last year.**

from 2 to 9 p.m.

  to … 없이 **from ~**만 쓸 수도 있다.
  - Call me in the afternoon. I'll be in my office **from 12 p.m.** (오후 12시부터)
  - Our class will begin doing group projects **from November.** (11월부터)

  from ~ to …와 같은 의미로 **from ~ until** …을 쓸 수 있다.
  - It usually snows a lot here **from December until February.** (12월부터 2월까지)
  - Dr. Kim sees patients **from 9 a.m. until 6 p.m.** (오전 9시부터 오후 6시까지)

② **since**: ~부터 (계속)

since는 특정 시점부터 어떤 행동이나 상황이 계속된다고 할 때 쓴다.

- This museum has been open **since 1970.** (1970년부터)
- Tom has been on vacation **since Tuesday.** (화요일부터)
- I'm hungry. I haven't eaten anything **since breakfast.**
- Betty has had short hair **since high school.**

since 1970

③ **by**: (늦어도) ~까지

by는 늦어도 정해진 시점까지 어떤 행동이나 상황이 끝난다고 할 때 쓴다.

- You should drink this milk **by June 17.** (늦어도 6월 17일까지)
- I'm going to be late. I can't get there **by 8.** (8시까지)
- "Could you finish this work **by next Wednesday**?" "Sure. I can do it."
- "Have our guests arrived yet?" "No, but they will arrive **by noon.**"

by June 17

④ **until**: ~까지 계속

until은 특정 시점까지 어떤 행동이나 상황이 계속된다고 할 때 쓴다.

- The road will be closed **until Friday.** (금요일까지 계속)
- I won't be home **until 9 p.m.** tonight. (오후 9시까지 계속)
- "Can I keep this book **until Saturday**?" "Yes, that's fine."
- "When can we meet?"
  "Is Friday OK? I won't have any time **until Thursday.**"

until Friday

PRACTICE

A. 그림을 보고 from ~ to …를 사용하여 문장을 완성하세요.

1	2	3	4	5

1. The class is *from 9 a.m. to 11 a.m.* _____.
2. The road is closed _____.
3. The store is open _____.
4. Drivers cannot park _____.
5. The tickets will be on sale _____.

B. 괄호 안에 주어진 동사와 since를 사용하여 Brian에 대한 문장을 완성하세요. 현재완료 시제로 쓰세요.

1. I'm in Egypt. I came here last week.
2. I met Jason in high school.
3. I don't smoke anymore. I quit last year.
4. I got married in July.
5. I have a car. I bought it in 2014.

BRIAN

(be) He *has been in Egypt since last week* ____.
(know) He _____.
(not smoke) He _____.
(be married) He _____.
(have) He _____.

C. by 또는 until을 써넣으세요.

1. I studied *until* 11 o'clock last night. I have an important test today.
2. This coupon must be used _____ August 3, and it can only be used once.
3. Some of my friends are coming to visit. They will stay with me _____ Friday.
4. "I have to write an essay _____ next Monday." "I'll help you with it."
5. The plane leaves at 3:30 p.m. We should arrive at the airport _____ 2 p.m.
6. The football game lasted _____ midnight. It was so long but exciting.

D. 다음은 The Rock Stars의 공연을 소개하는 블로그입니다. from ~ to …/by/until을 써넣으세요.

The Rock Stars Come to Springfield

THE ROCK STARS
COME TO SPRINGFIELD

From July 1st to July 7th

The Rock Stars are finally coming to town!
1. Ticket sales began last month and will end *by* July 1.
The band will play five concerts.
2. The concerts are _____ July 2 _____ July 6. They start at 8 p.m.
3. The concert hall will be very crowded, so if you want a good seat, you should arrive _____ 7:30.
4. Note: Please do not take any pictures _____ the end of the show.

정답 p.283, REVIEW TEST 12 p.238

UNIT
082

Grammar Gateway Basic

He is running **with** a dog. 기타 전치사 with, without, by

🎧 083.mp3

① **with**: ~와 함께, ~을 가진

- He is running **with a dog.** 그는 개와 함께 달리고 있다.
- The house **with the purple roof** is ours. 보라색 지붕을 가진 집이 우리 집이다.
- "Would you like to have tea **with us**?" "Sure. I'd love to."

with a dog

'(신체적 특징)을 가진'이라는 의미로 말할 때도 **with**를 쓴다.

- Patrick is the only boy **with green eyes** in his class.
  Patrick은 반에서 녹색 눈을 가진 유일한 소년이다.

'(도구)를 사용하여'라는 의미로 말할 때도 **with**를 쓴다.

- You have to write your answers **with a pen.** 너는 펜을 사용하여 답을 적어야 해.

② **without**: ~ 없는/없이

- I can't imagine life **without the Internet.** 나는 인터넷이 없는 삶을 상상할 수 없다.
- You must not drive **without a license.** 면허증 없이 운전해서는 안 된다.
- We have to start the meeting **without Jenny.** She's going to be late.

③ **by** + taxi, bicycle 등 (교통수단): ~을 타고

- "How did you get here?" "We came **by taxi**." 우리는 택시를 타고 왔어.
- I sometimes go to school **by bicycle**. 나는 가끔 자전거를 타고 학교에 간다.
- "Are you driving to Chicago?" "No. I'm going **by train**."

on foot   **by taxi**

'걸어서'라는 의미로 말할 때는 주로 **on foot**을 쓴다.

- I go to work **on foot**. It takes 20 minutes from my house. 나는 걸어서 회사에 간다.

④

about	~에 대한/대해
for	~에 대해
like	~처럼
of	~의

- "Can I help you?" "Yes. I'm looking for a book **about Peru**." (페루에 대한)
- "Thank you **for the advice**." "You're welcome." (조언에 대해)
- "What does Matt do?" "He's a doctor, **like his father**."
- "What's the name **of this band**?" "It's the White Tigers."

⑤ 전치사 (without, about 등) + -ing

전치사 뒤에 **-ing**를 쓸 수 있다.

- "Betty left **without saying** goodbye." Betty는 작별인사도 없이 떠났어. "Oh, I'm surprised."
- "Please tell me **about working** at the gym." 헬스장에서 일하는 것에 대해 말해주세요. "It's interesting."
- Robert is very good **at singing**. I want him to sing at my wedding.

이때, 전치사 뒤에 동사원형을 쓰지 않는 것에 주의한다.

- Tourists asked me how to get to the station, so I helped them **by showing** them the way.
  (by show로 쓸 수 없음)

PRACTICE

A. 그림을 보고 주어진 표현과 with 또는 without을 사용하여 문장을 완성하세요.

a helmet	~~a knife~~	a swimming pool	his glasses

1. He is cutting the bread _with a knife_ .
2. He is reading _____ .

3. She has a house _____ .
4. She is riding a motorcycle _____ .

B. 괄호 안에 주어진 표현과 with/without/by/about 등을 사용하여 문장을 완성하세요.

1. (my brother) "Do you live alone?" "No. I live _with my brother_ ."
2. (subway) The best way to get to City Hall is _____ .
3. (brown hair) "Who is Teresa?" "She's the girl _____ over there."
4. (a ticket) The concert is free. You can attend _____ .
5. (plane) We're going to Las Vegas _____ . It's the quickest way to get there.
6. (this pair of jeans) "What's the price _____ ?" "It's $40."
7. (foot) "How far is the mall from here?" "It's close enough to go _____ ."
8. (my wallet) Can I borrow a few dollars? I left home _____ this morning.
9. (the meeting) "Did you tell Matt _____ ?" "Oh, no! I forgot."
10. (a fish) Carmen is a good swimmer. She swims _____ .

C. 괄호 안에 주어진 전치사를 사용하여 예시와 같이 문장을 완성하세요.

1. I feel sorry. I'm late.
   → (for) I feel sorry _for being late_ .

2. We drove for 10 hours. We didn't stop.
   → (without) We drove for 10 hours _____ .

3. Turn off the lights to save energy.
   → (by) We can save energy _____ .

4. I can't skate. I'm terrible at it.
   → (at) I'm terrible _____ .

5. Paula is going to get a promotion. She's happy.
   → (about) Paula is happy _____ .

6. You joined our book club. I'd like to thank you.
   → (for) I'd like to thank you _____ .

정답 p.283, REVIEW TEST 12 p.238

We're **excited about** the trip. 형용사 + 전치사

🎧 084.mp3

① 형용사 + 전치사(about, at 등)

다음과 같이 형용사와 전치사를 함께 쓸 수 있다.

about

excited about ~에 대해 흥분한	◉ We're **excited about** the trip. 우리는 여행에 대해 흥분해 있다.
sorry about ~에 대해 미안한	◉ I'm **sorry about** the noise last night. I had a party. 어젯밤 소음에 대해 미안해요.
sure about ~에 대해 확신하는	◉ "Sally said she won't come back here." "Are you **sure about** that?"

at

angry/mad at ~에게 화가 난	◉ "Why is Ryan **angry at** you?" 왜 Ryan이 네게 화가 났니? "I broke his glasses."
good at ~을 잘하는	◉ Michelle is very **good at** math. Michelle은 수학을 매우 잘한다.
surprised at ~에 놀란	◉ Everyone was **surprised at** my decision to move to another city.

for

famous for ~으로 유명한	◉ This bakery is **famous for** its apple pies. 이 빵집은 애플파이로 유명하다.

from

different from ~와 다른	◉ How is the movie **different from** the book? 그 영화는 책과 어떻게 다른가요?

in

interested in ~에 관심 있는	◉ Jay is **interested in** fashion. He dresses well. Jay는 패션에 관심이 있다.

of

afraid of ~을 무서워하는	◉ When I was young, I was **afraid of** spiders. 나는 어렸을 때 거미를 무서워했다.
full of ~으로 가득한	◉ "Why is the store **full of** people?" 왜 가게가 사람들로 가득하지? "There's a sale."
proud of ~을 자랑스러워 하는	◉ You did a great job. I am very **proud of** you.
short of ~이 부족한	◉ I'm **short of** cash this week. Could I borrow $50?
tired of ~에 질린	◉ "I'm **tired of** the rain." "I know. It's been two weeks now."

to

married to ~와 결혼한	◉ Laura got **married to** Greg last month. Laura는 지난달에 Greg와 결혼했다.
similar to ~와 비슷한	◉ Brad looks quite **similar to** his mother. Brad는 그의 엄마와 꽤 비슷해 보인다.

with

busy with ~으로 바쁜	◉ Darcy has been **busy with** his studies lately. Darcy는 최근에 학업으로 바빴다.
careful with ~을 주의하는	◉ You have to be **careful with** that knife. It's very sharp. 너는 그 칼을 주의해야 해.
familiar with ~에 익숙한	◉ "Have you heard this song?" "No. I'm not **familiar with** it."

더 많은 형용사 + 전치사 표현: 부록 p.255 참고

PRACTICE

A. 적절한 전치사를 써넣으세요.

1. Frank is excited _about_ the football game today.
2. "Emily quit her job." "Yes. I was surprised _____ the news."
3. "You shouldn't bring food into the library." "I'm sorry _____ that. I didn't know."
4. I'm tired _____ pizza. Let's have Japanese food tonight.
5. Your shirt is similar _____ mine. Where did you buy it?
6. Jeremy doesn't want to come to the gallery with us. He's not interested _____ art.
7. Fifth Avenue in New York is famous _____ its shops.
8. Jake is afraid _____ the water, so he doesn't swim.

B. 그림을 보고 주어진 형용사와 적절한 전치사를 사용하여 문장을 완성하세요.

| different | full | ~~good~~ | proud | sure |

We are brothers.

1. Chad is _good at_ _____ basketball.
2. Jim's hair color is _____ his brothers'.
3. She must be _____ herself.
4. The cup is _____ coffee.
5. He is not _____ the answer.

C. 주어진 단어들을 하나씩 사용하여 문장을 완성하세요. 적절한 전치사를 함께 사용하세요.

| ~~angry~~ familiar married short similar | + | ~~himself~~ Italian food Julia money this city |

1. Adam was _angry at himself_ _____. He forgot to bring his homework to school.
2. "Is Greek food _____?" "No. They're very different."
3. Grace bought an expensive laptop, so she's _____ this month.
4. "Martin is getting _____ next week." "Are you going to their wedding?"
5. I'm not _____. I've never been here before.

D. 괄호 안에 주어진 형용사와 적절한 전치사를 사용하여 Linda와 Justin의 대화를 완성하세요.

LINDA: Justin! Your room is so dirty.
JUSTIN: ¹· I'm _sorry about_ that, Mom. (sorry)
² · But I'm so _____ my homework these days. (busy)
LINDA: ³· Are you _____ that? (sure)
You're always playing computer games.
JUSTIN: ⁴· Don't be _____ me, Mom. (mad)
I'll clean it tomorrow.

LINDA

JUSTIN

정답 p.283, REVIEW TEST 12 p.238

UNIT 085 | Did you **know about** the meeting? 동사 + 전치사

🎧 085.mp3

① 동사 + 전치사(**about, at** 등)

다음과 같이 동사와 전치사를 함께 쓸 수 있다.

about

know about ~에 대해 알고 있다	● Did you **know about** the meeting? 그 회의에 대해 알고 있었나요?
talk about ~에 대해 말하다	● Julie often **talks about** her children. Julie는 그녀의 아이들에 대해 자주 말한다.
think about ~에 대해 생각하다	● "What do you **think about** Pam?" "She's very sweet."
worry about ~에 대해 걱정하다	● Don't **worry about** the interview. You'll do great.

at

look at ~을 보다	● **Look at** that baby. He's so cute. 저 아기 좀 봐.
shout at ~에게 소리치다	● Ben **shouted at** us from across the street. Ben이 길 건너에서 우리에게 소리쳤다.
work at ~에서 일하다	● "How long have you **worked at** this company?" "For three years."

for

apply for ~에 지원하다	● I **applied for** a new job. Wish me luck! 나는 새로운 일자리에 지원했어.
ask for ~을 요청하다	● "I'm hungry." "I just **asked for** the menu." 내가 방금 메뉴를 요청했어.
look for ~을 찾다, ~을 구하다	● "What are you **looking for**?" "My scarf. Have you seen it?"
search for ~을 찾다	● The police are **searching for** the lost boy.
wait for ~을 기다리다	● "Who are you **waiting for**?" "Mr. Myers."

on

depend on ~에 의지하다, ~에 달렸다	● Ian is my best friend. I always **depend on** him. 나는 그에게 항상 의지한다.
spend ... on ~에 (돈/시간 등)…을 쓰다	● Don't **spend** too much money **on** clothes. 옷에 너무 많은 돈을 쓰지마.

to

belong to ~의 것이다, ~에 속하다	● "Is this your jacket?" "No. It **belongs to** Jerry." 그것은 Jerry의 것이야.
happen to ~에게 일어나다	● "What **happened to** Sam?" Sam에게 무슨 일이 일어났니? "I don't know."
listen to ~을 듣다	● I often **listen to** the radio while I drive.
talk to ~에게 말하다	● Can I **talk to** you for a few minutes? It won't take long.
write to ~에게 편지를 쓰다	● "Who are you **writing to**?" "My parents."

더 많은 동사 + 전치사 리스트: 부록 p.258 참고

② 다음과 같은 동사 뒤에는 전치사를 쓰지 않는 것에 주의한다.

answer ~에 답하다	● Kathy didn't **answer** my question. (answer to my question으로 쓸 수 없음)
call ~에게 전화하다	● Will you **call** me when you get home? (call to me로 쓸 수 없음)
discuss ~에 대해 논의하다	● We'll **discuss** the schedule tomorrow.
reach ~에 도착하다, ~에 닿다	● You can **reach** the airport easily from the train station.

PRACTICE

A. 그림을 보고 주어진 동사와 적절한 전치사를 사용하여 문장을 완성하세요. 현재진행 시제로 쓰세요.

ask	look	~~talk~~	write

1

Excuse me.

2

They're beautiful!

3

Salad, please.

4

DEAR FRIEND,

1. He *'s talking to OR is talking to* _____ a police officer.
2. They _____ the stars.
3. She _____ a salad.
4. She _____ a friend.

B. 괄호 안에 주어진 동사를 사용하여 문장을 완성하세요. 필요한 경우 적절한 전치사를 함께 쓰세요.

1. (shout) You don't have to *shout at* _____ me. I can hear you.
2. (apply) "Did you _____ the job?" "Yes. They're going to call back next week."
3. (answer) "I called Betty, but she didn't _____ the phone." "Maybe she's busy."
4. (depend) "Will you be home before dinner time?" "Well, it _____ my work schedule."
5. (belong) Peter _____ a book club. The members meet once a month.
6. (reach) "Can you help me? I can't _____ the top shelf." "Sure."
7. (worry) "You look sad. What's wrong?" "I'm OK. Don't _____ me."
8. (discuss) Today, we're going to _____ the history of America.

C. 다음 문장을 읽고 틀린 부분이 있으면 바르게 고치세요. 틀린 부분이 없으면 O로 표시하세요.

1. Students must listen the teacher carefully during class.   *listen → listen to*
2. We spent enough time on this matter. What should we discuss next?   _____
3. Mr. Pond called to you while you were on vacation.   _____
4. "What are you doing here?" "I'm waiting Sue."   _____
5. What happened to you? You look terrible.   _____
6. We reached to the top of the mountain by sunset.   _____

D. 괄호 안에 주어진 동사를 적절한 형태로 사용하여 Paul과 Chris의 대화를 완성하세요. 적절한 전치사를 함께 쓰세요.

PAUL

CHRIS

PAUL: ^1. I'm *searching for* _____ a part-time job this summer. (search)
CHRIS: ^2. You should _____ a job at Tino's Restaurant. (apply)
          ^3. They are _____ a waiter. (look)
PAUL: Really? ^4. Who should I _____? (talk)
CHRIS: Mr. Tino is the owner. You can call the restaurant.
PAUL: How much is the pay?
CHRIS: I'm not sure. ^5. It _____ your working hours. (depend)

정답 p.284, REVIEW TEST 12 p.238

UNIT
085

Grammar Gateway Basic

UNIT 086 | She is **trying on** a hat. 구동사

🎧 086.mp3

①

She is **trying on** a hat.
그녀는 모자를 써보고 있다.

try on은 구동사이다.

---

② 동사와 **on, out, up** 등을 함께 써서 하나의 의미를 갖는 구동사를 쓸 수 있다.

on

get on (비행기/버스/기차 등)에 타다	● Passengers should **get on** the plane now. 탑승객들은 지금 비행기에 타야 한다.
hold on 기다리다	● "We need to leave now." "**Hold on.** I'm almost ready." 기다려주세요.
try on ~을 입어보다, ~을 써보다	● "Can I **try on** this jacket?" "Of course. Go ahead."
turn on ~을 켜다	● Can you **turn on** the lights? It's getting dark.

out

eat out 외식하다	● I don't want to cook dinner tonight. Can we **eat out**? 우리 외식할까?
get out of (차/택시 등)에서 내리다	● I'll stop here, and you can **get out of** the car. 여기 설 테니, 넌 차에서 내리면 돼.
go out (밖으로) 나가다, 외출하다	● "Let's **go out** tomorrow evening." "I can't. I have to work late."
hand out ~을 나눠주다	● The teacher will **hand out** schedules before the class.
take out ~을 꺼내다, ~을 빼다	● Can you **take out** the dishes from the cupboard?

up

clean up ~을 깨끗이 청소하다	● Billy, please **clean up** your room. Billy, 제발 네 방을 깨끗이 청소해라.
get up 일어나다	● "What time do you usually **get up**?" 너는 보통 몇 시에 일어나니? "At 6:30."
wake up 깨어나다, ~을 깨우다	● **Wake up**, Hector! It's time for school.
pick up (수화기 등)을 들다, ~을 사다	● "Did you call Esther?" "Well, someone **picked up** the phone, but they didn't say anything."

더 많은 동사 + 전치사 리스트: 부록 p.258 참고

---

③ 구동사와 목적어를 함께 쓰는 경우 다음과 같이 두 가지 형태로 쓸 수 있다.

	목적어				목적어
● Cathy **put**	her socks	**on.**		Cathy **put on**	her socks.
● Please **turn**	your phone	**off.**	또는	Please **turn off**	your phone.
● Can you **slow**	the car	**down**?		Can you **slow down**	the car?

단, **it/them** 등의 대명사를 목적어로 쓰는 경우에는 동사와 **off, up** 등의 사이에 쓰는 것에 주의한다.

● "It's so hot." "Why are you wearing a sweater? **Take it off.**" (Take off it으로 쓸 수 없음)

● The office desks are dirty. We need to **clean them up.** (clean up them으로 쓸 수 없음)

PRACTICE

A. 주어진 구동사를 사용하여 문장을 완성하세요.

| get up | go out | ~~grow up~~ | hold on | slow down | work on |

1. "Where did you _grow up_____?" "I was raised in Florida."
2. Erica can't come today. She has to _____ her essay.
3. "What are you going to do on weekends?" "I might _____ with Amanda on Sunday."
4. Can you _____? You're driving too fast.
5. I should go to bed now. I need to _____ early in the morning.
6. Can you _____ for a moment? I can't find my credit card.

| come back | eat out | get on | get out of | hand out | take off |

7. My parents are traveling in Europe now. They'll _____ home next Saturday.
8. I couldn't _____ the bus because it was full. I have to catch the next one.
9. "Do you _____ for lunch often?" "No. I always bring my lunch to work."
10. You have to pay before you _____ a taxi.
11. Could you _____ these menus to the customers, please?
12. Please _____ your shoes before coming inside the house.

UNIT 086

B. 괄호 안에 주어진 단어들을 적절히 배열하여 문장을 완성하세요.

1. (wake / up / me) "Can you _wake me up_____ at 6 o'clock?" "OK."
2. (this report / in / hand) "When should I _____?" "By Friday."
3. (away / take / them) I've finished reading these magazines. You can _____.
4. (up / it / clean) The house is a mess! We need to _____ now.
5. (turn / the oven / on) Oh, no! I forgot to _____!
6. (down / write / it) Here's my address. You should _____ before you forget.
7. (out / took / our trash) My brother _____ this morning.
8. (the light / on / switch) It's dark inside. Can you please _____?
9. (her / call / back) Emma called and left a message. Are you going to _____?
10. (the volume / up / turned) I couldn't hear the radio, so I _____.

C. 괄호 안에 주어진 단어들을 적절히 배열하여 Linda와 James의 대화를 완성하세요. 필요한 경우 동사의 형태를 바꾸세요.

LINDA

LINDA: [1.] James, I need to _pick up a hat_ OR _pick a hat up_____.
(a hat / up / pick)
[2.] Can you _____ at the mall? (off / me / drop)
JAMES: Why are you buying the hat? You already have so many.
LINDA: [3.] Well, I _____ yesterday, and it was really nice. (try / on / it)
JAMES: But my favorite show is on TV now.
LINDA: Come on, James. [4.] _____, and let's go. (the TV / turn / off)

JAMES

UNIT 087 The door opened, **and** he came in.

and, but, or, because와 so

087.mp3

①

The door opened. He came in.

The door opened, **and** he came in.

문이 열렸고, 그가 들어왔다.

② 두 문장을 하나로 연결하기 위해 **and, but, or**를 쓸 수 있다.

and: 그리고, ~이고

- I met Tony, **and** we had dinner. 나는 Tony를 만났고, 우리는 저녁을 먹었다.
- Ms. Morris is a teacher, **and** her two sons are also teachers. Morris씨는 선생님이고, 그녀의 두 아들들도 선생님이다.

but: 그러나, ~이지만

- It was cloudy this morning, **but** the sky is clear now. 오늘 아침에는 흐렸지만, 지금은 하늘이 맑다.
- Michael can speak Spanish well, **but** he can't speak French. Michael은 스페인어를 잘하지만, 프랑스어는 하지 못한다.

or: 또는, 아니면

- Are you using this chair, **or** can I use it? 이 의자를 사용하고 있나요, 아니면 제가 사용해도 될까요?
- Have you been to Denmark before, **or** is it your first time? 너는 전에 덴마크에 가본 적이 있니, 아니면 이번이 처음이니?

and, but, or 뒤에서 반복되는 내용은 생략하고 말할 수 있다. 이때, **콤마(,)**는 쓰지 않는다.

- I start work at 9 **and** finish at 6. (= , and I finish work at 6)
- We can watch a comedy **or** an action movie. (= , or we can watch an action movie)

③ **because**: 왜냐하면, ~이기 때문에

- Adam doesn't talk much **because** he is shy. (수줍음을 많이 타기 때문에)
- I tell my secrets to my sister **because** I trust her. (그녀를 믿기 때문에)

so: 그래서, ~해서

- Adam is shy, **so** he doesn't talk much. (그래서 말을 많이 하지 않음)
- I forgot my wallet, **so** I went back home. (그래서 집에 돌아갔음)

because는 다음과 같이 문장의 맨 앞에 쓸 수 있으며, 이때 뒤에 **콤마(,)**를 쓴다. 단, **so**는 문장 맨 앞에 쓸 수 없다.

- **Because** we woke up late, we missed the train. (늦게 일어났기 때문에)
- The opera was boring, **so** we didn't enjoy it. (So we didn't enjoy the opera, it was boring으로 쓸 수 없음)

because of도 이유를 말할 때 쓸 수 있다. **because**는 문장을 연결할 때 쓰지만, **because of** 뒤에는 명사를 쓴다.

- The flight was canceled **because there was a storm.** (because of there was a storm으로 쓸 수 없음)
  The flight was canceled **because of the storm.** (because the storm으로 쓸 수 없음)

PRACTICE

A. 주어진 문장과 and/but/or를 사용하여 문장을 완성하세요.

do you need more time	do you want to drive yours	he couldn't attend
it hurt a lot	it tasted terrible	~~they won the game~~

1. The soccer team played well, *and they won the game* .
2. Are you ready to order, _____?
3. I cut my finger, _____ .
4. Wendy invited John to the wedding, _____ .
5. The soup smelled delicious, _____ .
6. Should we take my car, _____?

B. 그림을 보고 주어진 문장과 so와 because를 각각 한 번씩 사용하여 예시와 같이 문장을 완성하세요.

he was very tired	she bought a new one	she took some medicine	~~she washed it~~

1-2    3-4

5-6    7-8

1. Her shirt got dirty, *so she washed it* .
   → 2. *She washed her shirt because it got dirty* .
3. Her TV wasn't working, _____ .
   → 4. _____ .
5. He ran for an hour, _____ .
   → 6. _____ .
7. She had a headache, _____ .
   → 8. _____ .

C. because 또는 because of를 써넣으세요.

1. I like swimming *because* it's fun and good for my health.
2. Leo is not going to come tonight _____ his another appointment.
3. Ben couldn't go to school _____ he was sick.
4. I need to leave now _____ I have a class in 30 minutes.
5. We couldn't sleep yesterday _____ the baby. She cried all night.
6. Megan is moving to China _____ her new job.

정답 p.284, REVIEW TEST 13 p.240

🎧 088.mp3

①

She was watching TV **when he came in**.
그가 들어왔을 때, 그녀는 TV를 보고 있었다.

He fell asleep **while his boss was talking**.
상사가 말하는 동안, 그는 잠이 들었다.

② **when**: ~할 때

- My family moved to Arizona **when I was six years old**. 내가 여섯 살 때 우리 가족은 애리조나로 이사했다.
- Could you turn off all the lights **when you leave the house**? 집을 떠날 때 모든 불을 꺼주시겠어요?
- I was driving to work **when I saw an accident**.
- Emily and I were best friends **when she lived next door to me**.
- I always get nervous **when I have to speak in front of a lot of people**.

③ **while**: ~하는 동안

- Carol usually listens to music **while she's exercising**. Carol은 운동하는 동안 보통 음악을 듣는다.
- "Did anyone call **while I was in the meeting**?" 제가 회의 중일 때 누군가 전화했나요? "Yes. Mr. Owens called."
- My parents met **while they were working at the same company**.
- "Can you mop the floor **while I'm doing the laundry**?" "Of course."
- Jennifer had a lot of visitors **while she was in the hospital**.

④ **when**과 **while**은 다음과 같이 문장의 맨 앞에 쓸 수도 있다. 이때, 뒤에 **콤마(,)**를 쓴다.

- **When I arrived,** nobody was at home.
  (= Nobody was at home when I arrived.)
- **While you're waiting for a table,** would you like to look at the menu first?
  (= Would you like to look at the menu first while you're waiting for a table?)
- **When we were in high school,** we joined the chess club.
- **While I'm away,** Matthew will take care of my dog.

⑤ **when**과 **while** 다음에 미래의 일을 말할 때는 미래 시제가 아니라 현재 시제를 쓰는 것에 주의한다.

- What do you want to be **when** you **grow up**? (자라는 것은 미래의 일이지만 when you'll grow up으로 쓸 수 없음)
- It'll be warm and sunny **while** we **are** on vacation. (휴가를 가는 것은 미래의 일이지만 while we will be로 쓸 수 없음)
- I'll call you **when** I **have** time.
- Thomas will read the book **while** he's on the train.

PRACTICE

A. 그림을 보고 주어진 문장과 when을 사용하여 문장을 완성하세요.

he sat on the chair	~~he saw Daniel and Kelly~~	he woke up
it started to rain	they arrived at the theater	

1. _When he saw Daniel and Kelly_____, they were going to play tennis.
2. _____, it broke.
3. The movie was already playing _____.
4. Patty was running in the park _____.
5. It was 2 o'clock in the afternoon _____.

B. 두 문장을 적절히 연결하여 문장을 완성하세요.

1. While I was listening to the radio   •   •   he got injured
2. Do not use your cell phone   •   •   while you find a parking space
3. Can you set the table   •   •   while I make dinner
4. While I was taking a shower   •   •   I fell asleep
5. I'll get a shopping cart   •   •   Tom called me
6. While Matt was playing soccer   •   •   while you're driving

1. _While I was listening to the radio, I fell asleep_____.
2. _____.
3. _____?
4. _____.
5. _____.
6. _____.

C. 괄호 안에 주어진 동사를 사용하여 문장을 완성하세요. 현재 시제로 쓰거나 will을 함께 사용하세요.

1. (have) I'm going to take a dance class when I _have_____ some free time.
2. (meet) We _____ Jane while we visit Seattle next week.
3. (go) When I _____ to the post office, I'll get you some stamps.
4. (wait) While you buy some groceries, I _____ in the car.
5. (cook) While Kevin _____ the steak, Laura will make the salad.
6. (come) Can you call me when you _____ home?
7. (see) Have a safe flight. I _____ you when you're back.
8. (save) When Molly _____ enough money, she'll travel to Greece.

정답 p.284, REVIEW TEST 13 p.240

UNIT
088

Grammar Gateway Basic

🎧 089.mp3

①

The store closed **before they arrived**.
그들이 도착하기 전에 가게가 닫았다.

They arrived **after the store closed**.
그들은 가게가 닫은 후에 도착했다.

---

② **before**: ~하기 전에
- Please come to my office **before you leave**. 떠나기 전에 제 사무실로 와주세요.
- "What did you do **before you became a writer**?" 당신은 작가가 되기 전에 무엇을 했나요? "I was a teacher."
- Jess! You need to wake up **before it's too late**.
- That restaurant is very popular. We should make a reservation **before we go there**.
- "Should we get some drinks **before the concert starts**?" "Sure."

---

③ **after**: ~한 후에
- Let's go out to eat **after we do the cleaning**. 청소를 한 후에 외식하러 나가자.
- We took a picture **after we reached the top of the mountain**. 우리는 산의 정상에 도착한 후에 사진을 찍었다.
- I'll finish the report **after I come back from lunch**.
- My sister moved to another city **after she got married**.
- "Turn off the TV **after you watch the movie**." "Don't worry. I will."

---

④ **before**와 **after**는 다음과 같이 문장의 맨 앞에 쓸 수도 있다. 이때, 뒤에 **콤마(,)**를 쓴다.
- **Before David does something,** he always makes a plan first.
  (= David always makes a plan first before he does something.)
- **After I graduate from high school,** I'm going to get a job.
  (= I'm going to get a job after I graduate from high school)
- **"Before you joined the team,** who was the leader?" "It was Tony."
- **After we finish this,** we should take a break.

---

⑤ **before**와 **after** 다음에 **명사** 또는 **-ing**를 쓸 수도 있다.
- You should be home **before midnight**. 너는 자정 전에 집에 와야 한다.
- Everyone was excited **after hearing** about the prize. 상품에 대해 들은 후에 모두들 흥분했다.
- Read the document very carefully **before signing** it.
- "How about taking a walk **after dinner**?" "That sounds like a good idea."

PRACTICE

A. 주어진 문장을 보고 before 또는 after를 사용하여 문장을 완성하세요.

1. Andy goes to school. Then he goes to the library.
   → *Before Andy goes to the library*_____, he goes to school.
2. I took a shower. Then I put on my clothes.
   → I put on my clothes _____.
3. I had to wait in line. Then I ordered a cup of coffee.
   → I had to wait in line _____.
4. I locked the door. Then I left home.
   → _____, I locked the door.
5. Diane entered the room. Then she turned on the light.
   → _____, she turned on the light.
6. The thieves ran away. Then the police arrived.
   → The thieves ran away _____.
7. My brother eats breakfast in the morning. Then he goes to the gym.
   → My brother goes to the gym _____.
8. The visitors checked out of the hotel. Then they went to the art museum.
   → _____, they went to the art museum.

B. 주어진 표현과 before 또는 after를 사용하여 문장을 완성하세요.

drive	~~go~~	our wedding	read	the exam	the show

1. Brush your teeth *before going*_____ to bed.
2. I cried _____ the book. The ending was so sad.
3. I studied a lot _____, so I was prepared for it.
4. People should not drink alcohol _____ a car.
5. Dave is watching TV right now. He'll help me with my homework _____.
6. We're going to Hawaii _____. It will be a fun honeymoon.

C. 다음은 Bella's 머핀 믹스 조리법입니다. 괄호 안에 주어진 표현과 before 또는 after를 사용하여 문장을 완성하세요.

Bella's Chocolate Chip Muffins
You'll need: Bella's Muffin Mix, 1 cup of water, 2 eggs, chocolate chips

1. Bella's muffins are the perfect dessert *after a meal*_____. (a meal)
2. _____, heat the oven to 190 ℃. (baking the muffins)
3. _____ into a bowl, add two eggs and a cup of water to the mix in the bowl. (pouring the muffin mix)
4. Finally, add chocolate chips _____ into the oven. (putting the mixture)
5. Your delicious muffins will be ready _____! (25 minutes)

정답 p.284, REVIEW TEST 13 p.240

The city has changed **since** she arrived. since와 until

🎧 090.mp3

①

I just arrived.

It's been 10 years!

과거   지금

The city has changed **since she arrived**.

그 도시는 그녀가 온 이후로 지금까지 변해왔다.

since: ~한 이후로 지금까지

- I've played cello **since I was 12 years old**. 나는 12살 이후로 지금까지 첼로를 연주해왔다.
- Many people have visited the zoo **since it opened**. 동물원이 개장한 이후로 지금까지 많은 사람들이 그곳을 방문했다.
- Martin has been very busy **since he started his new job**.
- "How long has it been **since you quit smoking**?" "Three years."

since는 현재완료 시제와 주로 함께 쓴다. 이때, **since** 뒤에는 과거 시제를 쓴다.

- How have you been? It'**s been** a while **since** we **saw** each other. 우리가 서로를 본 지 한참 되었다.
- "Do you know Alice?" "Yes. I'**ve known** her **since** she **was** young." 나는 그녀가 어렸을 때부터 그녀를 알아왔어.

②

We were waiting for you.

They didn't eat dinner **until he arrived**.

그가 집에 올 때까지 그들은 저녁을 먹지 않았다.

until: ~할 때까지 (계속)

- We won't start the class **until everyone gets here**. 우리는 모두가 여기에 올 때까지 수업을 시작하지 않을 것이다.
- Mr. Simpson worked for our company **until he retired**. Simpson씨는 퇴직할 때까지 계속 우리 회사에서 일했다.
- We stayed at the beach **until it started raining**.
- "Where is the library?" "Go straight **until you see the hospital**. Then turn left."

until 다음에 미래의 일을 말할 때는 미래 시제가 아니라 현재 시제를 쓰는 것에 주의한다.

- "When should I put the eggs in the water?" "Wait **until it boils**."
  (물이 끓는 것은 미래의 일이지만 until it will boil로 쓸 수 없음)
- Please do not leave your seat **until the bus stops**.
  (버스가 멈추는 것은 미래의 일이지만 until the bus will stop으로 쓸 수 없음)

③ **since**와 **until** 다음에 명사를 쓸 수도 있다.

- I haven't seen Connor and Julie **since their wedding**. 나는 결혼식 이후로 Connor와 Julie를 보지 못했다.
- Mr. Brooks is on vacation now. He won't be back **until next Thursday**. 그는 다음 주 목요일까지 돌아오지 않을 것이다.

PRACTICE

A. since 또는 until을 써넣으세요.

1. Please turn off your cell phones _until_ the test is over.
2. You have learned a lot _____ you joined Spanish class.
3. Can you wait for me here _____ I finish my meeting?
4. "Did you arrive late?" "No. I've been here _____ 8 o'clock."
5. I've been happier _____ I moved to my new apartment.
6. Ruth is going to stay with us _____ Sunday. She's leaving next Monday.

B. 괄호 안에 주어진 단어들과 적절한 시제를 사용하여 문장을 완성하세요.

1. (meet at work) Jerry and Karen have been good friends since they _met at work_ .
2. (not call me) "Did you hear anything from Dad?" "No. He _____ since he left home."
3. (open last month) This restaurant has become popular since it _____ .
4. (break my leg) I haven't gone to the gym since I _____ .
5. (not travel anywhere) Since our son was born, we _____ .
6. (lose 10 pounds) I _____ since I started exercising in June.

C. 주어진 표현과 until을 사용하여 문장을 완성하세요.

she returned from vacation	it turns brown	she showed them the proof
the paint dries	~~the rain stops~~	we arrived at the theater

1. Don't play outside _until the rain stops_ . You'll get wet.
2. Luckily, the movie didn't start _____ .
3. The police didn't believe Ms. Wade _____ .
4. You should leave the bread in the oven _____ .
5. Matt had to do Sarah's job _____ .
6. We've just painted the wall. Please do not touch it _____ .

D. 주어진 그래프를 보고 since 또는 until을 사용하여 문장을 완성하세요.

TED — lost his camera / now — enjoy his trip ↓ not enjoy his trip

1. Ted enjoyed his trip _until he lost his camera_ .
2. Ted hasn't enjoyed his trip _____ .

JASON — moved to Taiwan / now — work at a bar ↓ work at a hotel

3. Jason worked at a bar _____ .
4. Jason has worked at a hotel _____ .

SANDRA — bought a car / now — take the bus ↓ not take the bus

5. Sandra took the bus _____ .
6. Sandra hasn't taken the bus _____ .

CINDY — got married / now — live in London ↓ live in Paris

7. Cindy lived in London _____ .
8. Cindy has lived in Paris _____ .

정답 p.285, REVIEW TEST 13 p.240

UNIT 090

Grammar Gateway Basic

🎧 091.mp3

①

If it rains, she'll stay at home.
비가 오면, 그녀는 집에 머물 것이다.

If it doesn't rain, she'll go hiking.
비가 오지 않으면, 그녀는 하이킹을 하러 갈 것이다.

If it rains, I'll stay at home.   If it doesn't rain, I'll go hiking.

② **if**: ~하면

if를 사용하여 '~하면 …할 것이다'라는 의미로 말할 때 다음과 같이 쓴다.

> **If + 주어 + 현재 시제,   주어 + will/can** 등 **+ 동사원형**

- **If you ask** the teacher, **he will answer** your question.   선생님께 물어보면, 네 질문에 답해주실거야.
- **If you don't like** seafood, **we can eat** something else.   네가 해산물을 좋아하지 않으면, 우리는 다른 것을 먹을 수 있어.
- **If Mr. Lewis calls, can you take** a message for me?
- **If I order** the clothes now, **the delivery will come** on Tuesday.
- **If Ms. Roy and Mr. Lee agree, I will cancel** today's meeting.

if는 다음과 같이 문장의 중간에 쓸 수도 있다. 이때, 콤마(,)를 쓰지 않는다.

- You can come to my house **if you get bored.** I'll be home all day.   네가 심심하면 우리 집에 와도 돼.
- Sharon will miss the flight **if she doesn't leave** soon.   Sharon이 곧 떠나지 않으면 그녀는 비행기를 놓칠 거야.
- You'll get your driver's license **if you pass** this test.
- We can go to the movies **if we're not busy** on Sunday.
- Should I take a taxi **if I want** to get there quickly?

③ **if** 다음에 미래의 일을 말할 때는 현재 시제를 쓴다. 이때, 미래 시제를 쓰지 않도록 주의한다.

- Will you wake me up **if** you **get up** early tomorrow?
  (내일 일찍 일어나는 것은 미래의 일이지만 if you'll get up으로 쓸 수 없음)
- **If** Erin **helps** us, we'll finish the work quickly.
  (Erin이 우리를 돕는 것은 미래의 일이지만 If Erin will help로 쓸 수 없음)
- I'll let you know **if** I **hear** from Jess.
- **If** you **do** the laundry, I'll do the dishes.

PRACTICE

A. 주어진 표현과 if를 사용하여 문장을 완성하세요.

| I get this job | the guests arrive | the supermarket isn't closed |
| the traffic is bad | we are in the same class | ~~we have enough time~~ |

1. *If we have enough time* _____, we can visit Olympic Park.
2. _____, we're going to be late.
3. _____, can I share your book? I forgot mine today.
4. _____, I'm going to work full-time.
5. _____, can you open the door for them?
6. _____, we should get some milk.

B. Judy는 자신의 미래에 대해 상상하고 있습니다. if를 사용하여 예시와 같이 문장을 완성하세요.

I'll go to a design school!

1. → study hard   *I'll study hard if I go to a design school* _____.
2. → become a famous designer   _____ if I study hard.
3. → make a lot of money   _____.
4. → help poor children   _____.
5. → feel happy   _____.

C. 괄호 안에 주어진 단어들을 사용하여 예시와 같이 문장을 완성하세요. 현재 시제로 쓰거나 will을 함께 사용하세요.

1. (I, take, you, to a game) If you like football, *I'll take you to a game* _____.
2. (Holly, forget, our appointment) I'll be upset if _____ again.
3. (You, feel, better) _____ if you take this medicine.
4. (Brandon, get, it) If I send this letter today, _____ tomorrow.
5. (your sister, come, to Toronto) If _____, she can stay with me.
6. (you, be, with me) Everything will be fine if _____.

D. 괄호 안에 주어진 단어들을 사용하여 Kate와 Amy의 대화를 완성하세요. 적절한 시제를 사용하세요.

KATE: What are your plans for Saturday?
AMY: [1.] Well, *I'll go* _____ hiking if the weather is nice. (I, go)
KATE: I heard it's going to rain.
AMY: [2.] If _____, I'll just stay at home. (it, rain)
KATE: [3.] If you don't go hiking, _____ you. We can watch movies! (I, visit)
AMY: Great! [4.] We can also bake cookies if _____. (you, want)

KATE

AMY

정답 p.285, REVIEW TEST 13 p.240

UNIT 092 | If he **had time**, he would eat breakfast. if (2)
if + 과거 시제

🎧 092.mp3

①

Sorry, I have no time.

If he had time, **he would eat** breakfast.
만약 시간이 있다면, 그는 아침을 먹을 텐데.
(시간이 없어서 아침을 먹지 못함)

---

② if를 사용하여 '만약 ~한다면 …할 텐데'라는 의미로 현재 사실과 다른 상황을 가정해서 말할 때 다음과 같이 쓴다.

> **If + 주어 + 과거 시제,   주어 + would(= 'd)/could 등 + 동사원형**

○ **If I knew** Harry's phone number, **I would call** him.
만약 내가 Harry의 전화번호를 안다면, 그에게 전화할 텐데. (전화번호를 몰라서 전화하지 못함)

○ **If we went** to Egypt, **we could see** the pyramids.
만약 우리가 이집트에 간다면, 피라미드를 볼 수 있을 텐데. (이집트에 가지 않아서 피라미드를 보지 못함)

○ **If Donna was** here, **she'd enjoy** this meal.

이때, **if** 뒤에 과거 시제를 써도 과거의 의미가 아닌 것에 주의한다.

○ **If you didn't own** a pet, **you could rent** that apartment.
만약 네가 애완동물이 없으면, 저 아파트를 임대할 수 있을 텐데. (과거에 애완동물이 없었다는 의미가 아님)

○ **If I had** long hair like you, **I wouldn't cut** it.
만약 내가 너처럼 긴 머리를 가졌으면, 그것을 자르지 않을 텐데. (과거에 긴 머리를 가지고 있었다는 의미가 아님)

이때에도 **if**는 문장의 중간에 쓸 수 있다. 이때, **콤마(,)**를 쓰지 않는다.

○ I could drive to work every day **if I had** a car. 만약 내가 차가 있다면 매일 회사로 운전해서 갈 텐데.
○ Aria would have more parties **if she didn't have** roommates. 만약 Aria가 룸메이트가 없다면 더 많은 파티를 열 텐데.
○ My life would be different **if I didn't meet** my best friend earlier.
○ We could save money **if both of us worked**.

---

③ 이때, 주어가 **I/he/she/it**인 경우 if 다음에 was 대신 **were**를 쓸 수도 있다.
○ **If I were** rich, I'd open my own restaurant. 만약 내가 부자라면, 내 소유의 음식점을 열 텐데.
○ **If Jerry were** taller, he could be a basketball player. 만약 Jerry가 키가 더 크다면, 농구 선수가 될 수 있을 텐데.
○ **If Megan were** younger, she would go back to university.

---

④ **If I were/was you, I'd ~**: 만약 내가 너라면, ~할 거야
○ **If I were/was you, I'd talk** to Benny about your problem. 만약 내가 너라면, 네 문제에 대해 Benny에게 이야기해볼 거야.
○ **If I were/was you, I wouldn't see** that movie. It's boring. 만약 내가 너라면, 그 영화를 보지 않을 거야.
○ "I'm going out for coffee." "**If I were/was you, I'd go** later. The café is usually crowded at this time."
○ "What do you think about this jacket?" "**If I were/was you, I wouldn't buy** it."

PRACTICE

A. 주어진 문장과 if를 사용하여 예시와 같이 문장을 완성하세요.

I am in Paris	~~I have enough money~~	I have more free time	it is sunny

1. *If I had enough money*, I'd buy a new suit.
2. _____, I'd go to the park.
3. _____, I'd visit the Eiffel Tower.
4. _____, I'd play tennis often.

B. 괄호 안에 주어진 단어들을 적절한 형태로 사용하여 문장을 완성하세요. 필요한 경우 would를 사용하세요.

1. (the seminar, be) I have meetings on Friday. If _the seminar were OR the seminar was_ on Saturday, I'd go.
2. (it, not be) "Are you having fun at camp?" "_____ boring if you were here."
3. (she, get up) Ashley is late for class. If _____ earlier, she wouldn't be late.
4. (Ryan, become) _____ a lawyer if he weren't a journalist.
5. (I, win) I'd get a gold medal if _____ the race.
6. (we, not wear) If it wasn't cold, _____ jackets.

UNIT 092

Grammar Gateway Basic

C. 주어진 표현과 If I were you, I'd ~를 사용하여 대화를 완성하세요.

~~be excited~~	not drink it	not drive	say sorry to her

1. I'm nervous about moving to a new city.
2. The traffic seems very bad today.
3. I had a fight with my girlfriend.
4. I bought this juice three weeks ago.

If I were you, I'd be excited _____.
_____.
_____.
_____.

D. 주어진 문장을 보고 if를 사용하여 예시와 같이 다시 말해보세요.

1. My parents don't live near here, so I don't see them on weekends.
   → *If my parents lived near here, I'd see them on weekends* .
2. Ted works in the afternoons, so he doesn't get up early.
   → _____ .
3. Brenna isn't busy, so she can meet us.
   → _____ .
4. Dan has a knee injury, so he can't play soccer.
   → _____ .

UNIT 093 | **if | do** vs. **if | did** if (3) if + 현재 시제와 if + 과거 시제 비교

🎧 093.mp3

If she **is** here, he**'ll be** happy.

그녀가 있다면, 그는 기쁠 것이다.
(그녀가 있을 수도 없을 수도 있음)

If she **was** here, he**'d be** happy.

만약 그녀가 있다면, 그는 기쁠 텐데.
(그녀가 없음)

---

② **if | do**와 **if | did**

어떤 일이 실제로 일어날 가능성이 있는 경우에 **if + 현재 시제**를 쓴다.

- **If** the weather **is** warm, I**'ll go** for a walk.
  날씨가 따뜻하다면, 나는 산책할 것이다.
  (날씨가 따뜻할 수도 아닐 수도 있음)

- **If** Eric **exercises** every day, he**'ll be** healthier.
  Eric이 운동한다면, 그는 건강해질 것이다.
  (Eric이 운동할 수도 안 할 수도 있음)

- **If** we **decide** to go to the party, we**'ll let** you know.

- **If** the store **is closed**, we **can park** our car in front of it.

- Jim **will wear** the pants **if** they **aren't** too big.

- We **can walk** to the station together **if** you **take** the subway home.

- **Can** you **bring** the letter to my office **if** it **arrives**?

- You **can ask** me for advice **if** you **have** any problems.

어떤 일이 실제로 일어날 가능성이 없는 경우에는 **if + 과거 시제**를 쓴다.

- **If** the weather **was** warm, I**'d go** for a walk.
  만약 날씨가 따뜻하다면, 나는 산책할 텐데.
  (날씨가 따뜻하지 않음)

- **If** Eric **exercised** every day, he**'d be** healthier.
  만약 Eric이 운동한다면, 그는 건강해질 텐데.
  (Eric이 운동하지 않음)

- **If** today **were** a holiday, we **could go** on a picnic.

- **If** Anna **studied** harder, she **could get** a good grade on the test.

- I**'d buy** that bag **if** it **weren't** sold out.

- The room **would look** better **if** this wall **was** a different color.

- We **could leave** work early **if** we **didn't have** a meeting today.

- I**'d take** a trip to China alone **if** I **spoke** Chinese well.

PRACTICE

A. 주어진 표현과 if를 사용하여 대화를 완성하세요. 현재 시제 또는 과거 시제로 쓰세요.

> | Ashley isn't so tired | I find it | the mall is open | ~~we leave now~~ |
> | --- | --- | --- | --- |

1. A: What time is it?
   B: It's 6:30. *If we leave now* , we'll catch the train.

2. A: _____ ,
   we could go shopping.
   B: I know! But it closed early today.

3. A: I think I left my ring at your house yesterday.
   B: OK. _____, I'll give it back to you.

4. A: _____ tonight,
   she would go to the movies with us.
   B: That's OK. She can join us next time.

> | I see him | she doesn't sleep late | the restaurant isn't full | we take 4th Avenue |
> | --- | --- | --- | --- |

5. A: _____, we could eat there.
   B: Do you know any other place to have dinner?

6. A: _____ ,
   we'd come home earlier.
   B: You're right. Let's use that road next time.

7. A: Where's Max? I've waited here for an hour.
   B: _____, I'll tell him you are here.

8. A: I hope Sarah won't be late tomorrow.
   B: _____ ,
   she will be on time.

B. 괄호 안에 주어진 표현을 적절한 시제로 사용하여 문장을 완성하세요. 필요한 경우 will 또는 would를 사용하세요.

1. (help you) If you ask Mike, he *'ll help you* OR *will help you*   with your essay.
2. (be fresh) Those vegetables look old. I would buy some if they _____ .
3. (attend) If the wedding wasn't on Friday, I _____ . I have an appointment that day.
4. (pick you up) If you call me at the airport, I _____ .
5. (have a car) I wouldn't take the bus if I _____ . The bus is always crowded.
6. (not like coffee) If Hannah _____ , she can have tea.
7. (be healthier) I don't go to the gym regularly. If I exercised every day, I _____ .
8. (not take an umbrella) If you _____ with you, you'll get wet.

C. 다음은 Amy가 Sandra에게 보낸 이메일입니다. 둘 중 맞는 것을 고르세요.

Subject	Hi, Sandra
To	sandra77@gotmail.com
From	amy318@gotmail.com

Hi, Sandra. How are you doing in Seattle?
I'm going to a music festival today. [1.] If you were here, it (will /(would)) be more fun.
The concert is at the park. I am glad the weather is nice.
[2.] If it (rains / rained) during the concert, the show can be canceled.
Many bands are going to play, but my favorite one is not coming.
[3.] If it (performs / performed), I would be happier.
I heard it might play next year. [4.] If that is true, I (will come / would come) again.

Love, Amy

정답 p.285, REVIEW TEST 13 p.240

UNIT
093

Grammar Gateway Basic

He knows the girl **who** won the race.

관계대명사
who/which/that (1) 주격

🎧 094.mp3

①

I know the girl **who** won the race.

He knows **the girl**. <u>She</u> won the race.
　　　　　　　　　　주어

He knows **the girl** <u>who</u> won the race.
　　　　　　　　　　관계대명사

그는 경기에서 우승한 소녀를 안다.

---

② 말하고 있는 대상이 어떤 사람 또는 사물인지 설명할 때 명사 뒤에 관계대명사 **who/which/that**을 쓸 수 있다.

	명사	who/which/that		
●	Do you know **the woman**	who	is standing there?	(저기 서 있는 여자)
●	The flight	which	goes to Boston	was canceled. (보스턴으로 가는 비행편)
●	I always eat **chocolate**	that	is from Italy.	

---

③ 사람에 대해 설명할 때는 관계대명사 **who**를 쓴다.

	사람	who		
●	Peter is married to **a woman**	who	is a lawyer.	(변호사인 여자)
●	Do you know **anyone**	who	can speak German?	

사람	who		
My uncle	who	lives in Dallas	is coming to visit. (댈러스에 사는 내 삼촌)
The man	who	is sitting next to Jamie	is my brother.

사물에 대해 설명할 때는 관계대명사 **which**를 쓴다.

	사물	which		
●	This is **the sweater**	which	was made by my mother.	(어머니에 의해 만들어진 스웨터)
●	Easy Film is **a company**	which	is famous for its digital cameras.	

사물	which		
The bus	which	goes to 10th Avenue	has just left. (10번가로 가는 버스)
The keys	which	are on the table	are mine.

관계대명사 **that**은 사람과 사물에 모두 쓸 수 있다.

	사람·사물	that		
●	I bought **an apartment**	that	is close to a park.	(아파트에서 가까운 공원)
●	Do you know **anyone**	that	knows about computers?	

사람·사물	that		
The tour group	that	visited the museum	had a great time. (박물관을 방문했던 단체 관광객)
The toys	that	are on sale	are on this shelf.

PRACTICE

A. Bill은 지금 여행 중입니다. 그림을 보고 who를 사용하여 Bill이 오늘 만난 사람들에 대한 문장을 완성하세요.

1

I can speak English.

2

I have six children.

3

I play the violin.

4

We are very famous.

5

I fix cars.

6

I am 99 years old.

1. Bill met a man *who can speak English* .
2. He sat next to a woman _____ .
3. He saw a man _____ .
4. He saw two women _____ .
5. He met a man _____ .
6. He visited a woman _____ .

B. who 또는 which를 써넣으세요.

1. Do you know the girl *who* _____ has red hair over there?
2. The name of the person _____ called yesterday was Samantha Smith.
3. The books _____ were newly published are in the New Arrivals section.
4. Patrick has a friend _____ comes from Spain.
5. I went to a restaurant _____ makes excellent soups.
6. Hanna is a person _____ cares about others.
7. Have you seen my bag _____ has green and blue stripes?
8. The pictures _____ were taken by Eric are hanging on the wall.

C. who/which/that을 사용하여 주어진 두 문장을 한 문장으로 바꾸어 쓰세요.

1. That building is really tall. It was built recently. → *That building which (OR that) was built recently is really tall* .
2. I bought a new sofa. It was on sale. → _____ .
3. The store sells magazines. It's around the corner. → _____ .
4. The people are very nice. They live downstairs. → _____ .
5. I found a suitcase. It belongs to Mr. Harris. → _____ .
6. Sarah taught the students. They graduated last year.
   → _____ .
7. A man just waved to us. He is standing across the street.
   → _____ .
8. We're excited about the festival. It will begin next week.
   → _____ .

정답 p.285, REVIEW TEST 13 p.240

UNIT 094

Grammar Gateway Basic

They love the food **which** he made.

관계대명사
who/which/that (2) 목적격

🎧 095.mp3

We really loved the food, James!

They love **the food. He made** <u>it</u>.

목적어

They love **the food** <u>which</u> **he made.**

관계대명사

그들은 그가 만든 음식을 아주 좋아한다.

---

② 관계대명사 **who/which/that**은 목적어로 쓸 수 있다.

who/that

○ Jane is **the girl** | who/that | **Harry likes.** (who/that을 likes의 목적어로 썼음)
○ My father is **the person** | who/that | **I respect the most.**

who/that

○ **The man** | who/that | **you met in the lobby** is my boss. (who/that을 met의 목적어로 썼음)
○ **The employees** | who/that | **I worked with** were helpful.

which/that

○ Dave likes **the new phone** | which/that | **Alice bought for him.** (which/that을 bought의 목적어로 썼음)
○ Anna often buys **clothes** | which/that | **she never wears.**

which/that

○ **The earrings** | which/that | **I lost yesterday** were expensive. (which/that을 lost의 목적어로 썼음)
○ **The book** | which/that | **my friend lent me** was really interesting.

다음과 같이 관계대명사 **who/which/that**은 주어로도 쓸 수 있다.

who/that

○ **The lady** | who/that | **lives next door** is friendly. (who/that을 lives의 주어로 썼음)
○ **The student** | who/that | **won the contest** will receive $100.

which/that

○ We visited **an old church** | which/that | **was built** in 1650. (which/that을 was built의 주어로 썼음)
○ I bought **a camera** | which/that | **works** under water.

---

③ 관계대명사 **who/which/that**을 목적어로 쓰는 경우 생략할 수 있다.

○ **Most people** (who/that) **I know** are from Las Vegas. (내가 아는 대부분의 사람들)
○ Can I use **the scissors** (which/that) **you have?** (네가 가지고 있는 가위)
○ I can't remember **the dream** (which/that) **I had last night.**

그러나 **who/which/that**을 주어로 쓰는 경우 생략할 수 없는 것에 주의한다.

○ I have **a friend** who/that **works at the hospital.** (a friend works at the hospital로 쓸 수 없음)
○ **The café** which/that **is on Pine Street** is always crowded. (The café is on Pine Street으로 쓸 수 없음)
○ This is **a song** which/that **is very popular these days.**

PRACTICE

A. 주어진 표현을 하나씩 사용하여 예시와 같이 문장을 완성하세요. who 또는 which를 함께 사용하세요.

the book	~~the boy~~	the cake		Brian Smith wrote	~~I met~~	I wore
the dress	the show		+	you're baking		you were watching

1. "Did I tell you about *the boy who I met* _____ during the trip?" "No. Tell me about him."
2. _____ to the party was too tight. It wasn't comfortable.
3. I can't wait to taste _____. It smells so good.
4. "_____ is over. Can I change the channel?" "OK."
5. _____ was great. I finished reading it last night.

B. that을 사용하여 예시와 같이 주어진 두 문장을 한 문장으로 바꾸어 쓰세요. 가능한 경우 that을 생략하세요.

1. Jamie gave me some shoes. She didn't want them. → Jamie *gave me some shoes she didn't want* _____.
2. I used to have a friend. I trusted him. → I _____.
3. I know a neighbor. He has many pets. → I _____.
4. The girl drove us to school. She isn't my sister. → The girl _____.
5. Paul ate all of the chocolate. He bought it in Belgium.
   → Paul _____.
6. I saw the art exhibit last night. It is open until next week.
   → The art exhibit _____.
7. We went to a restaurant. It's famous for its dessert.
   → We _____.
8. The boss introduced that man to us today. He's going to attend the next meeting.
   → That man _____.

C. 다음 문장을 읽고 틀린 부분이 있으면 바르게 고치세요. 틀린 부분이 없으면 O로 표시하세요.

1. I've talked to the man owns that store.   *owns → who (OR that) owns*
2. The house was sold last week is empty right now. _____
3. We stayed at the hotel many tourists recommended. _____
4. People exercise regularly live longer.   _____
5. Where is the book was on the table?   _____
6. Is that the train that you're waiting for?   _____

D. 괄호 안에 주어진 단어들과 who 또는 which를 사용하여 이웃과 James의 대화를 완성하세요. 가능한 경우 who 또는 which를 생략하세요.

Neighbor

Neighbor: ¹·We loved the food *you made* _____, James. (you, made)
JAMES: Thanks! ²·Next time, let's go to a restaurant _____ recently. (open)
³·My friend _____ cooking in Italy owns it. (studied)
Neighbor: ⁴·Is that the restaurant _____ last week? (you, visited)
JAMES: Yes. I had pasta there and it was very good.

JAMES

정답 p.286, REVIEW TEST 13 p.240

UNIT 095

Grammar Gateway Basic

UNIT 096 | **There is** a boat in the ocean. there + be동사

🎧 096.mp3

①

There is a boat in the ocean.
바다에 배 한 척이 있다.

There are a lot of people on the beach.
해변에 많은 사람들이 있다.

---

② '~이 있다'라는 의미로 말할 때, **there + be동사**를 쓸 수 있다.

긍정·부정			의문		
there	is are	(not)	Is Are	there ...?	

- **There is** a new shopping mall in town. 시내에 새로운 쇼핑몰이 있다.
- I can't make a cake. **There aren't** any eggs. 달걀이 하나도 없다.
- "**Are there** any shirts you want to buy?" "That green one."

---

③ **there is** + 단수/셀 수 없는 명사
- **There is a package** for you at the front desk. 안내 데스크에 당신에게 온 소포가 있어요.
- We can't buy that sofa because **there isn't enough space** in our apartment. 우리 아파트에 충분한 공간이 없다.

there are + 복수명사
- **There are lots of parties** during the holidays. 휴일 동안 많은 파티들이 있다.
- "**Are there any direct flights** from Seoul to Madrid?" 서울에서 마드리드까지 직항 항공편이 있나요? "Let me check."

---

④ **there was/were** ~: (과거에) ~이 있었다

긍정·부정			의문		
there	was were	(not)	Was Were	there ...?	

- **There was** a bookstore here, but it moved to Main Street. 여기에 서점이 있었는데 Main가로 옮겼다.
- The class finished early because **there weren't** any questions. 질문이 없었기 때문에 수업이 일찍 끝났다.

---

⑤ **there have/has been** ~: (과거부터 지금까지) ~이 있었다

긍정·부정				의문			
there	have has	(not)	been	Have Has	there	been ...?	

- "**Have there been** any calls for me?" 저한테 온 전화가 있었나요? "Yes. The manager called."
- "Where is the train?" "**There has been** a delay. It'll be here soon." 지연이 있었어요.

PRACTICE

A. 그림을 보고 주어진 표현과 there is 또는 there are를 사용하여 문장을 완성하세요.

a lake	~~a man~~	some fish	some people

1    2    3    4

1. *There is a man* _____ at the door.
2. _____ on the bridge.
3. _____ in the water.
4. _____ in the park.

B. there is/are 또는 there was/were를 사용하여 문장을 완성하세요. 필요한 경우 부정문으로 쓰세요.

1. " *Is there* _____ anybody at home?" "Rick might be back from work."
2. _____ an empty seat near the door, so I sat there.
3. I want to check my e-mail, but _____ any computers in this hotel.
4. _____ any bread to make sandwiches, so I had to go to the store.
5. Can you help me? _____ some problems with my new cell phone.
6. I want to see a movie tonight, but _____ anything to watch.
7. _____ any questions before we start today?

C. 괄호 안에 주어진 표현과 there have/has been을 적절한 형태로 사용하여 문장을 완성하세요.

1. (two storms) *There have been two storms* _____ since Monday.
2. (any visitors) " _____ here recently?" "Yes, but not many."
3. (a lot of accidents) _____ on the road these days. Drive slowly.
4. (a change) " _____ to my schedule?" "No. It's still the same."
5. (not, many tourists) _____ in the city this year.
6. (not, any rain) _____ this month. The weather is very dry.

D. Paul과 Chris는 해변에 갔습니다. 괄호 안에 주어진 표현과 there is/are 또는 there was/were를 사용하여 Paul과 Chris의 대화를 완성하세요.

PAUL: 1. *There are a lot of people* _____ on the beach today. (a lot of people)
CHRIS: I know. 2. _____ here yesterday. (not many people)
PAUL: Well, the weather is very nice today.
   3. _____ in the sky. (not a cloud)
CHRIS: Look! There is a boat there. It's a perfect day for a boat ride.
   4. _____ around here? (a rental shop)
PAUL: 5. _____ before, but I'm not sure if it's still here. (one)
CHRIS: OK. Let's check.

PAUL

CHRIS

정답 p.286, REVIEW TEST 14 p.242

UNIT 097 | He **gave his wife a ring.** 동사(give/make 등) + 사람 + 사물

🎧 097.mp3

①

He gave **his wife a ring**.
　　　　　사람　　사물

또는 He gave **a ring** to **his wife**.
　　　　　사물　　　　사람

그는 아내에게 반지를 주었다.

---

② 다음과 같은 동사 뒤에 사람 + 사물을 쓸 수 있다.

give (~에게 …을 주다) 　**make** (~에게 …을 만들어주다) 　**send** (~에게 …을 보내다)
show (~에게 …을 보여주다) **buy** (~에게 …을 사주다) 　**teach** (~에게 …을 가르치다)

- I **gave Kathy my phone number**. We'll talk about the project over the phone.　나는 Kathy에게 내 전화번호를 주었다.
- Josh **made me an omelet** this morning. It was very good.　Josh는 오늘 아침에 나에게 오믈렛을 만들어주었다.
- Richard **sent us a wedding invitation**. He's getting married next month.
- "Can you **show me your ticket**, please?" "Sure. Here you go."
- Fiona **will buy her boyfriend a box of chocolates** on Valentine's Day.
- My father **taught me French** when I was young. He's from France.

---

③ to 또는 for를 사용하여 다음과 같이 쓸 수도 있다.

give/send/show/teach + 사물 + to + 사람

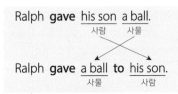

Ralph **gave** his son a ball.
　　　　　　사람　　사물

Ralph **gave** a ball **to** his son.
　　　　　　사물　　　　사람

- I **sent** my friends gifts.　　　　→ I **sent** gifts **to** my friends.　나는 친구들에게 선물을 보냈다.
- Could you **show** me the city map?　→ Could you **show** the city map **to** me?　저에게 시내 지도를 보여주시겠어요?
- Ms. Brown **teaches** us science.　　→ Ms. Brown **teaches** science **to** us.

make/buy + 사물 + for + 사람

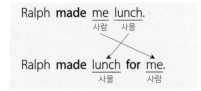

Ralph **made** me lunch.
　　　　　　사람 사물

Ralph **made** lunch **for** me.
　　　　　　사물　　사람

- Will you **buy** me a cup of coffee?　→ Will you **buy** a cup of coffee **for** me?　나에게 커피 한 잔을 사줄래?
- Joan **will make** Rick a sandwich.　→ Joan **will make** a sandwich **for** Rick.　Joan은 Rick에게 샌드위치를 만들어 줄 것이다.
- We **bought** Mr. Lee some fruit.　　→ We **bought** some fruit **for** Mr. Lee.

PRACTICE

A. 그림을 보고 주어진 표현을 사용하여 예시와 같이 문장을 완성하세요. 과거 시제로 쓰세요.

| a doll | his room | ~~some flowers~~ | some coffee |

1 — LUCY — These are for you.
2 — JEN — Thank you, mom!
3 — KIM — This is my room.
4 — JAKE — Here you are.

1. (give) He _gave Lucy some flowers_ .
2. (buy) She _____ .

3. (show) He _____ .
4. (make) He _____ .

B. 주어진 표현과 to 또는 for를 적절한 형태로 사용하여 예시와 같이 문장을 완성하세요.

| buy an apartment | ~~give her address~~ | make breakfast |
| send Christmas cards | show my new car | teach music |

1. (me) Victoria _gave her address to me_ . You don't have to ask her again.
2. (him) "Does your son still live with you?" "No. We _____ ."
3. (students) Mr. Franks had another job before he was a banker. He _____ .
4. (you) "Did I _____ ?" "No. Is it the one in front of the house?"
5. (me) My husband _____ last weekend. It was good.
6. (his friends) "Does Paul _____ every year?" "Yes. He makes them himself."

C. 주어진 문장의 형태를 바꾸어 쓰세요. 필요한 경우 to 또는 for를 지우거나 함께 쓰세요.

1. The doctor gave Ryan some medicine. _The doctor gave some medicine to Ryan_ .
2. Did Tim send those gifts to you? _____ ?
3. Money can't buy happiness for us. _____ .
4. Laura teaches students yoga. _____ .
5. Can you show me your passport? _____ ?
6. My mother made me a sweater. _____ ?

D. 괄호 안에 주어진 단어들을 적절히 배열하여 Amy와 Linda의 대화를 완성하세요.

AMY

AMY: Mom, did Dad do anything special for your birthday?
LINDA: Yes! 1. He _bought me dinner_ at a nice hotel. (dinner / me / bought)
    2. And he _____ . (me / a ring / to / gave)
AMY: A ring? Wow!
LINDA: Well, it's also for our 30th wedding anniversary.
AMY: I forgot about that! We should have a party.
    3. I'll _____ . (send / invitations / your friends)
    4. I can _____ too! (you / a cake / make / for)

LINDA

정답 p.286, REVIEW TEST 14 p.242

UNIT 097

Grammar Gateway Basic

① '~하라'라고 상대방에게 말할 때 동사원형(come, be 등)을 문장 처음에 쓴다.

- **Come** here. 이리 와라.
- The knife is really sharp. **Be** careful. 조심해라.
- "Where is the bank?"
  "**Go** straight and **turn** right at the next corner."
- **Hurry** up! We'll be late for class!

Come here!

'~하지 말아라'라고 할 때는 **don't** + 동사원형을 쓴다.

- The wall was just painted. **Don't touch** it. 그것을 만지지 말아라.
- **Don't leave** your bag there. Someone might take it. 거기에 가방을 두지 말아라.
- It's warm enough in here. **Don't turn** on the heater.
- **Don't forget**. It's Mom's birthday tomorrow.

② '(함께) ~하자'라고 상대방에게 권유할 때 **let's** + 동사원형을 쓴다.

- **Let's go** inside. 안으로 들어가자.
- **Let's take** a break for a few minutes. 몇 분 동안 쉬자.
- "I'm really hungry. **Let's order** something."
  "OK. How about Thai food?"
- "Where is Brian right now? Is he coming soon?"
  "I don't know. **Let's call** him."

Let's go inside!

'~하지 말자'라고 할 때는 **let's not** + 동사원형을 쓴다.

- We have a lot to do. **Let's not waste** time. 시간을 낭비하지 말자.
- It's going to rain this afternoon. **Let's not wash** the car today. 오늘 세차하지 말자.
- **Let's not discuss** this now. We can do it later.
- I'm tired. **Let's not stay** too long at the party.

③ '정말 ~하구나!'라고 감탄이나 놀라움을 나타낼 때 **How** + 형용사를 쓴다.

- Look at the view. **How wonderful!** 정말 멋지구나!
- "Dad, I made this card for you. Happy Father's Day!"
  "**How kind!**" 정말 친절하구나!
- "Emily lost her grandmother last Saturday."
  "**How sad!** Is she OK?"
- This soup is great. **How delicious!**

How wonderful!

What (+ a/an) + 형용사 + 명사로도 감탄이나 놀라움을 나타낼 수 있다.

- I have four meetings today. **What a busy day!** 정말 바쁜 날이구나!
- "I got a promotion yesterday!" "**What great news!**" 정말 좋은 소식이구나!
- "Have you heard? Jim won the lottery." "Really? **What a lucky guy!**"
- **What an interesting painting!** Who is the artist?

PRACTICE

A. 주어진 동사를 사용하여 상황에 맞게 명령문을 완성하세요.

be	~~close~~	do	slow	wake

1. The window is open. You feel cold.
2. Your friend is driving too fast.
3. It's already noon, but your brother is still in bed.
4. Your sister wants to play games, but she has homework.
5. Your friends are talking loudly in the library.

> *Close* _____ the window.
> _____ down.
> _____ up.
> _____ your homework.
> _____ quiet.

B. 그림을 보고 주어진 동사와 don't를 사용하여 문장을 완성하세요.

~~sit~~	smoke	swim	take

1. *Don't sit* _____ on the bench!

2. _____ pictures here.

3. _____ in the river.

4. Please _____ here.

C. 주어진 동사와 let's 또는 let's not을 사용하여 문장을 완성하세요.

ask	~~buy~~	go	listen	start	watch

1. A: This lamp doesn't work.
   B: It's old. *Let's buy* _____ a new one.

2. A: _____ to some music.
   B: Good idea. I'll turn on the radio.

3. A: This movie doesn't look interesting.
   B: _____ it then.

4. A: When are we having the meeting?
   B: _____ at 3:30.

5. A: _____ jogging today. I'm tired.
   B: OK. Let's relax at home.

6. A: Do you know the answer to this question?
   B: No. _____ Philip. He might know.

D. 1–3번은 How를, 4–6번은 What을 사용하여 상황에 맞게 감탄문을 완성하세요.

1. Your friend told you a funny joke.
2. You saw a very expensive bag.
3. You watched an exciting baseball game on TV.
4. Your friend has a nice car.
5. You just received lovely flowers from someone.
6. You're in a hotel room, and it has a great view.

> *How funny* _____ !
> _____ !
> _____ !
> _____ !
> _____ !
> _____ !

정답 p.286, REVIEW TEST 14 p.242

UNIT
098

Grammar Gateway Basic

UNIT 099 | He **said that** I could use his car. 다른 사람의 말을 전달하기

🎧 099.mp3

①

"You can use my car."

JAMES

KATE

He said that I could use his car.

"**You can** use my car."

He **said that I could** use his car.

그는 내가 그의 차를 사용해도 된다고 말했어.

James가 한 말을 Kate에게 전달하기 위해 said that을 썼다.

---

② 다른 사람의 말을 전달할 때 **said that**을 쓸 수 있다. 이때, 주어를 바꾸고 동사의 시제는 과거로 쓴다.

어제   오늘

- Katie: "**I am** so excited."   →   Katie **said that** | **she was** | so excited.
- John: "**I want** to play outside."   →   John **said that** | **he wanted** | to play outside.
- Chris: "**I will** lend you my camera." →   Chris **said that** | **he would** | lend me his camera.
- Mom: "**You have to** be home by 11." →   Mom **said that** | **I had to** | be home by 11.
- The boss: "**You can** leave early."   →   The boss **said that** | **we could** | leave early.

이때, **that**을 생략할 수도 있다.

- Gino just called. He **said** his flight was delayed. (= He said that his flight was ~)
- The news **said** it snowed heavily in Seattle today. (= The news said that it snowed ~)

---

③ 다른 사람의 말을 전달할 때 **told**를 쓸 수도 있다. **told** 뒤에는 사람 + that을 쓴다.

사람 + that

- I **told** | Dad that | I was ready for school. 나는 아빠에게 학교 갈 준비가 되었다고 말했다.
- Matt **told** | me that | he made some pasta for me. Matt는 나에게 날 위해 파스타를 만들었다고 말했다.
- Tom **told** | us that | he didn't need our help.
- "You **told** | me that | you wouldn't be late again." "I'm sorry."
- Ella and Dan **told** | you that | it was their wedding anniversary yesterday, didn't they?

이때에도 **that**을 생략할 수 있다.

- The doctor **told me** I should exercise twice a week. (= The doctor told me that I should ~)
- Wendy **told her friends** she was going to leave. (= Wendy told her friends that she was ~)

---

④ **told** 뒤에는 사람을 반드시 쓰고, **said** 뒤에는 사람을 쓰지 않는 것에 주의한다.

- Lisa **told me** she couldn't come to work this morning. (Lisa told she couldn't ~로 쓸 수 없음)
  Lisa **said** she couldn't come to work this morning. (Lisa said me she couldn't ~로 쓸 수 없음)
- You **told me** everything would be fine.
  You **said** everything would be fine.

PRACTICE

A. 다음의 사람들이 하는 말을 보고 said를 사용하여 다시 말해보세요.

1
I have a headache.

2
We're getting married.

3
I am on vacation.

4
We're going out.

5
BETTY
I'll call later.

6
I can't find my dog.
MARK

> 1. *He said (that) he had a headache* .
> 2. _____ .
> 3. _____ .
> 4. _____ .
> 5. _____ .
> 6. _____ .

Grammar Gateway Basic

B. A의 문장을 told를 사용하여 다시 말해보세요. 1–4번은 me를 함께 사용하세요.

> 1. *He told me (that) he had a headache* .
> 2. _____ .
> 3. _____ .
> 4. _____ .
> 5. _____ .
> 6. _____ .

C. said 또는 told를 써넣으세요.

1. Nicole *said* she didn't know Kim's phone number.
2. "Kevin _____ me that he could spend Christmas with us." "Really? That's great!"
3. Ms. Hill _____ that she worked at a museum.
4. "How are you getting to the airport?" "Todd _____ he would take me."
5. "I liked the book that you gave me." "I _____ you it was good."
6. Larry _____ me he could take care of our children this weekend.
7. Kelly _____ she was busy. Let's just go to the bar without her.
8. "How long do we have to wait?" "The waiter _____ me 10 minutes would be enough."

정답 p.287, REVIEW TEST 14 p.242

I like it **too**. I don't like them **either**.

too와 either, so와 neither

🎧 100.mp3

①

I like pizza. I like it too.

I **like** it **too**.
나도 역시 그것을 좋아해.

I don't like onions. I **don't** like them **either**.

I **don't** like them **either**.
나도 역시 그것을 좋아하지 않아.

---

②

too: ~도 역시 …하다

too는 긍정문에 쓴다.

- Kenneth is from Canada. His wife **is too**.
  그의 아내도 역시 캐나다 출신이다.
- "I want to go to Europe this summer."
  "I **do too**." 나도 역시 가고 싶어.
- "I'm going to have coffee. What about you?"
  "I'**ll** have coffee **too**."
- "I've met Stacy."
  "I **have too**. She's very nice."

either: ~도 역시 …하지 않다

either는 부정문에 쓴다.

- "John and Jane weren't at the party."
  "Bob **wasn't either**." Bob도 역시 파티에 없었어.
- We didn't have any wine, and we **didn't** have any beer **either**. 우리는 맥주도 역시 없었다.
- "I shouldn't spend too much money today."
  "I **shouldn't either**."
- "I've never run in a marathon before."
  "I **haven't either**. This is my first time."

---

③

'~도 역시 …하다'라는 의미로 말할 때 **so**를 쓸 수도 있다.

A: I **am** hungry.　　　　　B: **So am** I.

A: I **like** pizza.　　　　　B: **So do** I.

- "I **was** angry with Nate yesterday."
  "**So was** I." 나도 역시 어제 Nate에게 화가 났어.
- "We **watched** the Olympics this year."
  "**So did we**." 우리도 역시 올림픽을 봤어요.
- "Bill **can** speak Japanese."
  "**So can his brother**. They lived in Japan."

'~도 역시 …하지 않다'라는 의미로 말할 때 **neither**를 쓸 수도 있다.

A: I **am not** hungry.　　　B: **Neither am** I.

A: I **don't** like pizza.　　B: **Neither do** I.

- "I **don't** exercise often."
  "**Neither do** I." 나도 역시 자주 운동하지 않아.
- "Grace **won't** be ready until 7 o'clock."
  "**Neither will Leo**." Leo도 역시 7시까지 준비하지 못할 거야.
- "I **haven't** seen Ross for a long time."
  "**Neither have** I. He has been very busy."

이때, **So I am, Neither I do** 등과 같은 순서로 쓰지 않도록 주의한다.

- "I'm 21 years old." "**So am I**." (So I am으로 쓸 수 없음)
- "I don't like vegetables." "**Neither do I**." (Neither I do로 쓸 수 없음)

PRACTICE

A. too 또는 either를 써넣으세요.

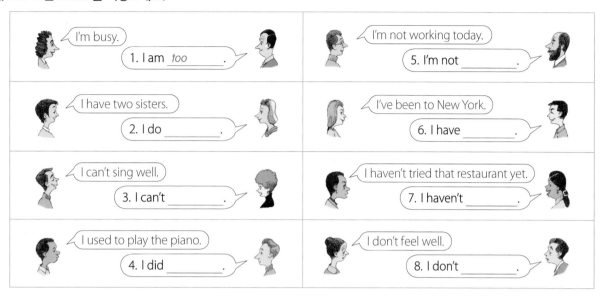

I'm busy.
1. I am _too_ .

I have two sisters.
2. I do _____ .

I can't sing well.
3. I can't _____ .

I used to play the piano.
4. I did _____ .

I'm not working today.
5. I'm not _____ .

I've been to New York.
6. I have _____ .

I haven't tried that restaurant yet.
7. I haven't _____ .

I don't feel well.
8. I don't _____ .

UNIT **100**

Grammar Gateway Basic

B. 괄호 안에 주어진 단어와 so 또는 neither를 사용하여 예시와 같이 문장을 완성하세요.

1. I'm sleepy.
2. I haven't gone skiing before.
3. I can ride a motorcycle.
4. Fred isn't married.
5. Sue and I are British.
6. My roommate doesn't talk a lot.
7. The soup wasn't very good.
8. Alice and Ron live in San Diego.

(I) _So am I_ .
(I) _____ .
(Brian) _____ .
(Maria) _____ .
(we) _____ .
(mine) _____ .
(the salad) _____ .
(Jim and Emily) _____ .

C. too/either/so/neither를 써넣으세요.

1. "That was a very funny movie." "I enjoyed it _too_ ."
2. Erica doesn't like dogs, and she doesn't like cats _____ .
3. "I should get up early tomorrow." "_____ should I."
4. This bread smells great. I hope it tastes good _____ .
5. "We're going to have a Halloween party tonight." "_____ are we."
6. We don't have a TV, and we don't have a computer _____ .
7. "I haven't talked to Ms. Williams lately." "_____ have I."
8. We visited a zoo last weekend. We went to an art museum _____ .
9. "Mark isn't good at sports." "_____ is Roy."
10. "Martin can fall asleep in noisy places." "I know! _____ can Harry."

정답 p.287, REVIEW TEST 14 p.242

REVIEW TEST

지금까지 학습한 내용을 통합해서 연습할 수 있는 REVIEW TEST입니다.
틀리거나 확실히 잘 모르는 문제는 해당 UNIT으로 돌아가 복습하세요.
그럼 마무리 연습을 시작해볼까요?

다양한 직업을 가진 사람들이 지금 각기 다른 행동을 하고 있습니다. 괄호 안에 주어진 동사들을 한 번씩 사용하여 문장을 완성하세요. 현재 시제 또는 현재진행 시제로 쓰세요.

Name: ALBERT
Job: Writer

Name: ANGELA
Job: Chef

Name: KEVIN
Job: Teacher

Name: SIMONE
Job: Nurse

1. (write, drink) Albert _writes_ novels. He _'s drinking_ OR _is drinking_ coffee.
2. (work, listen) Angela _____ at a restaurant. She _____ to music.
3. (read, teach) Kevin _____ a newspaper. He _____ at a high school.
4. (shop, help) Simone _____. She _____ sick people.

괄호 안에 주어진 단어들을 적절히 배열하여 문장을 완성하세요.

5. (is / he / busy)
   Tom is working hard. _He's busy_ OR _He is busy_ _____ today.

6. (Mom / is / pancakes / making)
   "_____?" "No, Dad is making them."

7. (do / not / we / use / it)
   Let's give Eric our camera. _____ anymore.

8. (you / know / him / do)
   "Why is that man waving at us? _____?" "Yes. He's my neighbor."

9. (are / Lisa and Anton / from England / not)
   _____. They are French.

10. (not / wear / Julia / does / glasses)
    "Are these glasses Julia's?" "No, they're Nick's. _____."

괄호 안에 주어진 단어들을 사용하여 현재 시제 또는 현재진행 시제 의문문을 완성하세요.

11. (I, late) _Am I late_ _____ for the party?	No, you're not.
12. (you, practice) _____ the violin every day?	Yes, I do.
13. (birds, eat) _____ worms?	Yes, they do.
14. (it, rain) _____ right now?	Yes, it is.
15. (Brian, take) _____ the bus to school?	No, he doesn't.
16. (you, watch) Why is the TV on? _____ it?	Yes, I am.
17. (she, work) Who is that woman? _____ here?	No, she doesn't.
18. (you, ready) _____ for the meeting?	No, I'm not.

보기 중 맞는 것을 고르세요.

19. "You look tired. Are you OK?" "I _____ sick."
    a) am   b) is   c) are

20. Sally _____ a good singer. I like her songs very much.
    a) am   b) is   c) are

21. It's rainy today, but it _____ cold.
    a) am not   b) is not   c) are not

22. I _____ tall, but I'm good at basketball.
    a) am not   b) is not   c) are not

23. "I like those pants. _____ they expensive?" "No, they're not."
    a) Is   b) Are   c) Am

24. "I lost my eraser." "_____ one in my pencil case. You can use mine."
    a) I'm having   b) I'm have   c) I have

25. Andrew doesn't have a car. He _____ the subway every day.
    a) take   b) takes   c) don't take

26. In Fiji, it _____ in the winter.
    a) is not snowing   b) don't snow   c) doesn't snow

27. "_____ fish for dinner tonight?" "No, I don't like fish."
    a) Do you want   b) Are you wanting   c) You are want

28. Emma _____. Her husband makes their meals.
    a) is not cook   b) doesn't cook   c) don't cook

29. I don't want to go out today. _____ too much.
    a) It's snowing   b) It's not snow   c) It's snow

30. "What are you and Mark doing?" "_____ a game."
    a) We're playing   b) We're play   c) We play

31. Is that Bill? He _____ his glasses today.
    a) is not wearing   b) is not wear   c) doesn't wear

32. My parents _____ well. They both have a cold.
    a) are feel   b) aren't feel   c) aren't feeling

33. "_____ right now?" "No, she's reading a book."
    a) Is Margaret studying   b) Is Margaret study   c) Does Margaret study

정답 p.288

틀리거나 확실하지 않은 문제는 아래의 표를 확인하여 해당 UNIT으로 돌아가 복습하세요.

문제	1	2	3	4	5	6	7	8	9	10	11	12	13	14	15	16
UNIT	10	10	10	10	1	5	8	9	2	8	3	9	9	5	9	5
17	18	19	20	21	22	23	24	25	26	27	28	29	30	31	32	33
9	3	1	1	2	2	3	10	6	8	9	8	4	4	5	5	5

TEST 2 과거와 과거진행 (UNIT 11-17)

 프랑스를 여행 중인 Jenny가 엽서를 보냈습니다. 주어진 동사를 사용하여 과거 시제 문장을 완성하세요.

~~arrive~~   buy   see   take   visit   walk

Dear Brian,

How are you? I'm in France!
1. I _arrived_ in Paris last Saturday.
2. On Sunday, I _____ along the river.
3. The next day, I _____ an art museum with my friend.
4. I _____ many beautiful paintings.
5. I _____ lots of photos.
6. This morning, I _____ some gifts for you.

Best wishes,
Jenny

괄호 안에 주어진 단어들을 사용하여 현재 시제 또는 과거 시제 문장을 완성하세요.

7. (I, make) _I made_ spaghetti for you.
8. (I, not see) _____ you yesterday.
9. (Susie, be) _____ your friend in college?
10. (I, have) _____ a headache.
11. (you, go) _____ to the concert last weekend?
12. (he, be) Who is that handsome man? _____ a freshman?
13. (I, not know) _____ the way to City Hall. Can you give me directions?

Thanks, Grace!
I was sick.
Yes, she was.
Take this medicine.
No. I stayed at home.
He's my brother!
Sure, follow me.

괄호 안에 주어진 단어들을 적절히 배열하여 문장을 완성하세요.

14. (was / he / not)
Jacob didn't eat dinner. _He wasn't OR He was not_ hungry.

15. (did / Lucy / go / not)
_____ to school yesterday. It was Sunday.

16. (Ben / clean / did)
"_____ the bathroom yesterday?" "Yes, he did."

17. (you / were / studying)
"I saw you at the library yesterday. _____?" "Yes. I had an exam today."

18. (waiting / were / we)
"Why were you and Joseph at the airport last night?" "_____ for Jenna."

218 예문 해석 무료 영어 학습 컨텐츠 제공 Hackers.co.kr

보기 중 맞는 것을 고르세요.

19. "What were you doing at 6 yesterday?"   "I _____."
   a) am worked   b) was working   c) am working

20. Last Tuesday _____ Tracy's birthday. She's 20 years old now.
   a) was   b) were   c) is

21. Sally _____ at home this morning. She didn't answer the door.
   a) wasn't   b) weren't   c) isn't

22. " _____ jogging when you saw them last week?"   "Yes, they were."
   a) Was Tom and Jane   b) Were Tom and Jane   c) Are Tom and Jane

23. "This sandwich is amazing! Did you make it?"   "No, I _____ it at a store."
   a) bought   b) was buying   c) buy

24. Kyle and I _____ butterflies every day, but we're too busy these days.
   a) used to catching   b) were catching   c) used to catch

25. Jason _____ to school yesterday. He took the bus.
   a) didn't walk   b) walks   c) doesn't walk

26. _____ in Taiwan?"   "Yes. I was there for two years."
   a) Did you use to live   b) Do you used to live   c) Are you living

27. "Sorry I called you so late last night."   "That's OK. I _____ when you called."
   a) wasn't sleeping   b) was sleeping   c) am sleeping

28. "Was your team playing soccer at 2 this afternoon?"   "No, we _____ lunch."
   a) used to have   b) are having   c) were having

29. Last night at 11, Andrew and Rachel _____ TV. They were playing video games.
   a) aren't watching   b) watched   c) weren't watching

30. " _____ you this afternoon?"   "No, she didn't."
   a) Was Jennifer call   b) Did Jennifer call   c) Does Jennifer call

31. " _____ when you saw him?"   "Yes, he was."
   a) Was Thomas exercising b) Were Thomas exercising   c) Is Thomas exercising

32. I _____ swimming lessons on Tuesdays, but I quit.
   a) take   b) used to take   c) am taking

33. The store _____ on weekends. Now it opens on Saturdays.
   a) didn't use to open   b) use not to open   c) don't use to open

정답 p.288

틀리거나 확실하지 않은 문제는 아래의 표를 확인하여 해당 UNIT으로 돌아가 복습하세요.

문제	1	2	3	4	5	6	7	8	9	10	11	12	13	14	15	16
UNIT	13	13	13	13	13	13	13	14	12	6	14	3	8	12	14	14
17	18	19	20	21	22	23	24	25	26	27	28	29	30	31	32	33
16	15	15	11	12	16	13	17	14	17	16	15	16	14	16	17	17

괄호 안에 주어진 단어들을 적절히 배열하여 문장을 완성하세요.

1. (owned / a dog / you / have / ever)
   Have you ever owned a dog ?

2. (we / not / yet / eaten dinner / have)
   _____ .

3. (many concerts / has / Mark / been to)
   _____ .

4. (the snow / stopped / has / just)
   _____ ?

5. (made / some muffins / Aaron and Nick / have)
   _____ .

6. (not / Mandy / a roller coaster / ridden / has)
   _____ before.

 그림을 보고 주어진 표현을 사용하여 현재완료 시제 문장을 완성하세요. 필요한 경우 부정문으로 쓰세요.

| be sick | ~~have this camera~~ | know each other | rain |

7. I *'ve had this camera* since 2012.

8. We _____ for 10 years.

9. It _____ since last month.

10. He _____ for two days.

 괄호 안에 주어진 동사를 사용하여 과거 시제 또는 현재완료 시제 문장을 완성하세요.

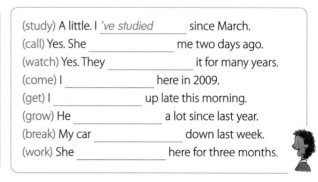

11. Do you speak French?
12. Have you talked to Cindy lately?
13. Do your parents like that TV show?
14. How long have you been in China?
15. Why are you late?
16. Your son is so tall now.
17. Where's your car?
18. When did Susan come to this company?

(study) A little. I *'ve studied* since March.
(call) Yes. She _____ me two days ago.
(watch) Yes. They _____ it for many years.
(come) I _____ here in 2009.
(get) I _____ up late this morning.
(grow) He _____ a lot since last year.
(break) My car _____ down last week.
(work) She _____ here for three months.

보기 중 맞는 것을 고르세요.

19. "_____ Tim and Lisa arrived at the party?" "Yes. They're dancing now."
    a) Have   b) Did   c) Do

20. "Have you already finished college?" "Yes. I _____ two years ago."
    a) have graduated   b) graduated   c) graduate

21. My baseball team lost again. We _____ a game since last year.
    a) haven't won   b) don't won   c) didn't win

22. I haven't seen my sister _____ five years. I miss her so much.
    a) since   b) ago   c) for

23. My daughter is at the hospital. She _____ her arm yesterday.
    a) has hurt   b) hurts   c) hurt

24. "What's wrong with the lamp?" "Jack _____ it."
    a) has broken   b) have broken   c) doesn't break

25. Jason and I _____ to the museum last Thursday.
    a) have gone   b) went   c) go

26. "Have you ever been to New Zealand?" "No. I _____ abroad."
    a) have traveled   b) haven't traveled c) hasn't traveled

27. "_____ your homework yet?" "I'll do it tomorrow."
    a) You done have   b) Have you done   c) Have done you

28. "Is Dad still at home?" "No. He _____ to work."
    a) has gone   b) has been   c) doesn't go

29. "How long have you been married?" "We've been married _____ 1998."
    a) since   b) ago   c) for

30. Martin is so smart. He _____ an exam.
    a) have never failed   b) has never failed c) hasn't never failed

31. "_____ come yet?" "Yes. It's on your desk."
    a) The mail did   b) Have the mail   c) Has the mail

32. "Am I late?" "No. The movie _____ yet."
    a) has started   b) hasn't started   c) haven't started

33. "Jessica looks upset." "_____ her watch."
    a) She has lost   b) She hasn't lost   c) Has she lost

정답 p.288

틀리거나 확실하지 않은 문제는 아래의 표를 확인하여 해당 UNIT으로 돌아가 복습하세요.

문제	1	2	3	4	5	6	7	8	9	10	11	12	13	14	15	16
UNIT	20	22	20	22	18	20	19	19	19	19	21	21	21	21	21	21
17	18	19	20	21	22	23	24	25	26	27	28	29	30	31	32	33
21	21	18	21	19	19	21	18	21	20	22	20	19	20	22	22	18

괄호 안에 주어진 단어들을 적절히 배열하여 문장을 완성하세요.

1. (like / Lisa / this ring / will)
   Will Lisa like this ring _____?

2. (going / marry her / he / to / is)
   Jake loves his girlfriend so much. _____.

3. (you / are / speaking)
   _____ at the seminar? I saw your name on the list.

4. (going / are / to / watch the fireworks / you)
   "_____ tonight?" "No. I'm tired."

5. (not / will / it / I / forget)
   "The password is 0922." "OK. _____."

6. (playing soccer / are / Alex and I / not)
   _____ this weekend. We're going to the beach instead.

 그림을 보고 주어진 표현과 be going to를 사용하여 문장을 완성하세요.

| drink some wine | ~~fall~~ | get on the train | stop at the light |

7   8   9   10

7. The tree _is going to fall_ _____.
8. She _____.
9. The car _____.
10. They _____.

 주어진 동사와 will을 사용하여 대화를 완성하세요. 필요한 경우 부정문으로 쓰세요.

| cook | meet | ~~open~~ | stay | tell | touch | turn on | write |

11. These gifts are for Janice.
12. Can I have your phone number?
13. You have to get up early tomorrow.
14. It's so cold.
15. I just painted that wall. It's still wet.
16. It's a secret.
17. I'm so hungry.
18. Let's see a movie tonight.

OK. I _won't open_ _____ them.
Sure. I _____ it down for you.
I know. I _____ up late.
You're right. I _____ the heater.
All right. I _____ it.
Don't worry. I _____ anyone.
I _____ something for you.
Sure. I _____ you at the theater.

보기 중 맞는 것을 고르세요.

19. Take this medicine. You _____ better.
    a) are going to get   b) were going to get   c) got

20. "You can get a 10 percent discount on this coat." "Really? _____ it!"
    a) I took   b) I take   c) I'll take

21. "Do you have any plans for this Sunday?" " _____ my grandparents."
    a) I visited   b) I visit   c) I'm going to visit

22. " _____ busy tomorrow?" "I'm not sure. Why?"
    a) Do you and Nate be   b) Will you and Nate be   c) You and Nate will be

23. We need to hurry. The bank _____ in 10 minutes.
    a) close   b) closes   c) closed

24. "This steak tastes awful." "Does it? I _____ it, then."
    a) won't eat   b) don't eat   c) didn't eat

25. "Did you book a ticket for Tokyo?" "Yes. _____ next Wednesday."
    a) I leave   b) I won't leave   c) I'm leaving

26. "Hurry up!" "Don't worry. We _____ late."
    a) will be   b) won't be   c) are

27. _____ the meeting this afternoon. She's sick.
    a) Jenny's attending   b) Jenny doesn't attend   c) Jenny's not attending

28. " _____ soon?" "I don't think so."
    a) Is the rain going to stop   b) Is the rain stop   c) Does the rain stop

29. Tina _____ the exam next week because she studied very hard.
    a) will pass   b) passes   c) passed

30. "We _____ to Seattle next month." "I'm glad you're staying here."
    a) don't move   b) aren't going to move   c) didn't move

31. I _____ with Kim next Sunday. Do you want to go with us?
    a) am going shopping   b) am not going shopping   c) was going shopping

32. " _____ to my birthday party?" "Of course. When is it?"
    a) Did you come   b) Do you come   c) Will you come

33. " _____ the car today?" "No. You can use it."
    a) Are you going to use   b) Are you use   c) Did you use

정답 p.288

틀리거나 확실하지 않은 문제는 아래의 표를 확인하여 해당 UNIT으로 돌아가 복습하세요.

문제	1	2	3	4	5	6	7	8	9	10	11	12	13	14	15	16
UNIT	23	24	25	24	23	25	24	24	24	24	23	23	23	23	23	23
17	18	19	20	21	22	23	24	25	26	27	28	29	30	31	32	33
23	23	24	23	24	23	25	23	25	23	25	24	23	24	25	23	24

TEST 5　조동사 (UNIT 26–32)

괄호 안에 주어진 단어들을 적절히 배열하여 문장을 완성하세요.

1. (can / teach / you / me)
   "I want to learn Spanish. _Can you teach me_ _____?" "OK."

2. (not / might / he / come)
   "Is Tom coming to the beach with us?" "I'm not sure. _____."

3. (think / get / should / he / I)
   Fred's hair is very long. _____ a haircut.

4. (would / like / you / to / dance)
   "_____ with me?" "Sure."

5. (do / have to / not / I / go)
   _____ to the hospital. I'm feeling much better.

그림을 보고 주어진 표현과 조동사를 사용하여 문장을 완성하세요. 필요한 경우 부정문으로 쓰세요.

| be scared | call the police | fall down the stairs |
| fix the roof | ~~turn off the stove~~ | use the car |

6. (should) You _should turn off the stove_.

7. (can) We _____.

8. (have to) We _____.

9. (might) Watch out! You _____!

10. (have to) You _____.
    I'm nervous.

11. (must) We _____.

괄호 안에 주어진 조동사를 사용하여 현재 시제 또는 과거 시제 문장을 완성하세요. 필요한 경우 부정문으로 쓰세요.

12. (must) "It's very cold today. You _must_ _____ wear a jacket!" "OK, I will."
13. (can) The view from the tower was amazing. We _____ see the entire city.
14. (have to) Hank _____ get up early yesterday. He didn't go to work.
15. (should) You _____ drive so fast. You could get in an accident.
16. (must) "That's the last train! We _____ miss it." "Let's run."
17. (have to) My new sweater was too big for me. I _____ return it last weekend.
18. (can) The teacher spoke too quickly. I _____ understand him.

보기 중 맞는 것을 고르세요.

19. "_____ David play the guitar?" "Yes, he can."
   a) Must   b) Should   c) Can

20. Phillip's car is very dirty. He _____ clean it often.
   a) must not   b) shouldn't   c) might

21. "_____ get a soda, please?" "Sure, here you go."
   a) Can I   b) Would I   c) Should I

22. "_____ use your pen?" "Of course. Go ahead."
   a) May I   b) Would you like to   c) Could you

23. "Western Hotel, how can I help you?" "_____ a reservation for two nights, please."
   a) I'd like make   b) Would you to make   c) I'd like to make

24. Sarah _____ do the laundry last night. She was too tired.
   a) can't   b) couldn't   c) might not

25. The plane will land now. All passengers _____ wear seatbelts.
   a) must   b) had to   c) shouldn't

26. Gary failed his driving test. He _____ take it again.
   a) have to   b) has to   c) doesn't have to

27. "Can you finish your homework tonight?" "I don't know. I _____ finish it."
   a) shouldn't   b) must not   c) might not

28. "_____ order some food for us?" "Yes! I'm hungry."
   a) Would you like   b) Would I   c) Should I

29. I _____ wash the dishes. My sister has done it already.
   a) must not   b) don't have to   c) doesn't have to

30. "_____ fix my computer for me, please?" "Sure."
   a) You would   b) Could you   c) Should you

31. Sam broke Melinda's cup. He _____ apologize.
   a) should   b) can   c) could

32. I'm new here. _____ show me around the office?
   a) Would you   b) May I   c) I'd like to

33. "_____ more wine?" "No, thank you. I've had enough."
   a) Would you like   b) Would you like to   c) Should I

정답 p.289

틀리거나 확실하지 않은 문제는 아래의 표를 확인하여 해당 UNIT으로 돌아가 복습하세요.

문제	1	2	3	4	5	6	7	8	9	10	11	12	13	14	15	16
UNIT	26	27	31	32	30	31	26	30	27	30	29	29	26	30	31	29
17	18	19	20	21	22	23	24	25	26	27	28	29	30	31	32	33
30	26	26	29	28	28	32	26	29	30	27	31	30	28	31	32	32

그림을 보고 주어진 동사를 사용하여 수동태 문장을 완성하세요. 과거 시제로 쓰세요.

| ~~catch~~ | make | steal | take | write |

1. The thieves   *were caught*   by the policeman.
2. The scarves _____ in Italy.
3. The letter _____ by Jackie.
4. The pictures _____ in New York.
5. The painting _____ by someone.

괄호 안에 주어진 단어들을 적절히 배열하여 문장을 완성하세요.

6. (it / visited / is)
   Michael's town is famous. *It is visited* _____ by many tourists each year.

7. (pets / allowed / not / are)
   "Can we take our dog with us?" "No, _____ in the museum."

8. (the house / not / was / sold)
   _____ yesterday. It's still for sale.

9. (the Mona Lisa / painted / was / Leonardo da Vinci / by)
   _____.

10. (These dishes / not / can / used / be)
    _____ in a microwave.

괄호 안에 주어진 단어를 사용하여 능동태 또는 수동태 문장을 완성하세요. 과거 시제로 쓰세요.

11. (prepare) "This pasta is amazing. Who made it?" "All the dishes *were prepared*   by Chef Antonio."
12. (cancel) "Did you go to the meeting yesterday?" "No, it _____."
13. (have) "Were you with Susie this morning?" "Yes, I _____ coffee with her."
14. (break) The window _____ by the storm last night.
15. (not finish) "Did you do your homework?" "I _____ it. I was too busy."
16. (invent) The light bulb _____ by Thomas Edison.
17. (watch) "What did Frank do on Saturday?" "He _____ movies all day."
18. (not wash) "Has Bruce washed the car yet?" "It _____ when I saw it this morning."

보기 중 맞는 것을 고르세요.

19. The apple pies in this bakery are fresh. They _____ every morning.
   a) baked   (b) are baked   c) are bake

20. I can't read this book. It _____ in German.
   a) is written   b) was writing   c) wrote

21. I sent flowers to my friend, but they _____ .
   a) were delivered   b) weren't delivered   c) don't deliver

22. "What instrument does Jane play?" "She _____ the flute."
   a) plays   b) is played   c) was played

23. Fred _____ tomatoes. He doesn't like them.
   a) isn't eaten   b) wasn't eaten   c) doesn't eat

24. "What's George's phone number?" "Sorry, I _____ ."
   a) don't know   b) am not known   c) wasn't known

25. "Thirty people _____ to the party, but only 10 people came." "That's too bad."
   a) invited   b) were invited   c) weren't invited

26. "Why was Jack crying this morning?" "He _____ for the soccer team."
   a) wasn't chosen   b) chose   c) isn't chosen

27. Thomas Neilson's books are very famous. They _____ every year.
   a) are read many people   b) read by many people   c) are read by many people

28. Samantha's house is very old. It _____ in 1964.
   a) was built   b) were built   c) built

29. "Where's your phone?" "I _____ it last night."
   a) am lost   b) was lost   c) lost

30. An office party _____ by Ms. Harper.
   a) will plan   b) is planning   c) will be planned

31. "Why were you late to work this morning?" "The road _____ by snow."
   a) blocked   b) was blocked   c) is blocked

32. "Where did you get that car?" "Tony _____ it to me."
   a) was lent   b) lent   c) is lent

33. "Who taught you math in high school?" "I _____ ."
   a) was taught by Mr. Adams   b) was taught Mr. Adams   c) taught by Mr. Adams

····· 정답 p.289

틀리거나 확실하지 않은 문제는 아래의 표를 확인하여 해당 UNIT으로 돌아가 복습하세요.

문제	1	2	3	4	5	6	7	8	9	10	11	12	13	14	15	16
UNIT	34	33	34	33	34	34	33	33	34	33	34	34	34	34	34	34
17	18	19	20	21	22	23	24	25	26	27	28	29	30	31	32	33
34	34	34	34	34	34	34	34	34	34	34	34	34	34	34	34	34

대화를 보고 who/what/where/when을 써넣으세요.

1. _Where_ are you from?
2. _____ does your brother do?
3. _____ is your favorite singer?
4. _____ did you meet your wife?
5. _____ does the next bus arrive?
6. _____ are those people in the picture?
7. _____ can I see the doctor?
8. _____ time does your plane leave?

I'm from Thailand.
He's a scientist.
Tracy Swift. Her songs are really good.
At our university. We were classmates.
In 10 minutes.
They are my neighbors.
At 11 o'clock tomorrow morning.
At 9 p.m.

각 사람이 궁금해 하는 내용을 보고 간접의문문을 사용하여 문장을 완성하세요.

9. Do you know _who that man is_ ?

Who is that man?

Why did you buy this hat?

11. I wonder _____ .

10. Can you tell me _____ ?

Where can I put this?

When will Erica get here?

12. Do you know _____ ?

괄호 안에 주어진 단어들을 적절히 배열하여 문장을 완성하세요.

13. (you / tried / have / Mexican food)
    Have you tried Mexican food before? It's really good.
14. (this necklace / much / does / cost / how)
    "_____?" "$70."
15. (many / here / work / people / how)
    "_____?" "Around a hundred."
16. (will / busy / whether / you / be)
    Can you tell me _____ next Saturday?
17. (go / when / Cindy / did)
    "_____ to Hong Kong?" "Last Friday."
18. (this / from / where / is / wine)
    "_____?" "It was made in Italy."

보기 중 맞는 것을 고르세요.

19. "_____ mine?" "This one."
    a) Cup which is   b) Which is cup   c) Which cup is

20. "_____ will you arrive?" "At about 4 o'clock."
    a) When   b) Where   c) Why

21. "That was a very long flight, _____?" "Yes. Nearly 10 hours!"
    a) isn't it   b) wasn't it   c) was it

22. "_____ do I turn on this machine?" "Press the green button."
    a) When   b) Who   c) How

23. "_____ would you like, beef or pork?" "Beef, please."
    a) Which   b) How   c) Who

24. I don't know _____ to school today.
    a) if Chris went   b) did Chris go   c) Chris went

25. "_____ are you calling?" "My boyfriend."
    a) What   b) Who   c) How

26. "Josh and Sharon just arrived." "_____ together?"
    a) They did came   b) Did they come   c) Did they came

27. _____ is my bag? I can't find it.
    a) Where   b) When   c) Why

28. "_____ from your house?" "About two miles away."
    a) How far is your school   b) How far your school is   c) How your school is far

29. "_____ did Catherine go back to the store?" "She left her purse there."
    a) When   b) Where   c) Why

30. "Can you tell me _____ for dessert?" "I want something sweet."
    a) what do you want   b) you want what   c) what you want

31. "I can't leave my car here, _____?" "No. You have to park over there."
    a) can I   b) can you   c) can't I

32. "_____ lived in Sydney?" "For 20 years."
    a) How long you have   b) How have you long   c) How long have you

33. "_____ the piano?" "No, but she can play the guitar."
    a) Jamie can play   b) Can Jamie play   c) Can play Jamie

정답 p.289

틀리거나 확실하지 않은 문제는 아래의 표를 확인하여 해당 UNIT으로 돌아가 복습하세요.

문제	1	2	3	4	5	6	7	8	9	10	11	12	13	14	15	16
UNIT	37	36	36	37	37	36	37	36	40	40	40	40	35	38	38	40
17	18	19	20	21	22	23	24	25	26	27	28	29	30	31	32	33
37	37	36	37	39	38	36	40	36	35	37	38	37	40	39	38	35

TEST 8 -ing와 to + 동사원형 (UNIT 41–45)

그림을 보고 주어진 표현을 사용하여 문장을 완성하세요.

cook	go to the museum	~~play soccer~~	read books	sing	wait in line

1. I love *playing soccer*
   OR *to play soccer*   .

2. I hate _____
   _____ .

3. I practice _____
   _____ every day.

4. I enjoy _____
   _____ .

5. I plan _____
   _____ .

6. I like _____
   _____ at cafés.

괄호 안에 주어진 동사를 사용하여 대화를 완성하세요. 필요한 경우 동사를 -ing나 to + 동사원형으로 쓰세요.

7. (play) "Do you go to the golf course every week?" "Yes. *Playing*_____ golf is my hobby."

8. (send) "Where are you going?" "I'm going to the bank _____ some money."

9. (make) "When will you return home?" "At about 6. I'll help you _____ dinner tonight."

10. (eat) "I want to lose weight." "You should avoid _____ snacks."

11. (stay) "Why didn't you come to the party?" "My dad made me _____ at home."

12. (move) "There is no space for the new printer." "Let's try _____ it to the other room."

13. (learn) "I'm studying Japanese these days." "Why did you decide _____ a foreign language?"

괄호 안에 주어진 단어들을 적절히 배열하여 문장을 완성하세요.

14. (writing / finished / I / my report)
    " *I finished writing my report*_____." "Great. Can I see it?"

15. (me / use / Aaron / let / his)
    My mobile phone wasn't working, so _____.

16. (to / buy / does / need / Kim)
    "_____ a new computer?" "Yes, hers is very old."

17. (taught / Nicole / to dance / me)
    "You're a great dancer." "Thank you. _____."

18. (good / swimming / is)
    _____ for your health.

보기 중 맞는 것을 고르세요.

19. "When did you decide _____ a book?" "About three years ago."
    a) to write   b) writing   c) write

20. "Jenna made Dale _____ yesterday." "What did she do?"
    a) to cry   b) crying   c) cry

21. "Mr. Smith offered _____ me chess." "That's great. You're going to enjoy it."
    a) to teach   b) teaching   c) teach

22. "Can you _____ these plants, please?" "Sure. Where should they go?"
    a) help me moving   b) help me move   c) help moving me

23. Why are you still watching TV? I told you _____ to bed an hour ago.
    a) to go   b) going   c) go

24. Sophie keeps _____ me text messages during class. I want her to stop.
    a) to send   b) sending   c) send

25. "What are you going to do next Saturday?" "I'm planning _____ Chad."
    a) visit   b) visiting   c) to visit

26. "_____ a cheesecake takes about an hour." "Really? It doesn't take very long."
    a) Bake   b) Baking   c) Baked

27. "Anna and Joe want me _____ their tennis club." "That sounds like fun."
    a) join   b) joining   c) to join

28. I don't enjoy _____ basketball outside when it's hot.
    a) to play   b) playing   c) play

29. _____ a taxi isn't easy on Fridays. Let's take a bus.
    a) Get   b) Got   c) Getting

30. "Why did you go to the supermarket in the morning?" "Emily had me _____ some milk."
    a) to buy   a) buying   c) buy

31. "I went to the library _____ a book." "What book did you borrow?"
    a) borrowing   b) borrow   c) to borrow

32. "Why did you stop _____ to the fitness center?" "I hurt my back."
    a) to go   b) going   c) go

33. "Do you have time _____ every day?" "Yes. I usually go to the gym after work."
    a) to exercise   b) exercising   c) exercise

정답 p.289

틀리거나 확실하지 않은 문제는 아래의 표를 확인하여 해당 UNIT으로 돌아가 복습하세요.

문제	1	2	3	4	5	6	7	8	9	10	11	12	13	14	15	16
UNIT	43	43	42	42	42	43	41	45	44	42	44	43	42	42	44	42
17	18	19	20	21	22	23	24	25	26	27	28	29	30	31	32	33
44	41	42	44	42	44	44	42	42	41	44	42	41	44	45	43	45

괄호 안에 주어진 단어들을 적절히 배열하여 문장을 완성하세요. 필요한 경우 명사를 복수로 쓰세요.

1. (dog / has / he / five)

   "Does Brian have any pets?" "_He has five dogs_____."

2. (many / attend / student / the concert)

   "Did _____ yesterday?" "No, not very many."

3. (snow / some / on / the road)

   There's _____. Please drive carefully.

4. (get / a / of / orange juice / glass)

   "Could I _____, please?" "Sure."

5. (ones / buy / new)

   "Your shoes are old!" "I know, I'm going to _____ tomorrow."

 그림을 보고 주어진 명사와 -'(s)를 사용하여 문장을 완성하세요.

~~book~~	house	office	seat	suitcases

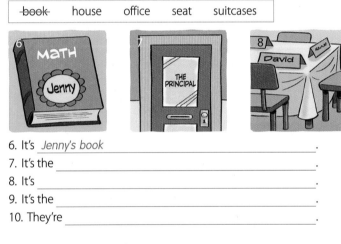

6. It's _Jenny's book_____.
7. It's the _____.
8. It's _____.
9. It's the _____.
10. They're _____.

 주어진 단어를 사용하여 문장을 완성하세요. 필요한 경우 a/an 또는 the를 함께 사용하세요.

airport	~~computer~~	drums	information	money	salt	taxi	umbrella

11. I'd like to buy _a computer_____. Could you help me choose a model?
12. "Did Clara take _____ with her? It's raining outside." "Yes, I gave her one."
13. "This soup needs some _____. Do we have any?" "Yes, we do. Here you are."
14. "We're going to be late. We should catch _____." "There's one over there."
15. "Can you play _____?" "No, I can't."
16. Mary's flight arrives in four hours. Let's wait for her at _____.
17. Can you lend me some _____? I want to get a soda.
18. "Could you give me some _____ about the test next Monday?" "Of course."

보기 중 맞는 것을 고르세요.

19. "I think my eyesight is getting worse." "You should get _____."
    a) new glasses   b) a new glasses   c) a new glass

20. "Do we have an exam tomorrow?" "No, _____ is next Friday."
    a) exam   b) an exam   c) the exam

21. Michael raises many _____ on his farm for their wool.
    a) a sheep   b) sheep   c) sheeps

22. "Do you need help with your bag?" "No, thanks. I can lift it by _____."
    a) me   b) mine   c) myself

23. "Have you seen _____ in my garden?" "Yes, they're beautiful!"
    a) the flowers   b) a flower   c) flowers

24. "Is there _____ nearby?" "Yes, there's one across the street."
    a) a bank machine   b) the bank machine   c) bank machine

25. "What's the highest mountain in _____?" "Mount Everest."
    a) world   b) a world   c) the world

26. "What were you doing when I called?" "I was having _____ with Jason."
    a) dinners   b) dinner   c) the dinner

27. "Where's Lisa?" "She _____."
    a) went to a work   b) went to work   c) went to the work

28. Eric is going to the airport too. You should get a ride with _____.
    a) him   b) his   c) he

29. "How's the weather in Chicago these days?" "_____ has rained for five days."
    a) The weather   b) Chicago   c) It

30. This letter has your name on it. It must be _____.
    a) your   b) you   c) yours

31. "Are you wearing my earrings?" "No. _____ are mine."
    a) This   b) Those   c) These

32. Matt's company is on _____.
    a) the fifth floor of the building   b) the fifth floor's building   c) the building of the fifth floor

33. "Can I borrow one of your hats today?" "Sure. _____?"
    a) Which ones   b) Which one   c) The ones

정답 p.290

틀리거나 확실하지 않은 문제는 아래의 표를 확인하여 해당 UNIT으로 돌아가 복습하세요.

문제	1	2	3	4	5	6	7	8	9	10	11	12	13	14	15	16
UNIT	46	46	47	48	57	54	54	54	54	54	49	49	47	49	50	50
문제	17	18	19	20	21	22	23	24	25	26	27	28	29	30	31	32	33
UNIT	47	47	48	49	48	55	49	49	50	50	50	51	52	53	56	54	57

TEST 10 수량 표현 (UNIT 58-64)

그림을 보고 some/any/no를 써넣으세요.

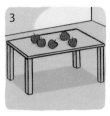

1. She took _some_____ photos.
2. There aren't _____ people in the park.
3. There are _____ apples on the table.
4. He didn't receive _____ mail today.
5. There is _____ water in the swimming pool.

둘 중 맞는 것을 고르세요.

6. Have you had dinner?	Yes, but I didn't eat ((much) / many) food.
7. Was traffic slow this morning?	No, there were (few / little) cars on the road.
8. Did you go to bed early last night?	No, I had (much / many) things to do.
9. Do you read many books?	Yes, I usually read six books (all / every) month.
10. How's the soup?	It needs (a little / a few) salt.
11. Let's go to Europe together!	I can't. I haven't saved (much / many) money.
12. How was the beach yesterday?	Terrible. It rained (all / every) day.
13. Have you finished fixing the car?	I couldn't. I had (little / a little) time today.

괄호 안에 주어진 단어들을 적절히 배열하여 문장을 완성하세요. 필요한 경우 of를 함께 사용하세요.

14. (friends / my / day / all)

"What are you going to do tomorrow?" "I'm meeting with _my friends all day_____."

15. (them / are / both)

"What color are Kate's cats?" "_____ white."

16. (my / live / cousins / most)

_____ in New York. Only one lives in Boston.

17. (has / none / he)

"Does Brandon have any brothers?" "No, _____."

18. (mine / them / is / neither)

"Which ball is yours, the red or blue one?" "_____. Mine is at home."

보기 중 맞는 것을 고르세요.

19. "Would you like _____ cookies?" "Yes, please. I love cookies."
   a) none   (b) some   c) no

20. "Do you have any bananas? I'd like to buy some." "I'm sorry, we have _____."
   a) no   b) none bananas   c) none

21. I haven't seen _____ movies this month. I've been too busy.
   a) any   b) some   c) no

22. _____ is knocking on the door. It might be John.
   a) Someone   b) Anything   c) Nowhere

23. "I think someone is crying. Do you hear _____?" "No, I don't."
   a) somewhere   b) anything   c) nothing

24. Jessica is popular. She has _____.
   a) many friends   b) much friends   c) all friends

25. "Do you have any rooms available?" "Yes, we have _____. Would you like to check in?"
   a) few   b) a little   c) a few

26. "How much milk do we have?" "Very _____. We should buy a carton tomorrow."
   a) a little   b) little   c) few

27. "Do you have any items on sale?" "Yes, _____ item is on sale."
   a) all of   b) all   c) every

28. Clark is very tired. He played soccer _____ day today.
   a) all   b) every   c) all of

29. I don't have to do much homework tonight. I have finished _____ it already.
   a) lot of   b) a lot   c) a lot of

30. "Did you do well on your history test?" "I think so, but _____ the questions were difficult."
   a) some   b) some of   c) most

31. I went to two different bakeries, but _____ them had bagels.
   a) neither   b) neither of   c) either of

32. "Do you want to go out for dinner or eat at home?" "_____ is fine."
   a) Both   b) Neither   c) Either

33. "Are any banks open at 6 p.m.?" "I'm not sure. _____ banks close before 5 p.m."
   a) Most   b) Most of   c) None

정답 p.290

틀리거나 확실하지 않은 문제는 아래의 표를 확인하여 해당 UNIT으로 돌아가 복습하세요.

문제	1	2	3	4	5	6	7	8	9	10	11	12	13	14	15	16
UNIT	58	58	58	58	59	60	61	60	62	61	60	62	61	62	64	64
17	18	19	20	21	22	23	24	25	26	27	28	29	30	31	32	33
59	64	58	59	58	58	58	60	61	61	62	62	60	64	64	63	64

그림을 보고 주어진 표현들을 하나씩 사용하여 예시와 같이 문장을 완성하세요. 형용사를 부사로 바꿔 쓰세요.

| ~~laugh~~ shout sit think | + | angry hard ~~loud~~ uncomfortable |

1. They _'re laughing loudly_____.
2. He _____.
3. She _____.
4. They _____.

괄호 안에 주어진 단어들을 적절히 배열하여 문장을 완성하세요.

5. (are / for / small / me / too)
   My old shirts _are too small for me_____. I need to buy new ones.

6. (rarely / is / crowded)
   "That café _____." "You're right. I often go there to study."

7. (to / tall / enough / not / ride)
   Thomas wanted to ride the roller coaster, but he was _____ it.

8. (tired / too / to / go)
   "I am _____ to the movies." "Let's stay at home, then."

9. (for / everyone / enough)
   "How many tickets did you buy?" "I bought _____."

10. (always / my car / can / use)
    You _____ if you need it.

괄호 안에 주어진 단어를 사용하여 문장을 완성하세요. 필요한 경우 주어진 단어를 비교급 또는 최상급으로 쓰세요.

11. (heavy) Can you help me carry these bags? They are too _heavy_____ for me.
12. (good) Something smells _____! What are we having for dinner?
13. (large) This skirt is too small for me. Do you have a _____ size?
14. (beautiful) I think roses are _____ than tulips.
15. (high) Mount Everest is the _____ mountain in the world.
16. (hot) "When is the _____ time of the day?" "Around 2 p.m."
17. (fast) "Can you run _____ than Nathan?" "No. He's the fastest in my school."
18. (strong) Susan is very strong, but she's not as _____ as her brother.

보기 중 맞는 것을 고르세요.

19. "Did you enjoy the movie?" "Yes, it was _____ the one we saw yesterday."
   a) the most interesting   b) more interesting than   c) interesting

20. "Did you make _____?" "Of course."
   a) pizza enough for the guests   b) pizza for the guests enough   c) enough pizza for the guests

21. I _____ in the ocean, but I want to try one day.
   a) never have swum   b) have never swum   c) have swum never

22. "Your shoes are so _____." "I know. I'm going to wash them tomorrow."
   a) dirty   b) dirtiest   c) dirtier

23. "Why are _____ at the shopping mall?" "It is having a sale."
   a) so much people   b) so many people   c) so many person

24. Ashley's house is _____ to school, so she always arrives at class first.
   a) the most close   b) more closer   c) the closest

25. My dad loves fishing. _____ me fishing on weekends.
   a) He takes often   b) Often takes he   c) He often takes

26. I'm telling you a _____ story. You have to believe me.
   a) true   b) truer   c) truly

27. Today is _____ yesterday. Let's go to the park.
   a) not as cold as   b) as not cold as   c) as cold as not

28. Troy has a stomachache. He ate dinner _____.
   a) too quickly   b) quickly too   c) too quicker

29. I finished work late yesterday. I was _____ usual.
   a) busier   b) busier than   c) the busiest

30. Did you do your homework _____ to get a good grade?
   a) enough good   b) well enough   c) enough well

31. It snowed a lot last night. You should drive _____.
   a) careful   b) carefully   c) more careful

32. "Please finish your work _____." "OK. I'll try my best."
   a) as sooner as possible   b) as soon as possible   c) as possible as soon

33. "That ring has a really big diamond." "It's _____ ring in the store."
   a) expensive   b) more expensive   c) the most expensive

정답 p.290

틀리거나 확실하지 않은 문제는 아래의 표를 확인하여 해당 UNIT으로 돌아가 복습하세요.

문제	1	2	3	4	5	6	7	8	9	10	11	12	13	14	15	16
UNIT	66	66	67	66	69	68	70	69	70	68	69	65	73	73	74	74
17	18	19	20	21	22	23	24	25	26	27	28	29	30	31	32	33
72	75	73	70	68	71	71	74	68	65	75	69	73	70	66	75	74

그림을 보고 주어진 장소와 at/in/on을 사용하여 문장을 완성하세요.

| ~~a bench~~ | home | the 4th floor | the bathroom | work |

1. They are sitting *on a bench*   .
2. They are   .
3. The hair salon is   .
4. He just arrived   .
5. He is changing his clothes   .

주어진 표현들을 사용하여 대화를 완성하세요.

| behind | by | down | for | from | in | ~~next to~~ | to |

6. Is City Hall near here?
7. When can you return my book?
8. How long have you known Tim?
9. When does the movie start?
10. Are you Chinese?
11. Where are you going for vacation?
12. Where is Scott?
13. Is there a bathroom on this floor?

(that building) It's right *next to that building*   .
(this Friday) I'll return it   .
(five years)   .
(10 minutes) It starts   .
(Korea) No, I'm   .
(Germany) I'm going   .
(the curtains) He's hiding   .
(the stairs) No. It's   .

괄호 안에 주어진 단어들을 적절히 배열하여 문장을 완성하세요.

14. (drinking / without / water)
    Kate is very thirsty. She ran for three hours *without drinking water*   .

15. (on / the / turn / air conditioner)
    "This room is hot." "Maybe you can   ."

16. (about / the trip / excited)
    We're going to Disneyland next week. We're very   .

17. (spends / on / unnecessary things / money)
    Robert likes to save money. He never   .

18. (the / up / clean / trash)
    All visitors to the park have to   before they leave.

보기 중 맞는 것을 고르세요.

19. "Where is your brother?" "He's standing _____ Colin and Ian."
   a) among   (b) between   c) under

20. "Do you know where the parking lot is?" "It's _____ the white building."
   a) behind   b) from   c) to

21. "Thank you _____ me home last night." "No problem."
   a) for drive   b) for driving   c) for drive to

22. It was raining, so we got _____ of the taxi and ran.
   a) in   b) off   c) out

23. I finished fixing your computer. You can _____ now.
   a) turn on it   b) turn it on   c) it turn on

24. "Where were you _____ 3 o'clock yesterday?" "I was at the shopping mall with Jake."
   a) in   b) on   c) at

25. The guests are coming soon. We need to finish cleaning the house _____ 20 minutes.
   a) within   b) during   c) at

26. "Are you good _____ swimming?" "No. What about you?"
   a) in   b) of   c) at

27. I went to school _____ my pencil case yesterday. I had to borrow a pen.
   a) with   b) by   c) without

28. "This question is so difficult." "How _____ Ms. Brown for help?"
   a) about ask   b) about to ask   c) about asking

29. "Can you hand _____ these free samples to the customers?" "Of course."
   a) on   b) out   c) to

30. The theater is famous _____ its comfortable seats, but the tickets are too expensive.
   a) at   b) for   c) to

31. "I might be late for our appointment." "OK. I'll wait _____ 8 p.m."
   a) by   b) during   c) until

32. "What is Jennifer doing?" "She's talking _____ Mr. Silver."
   a) for   b) to   c) at

33. I forgot to get the mail. Can you go to the mailbox and _____?
   a) pick it up   b) pick up it   c) it pick up

··· 정답 p.290

틀리거나 확실하지 않은 문제는 아래의 표를 확인하여 해당 UNIT으로 돌아가 복습하세요.

문제	1	2	3	4	5	6	7	8	9	10	11	12	13	14	15	16
UNIT	76	77	77	77	76	78	82	81	81	79	79	78	79	83	86	84
17	18	19	20	21	22	23	24	25	26	27	28	29	30	31	32	33
85	86	78	78	83	86	86	80	81	84	83	83	86	84	82	85	86

괄호 안에 주어진 표현과 and/but/or/so/because를 사용하여 문장을 완성하세요.

1. (they went to a café) Chris and Judy saw a movie, *and they went to a café* _____.
2. (should we take a bus) Do you want to drive, _____?
3. (I drank too much wine last night) I feel sick today _____.
4. (she couldn't come) Matt invited Cindy to his house, _____.
5. (she took some medicine) Christina had a headache, _____.

 괄호 안에 주어진 단어들을 적절히 배열하여 문장을 완성하세요. 현재 시제 또는 과거 시제로 쓰세요.

6. (sunny / if / it / be)
   If it is sunny OR *If it's sunny* _____ today, Ben will wash his car.

7. (work / finish / I / if)
   "Are you coming to the party tonight?" "I'll go _____ early."

8. (I / you / be / if)
   "My tooth hurts too much." "I'd see a dentist _____."

9. (she / since / leave / the company)
   I haven't seen Amanda _____.

10. (Martin / it / open / when)
    "What happened to our front door?" "It broke _____."

11. (while / she / on vacation / be)
    Rachel is going to stay at a resort _____ next month.

 그림을 보고 who 또는 which를 사용하여 문장을 완성하세요.

12. She is wearing a hat *which cost $120* _____.
13. He's pointing at the woman _____.
14. He's the man _____.
15. They're standing in front of a house _____.

보기 중 맞는 것을 고르세요.

16. On weekends, Evan goes to the library _____ reads some magazines.
   a) and   b) because   c) so

17. My new computer is expensive, _____ it's not very fast.
   a) so   b) but   c) while

18. "Why are you late?" "It was rush hour, _____ there were a lot of cars on the road."
   a) but   b) or   c) so

19. The girl _____ the race is my sister. I'm so proud of her.
   a) who she won   b) which won   c) who won

20. _____ I woke up, someone was knocking on the door.
   a) While   b) When   c) Since

21. Marvin is going to call Susie _____ work today.
   a) when he will finish   b) when he finish   c) when he finishes

22. He's the man _____ at Sophie's shop last week.
   a) that saw   b) which I saw   c) I saw

23. "Dad, will you buy me a new phone _____ a high score on my next exam?" "Yes, of course."
   a) if I get   b) if I'll get   c) if I got

24. _____ you if you don't finish cleaning the kitchen by noon.
   a) I help   b) I'll help   c) I would help

25. Nick _____ his friend's wedding if he weren't on a business trip.
   a) will attend   b) would attend   c) attends

26. Please turn down the music. I can't sleep _____ the noise.
   a) and   b) because   c) because of

27. Bill wanted to eat at a restaurant _____ Mexican food, but he couldn't find one.
   a) served   b) who served   c) that served

28. My uncle has taught English at this school _____ he was 25 years old.
   a) since   b) while   c) when

29. The picture _____ is great. I'll hang it on the wall in my living room.
   a) which drew   b) you drew   c) who you drew

30. You should brush your teeth _____ you go to bed.
   a) before   b) after   c) since

정답 p.291

틀리거나 확실하지 않은 문제는 아래의 표를 확인하여 해당 UNIT으로 돌아가 복습하세요.

문제	1	2	3	4	5	6	7	8	9	10	11	12	13	14	15	16
UNIT	87	87	87	87	87	91	91	92	90	88	88	94	94	95	95	87
17	18	19	20	21	22	23	24	25	26	27	28	29	30			
87	87	94	88	88	95	93	93	93	87	94	90	95	89			

그림을 보고 주어진 명사와 there is a 또는 there are two/three…를 사용하여 문장을 완성하세요. 필요한 경우 명사를 복수로 쓰세요.

bird	boy	glass	table	~~woman~~

1. _There is a woman_ _____ on the chair.
2. _____ in the tree.
3. _____ under the tree.
4. _____ on the table.
5. _____ in the water.

 괄호 안에 주어진 단어들을 적절히 배열하여 문장을 완성하세요.

6. (me / that pencil / give)
   "Could you _give me that pencil_ _____?" "Sure. Here you are."

7. (wanted / he / told / me)
   Mark _____ to go to the beach yesterday. Did he go?

8. (not / dinner / let's / cook)
   _____ tonight. I want to go to the Italian restaurant downtown.

9. (said / she / sleeping / that / was)
   Julia _____ when I called her.

10. (a / what / lunch / delicious)
    _____ ! Everything tasted great.

 too/either/so/neither를 사용하여 대화를 완성하세요.

11. I love classical music.
12. I haven't been to Japan before.
13. We'll visit our parents on Christmas.
14. Kim doesn't like beer.
15. We've just had lunch.
16. I wasn't good at math when I was young.
17. I didn't enjoy the movie.
18. Melvin and I watched the soccer game yesterday.

Ian does _too_ _____.
I haven't been there _____.
_____ will Sarah and I.
I don't like it _____. I prefer wine.
_____ have we. Let's get some tea.
_____ was my son.
_____ did I. It was boring.
Really? I did _____.

보기 중 맞는 것을 고르세요.

19. It is busy at the museum today. _____ a lot of visitors.
    a) There haven't been   (b) There have been   c) There is

20. I _____ from Boston. Did you get it?
    a) sent a postcard you   b) sent you to a postcard   c) sent you a postcard

21. "I tried calling Tim many times, but there is no answer." "_____!"
    a) How strange   b) How a stranger   b) What strange

22. "_____ many people at Molly's party?" "Yes. I had a good time with them."
    a) Were there   b) Was there   c) Is there

23. Cathy will _____ . Tomorrow is his birthday.
    a) buy a cake to her father   b) buy a cake her father   c) buy a cake for her father

24. Sharon likes sushi, and her husband does _____ .
    a) either   b) too   c) so

25. _____! Sue looks very cute in it.
    a) This picture look   b) This picture look at   c) Look at this picture

26. Tom said you speak Chinese well. Could you _____?
    a) teach Chinese to me   b) Chinese teach me   c) teach Chinese me

27. "I can't cook very well." "_____."
    a) I can either   b) Neither can I   c) Neither I can

28. I'm worried about Mike. He _____ a cold.
    a) he has said   b) had he said   c) said he had

29. _____ the pot! It's still hot.
    a) Do touch   b) Don't touch   c) Not touch

30. Lynn _____ to her house last night, but I was too busy.
    a) said I can come   b) said I could come   c) say I could come

31. "_____ a break." "OK. Let's sit on that bench for a minute."
    a) Let's take   b) Let's taking   c) Let's not take

32. _____ any onions in the grocery store, so I couldn't make onion soup.
    a) There were   b) There weren't   c) There wasn't

33. Steve _____ the meeting was canceled, so I stayed home.
    a) said me   b) told to me   c) told me

··· 정답 p.291

틀리거나 확실하지 않은 문제는 아래의 표를 확인하여 해당 UNIT으로 돌아가 복습하세요.

문제	1	2	3	4	5	6	7	8	9	10	11	12	13	14	15	16
UNIT	96	96	96	96	96	97	99	98	99	98	100	100	100	100	100	100
17	18	19	20	21	22	23	24	25	26	27	28	29	30	31	32	33
100	100	96	97	98	96	97	100	98	97	100	99	98	99	98	96	99

GRAMMAR GATEWAY BASIC

부록

영어 공부에 도움이 될 기본적인 사항들과 앞 UNIT에서 다룬 내용 중
추가 설명이 필요한 부분을 부록에 담았습니다.
그럼 같이 시작해볼까요? Let's start!

1 | 불규칙 동사 (UNIT 13, 18, 33)

영어에는 시제에 따라 형태가 불규칙하게 변하는 동사들도 있답니다. 자, 소리 내어 반복해 읽으면서 익혀볼까요?

현재	과거	과거분사
am/is/are (be동사) ~이다	was/were	been
awake 깨우다	awoke	awoken
beat 치다	beat	beaten
become ~이 되다	became	become
begin 시작하다	began	begun
bite 물다	bit	bitten
blow 불다	blew	blown
break 깨다	broke	broken
bring 가져오다	brought	brought
build 짓다	built	built
burn 불타다	burned/burnt	burned/burnt
buy 사다	bought	bought
catch 잡다	caught	caught
choose 고르다	chose	chosen
come 오다	came	come
cost (비용이) 들다	cost	cost
cut 베다	cut	cut
dive 잠수하다	dived/dove	dived
do 하다	did	done
draw 그리다	drew	drawn
dream 꿈꾸다	dreamed/dreamt	dreamed/dreamt
drink 마시다	drank	drunk

현재	과거	과거분사
drive 운전하다	drove	driven
eat 먹다	ate	eaten
fall 떨어지다	fell	fallen
feel 느끼다	felt	felt
fight 싸우다	fought	fought
find 찾다	found	found
fly 날다	flew	flown
forget 잊다	forgot	forgotten
forgive 용서하다	forgave	forgiven
freeze 얼다	froze	frozen
get 얻다	got	got/gotten
give 주다	gave	given
go 가다	went	gone
grow 성장하다	grew	grown
hang 걸다	hung	hung
have 가지고 있다	had	had
hear 듣다	heard	heard
hide 숨다	hid	hidden
hit 때리다	hit	hit
hold 들다	held	held
hurt 다치게 하다	hurt	hurt
keep 유지하다	kept	kept

현재	과거	과거분사
know 알다	knew	known
lay 놓다	laid	laid
lead 이끌다	led	led
learn 배우다	learned/learnt	learned/learnt
leave 떠나다	left	left
lend 빌려주다	lent	lent
let ~하게 해주다	let	let
lie 눕다	lay	lain
light 불을 붙이다	lit	lit
lose 잃다	lost	lost
make 만들다	made	made
mean 의미하다	meant	meant
meet 만나다	met	met
pay 지불하다	paid	paid
put 놓다	put	put
quit 그만두다	quit	quit
read[riːd] 읽다	read[red]	read[red]
ride 타다	rode	ridden
ring 울리다	rang	rung
rise 증가하다	rose	risen
run 달리다	ran	run
say 말하다	said	said
see 보다	saw	seen
sell 팔다	sold	sold
send 보내다	sent	sent

현재	과거	과거분사
set 놓다	set	set
shine 빛나다	shone	shone
shoot 쏘다	shot	shot
show 보여주다	showed	shown/showed
shut 닫다	shut	shut
sing 노래하다	sang	sung
sit 앉다	sat	sat
sleep 자다	slept	slept
speak 이야기하다	spoke	spoken
spend (돈을) 쓰다	spent	spent
stand 서다	stood	stood
steal 훔치다	stole	stolen
swim 수영하다	swam	swum
take 잡다	took	taken
teach 가르치다	taught	taught
tear 찢다	tore	torn
tell 말하다	told	told
think 생각하다	thought	thought
throw 던지다	threw	thrown
understand 이해하다	understood	understood
upset 속상하게 만들다	upset	upset
wake 잠이 깨다	woke	woken
wear 입다	wore	worn
win 이기다	won	won
write (글을) 쓰다	wrote	written

2 | 주의해야 할 형태 변화 (UNIT 4, 6, 13, 18, 33, 41, 46, 66, 73, 74)

영어의 동사, 명사, 형용사, 부사는 경우에 따라 형태가 변합니다. 복잡하게 느껴지지만, 규칙을 알면 조금도 어렵지 않답니다. 그럼 영어 단어의 형태 변화 규칙을 익혀볼까요?

A 동사의 형태 변화

동사에 -(e)s를 붙일 때 (현재 시제에서 주어가 he/she/it 등인 경우)

+ -s	bring → brings make → makes sleep → sleeps	eat → eats sing → sings meet → meets	walk → walks drink → drinks live → lives
-ss/-sh/-ch/-x + -es	pass → passes miss → misses kiss → kisses wash → washes wish → wishes	finish → finishes brush → brushes watch → watches catch → catches teach → teaches	reach → reaches search → searches fix → fixes mix → mixes relax → relaxes
-o + -es	go → goes	do → does	
자음 + y → y를 i로 바꾸고 + -es	study → studies carry → carries worry → worries reply → replies	copy → copies marry → marries bury → buries fly → flies	cry → cries hurry → hurries apply → applies try → tries
모음 + y → + -s	play → plays say → says	stay → stays pay → pays	buy → buys enjoy → enjoys

동사에 -ing를 붙일 때

+ -ing	go → going	be → being	know → knowing
-e → e를 빼고 + -ing	come → coming dance → dancing have → having make → making write → writing	take → taking leave → leaving live → living ride → riding shine → shining	smile → smiling prepare → preparing give → giving choose → choosing drive → driving
-ee + -ing	agree → agreeing	see → seeing	
-ie → ie를 y로 바꾸고 + -ing	die → dying	lie → lying	tie → tying
단모음 + 단자음으로 끝날 때 → 자음 한 번 더 쓰고 + -ing	run → running sit → sitting cut → cutting set → setting	put → putting hit → hitting stop → stopping swim → swimming	plan → planning shop → shopping begin → beginning refer → referring

동사에 -(e)d를 붙일 때

+ -ed	answer → answered want → wanted	help → helped watch → watched	clean → cleaned work → worked
-e/-ee/-ie + -d	create → created believe → believed	agree → agreed die → died	tie → tied lie → lied
자음 + y →y를 i로 바꾸고 + -ed	try → tried study → studied	cry → cried rely → relied	marry → married apply → applied
모음 + y → + -ed	enjoy → enjoyed	delay → delayed	play → played
단모음 + 단자음으로 끝날 때 →자음 한 번 더 쓰고 + -ed	prefer → preferred	stop → stopped	plan → planned

B 명사의 형태 변화

명사에 -(e)s를 붙일 때 (명사의 복수형)

+ -s	hat → hats flower → flowers	dog → dogs girl → girls	book → books tree → trees
-s/-ss/-sh/-ch/-x + -es	bus → buses glass → glasses	dish → dishes brush → brushes	sandwich → sandwiches box → boxes
-f(e) →f를 v로 바꾸고 + -es	shelf → shelves leaf → leaves	wolf → wolves wife → wives	knife → knives life → lives
자음 + y →y를 i로 바꾸고 + -es	baby → babies city → cities	lady → ladies family → families	berry → berries story → stories
자음 + o → + -es	potato → potatoes 예외) kilo → kilos	tomato → tomatoes piano → pianos	hero → heroes photo → photos
모음 + y → + -s	boy → boys	day → days	monkey → monkeys

C 형용사/부사의 형태 변화

형용사에 -ly를 붙여 부사로 만들 때

+ -ly	careful → carefully	quick → quickly	slow → slowly
-y → y를 i로 바꾸고 + -ly	angry → angrily lazy → lazily	noisy → noisily busy → busily	sleepy → sleepily lucky → luckily
-le → -ly	probable → probably	incredible → incredibly	

형용사/부사에 -(e)r을 붙여 비교급을 만들 때

1음절* 형용사/부사 + -er	fast → faster	cheap → cheaper	high → higher
1음절* 형용사/부사가 e로 끝날 때 → + -r	nice → nicer	close → closer	wide → wider
1음절* 형용사/부사가 단모음 + 단자음으로 끝날 때 → 자음 한 번 더 쓰고 + -er	big → bigger	hot → hotter	thin → thinner
2음절* 이상 형용사/부사가 y로 끝날 때 → y를 i로 바꾸고 + -er	easy → easier early → earlier	heavy → heavier happy → happier	hungry → hungrier pretty → prettier

* 영어의 음절은 소리 나는 모음의 개수를 단위로 구분합니다. 소리 나는 모음이 1개이면 1음절, 2개이면 2음절이 됩니다. 즉, 단어의 모음 개수가 아니라 '소리 나는 모음의 개수'에 따라 음절을 구분한다는 점에 주의해야 합니다. 예를 들어, cheap은 모음이 e, a로 두 개이지만, 발음은 [tʃiːp]으로 소리 나는 모음이 iː 하나이기 때문에 1음절의 단어입니다. beautiful 역시 모음이 e, a, u, i, u로 다섯 개이지만, 발음은 [bjúːtəfəl]로 소리 나는 모음이 úː, ə, ə로 세 개이기 때문에 3음절의 단어입니다.

형용사/부사 앞에 more를 써서 비교급을 만들 때

more + 2음절 이상 형용사/부사	beautiful → **more** beautiful	recently → **more** recently

형용사/부사에 the + -(e)st를 붙여 최상급을 만들 때

1음절 형용사/부사 + -est	fast → the fastest	cheap → the cheapest	high → the highest
1음절 형용사/부사가 e로 끝날 때 → + -st	nice → the nicest	close → the closest	wide → the widest
1음절 형용사/부사가 단모음 + 단자음으로 끝날 때 → 자음 한 번 더 쓰고 + -est	big → the biggest	hot → the hottest	thin → the thinnest
2음절 이상 형용사/부사가 y로 끝날 때 → y를 i로 바꾸고 + -est	easy → the easiest early → the earliest	heavy → the heaviest happy → the happiest	hungry → the hungriest pretty → the prettiest

형용사/부사 앞에 the most를 써서 최상급을 만들 때

most + 2음절 이상 형용사/부사	beautiful → the **most** beautiful	recently → the **most** recently

3 축약형 (UNIT 1, 2, 3, 8, 12, 14, 18, 23, 26, 31, 32)

일상 대화에서는 I am, she is 등을 I'm, she's 등과 같이 동사를 짧게 줄여서 자주 쓰는데, 이를 축약형이라고
합니다. 그럼 축약형을 함께 익혀볼까요?

A 축약형의 형태

	be (am/is/are)	have (have/has)	will	would
I	I'm	I've	I'll	I'd
he	he's	he's	he'll	he'd
she	she's	she's	she'll	she'd
it	it's	it's	it'll	it'd
we	we're	we've	we'll	we'd
you	you're	you've	you'll	you'd
they	they're	they've	they'll	they'd

B 부정어의 축약형

be	do	have	will, would 등
is not → isn't / 's not are not → aren't / 're not was not → wasn't were not → weren't	do not → don't does not → doesn't did not → didn't	have not → haven't / 've not has not → hasn't / 's not	will not → won't / 'll not would not → wouldn't / 'd not cannot → can't could not → couldn't should not → shouldn't

C 주의해야 할 축약형

is 또는 **has** → **'s**
- "Where is David?" "He**'s** in the garage. He**'s** fixing his car." (= He is in the garage. He is fixing his car.)
- My brother loves traveling. He**'s** been to almost every country in South Asia. (= He has been to ~)

yes를 써서 의문문에 짧게 답할 때는 축약형을 사용하지 않는 것에 주의합니다.
- "Are you Mr. Jones?" "Yes, **I am**." (Yes, I'm.으로 쓸 수 없음)
- "Is he a professor?" "Yes, **he is**." (Yes, he's.로 쓸 수 없음)

4 | 주의해야 할 명사와 the 용법 (UNIT 47, 50)

어떤 명사들은 셀 수 있을 것 같지만 셀 수 없기도 하고, the와 함께 쓰거나 함께 쓰지 않기도 합니다.
그럼, 셀 수 없는 명사들과 the를 쓰거나 쓰지 않는 명사들을 소리 내어 읽으면서 자신의 것으로 만들어 보세요.

A 셀 수 있을 것 같지만 셀 수 없는 명사

bread	cheese	chocolate	food	fruit	meat
paper	money	wood	furniture	luggage	ice
information	advice	news	work	cash	

- "Do you want some **bread**?" "Yes, please."
- We need to order some **paper**. We don't have any for the copy machine.
- I asked Tony for **information** about the seminar.

B the를 쓰지 않는 장소 표현

home	go home	(be) at home		
work	go to work	(be) at work	start work	finish work
school	go to school	(be) at school	start school	finish school
college	go to college	(be) in college		
bed	go to bed	(be) in bed		
church	go to church	(be) in church	(be) at church	
prison	go to prison	(be) in prison		

- Ms. Smith was very sick, so she had to **go home** early.
- Please call me after 3 p.m. I won't **be at work** until then.
- "When did your child **start school**?" "Last September."
- I **was in college** two years ago. I graduated last year.
- "I'm getting sleepy. I think I'll **go to bed**." "OK. Good night."
- The Morgans **are at church** now. They will come back in an hour.

C the를 쓰거나 쓰지 않는 이름

the를 항상 함께 쓰는 이름

대양·바다 이름	the Pacific	the Atlantic	the Black Sea	the Mediterranean Sea
강 이름	the Amazon	the Nile	the Thames	the Mississippi River

- **The Mediterranean Sea** is north of Africa.
- **The Amazon** is the second longest river in the world.

the를 쓰지 않는 이름

산 이름	Mount Fuji Mount Everest Mount Seorak Mount St. Helens 예외) 산맥 이름에는 **the**를 씀 the Himalayas the Alps the Andes the Rocky Mountains			
호수 이름	Lake Michigan	Lake Victoria	Lake Superior	Lake Titicaca
대륙 이름	Asia Australia	Africa Antarctica	Europe	North/South America
나라 이름	Italy France Korea Germany 예외) 연합국 · 공화국 이름에는 **the**를 씀 the United States of America the United Kingdom the Czech Republic			

- **Mount Fuji** is the highest mountain in Japan.
- I want to take a trip to **the Himalayas**.
- My family visited **Lake Michigan** during our vacation.
- People in **Asia** eat a lot of rice.
- "How long does it take to fly to **Italy**?" "I can check for you."
- Washington, D.C. is the capital of **the United States of America**.

5 | 사람과 사물을 가리키는 대명사 (UNIT 51, 53)

영어의 대명사는 문장에서 주어 역할을 할 때, 목적어 역할을 할 때, 소유를 나타낼 때 단어 형태가 달라집니다. 자, 그럼 다양한 대명사의 형태를 함께 익혀볼까요?

수	인칭	주격 (~은/는, ~이/가)	소유격 (~의)	목적격 (~을/를, ~에게)	소유대명사 (~의 것)
단수	1인칭 (나)	I	my	me	mine
	2인칭 (너)	you	your	you	yours
	3인칭 (그/그녀/그것)	he	his	him	his
		she	her	her	hers
		it	its	it	-
복수	1인칭 (나)	we	our	us	ours
	2인칭 (너희들)	you	your	you	yours
	3인칭 (그들/그것들)	they	their	them	theirs

6 알아두면 유용한 형용사 + 전치사 표현 (UNIT 84)

영어에서는 sorry about, good at 등과 같이 형용사와 전치사로 이루어진 표현들이 자주 쓰여요.
자, 그럼 소리 내어 반복해 읽으면서 익혀볼까요?

about	**angry about** ~에 대해 화가 난	
	○ Mr. Meyer is **angry about** the mistakes in the report.	
	excited about ~에 대해 흥분한	
	○ Brian is **excited about** the football game today.	
	nervous about ~에 대해 긴장되는	
	○ "Are you **nervous about** your first day at work?" "Not really."	
	sad about ~에 대해 슬퍼하는	
	○ Kristy is **sad about** moving. She'll miss her friends.	
	sorry about ~에 대해 미안한	
	○ I'm **sorry about** being late. It won't happen again.	
	sure about ~에 대해 확신하는	
	○ I asked how much the car was, but the salesperson wasn't **sure about** the price.	
	upset about ~에 대해 화가 난	
	○ We had a party, and our neighbors were **upset about** the noise.	
	worried about ~에 대해 걱정하는	
	○ "I'm so **worried about** tomorrow's exam." "I'm sure you'll do great."	
at	**angry at** ~에게 화가 난	
	○ I'm **angry at** Betty for losing my cell phone.	
	good at ~을 잘하는	
	○ Christine is really **good at** mathematics.	
	mad at ~에게 화가 난	
	○ My wife is **mad at** me for forgetting our anniversary.	
	surprised at ~에 놀란	
	○ John was **surprised at** his high score on the test.	
for	**bad for** (건강 등)에 나쁜	
	○ Coffee isn't **bad for** your health if you don't drink too much.	
	crazy for ~을 매우 좋아하는	
	○ Monica is **crazy for** romance novels.	
	famous for ~으로 유명한	
	○ This restaurant is **famous for** its pasta.	

from	**different from** ~과 다른 ○ "How is this apartment **different from** the other one?" "This one has an extra bathroom."
in	**dressed in** ~을 입은 ○ Edward is usually **dressed in** a suit at his office. **interested in** ~에 관심 있는 ○ I'm **interested in** art, so I often go to galleries.
of	**afraid of** ~을 무서워하는 ○ You don't have to be **afraid of** my dog. He won't bite. **certain of** ~을 확신하는 ○ Erica loves me. I'm **certain of** it. **full of** ~으로 가득한 ○ "Why is the store **full of** people?" "There's a sale today." **jealous of** ~을 질투하는 ○ A lot of people are **jealous of** Kenny because he's so popular. **proud of** ~을 자랑스럽게 여기는 ○ My sister won a prize. I am very **proud of** her. **sick of** ~에 싫증이 난 ○ I'm **sick of** eating the same thing every day. Let's try a new restaurant. **tired of** ~에 질린 ○ Brent was **tired of** waiting for his friend, so he went home.
to	**clear to** ~에게 분명한 ○ The instructions for my new camera aren't **clear to** me. **identical to** ~과 똑같은 ○ "What do you think of my new laptop?" "It looks **identical to** Jeremy's." **married to** ~와 결혼한 ○ Jeff has been **married to** his wife for six years. **nice to** ~에게 잘해주는 ○ Matt, you should be **nice to** your younger sister. **similar to** ~과 비슷한 ○ Your shoes look **similar to** mine.
with	**angry with** ~에게 화가 난 ○ I'm sorry I broke your glasses. Please don't be **angry with** me. **busy with** ~으로 바쁜 ○ Brenda had to quit the softball team. She was too **busy with** work. **careful with** ~을 조심하는 ○ Be **careful with** that plate. It's hot. **familiar with** ~에 익숙한 ○ I'm **familiar with** this neighborhood. I've lived here for a long time.

happy with ~에 대해 행복해하는
- Thomas is very **happy with** his new bicycle.

pleased with ~에 대해 기뻐하는
- "Are you **pleased with** your birthday gifts?"
  "Yes! I love them."

wrong with ~에 문제가 있는
- What's **wrong with** the TV? It doesn't work.

7 | 알아두면 유용한 동사 표현 (UNIT 85, 86)

영어에서는 talk about, look at 등과 같이 두 단어로 이루어진 동사 표현들이 자주 쓰여요.
자, 그럼 소리 내어 반복해 읽으면서 익혀볼까요?

about	**care about** ~에 관심이 있다	
	○ I don't **care about** music much.	
	hear about ~에 대해 듣다	
	○ "Have you watched the movie *Titan*?" "No, but I **heard about** it from my friend."	
	talk about ~에 대해 이야기하다	
	○ Everyone was **talking about** Clara's new car.	
	think about ~에 대해 생각하다	
	○ Donna **thought about** changing jobs, but she decided to stay.	
	worry about ~에 대해 걱정하다	
	○ "I'm sorry I'm late." "Don't **worry about** it. I didn't wait long."	
at	**arrive at** ~에 도착하다	
	○ We **arrived at** the station on time.	
	laugh at ~을 듣고 웃다, ~을 비웃다	
	○ I **laughed at** my friend's funny story.	
	look at ~을 보다	
	○ The visitors are **looking at** paintings in the gallery.	
	smile at ~에게 미소 짓다	
	○ Look! The baby is **smiling at** us.	
around	**go around** ~을 돌아가다	
	○ **Go around** the corner and you'll see the bank.	
	look around (~을) 둘러보다, (~을) 구경하다	
	○ "How can I help you?" "I'm just **looking around**."	
	pass around (물건 등)을 돌리다	
	○ Andy, could you **pass around** the snacks to the guests?	
	show around ~을 둘러보도록 안내하다	
	○ Could you **show** me **around** the city?	
	take around ~을 데리고 다니다, ~을 산책시키다	
	○ Follow me, and I will **take** you **around** the museum.	
	turn around 돌리다, 돌아서다, 뒤돌아보다	
	○ We're driving the wrong way! We have to **turn around**.	
away	**go away** 떠나다, 사라지다	
	○ I want to **go away** for my vacation.	
	keep away ~을 피하다, ~을 가까이하지 않다	
	○ Please **keep away** from that wall. The paint is still wet.	

	pass away 돌아가시다, 사망하다	
	⊙ My grandmother **passed away** last year.	
	put away ~을 치우다	
	⊙ Could you **put away** your books?	
	run away 도망가다	
	⊙ The dog jumped over the fence and **ran away**.	
	take away (감정·통증 등을) 없애다	
	⊙ The medicine will **take away** the pain.	
	throw away ~을 버리다	
	⊙ I **threw away** my old furniture before I moved here.	
back	**call back** 다시 전화를 하다	
	⊙ Tim will **call** you **back** in one hour.	
	come back 돌아오다	
	⊙ "When will you **come back**?" "In two hours."	
	get back 돌아가다, 물러나다	
	⊙ We **got back** from our trip to Rome this morning.	
	go back 되돌아가다	
	⊙ Can we **go back** home to get my bag?	
	look back 뒤돌아보다, (~을) 회상하다	
	⊙ I **looked back**, but nobody was there.	
	pay back ~에게 돈을 갚다	
	⊙ Can I borrow $50? I can **pay** you **back** tomorrow.	
	take back ~을 반품하다, ~을 되찾다	
	⊙ This hair dryer isn't working. I'm going to **take** it **back** to the store.	
	turn back 돌아오다, ~을 되돌리다	
	⊙ The traffic was bad, so we had to **turn back**.	
down	**break down** (자동차·기계 등이) 고장 나다, 분해하다	
	⊙ The photocopier **broke down**, so I couldn't copy the report.	
	calm down 진정하다, 가라앉히다	
	⊙ Ms. Ling told her children to **calm down** and be quiet.	
	fall down 넘어지다	
	⊙ Thomas **fell down** and hurt his leg.	
	lie down 눕다	
	⊙ I'm not feeling well. I'm going to **lie down** for an hour.	
	look down 내려다보다	
	⊙ **Look down** there! There are ducks under the bridge.	
	pass down ~을 물려주다	
	⊙ My older sister's clothes were **passed down** to me.	
	put down ~을 내려놓다, ~을 적어놓다	
	⊙ **Put down** that vase! You will break it.	

	shut down ~을 끄다, ~을 닫다	
	● Make sure to **shut down** the computer before you leave.	
	slow down 속도를 줄이다	
	● You need to **slow down**. You're driving too fast.	
	sit down 앉다	
	● Please **sit down** and wait for a few minutes.	
	take down (주소·전화번호 등을) 적어 놓다	
	● "Did you **take down** the salesperson's phone number?" "Yes."	
	turn down (TV·음악 등)의 소리를 줄이다	
	● "Dan, the music is too loud." "Sorry, I'll **turn** it **down**."	
	write down ~을 적다	
	● I'll **write down** some directions for you.	

for	**apply for** ~에 지원하다
	● Ms. Miller **applied for** the bank job, but she didn't get it.
	care for ~을 돌보다, ~을 좋아하다
	● My mom **cares for** me when I'm sick.
	look for ~을 찾다
	● "What are you **looking for**?" "My wallet."
	search for ~을 찾다
	● I **searched for** my keys all morning, but I couldn't find them.
	wait for ~을 기다리다
	● Don't **wait for** me. I'm going to be late.
	work for ~에 근무하다
	● Mr. Donald **works for** the restaurant.

in	**bring in** ~을 들여오다, ~을 가져오다
	● "It's raining now." "Really? We have to **bring in** the laundry!"
	check in (숙박·탑승) 수속하다, 체크인하다
	● Please **check in** at least an hour before your flight.
	fill in (빈칸 등)을 채우다
	● You need to **fill in** the blanks with your name and address.
	get in (택시·승용차 등)에 타다, ~에 들어가다
	● Hurry up and **get in** the car. It's getting late.
	hand in (서류 등)을 제출하다
	● Students must **hand in** their homework after class.
	stay in (나가지 않고) 안에 머무르다
	● It was snowing too hard, so we **stayed in**.

off	**call off** (계획 등)을 취소하다
	● Derek **called off** the party because he was sick.
	drop off (사람·짐 등)을 도중에 내려놓다
	● Can you **drop** me **off** at the mall? I need to buy some clothes.

	fall off 떨어지다
	● Cindy **fell off** the bicycle and hurt her knees.
	get off (버스·기차 등)에서 내리다
	● Daniel **got off** the train at Central Station.
	put off ~을 미루다
	● Mr. Jenkins **put off** the meeting. He changed it to next Monday.
	switch off (스위치 등을 눌러서) ~을 끄다
	● Please **switch off** your phones during the flight.
	take off (의복)을 벗다, 이륙하다
	● Please **take off** your shoes at the front door.
	turn off (전기·TV 등)을 끄다, (수도·밸브 등)을 잠그다
	● Did you **turn off** the heater when you left home?
on	**carry on** ~을 계속하다
	● The teacher told Jenny to be quiet, but she **carried on** talking.
	get on (버스·기차 등)에 타다
	● That's our bus. Let's **get on**.
	go on 계속하다
	● "Is my story too long?" "No. It's very interesting. Please **go on**."
	hold on 기다리다
	● "May I speak to Mr. Grey, please?" "**Hold on** and I'll connect you."
	keep on ~을 계속하다, ~을 유지하다
	● "Where's the bank?" "**Keep on** walking straight ahead."
	put on (의복)을 입다
	● Don't forget to **put on** your coat. It's very cold outside.
	switch on ~을 켜다
	● Don't **switch on** the light. I'm trying to sleep.
	try on (의복)을 입어보다
	● "Can I **try on** this shirt?" "Sure."
	turn on ~을 켜다
	● Dad **turned on** the TV to watch the news.
	work on ~에 착수하다, 노력을 들이다
	● I'll **work on** my science report after school today.
out	**bring out** (상품 등)을 내놓다
	● The company will **bring out** a new product next month.
	eat out 외식하다
	● "Shall we **eat out** tonight?" "That sounds good. What about Italian?"
	find out ~을 알아내다
	● Did you **find out** what happened to Sammy?
	give out ~을 나눠주다
	● My parents **give out** gifts every Christmas.

	go out 나가다, 외출하다
	● "What are you doing tonight?" "I'm **going out** with some friends."
	hand out ~을 나눠주다
	● We'll **hand out** the party gifts after the dinner.
	look out 조심하다, 주의하다
	● **Look out!** There's a car coming!
	put out (불 등)을 끄다
	● The men **put out** the fire at the office building.
	run out 다 써버리다, 다 떨어지다
	● We need to go to the gas station. We might **run out** of gas.
	take out ~을 가져가다, ~을 꺼내다
	● Would you **take out** the dishes from the dishwasher?
	watch out 주의하다, 조심하다
	● **Watch out!** There's a bee by your head.
	work out 운동하다
	● Todd **works out** at the gym every evening.
over	**get over** ~을 극복하다, ~을 넘다
	● Andrew **got over** his cold after only two days.
	go over ~을 복습하다
	● Kimberly **went over** her notes before the test.
	read over ~을 자세히 읽다, ~을 다시 읽다
	● We **read over** your report. It was very good.
	turn over (~을) 뒤집다, (~의) 방향을 바꾸다
	● The pancake was cooked on one side, so Judy **turned** it **over**.
through	**get through** ~을 통과하다, (전화 등으로) 연결되다, ~을 끝내다
	● Traffic was bad, so it took 20 minutes to **get through** the tunnel.
	go through ~을 통과하다, ~을 겪다
	● This train **goes through** Boston.
to	**belong to** ~의 것이다, ~에 속하다
	● "Whose car is that?" "It **belongs to** Tim."
	reply to ~에게 답하다
	● I asked Brenda a question, but she didn't **reply to** me.
	talk to ~에게 말하다, ~와 대화하다
	● I **talked to** the neighbors about the noise.
up	**break up** 헤어지다, 이별하다
	● Did you hear? Chad and Lisa **broke up**!
	bring up (문제 등)을 제기하다, ~을 기르다
	● You **brought up** a good point at the meeting.
	clean up ~을 청소하다
	● Marina **cleaned up** the kitchen this morning.

get up 일어나다
- When do you usually **get up** in the morning?

give up ~을 포기하다
- I want to **give up** smoking soon.

grow up 성장하다
- When Timmy **grows up**, he wants to be a singer.

hang up (전화를) 끊다
- Randy **hung up** the phone without saying goodbye.

hurry up 서두르다
- Bob, you need to **hurry up**. The train leaves in 10 minutes.

look up ~을 찾아보다
- "What does this word mean?" "**Look** it **up** in the dictionary."

pick up (수화기 등)을 들다, ~을 사다
- I called Joey three times, but he didn't **pick up**.

speak up 큰 소리로 말하다
- You need to **speak up**. I can't hear you well.

stand up 일어서다
- At the wedding, everyone **stood up** when the bride entered the room.

stay up 깨어 있다
- I never **stay up** late on weekdays.

turn up (TV·음악 등)의 소리를 높이다
- I like this song! Could you **turn up** the volume, please?

wake up 잠이 깨다, ~을 깨우다
- Tony, **wake up**! It's time for breakfast.

GRAMMAR GATEWAY BASIC

정답

PRACTICE Answers

REVIEW TEST Answers

PRACTICE Answers

UNIT 001

A

2. are; we're
3. am; I'm
4. is; it's
5. are; they're
6. is; he's

B

2. is a photographer
3. are in their car
4. are on the stage
5. is a repairman

C

2. I'm OR I am
3. It's OR It is
4. we're OR we are
5. You're OR You are
6. It's OR It is
7. I'm OR I am
8. She's OR She is

D

2. 'm 21 years old OR am 21 years old
3. is swimming
4. is a high school student
5. are my parents

UNIT 002

A

2. This water isn't
   OR This water is not
3. you're not OR you aren't
   OR you are not
4. Mark isn't OR Mark is not
5. we're not OR we aren't
   OR we are not
6. I'm not OR I am not
7. Sharon isn't OR Sharon is not
8. My books aren't
   OR My books are not

B

2. Richard isn't 23 years old
   OR Richard is not 23 years old
3. Sally and Alex aren't from Brazil
   OR Sally and Alex are not from
   Brazil
4. I'm not a nurse
   OR I am not a nurse
5. Tomorrow isn't Thursday
   OR Tomorrow is not Thursday

C

2. 're
3. 're
4. 'm
5. 's
6. 'm not
7. isn't
8. 'm not

D

2. isn't OR is not
3. are
4. 're not OR aren't OR are not

UNIT 003

A

2. Is
3. Are
4. Am
5. Is
6. Are
7. Are

B

2. Is it
3. Am I
4. Are you
5. Is today
6. Are Joel and Mary
7. Is she
8. Are we

C

2. No, I'm not

3. No, he's not OR No, he isn't
4. Yes, I am
5. No, they're not OR No, they aren't
6. No, it's not OR No, it isn't
7. Yes, she is

D

2. My name is Chun
3. Are you from China
4. I'm Chinese OR I am Chinese
5. Are you in this class
6. we're in the same class OR we are
   in the same class

UNIT 004

A

2. sitting
3. writing
4. having
5. coming
6. shopping
7. waiting
8. dying

B

2. 're eating popcorn
   OR are eating popcorn;
   're crying OR are crying
3. 's driving OR is driving;
   is ringing

C

2. is playing the violin
3. is entering the bank
4. are flying in the sky
5. is standing at the bus stop

D

2. He's having OR He is having
3. The children are helping
4. Mitchell is preparing
5. They're jogging
   OR They are jogging
6. I'm tying OR I am tying
7. We're selling OR We are selling

8. She's getting OR She is getting

UNIT 005

A

2. isn't moving OR is not moving
3. 're enjoying OR are enjoying
4. 're not wearing OR aren't wearing
   OR are not wearing
5. is teaching
6. 'm not swimming
   OR am not swimming

B

2. my sister is listening
3. Are you crying
4. Am I singing
5. Are you and Vicky baking
6. The wind is blowing
7. Are your brothers riding
8. Kyle is wearing

C

2. Yes, I am
3. No, I'm not
4. No, he's not OR No, he isn't
5. Yes, they are
6. Yes, it is

D

2. I'm having OR I am having
3. You're not OR You aren't drinking
   OR You are not drinking
4. we're selling OR we are selling

UNIT 006

A

2. shines
3. walk
4. ride
5. calls
6. work
7. costs
8. gets

B

2. carries
3. does

4. flies
5. has
6. reaches
7. goes
8. passes

C

2. does
3. has
4. speak
5. plays
6. cry
7. buy

D

2. Your father likes
3. we have
4. I prepare
5. Mom wants

UNIT 007

A

2. leaves home
3. starts work
4. goes to lunch
5. finishes work

B

2. Hannah washes
3. The post office opens
4. Pandas eat
5. My husband and I make
6. Water covers

C

2. collects
3. likes
4. bakes
5. need
6. close
7. jogs

D

2. has
3. live
4. cut
5. hunt
6. needs

UNIT 008

A

2. doesn't understand Chinese OR
   does not understand Chinese
3. don't look well
   OR do not look well
4. don't have a lot of homework OR
   do not have a lot of homework
5. doesn't watch TV
   OR does not watch TV
6. don't make any noise
   OR do not make any noise
7. doesn't clean OR does not clean

B

2. doesn't know OR does not know
3. remembers
4. don't want OR do not want
5. doesn't like OR does not like

C

2. work
3. shows
4. doesn't bite OR does not bite
5. don't buy OR do not buy
6. snows

D

2. don't eat OR do not eat
3. doesn't smell OR does not smell
4. hate
5. tastes

UNIT 009

A

2. Does Rosa have a boyfriend
3. Does Mr. Gill need more time
4. Do we know your phone number
5. Do you own a bicycle
6. Does the bus usually arrive
7. Do your kids like dogs

B

2. Do we know
3. Do your children go
4. Does Janet drive
5. Does Ted play
6. Does George work

7. Do you talk

C

2. Yes, I do
3. No, he doesn't
4. Yes, I do
5. No, she doesn't
6. Yes, we do

D

2. I want some mangoes
3. we don't have mangoes
4. Does it taste good

UNIT 010

A

2. is riding; works
3. is playing; designs
4. paints; 's sleeping OR is sleeping

B

2. Angela goes
3. I'm looking OR I am looking
4. The post office doesn't deliver OR The post office does not deliver
5. We buy
6. Jason and Fred aren't studying OR Jason and Fred are not studying
7. Mr. Smith's phone is ringing

C

2. 're swimming OR are swimming
3. spends
4. Do; remember
5. 's attending OR is attending
6. hates

D

2. O
3. shop → 're shopping OR are shopping
4. O
5. isn't having → doesn't have OR does not have
6. don't do → 'm not doing OR am not doing

UNIT 011

A

2. was at school
3. were at a restaurant
4. was at a store

B

2. The stars were
3. He was
4. These gloves were
5. My friends and I were
6. It was

C

2. was; 'm OR am
3. were; was
4. was; Is
5. are; were
6. was; 's OR is; 's OR is

D

2. was
3. were
4. was
5. is
6. are

UNIT 012

A

2. was asleep
3. wasn't on time OR was not on time
4. was angry
5. wasn't happy OR was not happy

B

2. weren't
3. wasn't
4. were
5. was
6. weren't

C

2. Was Howard at the meeting
3. Were you with Jessica
4. Kim and Lucy were there
5. The baseball game was exciting
6. Was your mom a cook

7. I was in Lisbon
8. Were you at the gym

D

2. I wasn't at school OR I was not at school
3. you were fine
4. The window was open
5. Were you cold

UNIT 013

A

2. played
3. invited
4. cried
5. went
6. worked

B

2. It closes
3. Laura and Nick got
4. Earth travels
5. We laughed
6. I forgot
7. Jeff flies
8. I need

C

2. O
3. meets → met
4. O
5. rains → rained
6. wins → won
7. O

D

2. took the bus
3. went to bed late
4. studied for our test

UNIT 014

A

2. She didn't read the newspaper OR She did not read the newspaper
3. She went to the gym
4. She didn't wash the car OR She did not wash the car

5. She attended a cooking class
6. She had lunch with Jackie

B

2. Did Sarah pass
3. Did you read
4. Did someone knock
5. Did you get
6. Did we miss
7. Did Dave grow up
8. Did the Smiths buy

C

2. Did you buy
3. My friends and I didn't visit
   OR My friends and I did not visit
4. Elena met
5. we didn't lock *OR* we did not lock
6. Jake found

D

2. I didn't like *OR* I did not like
3. Did you see
4. Paul watched

UNIT 015

A

2. were dancing
3. was carrying
4. were eating
5. was waving

B

2. was listening
3. were attending
4. were playing
5. was crossing

C

2. They're watching
   OR They are watching
3. Alice was lying
4. I was visiting
5. We were standing
6. He's holding *OR* He is holding

D

2. We were practicing

3. I was worrying
4. We were performing

UNIT 016

A

2. A woman wasn't sitting here
   OR A woman was not sitting here
3. I was meeting them outside
4. He wasn't carrying a bag
   OR He was not carrying a bag

B

2. Joe and I were enjoying the party
3. Evan was writing an e-mail
4. We were waiting for the bus
5. Was it snowing there
6. Was Sally going to the bank

C

2. Was Victor practicing
3. Eric and I weren't working
   OR Eric and I were not working
4. I was buying
5. Were you walking
6. We were cooking
7. I wasn't talking
   OR I was not talking
8. Was Clara swimming
9. I was sitting
10. Were you and Pete visiting

UNIT 017

A

2. used to be
3. used to like
4. used to live

B

2. didn't use to drink
   OR did not use to drink
3. used to eat
4. used to own
5. used to sell
6. didn't use to speak
   OR did not use to speak
7. used to be

C

2. exercises
3. used to listen
4. remember
5. used to go
6. used to take

D

2. used to have
3. used to come
4. used to be

UNIT 018

A

2. 's broken *OR* has broken
3. 's eaten *OR* has eaten
4. 's painted *OR* has painted
5. 've made *OR* have made
6. 's taken *OR* has taken

B

2. went; gone
3. bought; bought
4. ran; run
5. played; played
6. wrote; written
7. drove; driven
8. knew; known
9. sent; sent

C

2. hasn't eaten *OR* has not eaten
3. has grown
4. hasn't spoken *OR* has not spoken
5. 've ridden *OR* have ridden
6. haven't seen *OR* have not seen

D

2. Have you studied
3. Has Ben finished the report
4. Have you read
5. Has Amanda called you
6. Have the guests arrived

UNIT 019

A

2. 's stayed *OR* has stayed

3. 's driven *OR* has driven
4. 's grown *OR* has grown
5. 've lived *OR* have lived
6. 's caught *OR* has caught

B

2. have been married for
3. hasn't rained since
   OR has not rained since
4. has driven his car for
5. haven't talked to Ben for
   OR have not talked to Ben for
6. hasn't eaten anything since
   OR has not eaten anything since
7. 've known them for
   OR have known them for

C

2. How long has she played
3. How long have they attended
4. How long has she taken
5. How long has he been
6. How long have you had

UNIT 020

A

2. I've (never) played chess before
3. I've (never) lived in the country
4. I've (never) ridden a roller coaster
5. I've (never) seen a kangaroo
6. I've (never) had a pet

B

2. Have you ever watched an opera
3. Have you ever gone bungee
   jumping
4. Have you ever swum in the ocean
5. Have you ever been to Paris
6. Have you ever run a marathon

C

2. has been
3. 's gone *OR* has gone
4. 's gone *OR* has gone
5. 've been *OR* have been

D

2. Have you watched

3. Have you ever been
4. haven't been *OR* have not been
5. Have you eaten
6. 've never tried *OR* have never tried

UNIT 021

A

2. 've been *OR* have been
3. invented
4. saw
5. has grown

B

2. O
3. didn't use → haven't used
   OR have not used
4. knew → has known
5. O
6. have visited → visited

C

2. I haven't seen *OR* I have not seen;
   Brenna talked
3. Ms. Conner spoke; She's taken
   OR She has taken
4. I joined; We've worked
   OR We have worked
5. My plane hasn't arrived
   OR My plane has not arrived;
   It departed

D

2. My parents moved
3. How long have you been
4. I came
5. I've lived *OR* I have lived

UNIT 022

A

2. 's just dived *OR* has just dived
3. has just opened
4. 've just met *OR* have just met

B

2. We've already had
   OR We have already had

3. He's already read
   OR He has already read
4. I've already sent
   OR I have already sent

C

2. Have you visited him yet
3. He hasn't started it yet
   OR He has not started it yet
4. I haven't seen him yet
   OR I have not seen him yet
5. Has Lily called you back yet

D

2. I've already paid the money
   OR I have already paid the money
3. You haven't used it yet
   OR You have not used it yet
4. I've just given that one
   OR I have just given that one

UNIT 023

A

2. You'll find *OR* You will find
3. They'll win *OR* They will win
4. She'll return *OR* She will return
5. We'll need *OR* We will need
6. It'll help *OR* It will help

B

2. I'll drive
3. I'll lend you
4. I'll take it

C

2. won't take *OR* will not take
3. won't forget *OR* will not forget
4. 'll explain *OR* will explain
5. won't stop *OR* will not stop
6. won't sleep *OR* will not sleep
7. 'll call *OR* will call

D

2. We'll miss the train
   OR We will miss the train
3. Will you meet me at the airport
4. She'll be here in a minute
   OR She will be here in a minute

5. I'll have the chicken salad
   OR I will have the chicken salad
6. Will your family travel this fall
7. Will Jonathan pass the exam
8. I'll change it OR I will change it

UNIT 024

A

2. 're going to take
   OR are going to take
3. is going to leave
4. 's not going to graduate
   OR isn't going to graduate
   OR is not going to graduate
5. 're not going to be
   OR aren't going to be
   OR are not going to be
6. 'm going to relax
   OR am going to relax
7. 'm not going to rent
   OR am not going to rent

B

2. 's going to watch a movie
   OR is going to watch a movie
3. 're going to have a sale
   OR are going to have a sale
4. 's going to take an exam
   OR is going to take an exam

C

2. Is Tina going to meet
3. I'm going to see
   OR I am going to see
4. Are you going to buy
5. Brian is going to join
6. They're going to get
   OR They are going to get
7. Is it going to hurt

D

2. I'm going to cook
   OR I am going to cook
3. It's going to be OR It is going to be
4. Are you going to need
5. I'm not going to need
   OR I am not going to need

UNIT 025

A

2. 's seeing a movie
   OR is seeing a movie
3. 's taking a swimming lesson
   OR is taking a swimming lesson
4. 's visiting her grandparents
   OR is visiting her grandparents
5. 's attending Karen's wedding
   OR is attending Karen's wedding
6. 's leaving for Brazil
   OR is leaving for Brazil

B

2. leaves at 2:15
3. arrives at 2:00
4. begins at 9:00

C

2. Are you staying
3. The plane departs
4. Brenda is moving
5. It begins
6. The meeting finishes
7. I'm meeting OR I am meeting

D

2. leaves
3. 'm visiting OR am visiting
4. starts

UNIT 026

A

2. can fix
3. can talk
4. can't join OR cannot join
5. can't wear OR cannot wear
6. can stay
7. can't understand
   OR cannot understand

B

2. Can your parrot talk
3. Can Karen help
4. Can you attend
5. Can your husband drive
6. Can you tell

C

2. can't see OR cannot see
3. can walk
4. could buy
5. can't remember
   OR cannot remember
6. couldn't ride OR could not ride
7. can have
8. couldn't answer
   OR could not answer

D

2. he could understand
3. I could speak
4. I can't remember
   OR I cannot remember
5. Can I join
6. You can come

UNIT 027

A

2. might travel by train
3. might go to Martin's wedding
4. might move next month

B

2. might help
3. might not come
4. might try
5. might not fit
6. might not like
7. might invite
8. might not buy
9. might be
10. might rain

C

2. might not have
3. might go
4. might not be

UNIT 028

A

2. Can I take this seat
3. Can I get some water
4. Can I close the window

B

2. May I help
3. Can you call
4. May I look
5. May I borrow
6. Can you check
7. Can you buy

C

2. Could you come to my office
3. Could you sign this form
4. Could you read me another story
5. Could you move your car
6. Could you tell me your name

D

2. can you tell me
3. Can you say the number
4. Can I see it

UNIT 029

A

2. must stop
3. must not smoke
4. must not take
5. must turn off

B

2. had to
3. had to
4. must
5. had to
6. must

C

2. must not feel
3. must miss
4. must not know
5. must hurt
6. must not have
7. must read

D

2. must not forget
3. must check
4. must not go

UNIT 030

A

2. have to see
3. have to wait
4. have to use

B

2. have to teach
3. doesn't have to take
4. doesn't have to call
5. have to ask
6. don't have to pay
7. has to attend

C

2. doesn't have to write
3. don't have to run
4. have to be *OR* must be
5. must not park
6. have to pack *OR* must pack
7. don't have to bring
8. has to leave *OR* must leave

D

2. We had to stop at the gas station
3. I didn't have to tell John
4. Allan didn't have to buy a ticket
5. I had to change my clothes

UNIT 031

A

2. should buy
3. should speak
4. should wash

B

2. Children shouldn't watch
   OR Children should not watch
3. you should return
4. We should take
5. I shouldn't go *OR* I should not go
6. We shouldn't make
   OR We should not make

C

2. Should I find a new job
3. should I go to the airport
4. Should I change the channel?

5. Should I invite

D

2. I think she should stay at home
   OR I don't think she should stay at home
3. I think he should sell his computer
   OR I don't think he should sell his computer
4. I think she should go out for dinner *OR* I don't think she should go out for dinner

UNIT 032

A

2. Would you turn off
3. Would you bring
4. would you answer
5. Would you drive
6. Would you show

B

2. Would you like some wine
3. Would you like some ice cream
4. Would you like an orange

C

2. Would you like to go shopping
3. Would you like some bread
4. Would you like a map
5. Would you like to see the menu
6. Would you like to play golf

D

2. I'd like to study biology
   OR I would like to study biology
3. I'd like a ticket
   OR I would like a ticket
4. I'd like to invite you
   OR I would like to invite you
5. I'd like that blue sweater
   OR I would like that blue sweater
6. I'd like to visit Europe
   OR I would like to visit Europe

UNIT 033

A

2. 's written *OR* is written
3. aren't required
   OR are not required
4. Are; made
5. 's delivered *OR* is delivered
6. isn't used *OR* is not used
7. Are; baked

B

2. It was built
3. My dog is washed
4. It was canceled
5. His paintings are displayed
6. These photos were taken

C

2. can be worn
3. can't be shown
   OR cannot be shown
4. won't be announced
   OR will not be announced
5. must be paid

D

2. needs
3. start
4. aren't allowed
5. be used

UNIT 034

A

2. were sent
3. hit
4. was grown
5. found

B

2. was told
3. 's kept *OR* is kept
4. was repaired
5. are used
6. were worn

C

2. will deliver → will be delivered
3. were enjoyed → enjoyed

4. must cook → must be cooked
5. stole → were stolen
6. O
7. Does food allow → Is food
   allowed
8. was broken → broke

D

2. I was invited by the Millers
3. Those buildings were designed by
   Mr. Lee
4. The book will be signed by the
   author
5. This place is visited by many
   tourists
6. The television was invented by
   John Baird
7. A traffic jam can be caused by an
   accident

UNIT 035

A

2. The cookies are
3. Has Ted done
4. Does Mitchell live
5. Was Julie sleeping
6. We should take
7. Have you found
8. can I ask you

B

2. Have
3. Does
4. Did
5. Are
6. Has
7. Were
8. Do

C

2. O
3. was → did
4. O
5. Who the girl is → Who is the girl
6. O
7. you bought → did you buy

D

2. When are you moving to Australia
3. Where will you meet him
4. Can you come to my office

UNIT 036

A

2. What did John send
3. Who did they visit
4. What did he eat

B

2. What sports do you play
3. Who are you inviting
4. What fruit does that store sell
5. Who should I contact
6. What is the problem

C

2. Which book
3. Which car
4. Which shirt

D

2. Which
3. What
4. Who
5. Which
6. What
7. Which
8. What

UNIT 037

A

2. Why
3. When
4. Where
5. Why
6. Where

B

2. When will your parents be
3. Where do you live
4. Why should I wear
5. Why are you bringing
6. Where is she from
7. When is Sharon leaving

C

2. When did Ivan leave the office
3. When does the bus come
4. Why is the mall closed
5. Where can I find the elevator

D

2. Where
3. When
4. Where
5. why

UNIT 038

A

2. How did you come
3. How can I turn off
4. How do your kids get to
5. How should we prepare

B

2. How was the concert
3. How is the food
4. How are your parents
5. How was your holiday

C

2. How old
3. How much
4. How often
5. How far
6. How long
7. How much
8. How tall
9. How many

D

2. How is the scent
3. How much is it
4. How long will it take

UNIT 039

A

2. didn't you
3. don't they
4. hasn't she
5. can't you
6. isn't it

B

2. have you
3. am I
4. can he
5. are you
6. do we

C

2. wasn't it
3. can you
4. is it
5. haven't you
6. does she
7. aren't they

D

2. No
3. Yes
4. No
5. No
6. Yes

E

2. isn't it
3. didn't you
4. haven't you

UNIT 040

A

2. why Emily was late
3. where I parked my car
4. what I should write in the report
5. when John will be back
6. why the manager called me
7. how you can answer this question

B

2. Do you know where they lived before
3. Do you know what Tony does
4. Do you know how many children they have
5. Do you know what their hobbies are

C

2. if (*OR* whether) many people came to the party

3. if (*OR* whether) Annie is going to visit us tomorrow
4. if (*OR* whether) you've seen my brother *OR* if (*OR* whether) you have seen my brother
5. if (*OR* whether) Joey can play the violin
6. if (*OR* whether) Hannah has gone home

D

2. where the station is
3. how I can buy a ticket
4. if I'll arrive at the airport
   OR if I will arrive at the airport

UNIT 041

A

2. Losing
3. making
4. Wearing
5. watching
6. Swimming
7. Planting

B

2. reading that book
3. talking about her
4. Eating too much food
5. Running with these old shoes

C

2. Riding a roller coaster is exciting
   OR Riding a roller coaster is scary
3. Taking a taxi is cheap
   OR Taking a taxi is expensive
4. Traveling alone is safe
   OR Traveling alone is dangerous
5. Playing chess is fun
   OR Playing chess is boring

D

2. promises to be home by 6
3. needs to finish the report by Monday
4. plans to visit her grandparents tomorrow
5. hopes to win a Nobel Prize

6. expects to get the job

A

2. hiring
3. to do
4. to help
5. singing
6. to believe

B

2. opening the door
3. cleaning the bathroom
4. to buy this house
5. to play the flute
6. looking at me

C

2. choose to become
3. avoids driving
4. expect to spend
5. gave up smoking

D

2. enjoy going
3. hope to have
4. mind working

UNIT 043

A

2. going
3. feeling *OR* to feel
4. to join
5. writing *OR* to write
6. driving *OR* to drive
7. learning

B

2. stop laughing
3. stop to ask
4. Stop worrying
5. stop to buy
6. stop to take

C

2. to finish
3. going

4. taking
5. to call

D

2. to draw → drawing
3. O
4. moving → to move
5. to paint → painting
6. O

UNIT 044

A

2. want us to have
3. want me to move
4. want you to call

B

2. allowed Ben to use the camera
3. told Brian to answer the phone
4. expected David to call back soon
5. wanted Nick to speak louder
6. advised Nancy to go to bed

C

2. me run
3. him buy
4. me drive
5. us stay
6. them pay

D

2. help you find *OR* help you to find
3. help you carry
   OR help you to carry
4. help you answer
   OR help you to answer
5. help you wash
   OR help you to wash

UNIT 045

A

2. post office to send a package
3. hospital to visit his friend
4. library to return a book
5. zoo to see the pandas

B

2. to get some fresh air
3. to help him
4. to buy some ice cream
5. to stay healthy
6. to make an appointment

C

2. time to visit
3. questions to ask
4. games to play
5. book to read
6. snacks to share

D

2. things to do
3. work to finish
4. meetings to attend
5. time to talk

UNIT 046

A

2. feet
3. days
4. ladies
5. children
6. benches
7. parties
8. wives
9. knives
10. kilos
11. loaves
12. friends

B

2. a book
3. babies
4. tomatoes

C

2. loaf → loaves
3. child → children
4. O
5. peach → peaches
6. boy → boys
7. womans → women
8. O
9. photoes → photos

10. O

D

2. knife
3. knives
4. people
5. jacket

UNIT 047

A

2. air
3. rain
4. an umbrella
5. a taxi
6. salt
7. a man
8. an orange

B

2. apples
3. snow
4. a bicycle
5. sugar
6. a baby
7. a dog
8. music
9. water
10. flowers

C

2. O
3. egg → eggs
4. an information → information
5. teacher → a teacher
6. O
7. times → time

UNIT 048

A

2. pants
3. fish
4. a key
5. glasses
6. sheep
7. An apple

B

2. two cartons of milk
3. a piece of cake
4. three cans of soda
5. a loaf of bread

C

2. two box of cereals
   → two boxes of cereal
3. O
4. sock → socks *OR* a pair of socks
5. deers → deer
6. O
7. O
8. snows → snow
9. papers → paper

D

2. slices of pizza
3. cup of coffee; cans of soda
4. bottle of water

UNIT 049

A

2. an apple
3. a ticket
4. the office
5. the bill
6. a car

B

2. an accident
3. the cake
4. a funny joke
5. the window
6. the phone
7. a heater
8. an exam

C

2. a question
3. The water
4. an umbrella
5. the key
6. the book
7. a problem
8. a mountain
9. the suit

10. an orange

UNIT 050

A

2. the radio
3. golf
4. the moon
5. math

B

2. the ocean
3. history
4. the Internet
5. The government
6. baseball
7. breakfast
8. the world

C

2. go home
3. go to the airport
4. go to the movies
5. go to work
6. go to the bank

D

2. police → the police
3. O
4. sun → the sun
5. at the home → at home
6. O
7. the politics → politics

UNIT 051

A

2. it
3. He
4. me
5. They
6. us

B

2. her; She
3. He; him
4. you; you
5. We; us
6. They; them

C

2. It

3. him

4. us

5. They

6. We

D

2. Us → We

3. O

4. I → me

5. O

6. Them → They

UNIT 052

A

2. It's 12:30 *OR* It is 12:30

3. It's warm *OR* It is warm

4. it's close *OR* it is close

5. It's summer *OR* It is summer

7. It's Tuesday *OR* It is Tuesday

8. It's 15 miles *OR* It is 15 miles

9. It's December 25th

   OR It is December 25th

10. It's 8 o'clock *OR* It is 8 o'clock

B

2. It

3. they

4. you

5. It

6. We

7. It

8. It

C

2. Is it midnight

3. It's 2 p.m. *OR* It is 2 p.m.

4. It's summer *OR* It is summer;

   it's very warm *OR* it is very warm

UNIT 053

A

2. my bag

3. your key

4. our dog

5. his ball

B

2. his

3. hers

4. yours

5. theirs

C

2. its

3. your

4. Our

5. hers

6. theirs

D

2. Whose glasses; his

3. Whose wallet; yours

4. Whose scarf; hers

E

2. mine

3. yours

4. his

5. his

UNIT 054

A

2. Laura's husband

3. our kids' presents

4. your brother's boat

5. Richard's voice

6. her friends' problems

B

2. Scott's

3. The Andersons'

4. Lucy's

5. Kevin's

C

2. the price of this chair

3. the title of the book

4. the number of your hotel room

5. the top of the mountain

6. the start of the year

D

2. O

3. parents's → parents'

4. the page's top

   → the top of the page

5. Rose' → Rose's

6. O

7. Mr. Cowan → Mr. Cowan's

8. O

9. The best friend of Mia

   → Mia's best friend

10. O

UNIT 055

A

2. yourself

3. ourselves

4. myself

5. himself

B

2. herself

3. him

4. her

5. himself

6. himself

C

2. I made dinner by myself

3. He went to the park by himself

4. I was shopping by myself

5. She was playing games by herself

6. We're traveling by ourselves

   OR We are traveling by ourselves

D

2. me

3. yourself

4. yourself

5. them

6. myself

UNIT 056

A

2. that book

3. that painting

4. this ring

B

2. that

3. Those
4. this
5. that
6. This
7. those
8. These

C

2. How much are those socks
3. How much is that cake
4. How much are these spoons
5. How much is this perfume
6. How much are those sunglasses

D

2. that
3. these
4. those
5. Those

A

2. one
3. ones
4. one
5. one
6. ones

B

2. a new one
3. some cheap ones
4. an important one
5. some chocolate ones
6. a bigger one
7. an exciting one

C

2. Which ones
3. Which one
4. Which one
5. Which ones

D

2. big one
3. green ones
4. red ones

A

2. any snow
3. some paper
4. any sports
5. any trains
6. some friends
7. some rest
8. any money

B

2. any
3. some
4. any
5. any
6. some

C

2. something
3. Someone *OR* Somebody
4. somewhere

D

2. somewhere
3. someone *OR* somebody
4. anything
5. something
6. anywhere
7. Something
8. anyone *OR* anybody

A

2. no bread
3. no money
4. no tickets
5. no choice
6. No children
7. no rain
8. no windows

B

2. any; No
3. none
4. any
5. no
6. any
7. None

C

2. nowhere
3. nothing
4. nothing
5. nowhere
6. no one *OR* nobody

D

2. no
3. any
4. none

A

2. There isn't much space
3. There isn't much money
4. There are many kids
5. There isn't much bread

B

2. much interest
3. much furniture
4. many cups
5. many dogs
6. much information
7. much time

C

2. a lot of coffee
3. a lot of vegetables
4. a lot of fun
5. a lot of noise

D

2. much *OR* a lot of
3. a lot
4. a lot
5. much *OR* a lot of
6. a lot
7. a lot of
8. A lot
9. a lot of
10. much *OR* a lot of

A

2. a little water

3. a few roses
4. a few tickets

B

2. little information
3. Few cars
4. little sugar
5. little space
6. few letters

C

2. little
3. a little
4. a few
5. few
6. little
7. A little
8. few

D

2. few
3. a few
4. little
5. a few

UNIT 062

A

2. all
3. Every
4. All
5. every
6. All

B

2. All students
3. Every flower
4. Every seat
5. All men

C

2. All languages have
3. Every story has
4. All children need
5. All rain comes
6. Every table is

D

2. every weekend

3. every month
4. all week
5. all day
6. every morning

E

2. everywhere
3. everything
4. everyone *OR* everybody
5. everywhere

UNIT 063

A

2. Both women
3. Neither seat
4. Both cars
5. Neither store
6. Both babies

B

2. Both
3. either
4. Neither
5. both
6. either

C

2. Both novels
3. Both houses
4. Either month
5. Neither kind

D

2. Either
3. both
4. either
5. both

UNIT 064

A

2. Some of them
3. Most of them
4. None of them
5. Most of them
6. Some of them
7. None of them
8. All of them

B

2. Did you catch all of those fish
3. None of us liked it
4. I often visit some of my cousins
5. Most of the shops are expensive
6. None of these buildings were here
7. I put most of mine

C

2. Some animals
3. Most of the work
4. all animals
5. Most trees
6. some of these muffins
7. all of them
8. none of my friends

D

2. Both of our cars
3. Neither of his parents
4. either of the restaurants
5. neither of us
6. both of you

UNIT 065

A

2. long hair
3. old car
4. blue eyes

B

2. cold weather
3. pink roses
4. empty seats
5. medical school

C

2. smells delicious
3. feel scared
4. sounds good
5. tastes great
6. look happy *OR* feel happy

D

2. black
3. tall
4. kind

UNIT 066

A
2. quickly
3. nervously
4. comfortably
5. brightly

B
2. heavily
3. simply
4. perfectly
5. noisily
6. well
7. automatically

C
2. speak loudly
3. walk; angrily
4. drive safely
5. solve; quickly

D
2. well → good
3. O
4. quiet → quietly
5. beautifully → beautiful
6. O
7. terrible → terribly
8. O

UNIT 067

A
2. interesting
3. seriously
4. smart
5. completely
6. heavily
7. strange
8. regularly

B
2. fast
3. beautifully
4. hard
5. late
6. safely

C
2. easily → easy
3. frequent → frequently
4. O
5. sudden → suddenly
6. O
7. newly → new
8. noisy → noisily

D
2. quickly
3. nervous
4. long
5. late

UNIT 068

A
2. often
3. sometimes
4. never
5. rarely
6. always
7. usually

B
2. I sometimes exercise
   OR I rarely exercise
3. I often watch movies
   OR I sometimes watch movies
4. I always read books
   OR I never read books
5. I often clean my room
   OR I rarely clean my room
6. I often listen to music
   OR I sometimes listen to music

C
2. She's always smiling
   OR She is always smiling
3. Nick often plays
4. We'll never move
   OR We will never move
5. You should never leave
6. Danny sometimes meets
7. You can always talk
8. We rarely finish
9. I'm usually free
   OR I am usually free

D
2. 's rarely been *OR* has rarely been
3. 've always wanted
   OR have always wanted
4. 's never ridden
   OR has never ridden
5. 've sometimes felt
   OR have sometimes felt

UNIT 069

A
2. too fast
3. too dark
4. too long
5. too high

B
2. too expensive for us
3. too spicy for me
4. too hard for him
5. too early for them

C
2. too sick to go
3. too heavy to lift
4. too large to see
5. too busy to take

D
2. too much rain
3. too many words
4. too many cars
5. too much food
6. Too many tourists

UNIT 070

A
2. loud enough
3. large enough
4. tall enough
5. long enough

B
2. hungry enough
3. close enough
4. enough information
5. enough paper

6. hard enough
7. enough doctors
8. wide enough

C

2. big enough for two people
3. old enough to drink
4. comfortable enough for me
5. lucky enough to meet

D

2. enough books for the students
3. enough time to get to the station
4. enough exercise to stay healthy
5. enough toys for all of our cousins

UNIT 071

A

2. so tall
3. so heavy
4. so long
5. so small

B

2. so many passengers
3. so much food
4. so many questions

C

2. so many clothes
3. so many languages
4. so much gas
5. so much water
6. so much sugar
7. so many countries
8. so many sisters

D

2. so quiet
3. so many people
4. so high
5. so much time

UNIT 072

A

2. smaller
3. sweeter

4. colder
5. sooner
6. older

B

2. shorter than David
3. warmer than New York
4. longer than the Amazon

C

2. has lower grades than Theo
3. has darker hair than Beth
4. is weaker than steel
5. is noisier than the countryside

D

2. smarter than me
   OR smarter than I am
3. taller than us *OR* taller than we are
4. faster than her
   OR faster than she is
5. deeper than me
   OR deeper than I can
6. harder than them
   OR harder than they do

UNIT 073

A

2. thinner
3. easier
4. more interesting
5. worse
6. lower
7. earlier
8. bigger
9. more serious
10. farther
11. wider
12. closer
13. better
14. stronger
15. more important

B

2. more expensive than the brown cap
3. farther than Seattle
4. faster than the man

5. heavier than the white box

C

2. more carefully
3. hotter
4. more useful
5. larger
6. cheaper
7. happier

D

2. O
3. more easy → easier
4. O
5. dangerous → more dangerous
6. good → better

UNIT 074

A

2. more beautiful; the most beautiful
3. better; the best
4. cleaner; the cleanest
5. hotter; the hottest
6. happier; the happiest
7. larger; the largest
8. worse; the worst

B

2. the most creative person
3. the strongest animals
4. the busiest man
5. the most delicious dish
6. the freshest vegetables

C

2. more expensive than;
   the most expensive
3. the youngest; younger than
4. higher than; the highest

D

2. is the oldest
3. is the best
4. is the heaviest
5. is the shortest

A

2. as fast as
3. as cheap as
4. as tall as
5. as heavy as
6. as new as

B

2. can't eat as much as Jim
   OR cannot eat as much as Jim
3. isn't as far as the mall
   OR is not as far as the mall
4. doesn't go to work as early as Ian
   OR does not go to work as early
   as Ian
5. isn't as high as that tower
   OR is not as high as that tower
6. isn't as cold as Beijing
   OR is not as cold as Beijing

C

2. can eat much more than me
3. is farther than the park
4. goes to work earlier than Sally
5. is higher than this tower
6. is colder than Tokyo

D

2. as carefully as possible
3. as often as possible
4. as loud as possible
5. as quickly as possible

UNIT 076

A

2. on
3. on
4. in
5. at
6. at
7. in
8. in
9. on
10. at

B

2. in
3. At
4. on
5. on
6. At
7. on
8. in

C

2. at his desk
3. in the living room
4. at the mall
5. on the table

UNIT 077

A

2. on 2nd Avenue
3. at a birthday party
4. in the sky
5. on the bus

B

2. at
3. on
4. at
5. on
6. in

C

2. at the concert
3. on the train
4. at Ann's house
5. In a book
6. in prison
7. on the first floor

D

2. in bed
3. at the doctor's office
4. on Main Street
5. at home

UNIT 078

A

2. by *OR* next to
3. behind
4. in front of
5. behind

B

2. over
3. among
4. under
5. between

C

2. in front of
3. next to
4. behind
5. among
6. by
7. over
8. under

D

2. behind
3. next to
4. between

UNIT 079

A

2. is going over
3. 're getting out of
   OR are getting out of
4. is driving along
5. 's walking up *OR* is walking up
6. is passing through
7. is going past
8. 's falling off *OR* is falling off
9. 's walking across
   OR is walking across
10. is driving around

B

2. down
3. under
4. over
5. to
6. into
7. from
8. toward
9. on
10. off
11. through

12. out of

UNIT 080

A

2. at 7:18 p.m. *OR* at 7:18
3. in 1879
4. at night
5. on April 10

B

2. on
3. at
4. On
5. in
6. in
7. at
8. on

C

2. in February
3. at lunch
4. at 10 a.m.
5. on our anniversary
6. in the 20th century
7. in the evening
8. on Saturday night

D

2. on the weekend
3. at 11 o'clock
4. in the morning
5. in the afternoon; at night

UNIT 081

A

2. during
3. during
4. for
5. for
6. during

B

2. During the weekend
3. For eight years
4. During our meeting
5. During the winter
6. For five minutes

7. For about four months

C

2. in
3. during
4. for
5. during
6. within
7. in

D

2. for → during
3. within → in
4. during → for
5. O
6. in → within
7. O

UNIT 082

A

2. from June to July
3. from 10 a.m. to 7 p.m
4. from Monday to Friday
5. from April 20 to May 5

B

2. 's known Jason since high school
   OR has known Jason since high school
3. hasn't smoked since last year
   OR has not smoked since last year
4. 's been married since July
   OR has been married since July
5. 's had a car since 2014
   OR has had a car since 2014

C

2. by
3. until
4. by
5. by
6. until

D

2. from; to *OR* until
3. by
4. until

UNIT 083

A

2. without his glasses
3. with a swimming pool
4. without a helmet

B

2. by subway
3. with brown hair
4. without a ticket
5. by plane
6. of this pair of jeans
7. on foot
8. without my wallet
9. about the meeting
10. like a fish

C

2. without stopping
3. by turning off the lights
4. at skating
5. about getting a promotion
6. for joining our book club

UNIT 084

A

2. at
3. about
4. of
5. to
6. in
7. for
8. of

B

2. different from
3. proud of
4. full of
5. sure about

C

2. similar to Italian food
3. short of money
4. married to Julia
5. familiar with this city

D

2. busy with

3. sure about
4. mad at

A

2. 're looking at *OR* are looking at
3. 's asking for *OR* is asking for
4. 's writing to *OR* is writing to

B

2. apply for
3. answer
4. depends on
5. belongs to
6. reach
7. worry about
8. discuss

C

2. O
3. called to → called
4. waiting → waiting for
5. O
6. reached to → reached

D

2. apply for
3. looking for
4. talk to
5. depends on

A

2. work on
3. go out
4. slow down
5. get up
6. hold on
7. come back
8. get on
9. eat out
10. get out of
11. hand out
12. take off

B

2. hand in this report
   OR hand this report in
3. take them away
4. clean it up
5. turn on the oven
   OR turn the oven on
6. write it down
7. took out our trash
   OR took our trash out
8. switch on the light
   OR switch the light on
9. call her back
10. turned up the volume
    OR turned the volume up

C

2. drop me off
3. tried it on
4. Turn off the TV
   OR Turn the TV off

A

2. or do you need more time
3. and it hurt a lot
4. but he couldn't attend
5. but it tasted terrible
6. or do you want to drive yours

B

3. so she bought a new one
4. She bought a new TV because her TV wasn't working
5. so he was very tired
6. He was very tired because he ran for an hour
7. so she took some medicine
8. She took some medicine because she had a headache

C

2. because of
3. because
4. because
5. because of
6. because of

A

2. When he sat on the chair
3. when they arrived at the theater
4. when it started to rain
5. when he woke up

B

2. Do not use your cell phone while you're driving
3. Can you set the table while I make dinner
4. While I was taking a shower, Tom called me
5. I'll get a shopping cart while you find a parking space
6. While Matt was playing soccer, he got injured

C

2. 'll meet *OR* will meet
3. go
4. 'll wait *OR* will wait
5. cooks
6. come
7. 'll see *OR* will see
8. saves

A

2. after I took a shower
3. before I ordered a cup of coffee
4. Before I left home
5. After Diane entered the room
6. before the police arrived
7. after he eats breakfast in the morning
8. After the visitors checked out of the hotel

B

2. after reading
3. before the exam
4. before driving
5. after the show
6. after our wedding

C

2. Before baking the muffins
3. After pouring the muffin mix
4. before putting the mixture
5. after 25 minutes

UNIT 090

A

2. since
3. until
4. since
5. since
6. until

B

2. hasn't called me
   OR has not called me
3. opened last month
4. broke my leg
5. haven't traveled anywhere
   OR have not traveled anywhere
6. 've lost 10 pounds
   OR have lost 10 pounds

C

2. until we arrived at the theater
3. until she showed them the proof
4. until it turns brown
5. until she returned from vacation
6. until the paint dries

D

2. since he lost his camera
3. until he moved to Taiwan
4. since he moved to Taiwan
5. until she bought a car
6. since she bought a car
7. until she got married
8. since she got married

UNIT 091

A

2. If the traffic is bad
3. If we are in the same class
4. If I get this job
5. If the guests arrive
6. If the supermarket isn't closed

B

2. I'll become a famous designer
3. I'll make a lot of money if I become a famous designer
4. I'll help poor children if I make a lot of money
5. I'll feel happy if I help poor children

C

2. Holly forgets our appointment
3. You'll feel better
   OR You will feel better
4. Brandon will get it
5. your sister comes to Toronto
6. you're with me
   OR you are with me

D

2. it rains
3. I'll visit *OR* I will visit
4. you want

UNIT 092

A

2. If it were sunny *OR* If it was sunny
3. If I were in Paris *OR* If I was in Paris
4. If I had more free time

B

2. It wouldn't be *OR* It would not be
3. she got up
4. Ryan would become
5. I won
6. we wouldn't wear
   OR we would not wear

C

2. If I were you, I wouldn't drive
3. If I were you, I'd say sorry to her
4. If I were you, I wouldn't drink it

D

2. If Ted didn't work in the afternoons, he'd get up early
3. If Brenna were busy, she couldn't meet us *OR* If Brenna was busy, she couldn't meet us

4. If Dan didn't have a knee injury, he could play soccer

UNIT 093

A

2. If the mall were open
   OR If the mall was open
3. If I find it
4. If Ashley weren't so tired
   OR If Ashley wasn't so tired
5. If the restaurant weren't full
   OR If the restaurant wasn't full
6. If we took 4th Avenue
7. If I see him
8. If she doesn't sleep late

B

2. were fresh
3. 'd attend *OR* would attend
4. 'll pick you up
   OR will pick you up
5. had a car
6. doesn't like coffee
   OR does not like coffee
7. 'd be healthier
   OR would be healthier
8. don't take an umbrella
   OR do not take an umbrella

C

2. rains
3. performed
4. will come

UNIT 094

A

2. who has six children
3. who plays the violin
4. who are very famous
5. who fixes cars
6. who is 99 years old

B

2. who
3. which
4. who
5. which

6. who

7. which

8. which

C

2. I bought a new sofa which (*OR* that) was on sale

3. The store which (*OR* that) is around the corner sells magazines

4. The people who (*OR* that) live downstairs are very nice

5. I found a suitcase which (*OR* that) belongs to Mr. Harris

6. Sarah taught the students who (*OR* that) graduated last year

7. A man who (*OR* that) is standing across the street just waved to us

8. We're excited about the festival which (*OR* that) will begin next week

UNIT 095

A

2. The dress which I wore

3. the cake which you're baking

4. The show which you were watching

5. The book which Brian Smith wrote

B

2. used to have a friend I trusted

3. know a neighbor that has many pets

4. that drove us to school isn't my sister *OR* that drove us to school is not my sister

5. ate all of the chocolate he bought in Belgium

6. I saw last night is open until next week

7. went to a restaurant that's famous for its dessert *OR* went to a restaurant that is famous for its dessert

8. the boss introduced to us today is going to attend the next meeting

C

2. was sold → which (*OR* that) was sold

3. O

4. exercise → who (*OR* that) exercise

5. was → which (*OR* that) was

6. O

D

2. which opened

3. who studied

4. you visited

UNIT 096

A

2. There are some people

3. There are some fish

4. There is a lake

B

2. There was

3. there aren't *OR* there are not

4. There wasn't *OR* There was not

5. There are

6. there isn't *OR* there is not

7. Are there

C

2. Have there been any visitors

3. There have been a lot of accidents

4. Has there been a change

5. There haven't been many tourists *OR* There have not been many tourists

6. There hasn't been any rain *OR* There has not been any rain

D

2. There weren't many people *OR* There were not many people

3. There isn't a cloud *OR* There is not a cloud

4. Is there a rental shop

5. There was one

UNIT 097

A

2. bought Jen a doll

3. showed Kim his room

4. made Jake some coffee

B

2. bought an apartment for him

3. taught music to students

4. show my new car to you

5. made breakfast for me

6. send Christmas cards to his friends

C

2. Did Tim send you those gifts

3. Money can't buy us happiness

4. Laura teaches yoga to students

5. Can you show your passport to me

6. My mother made a sweater for me

D

2. gave a ring to me

3. send your friends invitations

4. make a cake for you

UNIT 098

A

2. Slow

3. Wake

4. Do

5. Be

B

2. Don't take

3. Don't swim

4. don't smoke

C

2. Let's listen

3. Let's not watch

4. Let's start

5. Let's not go

6. Let's ask

D

2. How expensive

3. How exciting
4. What a nice car
5. What lovely flowers
6. What a great view

UNIT 099

A

2. They said (that) they were getting married
3. She said (that) she was on vacation
4. They said (that) they were going out
5. He said (that) he would call (Betty *OR* her) later
6. She said (that) she couldn't find her dog

B

2. They told me (that) they were getting married
3. She told me (that) she was on vacation
4. They told me (that) they were going out
5. He told Betty (*OR* her) (that) he would call (her) later
6. She told Mark (*OR* him) (that) she couldn't find her dog

C

2. told
3. said
4. said
5. told
6. told
7. said
8. told

UNIT 100

A

2. too
3. either
4. too
5. either
6. too
7. either

8. either

B

2. Neither have I
3. So can Brian
4. Neither is Maria
5. So are we
6. Neither does mine
7. Neither was the salad
8. So do Jim and Emily

C

2. either
3. So
4. too
5. So
6. either
7. Neither
8. too
9. Neither
10. So

REVIEW TEST Answers

2. works; 's listening *OR* is listening
3. is reading; teaches
4. is shopping; helps
6. Is Mom making pancakes
7. We don't use it *OR* We do not use it
8. Do you know him
9. Lisa and Anton aren't from England
   OR Lisa and Anton are not from England
10. Julia doesn't wear glasses
    OR Julia does not wear glasses
12. Do you practice
13. Do birds eat
14. Is it raining
15. Does Brian take
16. Are you watching
17. Does she work
18. Are you ready

20. b)	21. b)
22. a)	23. b)
24. c)	25. b)
26. c)	27. a)
28. b)	29. a)
30. a)	31. a)
32. c)	33. a)

2. walked
3. visited
4. saw
5. took
6. bought
8. I didn't see *OR* I did not see
9. Was Susie
10. I have
11. Did you go
12. Is he
13. I don't know *OR* I do not know
15. Lucy didn't go *OR* Lucy did not go
16. Did Ben clean
17. Were you studying
18. We were waiting

20. a)	21. a)
22. b)	23. a)
24. c)	25. a)

26. a)	27. a)
28. c)	29. c)
30. b)	31. a)
32. b)	33. a)

2. We haven't eaten dinner yet
   OR We have not eaten dinner yet
3. Mark has been to many concerts
4. Has the snow just stopped
5. Aaron and Nick have made some muffins
6. Mandy hasn't ridden a roller coaster
   OR Mandy has not ridden a roller coaster
8. 've known each other *OR* have known each other
9. hasn't rained *OR* has not rained
10. 's been sick *OR* has been sick
12. called
13. 've watched *OR* have watched
14. came
15. got
16. 's grown *OR* has grown
17. broke
18. 's worked *OR* has worked

20. b)	21. a)
22. c)	23. c)
24. a)	25. b)
26. b)	27. b)
28. a)	29. a)
30. b)	31. c)
32. b)	33. a)

2. He's going to marry her *OR* He is going to marry her
3. Are you speaking
4. Are you going to watch the fireworks
5. I won't forget it *OR* I will not forget it
6. Alex and I aren't playing soccer
   OR Alex and I are not playing soccer
8. 's going to drink some wine
   OR is going to drink some wine
9. is going to stop at the light
10. 're going to get on the train
    OR are going to get on the train
12. 'll write *OR* will write

13. won't stay *OR* will not stay

14. 'll turn on *OR* will turn on

15. won't touch *OR* will not touch

16. won't tell *OR* will not tell

17. 'll cook *OR* will cook

18. 'll meet *OR* will meet

20. c)	21. c)
22. b)	23. b)
24. a)	25. c)
26. b)	27. c)
28. a)	29. a)
30. b)	31. a)
32. c)	33. a)

TEST 5

2. He might not come

3. I think he should get

4. Would you like to dance

5. I don't have to go

7. can't use the car *OR* cannot use the car

8. have to call the police

9. might fall down the stairs

10. don't have to be scared *OR* do not have to be scared

11. must fix the roof

13. could

14. didn't have to *OR* did not have to

15. shouldn't *OR* should not

16. must not

17. had to

18. couldn't *OR* could not

20. a)	21. a)
22. a)	23. c)
24. b)	25. a)
26. b)	27. c)
28. c)	29. b)
30. b)	31. a)
32. a)	33. a)

TEST 6

2. were made

3. was written

4. were taken

5. was stolen

7. pets aren't allowed *OR* pets are not allowed

8. The house wasn't sold *OR* The house was not sold

9. The Mona Lisa was painted by Leonardo da Vinci

10. These dishes can't be used
    OR These dishes cannot be used

12. was canceled

13. had

14. was broken

15. didn't finish *OR* did not finish

16. was invented

17. watched

18. wasn't washed *OR* was not washed

20. a)	21. b)
22. a)	23. c)
24. a)	25. b)
26. a)	27. c)
28. a)	29. c)
30. c)	31. b)
32. b)	33. a)

TEST 7

2. What

3. Who

4. Where

5. When

6. Who

7. When

8. What

10. where I can put this

11. why you bought this hat

12. when Erica will get here

14. How much does this necklace cost

15. How many people work here

16. whether you'll be busy *OR* whether you will be busy

17. When did Cindy go

18. Where is this wine from

20. a)	21. b)
22. c)	23. a)
24. a)	25. b)
26. b)	27. a)
28. a)	29. c)
30. c)	31. a)
32. c)	33. b)

TEST 8

2. waiting in line *OR* to wait in line

3. singing

4. cooking

5. to go to the museum

6. reading books *OR* to read books

8. to send

9. make OR to make

10. eating

11. stay

12. moving

13. to learn

15. Aaron let me use his

16. Does Kim need to buy

17. Nicole taught me to dance

18. Swimming is good

20. c)	21. a)
22. b)	23. a)
24. b)	25. c)
26. b)	27. c)
28. b)	29. c)
30. c)	31. c)
32. b)	33. a)

TEST 9

2. many students attend the concert

3. some snow on the road

4. get a glass of orange juice

5. buy new ones

7. principal's office

8. David's seat

9. Andersons' house

10. Sam's suitcases

12. an umbrella

13. salt

14. a taxi

15. the drums

16. the airport

17. money

18. information

20. c)	21. b)
22. c)	23. a)
24. a)	25. c)
26. b)	27. b)
28. a)	29. c)
30. c)	31. c)
32. a)	33. b)

TEST 10

2. any

3. some

4. any

5. no

7. few

8. many

9. every

10. a little

11. much

12. all

13. little

15. Both of them are

16. Most of my cousins live

17. he has none

18. Neither of them is mine

20. c)	21. a)
22. a)	23. b)
24. a)	25. c)
26. b)	27. c)
28. a)	29. c)
30. b)	31. b)
32. c)	33. a)

TEST 11

2. 's sitting uncomfortably

3. 's thinking hard

4. 're shouting angrily

6. is rarely crowded

7. not tall enough to ride

8. too tired to go

9. enough for everyone

10. can always use my car

12. good

13. larger

14. more beautiful

15. highest

16. hottest

17. faster

18. strong

20. c)	21. b)
22. a)	23. b)
24. c)	25. c)
26. a)	27. a)
28. a)	29. b)
30. b)	31. b)
32. b)	33. c)

TEST 12

2. at work

3. on the 4th floor

4. at home

5. in the bathroom

7. by this Friday

8. For five years

9. in 10 minutes

10. from Korea

11. to Germany

12. behind the curtains

13. down the stairs

15. turn on the air conditioner
   OR turn the air conditioner on

16. excited about the trip

17. spends money on unnecessary things

18. clean up the trash *OR* clean the trash up

20. a)	21. b)
22. c)	23. b)
24. c)	25. a)
26. c)	27. c)
28. c)	29. b)
30. b)	31. c)
32. b)	33. a)

7. told me he wanted

8. Let's not cook dinner

9. said that she was sleeping

10. What a delicious lunch

12. either

13. So

14. either

15. So

16. Neither

17. Neither

18. too

20. c)	21. a)
22. a)	23. c)
24. b)	25. c)
26. a)	27. b)
28. c)	29. b)
30. b)	31. a)
32. b)	33. c)

TEST 13

2. or should we take a bus

3. because I drank too much wine last night

4. but she couldn't come

5. so she took some medicine

7. if I finish work

8. if I were you *OR* if I was you

9. since she left the company

10. when Martin opened it

11. while she's on vacation *OR* while she is on vacation

13. who was on TV last night

14. (who) she met during the trip

15. (which) Ted's dad built

17. b)	18. c)
19. c)	20. b)
21. c)	22. c)
23. a)	24. b)
25. b)	26. c)
27. c)	28. a)
29. b)	30. a)

TEST 14

2. There is a bird

3. There is a table

4. There are three glasses

5. There are four boys

GRAMMAR GATEWAY BASIC

INDEX

영문 INDEX

한글 INDEX

한글 INDEX

INDEX에 있는 숫자는 **UNIT** 번호입니다. 괄호 안에 있는 숫자는 **UNIT** 내 섹션 번호입니다.

초보를 위한 기초 영문법

증보 1판 7쇄 발행 2023년 2월 6일
증보 1판 1쇄 발행 2019년 5월 27일

지은이	David Cho	언어학 박사, 前 UCLA 교수
펴낸곳	㈜해커스 어학연구소
펴낸이	해커스 어학연구소 출판팀

주소	서울특별시 서초구 강남대로61길 23 ㈜해커스 어학연구소
고객센터	02-537-5000
교재 관련 문의	publishing@hackers.com
동영상강의	HackersIngang.com

ISBN	978-89-6542-292-1 (13740)
Serial Number	01-07-01

외국어인강 1위,
해커스인강 (HackersIngang.com)

Ⅲ 해커스인강

· 본 교재 동영상강의 및 예문 음성 MP3
· 무료 스피킹·라이팅 훈련 워크북 및 워크북 MP3

영어 전문 포털,
해커스영어(Hackers.co.kr)

Ⅲ 해커스영어

· 무료 교재 예문 해석 자료
· 기초영어 및 영어 테스트 **무료 학습자료**

'영어회화 인강' 1위,
해커스톡(HackersTalk.co.kr)

왕초보영어 탈출
해커스톡

· 기초 영어회화 동영상강의
· 전문가의 1:1 스피킹 케어, 매일 영어회화 표현 등 무료 학습 콘텐츠